Postcolonial Insecurities

BORDERLINES

For more books in the series, see page vi.

Postcolonial Insecurities
India, Sri Lanka, and
the Question of Nationhood

SANKARAN KRISHNA

BORDERLINES, VOLUME 15

 University of Minnesota Press

Minneapolis

London

The University of Minnesota Press gratefully acknowledges permission to reprint the following. An earlier version of chapter 2 appeared as "Producing Sri Lanka: J. R. Jayewardene and Postcolonial Identity," in *Alternatives: Social Transformation and Humane Governance,* vol. 21, no. 3. Copyright 1996 by Lynne Rienner Publishers, Inc. Reprinted with permission. An excerpt from a poem of Sivaramani from "Poems of Sivaramani," introduced by Sitralega Maunaguru, which appeared in *Pravada* 1 (September 1992): 21–22 is reproduced in chapter 2 with permission from Pravada Publishers, Social Scientists' Association, Colombo, Sri Lanka. Chapter 3 was previously published as "Divergent Narratives," in *Sri Lanka: Collective Identities Revisited,* volume 2, edited by Michael Roberts (Colombo: Marga Institute, 1998); reprinted with permission.

Published by the University of Minnesota Press
111 Third Avenue South, Suite 290
Minneapolis, MN 55401-2520
http://www.upress.umn.edu

Printed in the United States of America on acid-free paper

Library of Congress Cataloging-in-Publication Data
Krishna, Sankaran.
    Postcolonial insecurities : India, Sri Lanka, and the question of nationhood / Sankaran Krishna.
        p.   cm. — (Borderlines ; v. 15)
    Includes bibliographical references and index.
    ISBN 0-8166-3329-0. — ISBN 0-8166-3330-4 (pbk.)
    1. Sri Lanka — Politics and government — 1978–   2. Tamil (Indic people) — Sri Lanka — Politics and government.   3. India — Foreign relations — Sri Lanka.   4. Sri Lanka — Foreign relations — India.
    I. Title.   II. Series: Borderlines (Minneapolis, Minn.) ; v. 15.
DS489.84.K77   1999
954.9303'2 — dc21   99-16845

The University of Minnesota is an equal-opportunity educator and employer.

11 10 09 08 07 06 05 04 03 02 01 00 99   10 9 8 7 6 5 4 3 2 1

For my parents

BORDERLINES

Long years ago we made a tryst with destiny, and now the time comes when we shall redeem our pledge, not wholly or in full measure, but very substantially. At the stroke of the midnight hour, when the world sleeps, India shall awake to life and freedom. A moment comes, which comes but rarely in history, when we step out from the old to the new, when an age ends, and when the soul of a nation, long suppressed, finds utterance. It is fitting that at this solemn moment we take the pledge of dedication to the service of India and her people and to the still larger cause of humanity.
— JAWAHARLAL NEHRU, AUGUST 14, 1947,
ON THE EVE OF INDIAN INDEPENDENCE FROM BRITAIN

We have failed in the essential task of nation-building.... In 1948, when our forefathers first set out along the path to freedom, they envisioned a truly free and united Sri Lanka.... We have failed to realize the dreams of our freedom fighters to build a strong and united nation. The silent majority watched in horror, whilst a great nation with an ancient civilization, steeped in one of the finest cultural and architectural heritages of the world, nurtured in the traditions of the noble Buddhist philosophy of peace, tolerance and love veered off into a terrifying era of ethnic, political and social violence.
— CHANDRIKA KUMARATUNGA, ON THE FIFTIETH ANNIVERSARY
OF SRI LANKA'S INDEPENDENCE FROM BRITAIN

This is not that long-looked-for break of day. Not that clear dawn in quest of which those comrades
Set out, believing that in heaven's wide void
Somewhere must be the stars' last halting place,
Somewhere the verge of night's slow-washing tide,
Somewhere an anchorage for the ship of heartache.
— FAIZ AHMAD FAIZ, ON INDEPENDENCE/PARTITION

Contents

Acknowledgments

One of the edifying consequences of having a rather ponderous research metabolism is that you accumulate a long list of people to thank by the time you are done. I would first like to acknowledge all my interviewees—without them this book could not have been written. They had differing reasons for wanting to get their side of the story out, and the end result may not please some, or any, of them. Although most are listed in the Appendix, a small handful chose to remain anonymous. My thanks to each and every one of them for their time and hospitality. The research trips undertaken for this project were variously supported by the National Endowment for the Humanities summer fellowships, the Program in Conflict Resolution, the Spark Matsunaga Institute of Peace, the College of Social Sciences, and the University Research Council—all administered through the University of Hawai'i at Manoa. My gratitude goes to these organizations for encouraging this project at a time when I was quite unsure where it was headed. Although the Indian government refused to clear this project for funding by the American Institute of Indian Studies, Pradeep Mehendiratta at the latter's New Delhi office conducted himself with real class.

My two brief trips to Sri Lanka were immensely enjoyable and productive, thanks mainly to Jayadeva Uyangoda, Vyvette, Deanne, the epicurean Eppyndra, and that phlegmatic Hegelian, Podi Mahattya. I learned a lot by hanging out at the Social Scientists Association in Colombo. The commitment of many there to both a high level of academic discourse and an active engagement with progressive causes left a deep imprint on my thinking. My many trips to New Delhi over the summers were memorable, thanks to Ena and the "saare Singh parivar." Ena's multiple roles as chauffeur, realtor, city guide, and "paan" connoisseur were invaluable, as was her genuine interest in the details of my research.

The longer my time in the academy the more I appreciate how fortunate I am to have so many supportive colleagues in the Department of Political Science at Manoa. My thanks to Jonathan Goldberg-Hiller, Manfred Henningsen, Kathy Ferguson, Jorge Fernandes, Cindy Kobayashi Mackey, Neal Milner, Carole Moon, Deane Neubauer, Nevzat Soguk, Phyllis Turnbull, S. P. Udayakumar, and many others for all their help over the years. I owe Mike Shapiro more than I can possibly express in words. It is not often that someone who was a distant intellectual guru of yours in graduate school goes on, serendipitously, to become a colleague, friend, and mentor. My thanks to the many graduate and undergraduate students who were often the first sounding boards for the ideas in this book. I would like to thank David Campbell, M. S. S. Pandian, Mrinalini Sinha, Raju Thomas, and Rob Walker for their help during various stages of this and other projects. I miss Harry Friedman, T. V. Satyamurthy, and Charlie Abeyesekera, who passed away during these last years; I am glad our paths did cross and I have the memory of our times together.

Early outtakes were presented at the International Studies Association and the Association of Asian Studies meetings, and, of course, at the annual South Asia bashes in Madison. I also did my shtick at the Center for International Politics and Disarmament at Jawaharlal Nehru University in Delhi, the Madras Institute of Development Studies in Madras, the departments of political science at the University of Minnesota and Macalester College, and the Center for South Asian Studies at the University of Wisconsin-Madison. Although responses ran the gamut from outraged incredulity to guarded enthusiasm, I would like to thank all my respondents; I learned much from their comments. Carrie Mullen has been very supportive and encouraging as I gradually tamed a sprawling first draft into a lean and (I hope) coherent narrative. My thanks to her, to Robin Moir, and to

Laura Westlund at the University of Minnesota Press for all their help, and to Annie Barva for her meticulous work as copy editor.

In some ways I feel as if this book were written with a telephone receiver in the crook of my shoulder. Itty Abraham and I have probably added a hefty amount to the long-distance bills of our respective institutions as we conversed about India, science, Nehru, postcoloniality, cricket, and just about everything under the sun. I no longer know which ideas are mine and which are his. That such ownership does not matter in the least is all that matters.

As in the story of the Arab, the camel, and the tent, this book gradually came to occupy an alarmingly large chunk of my life. That I have stayed sane and actually enjoyed much of the years gone by is largely due to Monomita and the boys, Arnav and Amrit. My debts to them are unredeemable. Finally, this book is dedicated to my parents, Rama and V. V. Sankaran, the two most unabashed and indulgent fans anyone could ask for.

Honolulu, Hawai'i
March 1999

Abbreviations

ACTC	All-Ceylon Tamil Congress
APC	All-Parties Conference
CRD	Committee for Rational Development
DDC	District Development Councils
DK	Dravida Kazhagam
DMK	Dravida Munnetra Kazhagam
DUNF	Democratic United National Front
ENLF	Eelam National Liberation Front
EROS	Eelam Revolutionary Organization
IB	Intelligence Branch
IPKF	Indian Peace Keeping Force
ISLA	Indo-Sri Lanka Agreement
JVP	Janatha Vimukthi Peramuna
LTTE	Liberation Tigers for Tamil Eelam
NEPC	Northeastern Provincial Council
PLOTE	Peoples Liberation Organization for Tamil Eelam
PUCL	Peoples Union for Civil Liberties
PUDR	Peoples Union for Democratic Rights
RAW	Research and Analysis Wing
SAARC	South Asian Association for Regional Cooperation
SLFP	Sri Lanka Freedom Party
SLMP	Sri Lanka Mahajan Party
TELO	Tamil Eelam Liberation Organization

TNA   Tamil National Army
TUF   Tamil United Front
TULF   Tamil United Liberation Front
UNP   United National Party

Introduction

. . . it is important to articulate the ideal to which your strategies of critical detachment are attaching you.
— WILLIAM CONNOLLY, THE ETHOS OF PLURALIZATION

THEMATIC CONCERNS

This book is about the troubled and violent journey of postcolonial nationalism in South Asia. It examines the interaction between the modern enterprise of nation building and the emergence of ethnic conflict in this area by focusing on a specific event: Indian political and military involvement in the struggle between Sinhalese and Tamils in Sri Lanka. It argues that the attempt to construct nation-states on the basis of exclusionary narratives of the past and univocal visions for the future has reached an impasse. The fixation with producing a pulverized and uniform sense of national identity (usually along majoritarian lines) has unleashed a spiral of regional, state, and societal violence that appears endless. The disciplines of history and international relations have rendered the narrative of the nation that undergirds the political imaginaire in South Asia as rational, realist, inevitable, and progressive. One finds the contemporary violences, both physical and epistemic, that accompany nation building repeatedly justified by the claim that the history of world politics has demonstrated such violence to be both inescapable and, indeed, necessary. It is perhaps time, however, to reexamine the journey embarked upon in South Asia in the late 1940s: the journey of modernist nationhood with singular conceptions of sovereignty and identity.

A central argument of this book is the need to conceive of South Asia as a space marked by highly decentralized nation-states with substantial degrees of provincial or regional autonomy and a pluralist sense of national identity. Whenever state elites in the region have attempted to ride roughshod over the rights and aspirations of so-called peripheral minorities (religious, linguistic, regional, or other), the result has been either a violent partition/secession or the emergence of ethnonationalist movements that have attempted to achieve those ends. The very process of national integration around a putative majoritarian identity constitutes the stimulus for various particularistic movements that demand a space within which they can achieve self-determination as nations. In contrast, on occasions when state elites have responded to the aspirations of such regional movements by according them greater autonomy and recognition of their distinctiveness, the result has been a strengthening and enriching of a pluralist sense of nationality.

In this book, I argue for a politics of *postcolonial engagement*, defined here as the simultaneous task of deconstructing, historicizing, and denaturalizing all identities (national, ethnic, linguistic, religious), *as well as* envisioning and struggling for a future that does not seek to transcend or escape identity politics so much as fight for justice and fairness in the worlds we do inhabit. A critical and engaged approach to international relations is indispensable in such a struggle that is simultaneously deconstructive and oriented toward the achievement of specific political goals and visions.

If the case for a South Asia marked by highly decentralized nation-states is an important normative argument of this text, a number of other themes recur as I make my case: (a) the notion of postcolonial anxiety; (b) the mutually constitutive character of identity and difference; (c) the idea of miscegenation and the always already adulterated nature of our received categories; (d) the altered character of statist and insurgent violence in recent times; and (e) the need to articulate a postcolonial politics of agency, one that has a complex and agonistic relationship with other genres of scholarship on world politics at this point in time. In the chapters to follow, I weave in and out of these other themes, not necessarily in any particular order. Rather, I find myself returning to them, picking away and trying to tease out various shades and accents even as I chart the Indian involvement in the Sri Lankan ethnic struggle. Such a strategy of iterative explorations punctuated by returns to a central theme does not always facilitate linear narrative. However, I submit there is something to be gained by these explorations. Here, I wish to summarize briefly my understanding of all but the last of the listed themes (that of postcolonial agency, which I explore in detail in the second section of this introduction), not in any totalizing or definitional sense but rather as an emblematic first cut into these issues—to convey their flavor, as it were.

By *postcolonial anxiety,* I refer to the fact that the social constructions of past, present, and future for state elites and educated middle classes in the third world are mimetic constructions of what has supposedly already happened elsewhere: namely, Europe or the west. The story of what once happened in Europe constitutes the knowledge that empowers state elites as they attempt to fashion their nations in the image of what are considered successful nation-states. Both the past and the future become an imitative and thankless quest to prove that supremely unworthy maxim: "We are as good as..." Premised on this narrative of what once happened "out there," postcolonial elites attempt to remake the recalcitrant clay of plural civilizations into lean, uniform, hypermasculine, and disciplined nation-states. I consider postcolonial anxiety to be this attempt at replicating historical originals that are ersatz to begin with.

I regard the politics of identity as a discursive process by which societies produce categories such as insider and outsider, safety and danger, domestic and foreign, self and other, nation and ethnic group. From its very inception, the politics of identity is in a dialectic with a politics of difference. Identity and difference mutually constitute each other, and no essentialist points, Archimedean or otherwise, serve as their foundations. In contrast to most works that regard ethnicity as a provincial and retrogressive force pitted against the universalist and progressive ideal of the nation, this work shows how ethnicity is both a danger to and an opportunity for the making and remaking of the nation. It is not so much an inferior and subversive counter to the nation as it is the supplement that allows for the construction of the nation in a specific way involving the production of a hierarchy of national belonging that empowers some and marginalizes others.

Identity politics is invariably premised on an originary moment of immaculate conception, when the self existed in solitary splendor. History becomes the story of the fall from Eden, when the pristine purity of identity was defiled by the arrival of the "other," and its eventual recovery was to be through annihilation of the impure outsiders. In contrast, I try in this narrative to point to the ineffably miscegenated character of our origins: not only in the theoretical sense of the debt that identity always owes to otherness, but also in the historical sense that every linguistic, religious, nationalist, and ethnic category is bastardized and adulterated from the very outset. Rather than cringe from the miscegenated character of our most fundamental identities, I argue that we ought to celebrate and revel in the fact of our inextricably intertwined and impure selves.

Modern conflict in South Asia (as elsewhere) has become deterritorialized in significant ways. First, it is increasingly fought not so much between soldiers in uniform over well-defined territories, but rather among shadowy intelligence organizations and covert armies, paramilitary forces and mercenary outfits, insurgents and terrorist groups, all aided and abetted by regimes in neighboring countries and by diasporic groups that span the entire globe. It has, moreover, suffused border areas as well as those areas deep within the territory of the countries in the region. Second, the majority of casualties in such conflicts in South Asia are ordinary citizens, not professional soldiers. The body counts for such purportedly low-intensity conflicts exceed the casualties of conventional war by many orders of magnitude. Examples of such conflicts in which the usual antinomies domestic/foreign, state/civil society, inside/outside, and soldier/civilian are rendered thoroughly problematic and difficult to maintain include Kashmir, Punjab, Assam, and all of Northeast India; Sind, Baluchistan, and the Northwest Frontier province in Pakistan; the northern and eastern provinces in Sri Lanka; and the Chittagong Hill Tracts in Bangladesh. Finally, modern conflict in South Asia is deterritorialized in the sense that much of the material and psychic sustenance of ethnonational movements comes from all corners of this planet as various diaspora monetize their nostalgia for home through financial and other forms of support. An ethnographer studying the Liberation Tigers for Tamil Eelam (LTTE), a militant group at the forefront of the Sri Lankan Tamil movement for self-determination, would have a hard time demarcating and entering the field of her proposed ethnography: the guerrillas' walkabouts now span Jaffna and Geneva, Sudumalai and Sydney.

As with any book, this one too emerges from and into a specific intellectual context. In the remaining sections of this Introduction, I discuss critical differences of emphasis between the postcolonial position outlined here and other available standpoints given elsewhere to analyze world politics. As erstwhile narratives that held out the hope for a better tomorrow (prominently socialism and third-world nationalism) have run aground in recent years, some have sought escape through a politics of nostalgia (by asserting the putative purity of class, for example), or a politics of deferred redemption (exemplified in the idea that violence and human rights violations in third-world countries are justifiable as they are temporary and necessary detours on the road to nation building), or a politics of ironic disengagement (by forcing a choice between either deconstructing modernity or being complicit with its institutions and regimes of power). Much of this occurs in a larger context in which the world as perceived by mainstream international relations scholarship is confined to a metropolitan West, whereas all other areas are either cast in the role of vernacular variations on central themes or simply ignored. Yet, as the works of a number of postcolonial authors (notably Said 1978, Chakrabarty 1992, Sinha 1995) remind us, the story of "how the west was one" (Klein 1994) has always been inextricable from the story of how the rest were rendered both multiple and voiceless. The emergence of a canonical western civilization and its valorization of "classical" antiquity were predicated upon the anxieties of the colonial encounter and the very creation and dissemination of the idea of the orient. This book, in contrast to many in mainstream international relations scholarship (from both western and non-western scholars), suggests such an alternative "worlding": one that sees east and west, orient and occident, first and third worlds, metropole and postcolony, north and south, as spaces that are nonfoundational and constantly reproduced in relational terms. They owe an unredeemable debt to each other as their supposedly essential natures and differences are played out in relation to each other and under the regimes of power and knowledge.

If the above paragraphs offer preliminary and terse summaries of some of the central themes of this book, in the next section I offer a more detailed discussion of my notion of postcolonial agency.

Among other things, it ought to indicate the specific space that this intervention into the discourse of international relations tries to clear for itself.

POLITICS, IRONY, AND AESTHETICS

I enter the discussion of a situated politics of postcolonial agency somewhat obliquely by examining Ashis Nandy's (1995, 237–66) critique of Salman Rushdie's political commentaries. Nandy discerns an intriguing self-partitioning among at least four artists of this century: Satyajit Ray, Salman Rushdie, H. G. Wells, and Rudyard Kipling. He finds in each of them a split between, on the one hand, a rather overdeveloped creative faculty that is unconventional and generally trashes the assumption of progress that informs the European Enlightenment and, on the other hand, a self that is staidly conventional, rational, scientific, politically correct (in the sense of conforming to the accepted social codes and mores of one's time), and modern, with an appropriate degree of deference for Enlightenment values. With his penchant for the counterintuitive, Nandy proceeds to nuance this split by showing, for example, that Ray's understated films emerge from his loose and creative side, whereas his fantastic (in the original sense of that word) and popular science fiction novels and crime thrillers pay homage to modern scientific and rationalist methods of the European Enlightenment. By way of contrast, Rushdie's novels reflect the creative, irreverent side, whereas his supposedly pedantic political commentaries show his conformist and modern persona.

One of Nandy's main points is that in a world that has bludgeoned all shamans (other than those singing the praises of instrumental rationality) into submission, the modern artist has to demonstrate his or her unequivocal allegiance to so-called correct values and beliefs in order to preserve a space in which their creative transgressions are allowed to roam free and to question precisely such values and beliefs. In other words, in a concession that says more about our times than it does about either cognitive dissonance or hypocrisy in the artist, the conformist political persona seems necessary to enable and free the creative, artistic persona. After appreciating Rushdie's fiction for its depiction of the polyglot popular culture of modern India, Nandy contrasts that fiction with his political commentaries, which he thinks

have all the "right" values in a predictable social-democratic for-
mat...[are] cliché-ridden and pathetically dependent on categories
derived from the popular Anglo-Saxon philosophy of the inter-war
years....when Rushdie writes on public issues in non-fictional form,
he...speaks in a tone that may be very comforting to the aging Left,
but that is not even good radical chic, being at least thirty years out
of date....Rushdie...driven by his internalization of the West, tries
in his non-fiction to be allegiant to Enlightenment values, to win
through such conformity the freedom to be more careless about such
values in serious fiction. (1995, 239, 260)

Now, some who have reveled in the free-wheeling prose of Rushdie's
fiction will probably feel a trifle let down on reading his forays into
serious sociopolitical commentary. (For instance, his stentorian lecture to Rajiv Gandhi for banning the *Satanic Verses* in India and his
review of Attenborough's movie *Gandhi* do, to a degree, bear out
Nandy's point.)[1] However, I would submit that it is possible to read
Rushdie's split self on an entirely different register, one that foregrounds the notion of postcolonial agency: a position that marks
the need to undertake simultaneously a metacritique of modernity
even as one uses its institutions and resources to struggle for fairness
and equity in the worlds we do inhabit. I elaborate later on this notion
and its import for the possibility of a critical international relations.

Rushdie the author brings to life a fabulous South Asia where
even as people so often riot and kill in the name of religion or community or language, they also share an awareness of our inextricably mixed, miscegenated origins, our thoroughly adulterated genealogies not only in South Asia but also in and with the west, and our
shared predicaments of life in a space so effulgent with madness of
one kind and another. A bond unites the peoples, religions, cultures,
languages, and eccentricities of this space, a bond that enables us to
come back together repeatedly after every bout of slaughter and
suffering and, against all odds, to recreate communities. There is in
the author of *Midnight's Children* a genuine empathy, an affection
for the subcontinent in all its diversity, orneriness, and irrationali-
ties. This is the Rushdie who is able to carry effortlessly with him,
like a whimsical tambourine man, millions in South Asia and elsewhere who hang on every word of his fiction.

In some part, the allure of his fiction lies in the ability both to
create and to evoke our shared selves as a people, with all the vio-

lence and love that simultaneously entails. Here is Rushdie's description of the frenetic hours to midnight August 14–15, 1947, the very moment Jawaharlal Nehru was (presumably) putting the finishing touches to his stirring "tryst with destiny" speech to the bloody new nation and inscribing it securely within the Enlightenment's narrative of progress and redemption:

> August in Bombay: a month of festivals, the month of Krishna's birthday and Coconut Day; and this year—fourteen hours to go, thirteen, twelve—there was an extra festival on the calendar, a new myth to celebrate, because a nation which had never previously existed was about to win its freedom, catapulting us into a world which, although it had five thousand years of history, although it had invented the game of chess and traded with Middle Kingdom Egypt, was nevertheless quite imaginary; into a mythical land, a country which would never exist except by the efforts of a phenomenal collective will—except in a dream we all agreed to dream; it was a mass fantasy shared in varying degrees by Bengali and Punjabi, Madrasi and Jat, and would periodically need the sanctification and renewal which can only be provided by rituals of blood. (Rushdie 1980, 129–30)

Few passages better illustrate the fragility and artifice of this new collective called the nation, as well as its allure and power over those in its thrall. In contrast, when Rushdie writes in the vein of social critic, the persona he inhabits (or is forced to inhabit) is often that of a "Paki" living in Thatcher country, the reluctant spokesman of a South Asian diaspora in a place that refuses to recognize them as even human in some instances, a doubting Muslim constantly appalled and belittled by the caricatures of Islam produced by the western media and increasingly by a Hinduizing India. Rushdie will not stand idly by as the Raj is filtered through the sepia-tinted lenses of imperialist nostalgia so that the horrors of British colonialism in India and elsewhere are effaced and replaced by the kitschy spectacle of high tea on the lawns, beturbaned bearers, chutney sandwiches, and noblesse oblige. Rushdie irritatingly and stridently reminds mainstream English culture that imperialism was mainly about racism, exploitation, and plunder. The pacifying of that history into Anglophilic nostalgia will not go quietly into the night.

Rushdie the activist-commentator cannot but engage with the political, economic, social, and cultural milieu of late modern Britain. In that context, he will fight for the rights of the people with whom he identifies (among others, prominently the South Asian diaspora), using the weapons available to him in the country in which he lives. As he notes about various diaspora in Britain: "We are. We are here. And we are not willing to be excluded from any part of our heritage; which heritage includes both a Bradford-born Indian kid's right to be treated as a full member of British society, and also the right of any member of this post-diaspora community to draw on its roots for its art, just as all the world's community of displaced writers has always done" (Rushdie 1991, 15). He demands that people — irrespective of race, ethnicity, color, gender, language, religion, or other baggage — be treated fairly, honestly, equally, or, in other words, be treated as any "full member of British society." If I might put it another way (mangling Paul Gilroy in the process), it's too bad there ain't no black in the Union Jack, but we're here and we're here to stay in all our brown-blackness, with our spices and curries, our smells and accents. This may not be your idea of England, it may completely ruin for some the majestic cadence of Shakespeare's insular England,[2] but for those of who have landed here through forces and currents we neither fully understand nor control, for good or for bad, England is one of our homes, and English one of our languages. Deal with it.

To ask to be treated as a "full member of British society" can only mean that one demands one's rights in an England made and remade by modernity with all its attendant values, including fundamental rights to freedom of speech, property, association, practice of religion, equality of opportunity, legal protection against discrimination: the whole baggage of modern, liberal society. In similar vein, Rushdie has critiqued the growing communalization of Indian political culture, the rise of Hindu fundamentalist parties, and the compromises made by avowedly secular parties and leaders with the retrogressive forces of both Hindu and Muslim persuasions. In such critiques, Rushdie does drop anchor in modern, liberal-democratic, pluralist values. Does his demand for equality of treatment and for fundamental rights of various minority groups in Britain or India under the regime of modernity *mesh uneasily* with his fantastic deconstructions of the modern condition, of religion and faith, of the idea of selfhood, of the nation? Perhaps. Does his deconstruction of all such identities *contradict or subvert* his politics of struggles for fairness, justice, and equality in a racist Britain and a Hinduizing India? Absolutely not. On the contrary, the simultaneous struggle for fairness and equality *within* a world created and reshaped by modernity *and* for a world that goes *beyond* modernity itself is a definitively postcolonial position, one that is indispensable in order to have any sense of agency at all under late modernity. This position is neither remarkable nor contradictory: various struggles, be they of women or blacks or gays and lesbians or *dalits* (a word meaning "oppressed" and a label preferred by so-called lower-caste Indians to *untouchable* or to Gandhi's neologism *harijan*, which means "children of god"), have combined a metalevel struggle against a world fragmented by divisive identities with a struggle for fairness and equity in a world in which some identities seem to be more equal than others.

I suspect that, to some degree, Nandy's fondness for the novelist and his impatience with the political commentator hinges on the issue of ironic distance. There is something seductive about the detachment afforded by a genealogical standpoint. The deconstruction of modernist narratives from a distant nonplace articulates a self that is at once fashionable and with-it: it matches the wry mood of (the sexiest) sections of contemporary academe and literature. Somehow, that self is seen as meshing uneasily with the political commentator who brazenly takes the stand and displays the ax he has to grind. Nandy probably regards himself as a modern-day shaman whose forte is exposing the pathologies and conceits of a modernity run amok. This business of prescribing solutions for societal ills (in his view, nearly all attributable to the juggernaut of modernity) is something of which he wants no part. If anything, he would aver, modern civilization has too many self-appointed problem solvers, social engineers who cannot leave well enough alone. It is among the so-called defeated civilizations (unmasked witch doctors, faith healers who have lost the allegiance of erstwhile wards, rainmakers standing forlorn amidst arid lands) that our world may yet find redemption. Nandy disengages himself with avuncular charm: "I shall leave the reader with these questions, in the belief that all questions cannot—and should not—be answered by those who raise them" (1995, 266). Not only can he get away with such a gentle evasion, but in some sense we want him to. After all, over the years his questions pace colonialism, modernity, identity, science, and development have been superbly insightful. To elevate him to a resident mystic or shaman of antimodernity seems entirely befitting. If he wants to keep his critique of modernity unsullied by "descent" into prescriptive social engineering, it seems a small price to pay: let us by all means indulge him such a request. By the same token, however, irony has its place. The necessary accompaniment to such an act of critical detachment ought to be a politics of engagement, a politics that raises the awkward and pragmatic issue of degree as Edward Said does:

> It is at precisely that nexus of committed participation and intellec-
> tual commitment that we should situate ourselves to ask *how much*
> identity, *how much* positive consolidation, *how much* administered
> approbation we are willing to tolerate in the name of our cause, our
> culture, our state.... In education, politics, history and culture, there
> is at the present time a role to be played by secular oppositional in-
> tellectuals, call them a class of informed and effective wet blankets,
> who do not allow themselves the luxury of playing the identity game...
> but who more compassionately press the interests of the unheard,
> the unrepresented, the unconnected people of our world, and, who
> do so not in the "jargon of authenticity" but with the accents of per-
> sonal restraint, historical skepticism and committed intellect. (Said
> 1988, 59, emphasis original)

This is a politics that never loses sight of the necessity to critique constantly and to move beyond identity politics, but that is also equally cognizant of the fact that within modern societies, struggles over equity, fairness, and tolerance are constituted by discourses that regard identity as legal and social vessels with meaning and rights.

Such a simultaneous struggle for a universalist notion of fairness within modernity and against the modern condition informs Kwame Anthony Appiah (1992) as he makes an important distinction be-tween the politics of postcolonialism and postmodernism. Appiah discerns a certain transition in the late 1960s and early 1970s in francophone and anglophone African literature. Whereas the early works of authors such as Chinua Achebe celebrated the emergence of the independent nation-state and regarded decolonization as the originary moment for each new African nation to come into its own finally, the novels of the later decades became disillusioned and bit-terly critical of nation building and development as they degener-ated into kleptocracy and ethnic fratricide. In their disenchantment with the narrative of the nation and in their experimentation with metropolitan styles of pastiche, parody, irony, and magic realism, postcolonial authors (such as Chinua Achebe, Ben Okri, Rushdie, Gabriel García Márquez) often seemed to be cut from the same cloth as western, postmodernist writers disenchanted with metanarratives *tout court*. Yet, there were crucial differences, in terms of politics, between these two genres of writing (which one might term provisionally, with Appiah, the *postcolonial* and the *postmodern*), differences that were ignored or elided under the universalization of the postmodern moment in literature itself. Appiah's summation of one of the crucial distinctions between postcolonialism and postmodernism on the question of political agency is succinct:

> Postcoloniality is *after* all this: and its *post,* like postmodernism's, is also a *post* that challenges earlier legitimating narratives.... But it challenges them in the name of the ethical universal; in the name of *humanism,* "le gloire pour l'homme." And on that ground it is not an ally for Western postmodernism but an agonist, from which I believe postmodernism may have something to learn.... For what I am calling humanism can be provisional, historically contingent, anti-essentialist (in other words, postmodern) and still be demanding. We can surely maintain a powerful engagement with the concern to avoid cruelty and pain while nevertheless recognizing the contingency of that concern. Maybe, then, we can recover within postmodernism the postcolonial writers' humanism—the concern for human suffering, for the victims of the postcolonial state...while still rejecting the master narratives of modernism. (1992, 155, emphasis original)

Throughout this volume, I keep returning to the idea that a politics of postcolonialism is premised on such a simultaneous engagement within and against modernity, and can serve as an agonistic encounter with postmodernism. To give a specific instance, I argue that even as we deconstruct "India" and "Sri Lanka," or "Tamil" and "Sinhala," or "Buddhist," "Hindu," and "Muslim," we ought to remain aware of the political import of each of these deconstructions in the contexts in which they are made. What might be the effect of demonstrating the historical artifices of the Tamil claim to a homeland in northeastern Sri Lanka at a time when the Sinhala-dominated government in Colombo is pursuing a politics of ethnic annihilation against the same Tamils? What sort of political gesture must this deconstruction be accompanied by for it to escape complicity with the Sri Lankan state? If one deconstructs the idea of the nation as just another vestige of modernity's spent narratives, what sort of alternative spatial imaginaire can one contemplate in its stead? If the postcolonial nation-state in its present avatar has reached a dead end, what sort of politics can we envisage to produce spaces of tolerance, plurality, and nonviolence?

These questions involve normative choices, a sensitivity to specific political contexts, and implications of suggested actions. A premature and exaggerated claim regarding the death of the narratives of modernity or of the futility of any form of identity politics based on the idea of a sovereign selfhood incapacitate our ability to deal precisely with such matters of degree. In an essay on the import of recent works in critical international relations, I argued that even works embarking from professedly critical postmodern and poststructural perspectives often replicate the Eurocentric ecumene of "world" politics. Emerging from a rather comfortably self-contained view of the west, they seem to contain little recognition that a totalizing critique of all forms of essentialism and identity politics might play out very differently for people situated outside putative mainstreams or that the demise of narratives such as the nation may have different political implications for those situated elsewhere. I argued the case for a provisional or strategic essentialism that ought to govern our political actions in late-modern times and suggested that posing the issue as a choice between *either* deconstructing the narratives of modernity *or* complicitous political activism in a world dominated by modernity was an impoverishing and naive way of conducting one's politics (1993; see Der Derian 1994 for a feisty rebuttal).

We seem to have allowed this seeming contradiction (between a belief in the progressive political steps that will carry us beyond modernity's violences and the fact that such a belief itself relies on the institutions and traditions of a modernist narrative) to paralyze us or, at any rate, to cloud our analysis. My notion of postcolonial agency avers that one has to engage constantly in identity politics without ever forgetting that the identity one inhabits is provisional, artificial, often impoverishingly reductionist, and only a single identity out of the many that one enters and leaves as circumstances both dictate and warrant. To put the same matter somewhat differently, a postcolonial perspective entails a radical acceptance of the open-ended character of our narratives even as it accepts responsibility to affect the trajectories along which those narratives seem headed. In articulating a postcolonial position that resists the temptations of narrative closure, I am asserting agency over that most fundamental of contested spaces: the future. I refuse the blackmail that suggests every attempt at social or political engineering must be either an instance of hubris or of unfashionable reformism.

In this context, I would like to return to Rushdie and Nandy, this time on the question of aesthetics and politics. Appropriately enough, I do so by analogy to a realm that enthuses both Rushdie and Nandy, South Asia and England: cricket. I see the ironist's distaste for explicit and strident political rhetoric in a controversy that dogged cricket in England earlier in this century (and, in different variations, elsewhere in the world) regarding the differences between so-called amateur, gentlemen players and an emerging class of more hard-bitten professionals. The former were usually Oxbridge, upper-crust, and supposedly more sportsmanlike, whereas the latter were often (again, supposedly) cut of rougher cloth. In a game remarkable for the interpretive character of its rules and the degree to which subjective judgments decide outcomes, much depends on players abiding by unwritten codes of conduct and fair play. In this milieu, the argument went, gentleman players were more likely to play with a straight bat than were professionals whose very livelihoods depended on their performance and, indeed, whose appreciation for the aesthetic of the game itself was thus clouded.

Of course, much of this debate was nothing but elitist humbug.[3] Yet, in some ways it was also about an attempt to recapture a pure, noninstrumental, and premodern sense of being in a Britain thoroughly disenchanted by industrialism and modernity. It was an effort to recapture what Walter Benjamin (1969) calls the "aura" of things profaned and secularized by the advent of modernity and mass production. Through the window of cricket, one discerns a romanticist reaction to the specialized professionals (the denizens of Weber's iron cage) and a longing for a simpler, less specialized, and enchanted world in which the gentleman was marked by his effortless ease in all fields while being a specialist in none. As with many romanticist moves, it retained a conservative tone as it buttressed the hierarchies of British society. In an analogous sense, I discern in the distaste for strident, engaged political writings of

Rushdie an antimodern preference for social commentary that does not brazenly espouse its cause. There is a fetishization of ironic distance, for an ideological argument at some remove from immediate material provocations. It is, in that sense, an aesthetic argument that tries to efface the traces of work or labor that produce the standpoint itself. To put it bluntly, the distance between the politics of irony and an aestheticized politics of disengagement is worryingly short.

Looking back from the distance of more than a decade, one can chart a trajectory in the case of critical international relations theory that is related to the above discussion on politics and aesthetics. The force of Richard Ashley's critique of mainstream international relations scholarship in his early works (specifically 1983 and 1984) arose from an arresting combination of Pierre Bourdieu and Antonio Gramsci—specifically their insights on habitus, economism, and doxa. This combination was effectively used by Ashley to depict how a supposedly contested discipline with its lore of legendary debates and sharply divergent ideological positions was in reality underlain by an enduring consensus (the habitus) on the way the world turns. Beneath the apparent divergences within mainstream international relations scholarship, Ashley argued, were an uncritical ingestion of the neoclassical economic model of asocial, utility-maximizing rational actors interacting in a milieu of anarchy as a metaphor for the system of nation-states; a fundamentally ahistorical perspective on the relationship between economy and nature, reifying an ephemeral and socially produced distinction between these domains into an eternal and uncontestable truth; and a view of the future as an extrapolation of scientifically discoverable laws and trends rather than as an open-ended consequence of engaged social and political interactions among sentient human beings. In essence, Ashley's critique of mainstream international relations scholarship reinstated political agency and the social within the increasingly unself-reflexive and ahistorical world of neorealist scholarship. However, by the late 1980s, the focus on political agency within critical international relations scholarship receded into the background, and one witnessed the enclosing of an already claustrophobic disciplinary debate between "dissident" and "mainstream" international relations rather than an engagement with the issues that should have been debated:

the altered character of north-south relations under conditions of newly energized global Fordism; the relevance of identity politics in a context wherein all identities seemed adrift in a sea of deconstruction; the construction of a politics of coalition to oppose a U.S. regime energized by its victory in the cold war and flexing its rejuvenated muscles in Iraq. The target of critical scholarship seemed to change from *neorealist practice and statecraft* with its impoverishing economism to the *works of various neorealist international relations scholars* who now stood in as disciplinary surrogates of such practice. Somewhere along the line, text overwhelmed (and became) context.

Indeed, even the lingering traces of Gramsci's notion of a committed, organic intellectual seemed fully exorcised when Ashley described a genealogical standpoint or critical attitude from where one could view international relations: "Eschewing any claim to secure grounds, the appropriate posture would aspire instead to an overview of international history in the making, a view from afar, from up high" (1987, 408). The whiff of Olympus that accompanied this avowedly coordinateless genealogical standpoint was strengthened when nearly every form of scholarship that provisionally and strategically sought a mooring in identity (gender, race, class, nation) or cause (the environment, human rights, peace) was deemed deficient either because it proceeded from an all too assured notion of a foundational truth or ethic, or because it was committed to some sovereign notion of subjectivity, or because it read social reality in a religious mode that desired to discipline ambiguity rather than celebrate it, or because it subscribed to a hypermasculine will to knowledge, and so on (Ashley and Walker 1990a, 1990b).[4] Whatever the intradisciplinary angst that motivated such a claustrophobic debate, one of the regrettable upshots of it was that it deflated possible alliances between critical international relations scholarship and other progressive intellectual-political movements. As in Ashley's work in the late 1980s, the retreat to an ethereal nonspace above and beyond the rough and tumble of everyday politics seems to echo the aesthetic pose I outlined in the context of Nandy's work. Any effort to anchor one's politics provisionally and contingently around a discourse of identity had to be deconstructed as a power move, leaving a disengaged total critique as the only option. There is a politics of purity at work here premised on a disenabling choice: either one deconstructs modernity in toto, or one must be complicit with it. The politics of postcolonial agency I offer here is an effort to go beyond that choice.[5]

OVERVIEW

My inquiry into the troubled journey of postcolonial nationalism in South Asia is structured in two parts. In part I, "Narratives in Contention: Indian, Sinhalese, and Tamil Nationalisms," I examine the discursive construction of identity/difference in the form of narrative. Specifically, I examine four distinct narratives: pan-Indian nationalism as reflected in the discourse of Indian foreign policy; Sinhala nationalism in Sri Lanka as read through the life and text of President J. R. Jayewardene; and Tamil nationalisms in both Sri Lanka and the Indian state of Tamil Nadu, read through the discourses of Eelam and Dravidianism, respectively. Together, these narratives of identity serve as a general historical background to the second part of the book, where the focus is more narrowly trained on Indian intervention into the Sri Lankan ethnic struggle.

In chapter 1, I examine the self-construction of India in the twentieth century through the discourse of foreign policy. I depict how something called *India* emerged in counterpoise to a colonial and imperial west, on the one hand, and to a certain construction of South Asia, on the other. The late-colonial experience and the nationalist movement imparted to the character of state power in India a powerful ideology that defined the nation in terms of secularism, a respect for diversity, and the reversal of underdevelopment by state-led industrialization. On all these counts, the Indian experience was inscribed as qualitatively superior and more progressive than the monological visions that supposedly underwrote the neighboring countries (religion in the case of Pakistan and Nepal, a growing majoritarian Sinhala-Buddhist identity in the case of Sri Lanka, monarchy in the case of Bhutan, and so on). Moreover, there was a strong belief among Indian state elites that with independence they also inherited the mantle of the British colonial administration as the strategic linchpin of the entire region and that the smaller powers essentially had to frame their policies in line with Indian interests. Such a notion of regional hegemony remained largely incipient during the 1950s and 1960s but received a sharp fillip in 1971 on the secession (with

India's help) of Bangladesh from Pakistan. I argue that this event (specifically, the way it narrated into the historical memory of Indian state elites) inaugurated a new and dangerous turn in the Indian state's regional and domestic policies. 1971 was interpreted as India's coming of age in the tough world of realpolitik and decisive proof of her hegemonic status in the region. At one level, India considered ethnic and other subnational movements a danger to the very principle of state sovereignty and a problem that it could assist its neighbors in resolving (as demonstrated when it helped Sri Lanka put down the Maoist Janatha Vimukthi Peramuna [JVP][6] insurgency in mid-1971). At another level, however, Bangladesh showed how ethnicity also represented an opportunity for India to put neighbors in their place, destabilize their regimes, and, indeed, promote the balkanization of their territories if need be. Whether India stood for the principle of statist sovereignty in the region (ethnicity as danger) or whether it regarded the fate of "kindred ethnic minorities" in neighboring countries as a useful cover under which to pursue its geopolitical domination of its neighbors (ethnicity as opportunity) was never satisfactorily resolved by her state elites in the decades after 1971. However, destabilizing neighboring regimes by aiding those kindred ethnic minorities became a staple of Indian regional policy thereafter.

Postcolonial Sri Lanka reflects a tension between the discourse of universal, equal citizenship for all within a nation and the claims of the majority community to special status. Chapter 2 argues that most Sinhala political leaders since 1948 have articulated a narrative that accords the majority community (the Sinhala Buddhists) a special place in the national hierarchy even as they push others (Tamils, Burghers, Moors) into their proper places. I depict the construction of Sri Lanka on a majoritarian ethos through a textual analysis of the writings, speeches, memoirs, policies, and actions of a leading politician whose life straddles the entire twentieth century: J. R. Jayewardene.

I next examine, in chapter 3, the narrative of Tamil identity in Sri Lanka by tracing the movement of Tamil politics from moderation and attempted federalism (1940s–1960s) to secession and self-determination (1970s) to the present politics of irredentist violence (1980s on). I show how Tamil nationalism enters a militant and violently exclusionary phase — initially as a reaction to Sinhalese repression and to the failure of moderate politics, but increasingly (especially in recent times) with a logic that can be understood mainly in a global context of such local movements. Perhaps the critical feature of the emergence of Tamil nationalism in Sri Lanka is that it is inextricably connected to the modernization of Ceylon. The enumeration and fixation of previously fluid identities, done supposedly to distribute economic and political assets equitably, and of policies of affirmative action — all mediated through the logic of electoral politics — have unleashed consequences that are superficially antimodern: the resurgence of supposedly primordial identities.

A narrative that plays a crucial role in Indo–Sri Lankan relations is Dravidian nationalism in the southern state of Tamil Nadu in India. I chart its movement from a progressive anti-Brahminism, anti-casteism (1930s and 1940s), and brief secessionism in its early years to its reconciliation with an (inadequate) federal dispensation in the Indian union from the 1950s on. By the late 1960s, the secessionist proclivities of the Dravidian movement had all but disappeared. Yet, in the 1980s, as Indira Gandhi's regime sought to intervene in Sri Lanka, the secessionist history of the Dravidian movement would serve as a crucial alibi for India. The tenuous connections between the Sri Lankan Tamil nationalist movement and the Dravidian movement in Tamil Nadu would be greatly exaggerated by Indian state elites to embellish the claim that India had legitimate security reasons to be actively interested in Sri Lanka's domestic affairs.

The two narratives of Tamil nationalism are critical to some of the overall theoretical arguments I make in this book. I use the case of Dravidian nationalism to establish my point that there is nothing essentialist about ethnicity, nor is any ethnic group inherently predisposed to secession. Whether or not a particular segment of society commences on an ethnonationalist path is an open-ended, political question. To a substantial degree, the trajectory that such movements (usually emergent in peripheral regions with nonmajoritarian language, religion, or culture as their markers) will embark upon is dependent on the way the center treats such a movement. If the center's response is one of tolerance, respect, and fair-mindedness, the trajectory tends to veer away from separatism and toward a federal spatial imaginaire, as happened with the Dravidian movement. When majoritarian conceptions of national space overwhelm difference and marginalize those outside the self-anointed national community, however, ethnicity and ethnonationalism become potent vehicles for mobilizing the multiple resistances to such discrimination, as demonstrated in the narrative of Tamil nationalism in Sri Lanka. Thus, in this work, ethnicity is not regarded as an always-already inferior and subversive counter to the nation as it is the supplementary principle that allows for the construction of the nation in specific ways.

These narratives of identity serve as the backdrop for part II, "Delusions of Grandeur: India, Tamil Nadu, and Sri Lanka," which represents an ethnography of the Indian political and military involvement in Sri Lanka (chapters 4 through 6) between 1980 and 1991. Relying primarily on more than sixty interviews conducted over three years in India and in Sri Lanka, and secondarily on the literature the Indian intervention has spawned, this section examines how the contending narratives of identity led to violent conflict. At one level, Indian motivations in Sri Lanka stemmed from a desire to see that country resolve its ethnic question by recognizing itself as a multiethnic society in which Tamils would not be discriminated against. But, at another level, the "kindred" Tamil minority in Sri Lanka and the growing militant movement there gave India an opportunity to destabilize Jayewardene's regime, which seemed oblivious to Indian pretensions to become regional hegemon. For much of the early 1980s, the Indian government encouraged the Sri Lankan Tamils, including militant groups, in their fight against the Sri Lankan state. It adopted what came to be called a twin-track policy: on the one hand, offering its good offices in helping the Sri Lankan government settle the ethnic question through negotiations with the Tamil political representatives, and on the other, aiding the Sri Lankan Tamil militants in order to demonstrate their ability to make life difficult for Jayewardene. Exactly where and how the two tracks would meet were never thought through, let alone specified. Diplomatic pressure on Colombo on the ethnic question was undercut by arming and training Tamil militants in India. Because of such covert support, both the Sri Lankan regime and Sinhala civil society had little faith in Indian neutrality or advice on the ethnic question. On the other side, the main militant group, the LTTE, was disappointed by the Indo–Sri Lanka Agreement (ISLA) of 1987, which, while allaying India's geopolitical concerns, forced (in their view) a settlement of the ethnic question that did not go as far as they would have liked. The contradictions between these two policy lines produced a military intervention to implement the agreement (the induction of the Indian Peace Keeping Force) that was disastrous for all concerned.

Chapter 7 ends by pointing to an aporia in postcolonial nationalism: the very micropolitics of producing the nation are responsible for its unmaking or unraveling. The desire to produce a strong and coherent nation—usually on the explicit or implicit principle of a majoritarian ethos—engenders alternative movements (ethnonationalist) for secession. Such movements become an integral part of each nation's efforts to destabilize their neighbors. Nation and ethnicity are locked in a productive and dialectical dyad that creates enunciative spaces for fashioning political careers, winning elections, coming to power, and so on. The mobilization of ethnic and other constituencies on the basis of a discourse of danger is rewarded by the very system (democratic, electoral politics) that is supposedly the solvent of such identities and promoter of a unified sense of national citizenship.

This aporia serves as the bridge to the concluding chapter of the book, wherein I return to the question of agency. Although most works classified as postcolonial are persuasive in their deconstruction of the multiple fictions that inform the nation, they are remarkably reticent about the vision of the future that animates their politics. If the postcolonial nation is indeed in crisis, caught twixt the twin pincers of growing ethnonationalist movements within and the dissolving, assimilative, neocolonialist forces of globalization without, what sorts of spatial configurations can we envisage or provisionally and contingently outline as a means to engage with the politics of our time? At the risk of sounding either gauche or like yet another modernist social engineer, I attempt an outline of my preferred South Asia. I do so by entering an ongoing debate that reimagines this region as one marked by decentralized nation-states with high degrees of regional or provincial autonomy. I suggest a countermemorial reading of two significant political events: the moment of Partition (in 1947) and the creation of Bangladesh (in 1971) to make my case for a highly decentralized and genuinely federal system of nation-states in this region. The contrasting examples of Dravidian and Sri Lankan Tamil nationalisms powerfully support my argument for reenvisioning South Asia along these lines. I end the book with a meditation on the narratives that currently constitute and dominate the spaces of India, Sri Lanka, and Eelam. At some level, they are all premised on an effort to recover a pure originary state of being where territory and identity coincide. Resisting this urge for recovery, I prefer to see the narratives that constitute us to be open-ended and miscegenated. Accompanying this resolute refusal to engage in a politics of transcendence is a normative commitment to create and maintain a democratic space for a pluralist ethos, one that respects alterity and refuses to banalize difference into synthesis.

I

*Narratives in Contention:
Indian, Sinhalese, and
Tamil Nationalisms*

Mimetic Histories:
Foreign Policy and the Narration of India

The event is not what happens. The event is that which can be narrated.

— ALLEN FELDMAN, FORMATIONS OF VIOLENCE

In a sense, to speak of foreign policy presupposes the availability of a given spatialization of the world in terms of us and them. Conventionally, foreign policy is the set of actions by "us" out "there." In the modern, post-Westphalian world of nation-states, foreign policy constitutes the actions of state elites who try to maintain, at minimum, something called "our national security" and to further at every opportunity something called "our national interest." This discourse of foreign policy is amnesiac about the relative novelty of its central identities and the dialectical character of its antinomies. It exemplifies the Nietzschean dictum regarding the truth of our depictions of social reality, that they are produced by "a mobile army of metaphors, metonyms and anthropomorphisms — in short, a sum of human relations, which have been enhanced, transposed, and embellished poetically and rhetorically, and which after long use seem firm, canonical and obligatory to a people: truths are illusions about which one has forgotten that this is what they are" (Nietzsche 1954, 46–47).

Conventional studies of foreign policy and international relations view the world as comprised of putatively unitary nation-states that

3

interact with each other in an anarchic milieu: the constituent units of this system are seen as unremarkable, unquestionable givens— things that go without saying because they came without saying. In his definitive work on the international system, Kenneth Waltz (1979) makes it clear that historicizing such a spatialization of the world is not germane to the issue at hand: namely, creating a parsimonious theoretical model that describes the world order. From a postcolonial perspective, it is unsurprising that he can blithely state, "Concern with international politics as a system requires concentration on the states that make the most difference. A general theory of international politics is necessarily based on the great powers" (1979, 73). His is a world far removed from that of Said (1993), who historicizes the emergence of great powers and third worlds as simultaneous and mutually constitutive events in an imperialist worlding of modern geography.

In their ahistorical and unself-reflexive depiction of the world, mainstream international relations scholars engage in a reductionism and reification that Richard Ashley (1983, 1984) describes insightfully in his critique of the economism that underlay most of their analyses. In this chapter, however, I regard foreign policy as a discursive practice that, far from being the actions of an always recognizable "us" on a "them," is historically emergent and produces and reproduces the very antinomies critical to identity itself: us/them, domestic/foreign, self/other, inside/outside.[1] Viewed thus, an entity called "India" is coeval with a discourse called "Indian foreign policy," and one can talk of the discourse of Indian foreign policy as an important and constitutive moment in the emergence of India itself. Foreign policy may then be regarded as a set of practices oriented toward the creation and maintenance of boundaries, borders, and distinctions between a self and other(s): a spatial, identity-forming discourse, an act of simultaneous self-fashioning and worlding.

I begin by examining the spatialization of India during the late-colonial period: how the accident of British administrative boundaries became endowed as the "natural" geographical frontiers of India. I then depict how the encounter between India and the west resulted in a paradoxical notion of decolonization: at one level, national redemption was impossible without independence from the British, but, at another, the tasks the postcolonial state set itself mirrored all that the west already was. I examine the tension between genuine decolonization and a mimetic vision of the future in three critical arenas: economic planning, science and the scientific temper, and national integration. The legacy of this tension has made for a national imaginaire that is strongly centralizing and regards every assertion of provincial or regional autonomy and identity to be the entering wedge of disintegration. This centralizing imperative became even stronger after the emergence of Bangladesh in 1971, which had enormous consequences for both Indian policy toward its regional neighbors and, within India, the central government's policies and attitudes toward state-level regimes. At the regional level, earlier incipient notions of India as hegemon received a strong fillip from what was perceived as a success in Bangladesh, while domestically the trend toward riding rough-shod over state rights through overcentralization gained momentum. Within and without the nation, ethnicity came to be regarded not merely as a danger to the principle of statist sovereignty, but equally as an opportunity that allowed for the acquisition and retention of state power in specific ways.

Throughout, I use the term *modulation* to refer to the way, under modernity, social reality is understood in the form of replicable narratives or scripts that govern our actions and enable us to find our way in the world. With ever-increasing ecumenes as technologies of print and of electronic audio-visual reproduction sweep across the world, this modulation of reality constitutes certain national experiences as originals and defines the task for latecomers as replicating the experience of such originals. From the complexity and contingency of what happened in Europe, the story of an ideal form of nation building is abstracted and becomes the model against which postcolonial pasts and futures are evaluated, found wanting, and, by closer imitation, redemption is sought. By a parallel logic, the complexity and contingency of India's role in 1971, culminating in the break-up of Pakistan and the creation of Bangladesh, gets modulated post facto into a script for the production of Indian identity through a hegemonic regional policy and an overcentralized, authoritarian style of governance. In this modulation of the events of 1971, ethnicity plays a crucial role. It becomes both a putative danger to the principle of pluralist nation building and an opportunity that can be effectively used to legitimize Indian intervention into neighboring countries and into states in the Indian union.

WORLDING INDIA

In the beginning, there was Geography. The discursive construction of India, like for many a nation, has often begun by highlighting the fact that nature, by a seismic throw of the dice, created a physical cradle for its emergence. The evocation of a divine cartography that separated this land from others is exemplified in the following quote from the opening paragraph of a book that was for a long time the definitive text on Indian history:

> India is the name given to the vast peninsula which the continent of Asia throws out to the south of the magnificent mountain ranges that stretch in a sword like curve across the southern border of Tibet. This huge expanse of territory... has the shape of an irregular quadrilateral.... The lofty mountain chain in the north... includes not only the snow-capped ridges of the Himalayas but also their less elevated offshoots.... These lead down to the sea and separate the country from the wooded valley of the Irrawaddy on the one hand and the hilly tableland of Iran on the other. (Majumdar, Raychaudhuri, and Datta, 1960, 1)

This notion of India as a naturalistic entity, a geographical expression of unity, is echoed by the man regarded as the architect of modern India, Jawaharlal Nehru:

> The accidents of geography have had a powerful effect on determining national character and history. The fact that India was cut off by the tremendous barrier of the Himalayas and by the sea produced a sense of *unity* in this wide area and at the same time bred exclusiveness. Over this vast territory a vivid and *homogenous civilization* grew up which had plenty of scope for expansion and development, and which continued to preserve a *strong cultural unity.*... Mountains and seas are no longer barriers, but they still determine *a* people's character and *a* country's political and economic position. (1946, 452, emphasis added)

The underlined phrases try to render the nation one against a historical record that just as easily lends itself to a story about the tremendous diversity of the region. Similarly, the enduring patterns of long-distance trade and of demographic and cultural movements give lie to the claim regarding the barrier presented by the mountains and seas. More importantly, Nehru (and the historians referred to earlier) elides a more political and discomfiting story regarding the origins of India—namely, that its boundaries were determined not so much by the enduring accidents of geography as they were by the ecumene of the British colonial empire in South Asia at the point of decolonization.

This point is best indicated by a brief counterfactual exercise. For all the invocations of divine cartography, hardly any Indian nationalist leader considered Nepal to be a legitimate part of India, although it would be firmly within the geographical ambit traced by Nehru and the historians in the above quotes. Similarly, with few exceptions, Ceylon was never considered legitimately part of India during the movement for independence. Such counterfactuals reflect that the imaginaire of India coincided with the administrative boundaries of the British Indian empire (Nepal remained a constitutional monarchy outside the direct rule of the Raj, and Ceylon was administered as a separate colonial state).

Along with these initial steps to naturalize the region go a discourse of danger that marks it as porous, offering endless opportunities for marauders of various hues to invade and subjugate India. K. M. Panikkar, a historian respected for his insights into matters geopolitical, notes in his definitive work that

> India is so situated that she could be attacked both from the land side and from the side of the sea. . . . [T]he invasions of India from the land side have been the result of unsettled conditions in Central Asia. . . . From the side of the sea the position is different. The fact that we have had numerous invasions from the land side and only one invasion from the sea side has made us believe that the danger from the land side is greater and more permanent and the danger from the sea is less important. That there has been only one invasion from the sea is due to the fact that the invasion route to India came to be discovered only in 1498. It is necessary to emphasize that from that historic day when Vasco Da Gama with his fleet of warships arrived at Calicut, India has ever been under the relentless pressure of sea power, steady and unseen over long periods, but effectively controlling our economic life and political life. In fact, since 1498, India has been blockaded. (1969, 115–16)[2]

Having isolated the specific points of vulnerability in the "geo-body" (Winichakul 1994) of India, Panikkar proceeds to outline what he considered indispensable for the protection of the realm, the minimum set of conditions that would ensure that the points of vulnerability would not become actual opportunities for entry and conquest. This discourse constructs the past in a specific manner and points to the task of the future: whenever the great land mass of India has been marked by political fragmentation and social disunity, the threat of external conquest has become a reality, whether in the repeated conquests through the northwest mountain passes or the consolidation of a British mercantile trading company into the world's largest colonial enterprise. Indian civilization and security have been at their apex, the narrative avers, only at the times when the subcontinental land mass has been united under a single polity, marked by both political integration and sociocultural renaissance. In the script of Indian history, the Golden Ages invariably refer to the subcontinental empires of the Mauryan dynasty and the reign of the Mughal emperor Akbar. The indispensable requirement for the future is clear: India as a nation will come into its own only when it is united, integrated, cohered. Panikkar's geopolitics ends with a reminder of this nonnegotiable fact of history:

> The only practical remedy to this permanent geographical weakness of India … is the strength of her own internal political and economic structure … a strong central government having full control of the resources of the nation, a very high level of industrialisation, a political and economic integration of the country, which could overcome the internal contradictions present in our society … as would raise us to the level of a powerful state. … Continuous vigilance is the price of freedom, but the vigilance we exercise must be based on an understanding of the elements of our strength and weakness. … Geopolitics has therefore to become an essential subject of study for all interested in the future of India, for … we could only neglect it at our peril. (1969, 118–20)[3]

This narrative reveals the simultaneous and dialectical production of self and the world. Based on such a worlding, the elements of national (re)generation are spelled out: unity; a strong, centralized government; political and economic integration; no internal contradictions; a high level of industrialization; and eternal vigilance.

"MADE IN INDIA": SCIENCE, PLANNING, AND CITIZENSHIP

Closely related to geopolitics are other arenas in which the centrality of the above attributes are reinforced, arenas one is not normally predisposed to consider in a discussion of foreign policy. On matters of science and the scientific temper, economic planning, and the project of national integration, one finds a recurring thread on the need for a strong, centralized government; a model of self-reliant economic development that would never again leave India vulnerable to external powers; and suspicion of any vision of citizenship or belonging outside the narrative of mainstream Indian nationalism.

In a postcolonial context, the enterprise of making the nation is vexed from the very outset by an incontrovertible fact: it has already happened elsewhere. Early on, the dominant perception of the nationalist elite regarding India was that it was a civilization left behind, one whose historical destiny was ever to play catch-up. Such an articulation of global space and India's location within it marked the emergence of that very familiar creature of our time: the developmental state.[4] The newly independent state located itself in a mediatory position between domestic, depicted as a violated and exploited space, and foreign, depicted as riven with hierarchy, dominated by more powerful nations responsible for colonization, but who, through their superior science and technology would yet be the wellspring for Indian regeneration. This position would prove to be one of enormous power and prestige for the postcolonial state. It would gain legitimacy by the deftness and finesse with which it mediated between inside and outside: on the one hand, playing the bipolar world of the 1950s and 1960s to gain concessions in terms of foreign aid, technical know-how, and political support, but, on the other, doing so in ways that retained a strong sense of national sovereignty and avoided all appearance of becoming a neocolonial satellite of either superpower. Of course, at a broader level, in east or west, the spatialization of the world in terms of contrasting constructions of inside and outside has had similar effects on state power: it has served as the basis of legitimacy, elevated certain skills and abilities to the level of the indispensable, and circulated practices that in the name of national security and development have justified and reinforced the power of some few at the expense of many others.

Someone as intelligent as Jawaharlal Nehru was not going to mimic anybody if he could help it. If he and others like him were engaged in an enterprise that looked suspiciously familiar, one could count on the fact that such mimesis would be accompanied by an arduous effort to differentiate it from so-called originals. The national movement in India, especially after the entry of Gandhi onto the scene in 1916, was accompanied by an incisive critique of modernity. The pathology of scientific, hypermasculine, industrial civilization, it was argued, was evident in the Europe of the interwar years, specifically in Nazism and fascism. The secularization of previous understandings of man's relation to nature, the utilitarian calculus that came to commodify both human nature and social relationships, the alienation of individuals under capitalist modernity, and the contribution of all of these to the genocidal violence of wartime Europe and later to the nuclear explosions over Japan were not lost on either Gandhi or Nehru. Against this background, the reinscription of western rationality and science as a means of rejuvenating India had to be done with careful attention to deflect the charge of mimicry and neocolonialism.

Gandhi's solution to this problem was characteristically idiosyncratic and prescient: he consistently interpreted his struggle for independence as not so much against the British as again what they represented in terms of a worldview that today one might describe as the "modern condition" and that he chose to call "industrial society." Hence, his wish that the Congress Party be disbanded on independence and the country return to a decentralized polity with non-industrialized, self-sufficient villages oriented toward the satisfaction of needs and not wants.[5] Nehru, staying within a postenlightenment, progressive narrative of scientific rationality, finessed the contradiction differently (Chatterjee 1986). I examine below how Nehru spatialized the world and India (his foreign policy, if you will), seeing the west as the source of redemption but doing so in such a way as to deflect any whiff of imitation. I examine this approach in three interrelated areas — science, economic planning, and national citizenship — to reveal their indispensability to the creation of, in Panikkar's terms, a geopolitically safe nation and citizen.

Nehru essentially argued for an abstraction of western science and rationality from the societal context in which they had emerged, namely, modern Europe. There could be a secular and selective appropriation of the scientific method, of the practice of science, without necessarily contaminating it with the alienation, commodification, and economistic calculus that accompanied it in the capitalist west. In his autobiography, Nehru reveals his somewhat unsure resolution: "Most of us were not prepared to reject the achievements of modern civilization, although we may have felt some variation to suit Indian conditions was possible.... It [India] will succumb to this newcomer, for the West brings science and science brings food to the hungry millions.... It may be that when India puts on her new garment, as she must, for the old is torn and tattered, she will have it cut in this fashion, so as to make it conform both to present conditions and her old thought. (1936, 77, 432)

Aside from this question of adaptation, Nehru goes on to suggest that there is a universalist core to science that can be abstracted away from its western-ness. In other words, the British in India were merely the carriers of this secular way of thinking that belonged to humanity at large and would come to India anyway. He thus notes, "In almost every country in the world the educational and material progress has been tremendous during the last century because of science and industrialism.... Are we needlessly cantankerous and perverse if we suggest that some technical progress would have come to us anyhow in this industrial age, and even without British rule?" (1936, 434). In making a careful distinction between science as a progressive and universalist legacy versus science as inextricably embedded in modern alienation, Nehru echoes a move with a long history. As Marshall Berman notes regarding capitalist modernity in his classic work, *All That Is Solid Melts into Air,* the pioneers in this regard may well have been the Russian populists of the mid–nineteenth century:

> But what if this culture were not universal after all, as Marx thought it would be? What if it turned out to be an exclusively and parochially Western affair? This possibility was first proposed in the middle of the nineteenth century by various Russian populists. They argued that the explosive atmosphere of modernization in the West—the breakdown of communities and the psychic isolation of the individual, mass impoverishment and class polarization, a cultural creativity that sprang from desperate moral and spiritual anarchy—might be a cultural peculiarity rather than an iron necessity inexorably awaiting the whole of mankind. Why should not other nations and civilizations achieve more harmonious fusions of traditional ways of life with modern potentialities and needs? (Berman 1982, 124)

Berman's work is a reminder that postcolonial mimesis is only the latest in a long line that began with the industrial revolution in the northwestern corner of Europe. Since then, the story of modernity can be written in terms of the global desire to emulate this original revolution in terms of the technological ease it promised, yet retain the supposed spirituality of traditional society and deflect the worst accompaniments of industrial society in the west. The sting of post-colonial mimicry is blunted as one realizes that, really, we are all mimics under modernity.

A critical step in the construction of the new nation-state was thus to split science from the politics of modernity, from the con-joined enterprises of colonialism and capitalism. Once independence was achieved, and science was rendered asunder from colonialism, it could be made to work for India.[6] This belief meshed well with the dominant trope of Nehru's years as prime minister of India (1947–64): the state as the promoter of a scientific temper in the country that would serve as antidote to various forms of traditional, religious, and superstitious ways of ordering the world. Specifically, the purpose of science was to promote the unity of India. Tenden-cies toward regionalism, separatism, and other forms of particular-ity were derided not merely as provincial but, more importantly, as reflecting nonscientific, irrational, and superstitious mindsets.

In a largely preliterate and diverse country, the modulation of shared national identity took the form of gigantic and mute sym-bols of statist megascience. The predominant nationalist symbols of these times, the 1950s and 1960s, were colossal hydroelectric pro-jects, steel mills, atomic power reactors, machine-tool factories — nearly all built and owned by the state. Every Indian who lived through these decades will recollect the ubiquitous, almost social-ist-realist calendars with glossy pictures of the Bhakra-Nangal Dam, the steel mills of Durgapur and Rourkela, the rocket-launching sta-tion at Thumba in Kerala, the Hindustan Machine Tools Factory in Bangalore, the Bhabha Atomic Research Center in Trombay, and other stoic milestones in the national journey toward self-reliance. The linguistic, religious, regional, and cultural specificities of each of these locations (Rourkela, Bangalore, Trombay, Thumba, and so on) were rendered ornamental as they were conjoined along a dif-ferent principle of unity: that of a uniform and homogenous national space on a singular trajectory of development.

The sundering of science from its western specificity was fur-thered by allying Indian development with the ideology of socialism (which, despite its western roots, was always regarded as less Euro-centric in all of Afro-Asia). The linearity of the developmental paradigm and the ignominy of bringing up its rear were thus mitigated by a (largely rhetorical) commitment to socialism.[7] The ideological undergirding of the immensely pervasive and centralizing state that came to characterize India after independence, in both the political and material realms, can be traced back to this period when it anointed itself as a scientific, rational unifier of a backward and fissiparous society.[8]

The construction of national unity can also be read through two related discourses in Nehru: economic planning and national citizenship. Most studies on planning in India highlight its contributions to the emerging field of development economics (Chakravarty 1987) or its indispensability given the legacy of colonialism (Byres 1982, Chandra 1979, Nayar 1972). What is interesting from my perspective is the degree to which the main proponent of planning was explicit regarding its importance as a symbolic act that would endow the nation with a sense of its own corporeality, a physical sense of being, something he felt was missing in the narrative of Indian history. Nehru's various speeches on the Five-Year Plans and on the quasi-autonomous (from the purview of Parliament and concerned minstries, such as finance or industry) Planning Commission are as full of references to the emotional and ideational importance of planning as to its economic importance. Thus, Nehru inaugurating the First Five-Year Plan (1951–56):

> We must remember that it is the first attempt of its kind to bring the whole picture of India — agricultural, industrial, social and economic — into one framework of thinking. . . . It has made us realise mentally and emotionally that we are a united nation. We tend to go off at a tangent and think along narrow provincial, communal, religious or caste lines. We have no emotional awareness of the unity of our country. Our Plan has challenged us to think in terms of the good of the nation as a whole apart from the separate problems which we have to face in respect of our villages, districts or provinces. (1956, 7–8)

The desire to endow the nation with a tangible, material reality — to fixate it as a united and coherent entity that could then be propelled along a trajectory of modernity — is palpable in this excerpt, which is equally explicit on the status of alternative self-conceptions (province, religion, caste) as narrow, inferior, and tangential to the main task of the times: national unity and development.

Turning to the question of the ideal citizen who would populate this new realm, Nehru was faced with a formidable intellectual challenge on account of Gandhi's dominance of the anticolonial movement. Thanks to the latter, the movement had been, in the main, nonviolent, which contributed to the idea that the new nation, India, represented a vastly different entity in a world dominated by realpolitik. Nehru, quite unwilling to give up on this legacy of nonviolence and its role in India's self-fashioning as a new and moral voice in the comity of nations, had the task of integrating into a nation various recalcitrances — princely states, diverse religions and languages, parties of the extreme right and left, a privileged and conservative class of landlords. The creation of Pakistan and the war that followed immediately over Kashmir (1948) further limited the context within which nonviolent and idealist politics could function. The resort to coercion or force was hardly something to be foregone ab initio in such a space. In a closely argued text written in anticipation of Indian independence, Nehru finesses this tension between claiming the idealist, nonviolent, satyagraha legacy of the national movement, on the one hand, and crafting a nation out of contentious spaces, on the other. The silent specter of Gandhi hovers behind these passages, but by the end, Nehru is able to exorcize his presence successfully.

He begins by noting that "it is impossible to ignore the fact that both government and social life necessitate some coercion.... They will have to exercise coercion...till such time when every human being in that State is perfect, wholly unselfish, and devoted to the common good" (1936, 542–43). Such an argument justifying statist coercion is unremarkable; it is at least as old as contractarian theories of the modern state. What is interesting is the way Nehru deals with Gandhi, who here serves as the archetypal idealist foil for Nehru's realpolitik. Essentially, his strategy is one that simultaneously memorializes and mutes Gandhi. In a key passage, he notes:

> The ideas of non-violent resistance and the non-violent technique of struggle are of great value to India as well as to the rest of the world, and Gandhiji has done a tremendous service in forcing modern thought to consider them. I believe they have a great future before them. It may be that mankind is not sufficiently advanced to adopt them in their entirety.... For the present, the vision may not materialise sufficiently, but like all great ideas its influence will grow and it will more and more affect our actions.... Gandhiji, of course,

continues to be a vital force whose non-violence is of a dynamic and aggressive character.... With all his greatness and contradictions and power of moving the masses, he is above the usual standards. One cannot measure him or judge him as we would others. (1936, 547–51)

By seemingly conceding the high moral ground to Gandhian idealism, Nehru reinscribes the low but practical, pragmatic, and powerful, enterprise of state building within the logic of realpolitik. Whatever the moral inclinations of the state builder, his conscience has to take a back seat to the more compelling historical imperative: nation building. Nehru continues, "The present conflicts in society can... never be resolved except by coercion.... [W]e must also realise that human nature being what it is, in the mass, it will not always respond to our appeals and persuasions, or act in accordance with high moral principles. Compulsion will often be necessary, in addition to conversion, and the best we can do is to limit this compulsion and use it in such a manner that its evil is lessened" (1936, 552). Nehru's explicit acceptance of the inherent morality of the idealist, Gandhian position, moreover, imparts an air of tragic grandeur to his own actions: a man forced by the inexorable logic of statecraft to separate his personal convictions from the enterprise of building India.

Underlying each of these three arenas (science, planning, national integration) is a recurring theme: the state as the repository of knowledge (in its role as scientific modernizer of the nation) and arbiter of morality (by its monopoly on deciding what furthers the making of the nation and what does not). Correspondingly, the citizen is regarded as, at best, an eventually educable ward and, at worst, someone prone to derail the national journey with his irrational and provincial proclivities. State and society are thus interpellated in an overall discourse of "developmentalism" that empowers certain visions of the nation and progress over other, alternative imaginings. The detailed discussion above is intended to display the imbrication of power and knowledge in a realist logic of statecraft: how a certain spatialization of the world and of "us" empowers state elites in specific ways, how it positions state above civil society, and how it makes certain practices, skills, and resources indispensable and others marginal.

The consequences of such a worlding were palpable at both the material and ideational levels. At a material level, by the early 1980s, the Indian state was economically pervasive to an unprecedented extent, exceeding most other states, barring socialist-communist ones.[9] Belying claims made from the 1950s through the 1970s that such a pervasive state was a precursor to an eventual transition to a home-grown variety of socialism, the reality was a highly unequal capital-ist economy on the one hand mired in bureaucratic overregulation and on the one other stunted by an overprotected, monopolistic, and inefficient private capitalist sector. The ideational legacy of this worlding was, however, far more critical and enduring. First, the story of India after 1947 was to be written mainly in terms of how the nation came (or did not come) into its own. There was no space in this narrative for the histories of the diverse regions and periph-eries *except* as variations on central themes. In other words, their histories now came to be read exclusively in terms of their role in the anticolonial struggle and their contribution to the reigning model of economic development in postcolonial India. Although the ani-mating vision was "Unity in Diversity," it was 'understood' (and re-sisted, as the violence that has accompanied the effort to unite India reveals) that diversity was appreciated only insofar as it embellished Indian unity or as long as it was a recognizable variation on the central theme. Second, the central attitude toward peripheral aspi-rations for linguistic or cultural or economic or fiscal or any other form of state autonomy was underlain by a suspicion that such as-pirations were the entering wedge for the unraveling of the nation. Buttressed by a discourse of danger whose genealogy was traced over millennia, national unity was a sine qua non. Any attempt at imagining a community outside the claustrophobic embrace of the nation-state elicited the charge of an antinational separatism or, at best, chauvinistic provincialism. It is this suspicion that has shaped a country whose constitution is ostensibly federal but whose actual political dispensation is highly centralized and a poor facsimile of any such federalist blueprint. Over the years, consequently, nation building in India (as everywhere else) has left a long and bloody trail in an endless quest for the perfect citizen.

In this section, I have attempted, through a brief examination of three facets of "making India" (science, planning, and national in-tegration) to understand some of its most important attributes in the period from 1947 to the recent past. These facets may not be recognized as foreign policy by conventional approaches. However, by showing how the content of India was always already crucially influenced by understandings of the outside world and what had happened there in history, and by detailing the precarious postcolonial project of straddling mimesis and originality, I have tried to argue that the very act of building a nation is intimately an act of foreign policy. In the next section, I turn to an enduring trope in postcolonial nationalisms, the oxymoronic idea of a society that is permanently in transition: between ex-colony and not yet nation. I suggest that the metaphor of transition is an important device to justify and recuperate the incredible degree of statist and societal violence accompanying the nation-building project.

THE LOGIC OF DEFERRENCE

In an important text, Jacques Derrida (1982) argues that social meaning arises from the simultaneous act of differentiating the thing from other(s) and endlessly deferring the very possibility of comprehending its presence in any final sense, outside the chain of signifiers of which it is part. This dual act of differentiating and endlessly deferring, which he outlines as his concept of différance, is arguably central to the production and dissemination of meaning in any social universe. What becomes appropriate then is not so much a logic of inquiry premised on uncovering a hidden "metaphysics of presence" (Derrida 1976, 101–40), but rather one that understands meaning as arising from an endless circulation of signs, from their "systematic play of differences" (Derrida 1982, 11). This notion of differentiation-deferral is of some utility in understanding how postcolonial states attempt to establish the discursive hegemony of nationalism in their societies.

Central to nationalisms everywhere is the metaphor of nation as journey, as something that is ever in the making but never quite reached. I call this social and political process by which outlined tasks are repeatedly postponed and defined destinations are never quite reached a *logic of deferrence*. The logic of deferrence secures the legitimacy of the postcolonial state by centering its historical role in the pursuit of certain desired futures. It situates state elites at the dangerous interstice of the domestic and the foreign, as they mediate this dialectic in the direction of security and development. It undergirds the legitimacy of the state by securing for it both time and space. Time in the idea that the journey toward achieving a nation has just begun. There is much that has to be reversed: the state literally buys time for itself as it deflects the adverse judgment of civil society "for the time being." It secures space for autonomous action by deploying the argument that divisiveness and difference would only delay the national journey.

In this logic of deferrence, postcolonial societies both resemble and differ from the nation-states of the west. In the latter, the endless deferment is on the question of extending the idea of community to a global space. A premature extension of the idea of domestic community beyond the border quickly draws the charge of a feminized, limp-wristed, irresponsible, woolly-headed idealism. Within the literature of international relations, the extension of *communitas* beyond the borderlines always has a limit that tends to infinity: it is a task that can never be completed because its completion can only imply the negation of the state itself and with it the entire hegemonic discourse of an insecurity-centered statist international relations. In other words, the discursive universe of international relations is built upon the endless reproduction of the inside/outside antinomy (Walker 1993). The deployment and reproduction of this opposition constitutes one of the fundamental principles of state legitimacy, autonomy, and monopoly over the instruments of coercion. The hegemonic density of this spatializing of the world arises from the fact that the very practices it entails ensure that its supposedly desired futures can never become reality.

In the space called the postcolony, the endless deferment is on the question of achieving national unity itself. In the attempt to pulverize alternative forms of self-identity into the uniform code of citizenship, the discourse of danger actually unleashes social and political movements built on ethnicity, religion, region, language, caste, and tribe. Even as such movements often rail against the nation-state, they replicate the unitary understandings and exclusivist understandings of identity, territory, and sovereignty that characterize the project of nation building. In other words, it is these alternative signs of belonging that give meaning and content to the idea of the nation itself, a process that embodies Derrida's notion of meaning as arising from différance. The process of nation building unleashes a cycle of state repression and societal reaction that is both violent and seemingly ceaseless. Although national integration is presented as the telos, the effort at cohering recalcitrant identities releases into circulation practices that further atomize and differentiate these multiple selves. Thus, the "moment of arrival" (Chatterjee 1986) as a nation is deferred endlessly in the postcolony.

A close reading of a recent, influential work on the "security predicament of the third world" by Mohammed Ayoob (1995) demonstrates the narration of postcolonial space as endless deferment. Ayoob's argument exemplifies all the elements that I have provisionally sketched above as entailing a logic of deferrence. His synopsis of the security predicament of third-world nation building projects is both terse and exemplary of the huge amount of literature on the topic. He begins with a disambiguated constant of world history against which postcolonial state-building projects will be evaluated. He notes there is something called a "process by which modern national states are created" (1995, 23). His detailing of this process is an illustration of what I mean by modulation:

> The national state in Europe as we know it today had a long and painful gestation period that took anywhere from four... to seven... centuries to reach its culminating stage. Unfortunately for third world state makers, their states cannot afford the luxury of prolonging the traumatic and costly experience of state making over hundreds of years, as was done in Western Europe. The demands of competition with established modern states and the demonstrated effectiveness of socially cohesive, politically responsive and administratively effective states in the industrialized world make it almost obligatory for third world states to reach their goals within the shortest time possible or risk international ridicule and permanent marginalization within the system of states. (1995, 30)

A contingent and open-ended set of events that happened across a continent over centuries is modulated, ex post facto, into a coherent and teleologically prescient "gestation" in Ayoob's description. Having established this modular version of "how nation-states are made," Ayoob predictably reifies it by analogies to both evolutionary theory and to systemic models (1995, 32). Unsurprising, too, is the dispensable status accorded to human rights in states that have to "telescope" the nation-building process:

> the concept of human rights owes its empirical validity to the successful functioning of the industrialized, representative and responsive states of Western Europe and North America.... But these states have generally successfully completed their state-building processes;

they are politically satiated, economically affluent and uncondition-
ally legitimate in the eyes of their populations. They can, therefore,
afford to adopt liberal standards of state behavior, because they are
reasonably secure in the knowledge that societal demands will not
run counter to state interests and will not put state structures and
institutions in any grave jeopardy. (1995, 84)

Besides the rather dewy-eyed portrayal of human rights in the
west, the concept of human rights is now firmly historicized within
a modular narrative of Europe, and its empirical validity has come
to depend on the fact that western countries have supposedly inter-
nalized it in their functioning. At the very least, one could argue that
the validity of something such as human rights can be grounded in
a discourse of ethics and morality that exceeds such a historicist argument. The narrative of what once happened in Europe has now
returned to stand in judgment over history and on what is permissible and what is not. In these excerpts, one discerns clearly the intertwined relationship of power and knowledge. Echoing Nehru's de-
ferral of nonviolence until such time as "every human being in that
State is perfect, wholly unselfish and devoted to the common good,"
Ayoob demands time for third-world states as they violently cohere
the realm: human rights norms are something "most third world
states, struggling to maintain political order, will not be able to meet
for many decades" (1995, 85).[10]

Reigning notions of territory, sovereignty, state, and citizenship—
contained within the discipline of state-centric international relations
and reproduced everyday in the practice of statecraft—acquire a
hegemonic, objective density.[11] The fragility and the ambivalences
of their originary moments are effaced as they are presented as the
facts of a long and sedimented history. The ongoing violence that
accompanies the reinscription of these facts of history, these imperatives of state making in both the west and the third world should
give us pause. The anchoring of ethics and morality around a modulation of history constitutes an escape from the normative choices
entailed in the politics of our time. The making of the nation serves
as the universal alibi for the violent unmaking of all alternative
forms of community.

The postcolonial present is thus eternally suspended in a space
labeled a "transition." Infantilizing this space (these are societies
yet to achieve maturity) deems it one in which proscriptions against

violence do not apply with the same force as they would in societies that have already arrived. Ultimately, as Joseph Conrad notes in regard to imperialism, the thing that separates this violence from murder, that redeems it in any way, is an "idea only. An idea at the back of it; not a sentimental pretence but an idea; and an unselfish belief in the idea — something you can set up, and bow down before, and offer sacrifice to" (quoted in Said 1993, 69).

MODULATING BANGLADESH

At independence, Indian state elites regarded their society as having emerged with some clear advantages over immediate neighbors. The commitment to secularism, democracy, independence in foreign affairs, and planned development was contrasted favorably with neighbors, which were deemed to be of a lesser order of legitimacy because they were founded on the principle of religion (Pakistan); were of a nondemocratic political order, such as a monarchy (Nepal, Bhutan, Sikkim); were betraying the anticolonial struggle by their alliance with world powers (Pakistan); or were moving in the direction of ethnic majoritarianism (Ceylon, which in any case was already delegitimated because independence was gained without much struggle). The conduct of free and fair elections based on universal mass suffrage from the early 1950s and the relatively peaceful resolution of the demand for linguistic states within the union (something Nehru had reluctantly acquiesced to) were further reasons for distinguishing India from the checkered experiments with democracy in other parts of the region (see the introduction to Bajpai and Cohen, eds., 1993, for a concise summary of Indian views in this regard). Moreover, considering India the largest legatee of the erstwhile colonial system of regional security, state elites regarded the region as in many ways their "backyard."[12]

For the most part in the early years after independence, however, Indian policy lacked the economic and military muscle to translate this self-understanding as a potential world power into reality. Nehruvian claims regarding peaceful international relations and of representing a new and moral voice in the comity of nations were matched by small defense budgets, low priority accorded to strategic and military matters, and neglect of the defense sector because the focus was on economic development. Stand-offs in wars with Pakistan (1948 and 1965) and a conclusive defeat by the Chinese (1962) indicated the limits of any pretension toward regional, let alone world, status in terms of realpolitik. If one were to generalize about India's policies toward the region in Nehru's time (1947–64), one could aver that there remained an unresolved tension between a self-fashioning as a peaceful, nonviolent country that represented a genuinely new force in the world and a self-fashioning as a regional power that inherited the British presence in the subcontinent and saw itself as a hegemon (see Kapur 1988 for an insightful elaboration of this tension). Although the defeat in 1962 by the Chinese resulted in a sharp diminution of idealist rhetoric, the incipient idea of regional hegemony gained currency and became the dominant self-perception of Indian state elites after 1971.

The crucial turning point in this process of self-fashioning from a pacifist nation to one of regional hegemon was the 1971 war with Pakistan leading to the emergence of Bangladesh. This event marked a critical rupture in the production of India, with important consequences for both India and the region in the decades thereafter. What really happened in 1971 is less important than the way those events were modulated or narrated within India. Prior, largely rhetorical claims to regional leadership and hegemony now become the actual parameters of policy. Equally important, a "script" that produces successful intervention into the affairs of neighboring countries, and into ethnic, religious, and linguistic movements within India, is culled from 1971 and thereafter strongly influences the conduct of both domestic and regional policy by Indian state elites.

The civil war between the Bengali-speaking populace of East Pakistan and the political center in West Pakistan peaked in mid-1971. In the months leading up to the civil war, evidence indicates that Indian state elites favored a solution to the crisis that would preserve the territorial integrity and sovereignty of that country. West Pakistani intransigence presented India with the opportunity to split the eastern wing away from the western. Yet, once December 1971 had passed into history, India's role in midwifing the emergence of Bangladesh was retroactively imputed with a long-standing intentionality and careful planning that it did not have, at least not until the summer of 1971 (see Sisson and Rose, 1990, 42 and 210, for details on this). Bangladesh was rapidly modulated into the following: an instance of Indian success in realpolitik, decisive proof that the creation of Pakistan in 1947 on the basis of religion was a fal-

lacy, an instance of the successful working of Indian regional hegemony, and an example of the script by which India ought to govern
its relations with neighboring states and with various domestic social and political movements.

The reasons for initial Indian hesitancy in favoring the breakup
of Pakistan are obvious. If the emergence of Bangladesh exposed
the fallacy of religious nationalism in South Asia, it demonstrated
equally well the fragility of most other narratives that underlie the
enterprise of nation making. For example, if East Bengali linguistic
and cultural nationalism warranted a separate realm, what could
be the counter to similar demands by Nagas or Oriyas or Punjabis
or any other group within the Indian union? Yet such ambivalence
and doubt were effaced as sections of the media, political elite, and
academic community gravitated to the view that Indian "success"
in Bangladesh was proof of its hegemony and the viability of the
Indian experiment in comparison with its neighbors.

According to the newly fashioned narrative, prior to 1971 India
had been militarily weak, which accounted for problems with neighboring countries. Once India showed itself capable of adroit realpolitik and of gaining military victory, her strategic problems either disappeared or became more tractable. The success in Bangladesh thus
came to be the main explanation for a whole series of other supposed successes in the realm of domestic and foreign policy that
followed in its wake; moreover, 1971 became the recipe for the continued production of such regional and domestic successes. As the
doyen of security studies in India, K. Subrahmanyam, puts it:

> Following India's military reverse in the border clashes with China
> in 1962 the image of India as a military power suffered a major set-
> back. This encouraged Pakistan to launch its operations in the Rann
> of Kutch in April 1965 and Operation Gibraltar in August 1965.
> The Naga hostiles got in touch with the Chinese for arms and the
> Mizos started their insurgency in 1966 with the active support of
> Pakistan.... The Indian image and stature regained their losses fol-
> lowing the Indian victory in the Bangladesh war and the Indian peace-
> ful nuclear explosion in 1974. It is not just a fortuitous coincidence
> that the Kashmir accord with Sheikh Abdullah, the Shillong agree-
> ment and the first dialogue with the Mizo leadership came after the
> above events. The Chinese too stopped their assistance to the Naga
> hostiles. Pakistan is likely to swear by the Simla Agreement as long

as there is a credible image of Indian military power adequate to deter any adventurism on their part. (1982, 122–23)

Subrahmanyam's characterization of 1971 as a turning point for the better regarding India's security position is echoed by Urmila Phadnis and Nancy Jetly as they contrast the pre- and post-1971 periods:

> 1971, in more ways than one, signifies a watershed in India's foreign policy in terms of a redefinition of its status and role in the South Asian region. Bangladesh demonstrated not only India's capabilities to restructure interstate relations in the subcontinent to its satisfaction but also revealed the limitations of the role of the outside Powers in the region. It witnessed the emergence of India as a preeminent Power in the region with a new military and political status after almost a decade of the 1962 debacle which had put India's aspirations for a regional role in complete disarray. 1971 also marked the emergence of Indira Gandhi as a leader of great stature capable of playing the cynical, at times ruthless, game of realpolitik with aplomb as also taking bold initiatives in pursuance of India's legitimate aspirations in the region. (1990, 155)

The above quotes are emblematic of the signficance attached to 1971 within India. What is critical, however, is that a certain model of conducting both regional and domestic policy was crafted and came to inform both Indian interactions with neighbors and the central government's dealings with states within India. In bald terms, the Indian state recognized, in a way it had not done before, that ethnicity was not merely a threat to the nation, but that under certain conditions 'dangerous' ethnicity could constitute an important component of statist policy making itself. In other words, with the utilization of the idea of the "nation in danger" on account of ethnicity, new ways to acquire and retain political power presented themselves. From there to the actual instigation of ethnic extremism in order to take advantage of the opportunities created thereby was but a short step.

Within the country, the central government sought to delegitimate opposition party–led state governments by promoting unrest and turmoil in these states through the state-level Congress parties and central intelligence agencies. This approach sometimes included aiding and assisting extremist ethnonational, religious, linguistic, and other social forces. Having thus discredited the state government, the center would step in, often by unseating the existing regime on grounds of instability and calling for new elections, which the Congress Party could then contest on the platform of restoring peace and stability. For example, in Punjab in the early 1980s, the regime in New Delhi promoted extremist, separatist groups in order to create instability and violent turmoil in the state. Such instability was used in a two-step process by the center: first, discrediting moderate elements of the ruling Akali Party by encouraging extremists, and second, using extremist provocations as reason for central government intervention—in this instance the army was sent, followed by elections in which the Congress Party hoped to triumph by promising to restore order and stability. A similar pattern of discrediting state regimes by fostering extremist movements, followed by the Congress Party campaigning on a slogan of the restoration of peace and national unity, was attempted with varying degrees of success in a number of other Indian states through the early 1980s.[13]

Externally, a similar pattern of decision making began to emerge after 1971. Covert intelligence agencies (especially the Research and Analysis Wing (RAW), an intelligence branch of the central government established by Mrs. Gandhi in the late 1960s, ostensibly for external purposes only), often in tandem with ethnic minorities opposed to the regime in that country,[14] sought to destabilize regimes perceived as acting in ways inimical to India's regional geopolitical interests. These regimes were at the same time subject to intense diplomatic pressure at the level of the government to change their policies in line with Indian interests. Ethnicity and nation were now locked in a discourse of danger that is usually enormously productive as far as the exercise of state power is concerned. In each instance, the danger of ethnic chauvinism or separatism was used as the justification for an authoritarian and hard-line response by the center. Yet, it was often the center itself that was responsible for fomenting such ethnic separatism in the first place: either directly, by its intelligence agencies supporting the extremist fringes of such movements, or indirectly, by a concentration of power and an increasingly majoritarian conception of national identity. It is this enormously productive and generative capacity of a dyad such as nationality/ ethnicity that needs to be highlighted and understood. Each pole of this antinomy energizes and propels the other, and in the process the nation is violently made and unmade, political careers are secured and squandered, elections are won and lost, and dominations attempted and resisted.

Indian intervention in Bangladesh is a classic instance of nothing succeeding like success. A legion of works extol the superb process of decision making exhibited by Mrs. Gandhi during that crisis.[15] An argument that runs through many of these works is that India succeeded in Bangladesh in large part because of the way the civilian leadership, the defense service chiefs, the intelligence agencies, and the diplomatic corps all worked as a tight unit. The core decision-making body consisted of a small handful of individuals who met regularly to discuss options and make choices. Such a tightly controlled decision-making process, whatever its efficacy in the short term in the instance of Bangladesh, proved to be politically authoritarian and regionally destabilizing, and it concentrated power in the prime minister and a small coterie around her, including the chiefs of the domestic and external intelligence agencies. This style of decision making was entirely in tune with the personality and politics of Mrs. Gandhi (prime minister from 1966 to 1977 and again from 1980 to 1984).[16] The personalization of power intensified over the years, and with impunity and increasing frequency she used Article 356 of the Constitution, which enabled her to dissolve state governments and declare President's Rule in them. For instance, under the first two prime ministers (Nehru and Lal Bahadur Shastri), President's Rule was imposed on state governments a total of eight times in nineteen years, whereas in Mrs. Gandhi's sixteen years as prime minister, it occurred forty-two times, mostly to topple legitimate state governments. The degree of federalism, quite limited to begin with, was sharply narrowed under her regime, and the locus of power shifted from the Parliament or cabinet exclusively to the prime minister's office.

I argue that this twin-track policy—overt pressure on recalcitrant regimes to get them to kowtow the preferred line, combined with covert pressure through dissident groups under the (incomplete) control of intelligence agencies—became a crucial legacy of the Bangladesh operation. To put it differently: after 1971, the overall *strategic* framework of regional policy sought the establishment and recognition of Indian hegemony, and the main *technique* to ensure this was a twin-track policy that combined overt diplomatic pressure with covert support of dissident groups within the neighbors.

Meshing with these developments within the country was an external shift in which the superpowers seemingly conceded India's regional dominance. In retrospect, it is obvious that this concession was not so much the anointing of a regional power as it was the retreat of a post-Vietnam United States and an increasingly beleaguered Soviet Union from (the increasingly marginal area of) South Asia. Yet, Indian elites saw the shift as one more instance of the benefits of the victory of 1971. As a result, there emerged a slew of works extolling India as a regional power worthy of serious attention (Mellor, ed., 1979, Cohen and Park 1978, Nayar 1975).

Bhabani Sen Gupta (1983) summarizes the altered Indian attitude toward the opportunities and dangers represented by this dyad of nationality/ethnicity since 1971 as the Indira Doctrine in South Asia. He notes that a critical change occurred after 1971: India now explicitly claimed it had a legitimate interest in the fate of "kindred" ethnic minorities in neighboring countries and would take appropriate actions to ensure their welfare and safety. Augmenting the interventionist implications of such a stance in a region rife with kindred ethnic minorities, Sen Gupta paraphrases the emerging view on the appropriate conduct for India's neighbors: "No South Asian government must . . . ask for external military assistance with an anti-Indian bias from any country. If a South Asian country genuinely needs external help to deal with a serious internal conflict situation or with an intolerable threat to a government legitimately established, it should ask for help from a number of neighboring countries including India. The exclusion of India from such a contingency will be considered to be an anti-Indian move on the part of the government concerned" (1983, 20).

What distinguishes the Indian effort to acquire regional hegemony after 1971 is that it is not conditioned by the pursuit of the territory of neighbor countries. Critics who charge India with territorial expansionism have a difficult time explaining Indian policy (for one unconvincing effort, see Dutt 1984). When presented with an opportunity to balkanize Pakistan or prolong the stay of Indian forces in Sri Lanka, Indian state elites have refrained from doing so,[17] which ought to clue one in on the conclusion that Indian self-fashioning in

South Asia is more as a hegemon in the Gramscian sense of the term: a consensual leader rather than a military or economic power intent on dominating neighbors. An instance of this pattern of eschewing territorial gains—what I would call the acquisition of moral or symbolic capital by a form of coitus interruptus—occurred in 1971 when India could have arguably trifurcated a demoralized West Pakistan after the latter's surrender in East Pakistan, but chose not to do so. (Instead, India declared a unilateral cease-fire in the western sector.)

This desire to be perceived as a hegemon in the Gramscian sense, rather than in the narrow security studies meaning of that term, gives Indian regional policy a dangerous edge. Indian state elites and those Anirudha Gupta (1990) describes as an "establishment elite" are convinced of the superiority of their model of nation building in comparison to the models followed by their neighbors. A regional policy that keeps external powers at bay and forces neighbors to recognize Indian suzerainty is underlain by a powerful self-fashioning as a self-reliant, secular, democratic, and peaceful nation that dates back to the national struggle. The few occasions on which Indian interventions into neighboring countries have been in favor of democratic regimes, a recognition of their inherently pluralist character, and against left-wing or military extremism have imparted to Indian policy making a moralistic conviction that can only be described as hubris.

Such hubris can be witnessed in the way that Indian intervention into East Pakistan in 1971, its stance against the Maoist JVP insurrection in Sri Lanka in 1971, its support for the Tamil militants in Sri Lanka between 1983 and 1987, and military action against the LTTE in that country between 1987 and 1990, its support for the king and democratic forces in Nepal in 1950–51 and in 1960–62, respectively, and its action against the coup attempt by mercenaries in the Maldives in 1988 have been rendered into a narrative of a benign India promoting legitimate regimes, democracy, and the principle of state sovereignty in the region.[18]

To summarize: although Indian self-fashioning had always aspired to the legacy of the British as subcontinental gendarme, it remained largely rhetorical until 1971. The victory in East Pakistan and the creation of Bangladesh imparted a powerful fillip to such an incipient ideology of regional hegemony. Most importantly, the opportunities and not merely the dangers inherent in the dyad nation/

ethnicity were perceived in a certain way for the first time. A process of decision making that supposedly characterized Indian actions in the months leading to that war was culled into a script seen as optimal and replicable. This script made little distinction between domestic and foreign affairs. In both, it promoted a highly centralized, concentrated method of exercising power involving a combination of overt diplomatic or political pressure on recalcitrant regimes with covert attempts at destabilization by playing extremist against moderate factions and trying to fish in the troubled waters thus created. Most importantly, the twin-track policy that emerged from this experience crucially reflects the generative power of identity/difference, in this instance represented by nation and ethnicity. Ethnicity was constantly used within a discourse of danger to the nation, which would then necessitate strongly centralizing and authoritarian responses from the state. Ironically, the very attribution of danger to ethnicity and ethnic consciousness often worked as a self-fulfilling prophecy, providing endless opportunities for the violent and bloody making of the nation.

CONCLUSION

In this chapter, I problematize a phrase such as "Indian foreign policy and its impact on South Asia," something that we banally take for granted. I argue that the settled identities in that phrase rest on a politics of forgetting. The terms *India, foreign,* and *South Asia* reflect an unsettled and violent spatialization of the world, one that is ongoing and contested. Foreign policy, rather than the actions of a pregiven nation on an outside, can be reread as a discursive process of producing and reproducing the very categories and identities upon which it rests. Much of what is regarded as intrinsic to the character of modern India — namely, planning, the dirigiste state as economic and social engineer, the role of science and development in making the nation, and the modernization project in a wider sense — can all be read against the grain as a careful spatialization of the self against an other, a process that I have described as *worlding.* The narrative of what once happened in Europe stands as both, the model in whose image an India is sought to be constructed and contrasted. Finally, the events of 1971 leading to the creation of Bangladesh marked a critical rupture in the self-fashioning of India. Previously incipient notions of regional hegemony and subcontinental gendarme received a powerful impetus when Bangladesh was modulated into an instance of Indian success in realpolitik. Throughout, the discursive construction of the self has been in dialogue with a world. The spatialization of India and the world has been intertwined with questions of power and knowledge. The consequences of such a worlding have not been merely foreign policy as it is conventionally understood. Rather, I have suggested that this worlding is a representational practice that has drawn boundaries; rendered spaces sacred and profane; elevated some interpretations of who we are, whence we came, and where we ought to be headed to the status of the truth, while marginalizing other stories as fable; and both imperfectly and incompletely created India. Finally, in the context of the voluminous literature on Indian foreign policy, this chapter has accomplished one more thing of significance: it has demonstrated that it is perfectly possible to write at length about that topic and yet use a certain ubiquitous word but once — *nonalignment.*

2

Producing Sri Lanka from Ceylon:
J. R. Jayewardene and Sinhala Identity

History has always been conceived of as a movement of a resumption of history, as a detour between two presences.
— JACQUES DERRIDA, WRITING AND DIFFERENCE

In this chapter, I examine the production of a modern nation in Sri Lanka through a process that has been extraordinarily violent in both physical and epistemic terms. I do this primarily through a close analysis of a particular text authored by a former Sri Lankan president whose political career spanned most of the twentieth century, J. R. Jayewardene. If we are the stories we tell about ourselves, Jayewardene's fable regarding the origins and evolution of Sri Lanka is interesting for the ways in which it produces a sense of identity out of difference. It is an encapsulation of history as understood and lived by the majority community in Sri Lanka, the Sinhala-speaking Buddhists. It is hardly surprising that this story is writ largely in terms of that community's difference from various minority groups, especially the Tamils, who are rendered both inferior and the age-old antagonists of the Sinhalese.[1]

Sri Lanka's movement from a peaceful, indeed idyllic Ceylon to a synonym for macabre ethnic violence is the story of a majority community's attempt to fashion a nation in its own image through monopolization of the state and of the consequent emergence of a secessionist ethnonational movement. Despite claims of ancient enmity and eternal difference, this ethnic conflict is a depressingly modernist tale. The effacement of alternative imaginations of the self and their attempted replacement by a single view one based on a modern, sovereign nation-state in Sri Lanka are unremarkable in the sense that such things have been happening everywhere for some time now. One could say that the pulverization of different ways of identifying the self into a uniform code of citizenship is pretty much what passes for the history of our times. To the extent that modernity is the disciplining of ambiguity and an intolerance for multiple or layered notions of identity, territory, and sovereignty, citizenship is invariably an either-or matter. Whether emanating from region, religion, language, or ethnicity, any alternative to the univocal idea of citizenship is rendered spurious, reactionary, vestigial, or, worse, traitorous.

This effort to produce an abstract, homogenous national space out of various forms of pre- and nonnational place is inscribed with all the anxieties of approximating modernity. It is a process Henri Lefebvre describes with insight when he notes that in the production of space under modernity, "*There is a violence intrinsic to abstraction.* . . . [A]bstraction's *modus operandi* is devastation, destruction. . . . The violence involved does not stem from some force intervening aside from rationality, outside or beyond it. Rather, it manifests itself from the moment any action introduces the rational into the real, from the outside, by means of tools which strike, slice and cut—and keep doing so until the purpose of their aggression is achieved" (1991, 289, emphasis original).[2]

Although the discourse of citizenship is superficially secular, with a small twist of perspective it can be regarded as one more in a long line of discourses that have sought to construct social reality and identity for a people in a given space and is accompanied by practices that are, in their own way, ritualistic and eschatological (Campbell 1992). Nandy reveals this metonymously religious character of modern nationalism when he observes that "the ideas of nation-building, scientific growth, security, modernization and development have become parts of a left-handed technology with a clear touch of religiosity—a modern demonology, a *tantra* with a built-in code of violence. . . . This package often plays the same role vis-à-vis the people of the society—sanctioning or justifying violence against the weak and the dissenting—that the church, the *ulema*, the *sangha*, or the Brahmans played in earlier times" (1990a, 134).

In the case of Sri Lanka, even the lip service paid to secularism is dispensed with. It is, after all, a country that in 1972 rewrote its constitution to give special place to Buddhism and explicitly avowed its sustenance as one of the charters of the state. The idea of the nation is heavily interlaced with the notion that it is a special land because it is consecrated by the Buddha and its manifest destiny is preservation of the Buddhist faith. The liberal-democratic idea of the fundamental equality of all citizens within the national space runs directly counter to the idea of Sri Lanka as ultimately the abode of the Sinhala Buddhists, a space divinely ordained for the preservation of their faith.

Jayewardene's story begins with the consecration of Sri Lanka by the Buddha and points to a future as a glittering, dynamic, entrepreneurial node in the circuits of world capitalism: an ersatz Singapore, if you will. At a superficial level, this meshing of the pastoral, idyllic notion of the abode of the Buddha, a just and moral island (the Dhammadipa), with the vision of an urbanized, hyperenergetic, capitalist export platform might seem uneasy or even self-contradictory. Yet, in the space called the postcolony such contradictions of development are not only common, but continually being finessed, as detailed in chapter 1.

I begin with a brief discussion of the idea of narrative and political rhetoric in the construction of the nation, with a focus on the role of individual political leadership in this process. I then undertake a textual analysis of an emblematic piece by President Jayewardene to illustrate how the nation is narrated. I weave in and out of the textual analysis by counterposing alternative constructions of the social reality that Jayewardene attempts to narrate in his text. Finally, I examine the production of a hierarchy of authenticity in the nation and its consequences for the ethnic struggle in Sri Lanka today.

NARRATIVE, RHETORIC, AND POLITICAL BIOGRAPHY

It helps to think of social reality as primarily encoded in the form of narrative. Whether we see ourselves as individuals or as social beings embedded in nation, tribe, or any other collective identity, our sense of our past, present, and future is marked by various rites of passage and rendered comprehensible or significant through the device of narrative. Narrative allows us to make sense of the meaningless seriality of everyday existence and see it instead as a "progressive elaboration" toward a "comprehensible form" (White 1978, 96). Elaborating on this idea, Hayden White notes how narratives are emplotted in various genres that make them socially recognizable:

> historical discourse should be viewed as a sign system which points in two directions simultaneously: first, toward the set of events it purports to describe and second toward the generic story form to which it tacitly likens the set in order to disclose its formal coherence considered either as a structure or as a *process*. Thus, for example, a given set of events, arranged more or less chronologically but encoded so as to appear as phases of a *process* with a discernible beginning, middle and end may be emplotted as a Romance, Comedy, Tragedy, Epic or what have you, depending on the valences assigned to different events in the series as elements of recognizable archetypal story-forms. (1978, 106, emphasis original)

I would like to emphasize the role of narrative in the production of a sense of belonging or identity: it is the intersubjective and societal recognition of the story line that is critical in determining the ecumene of the narrative. In other words, narratives not only endow space with identity, but establish degrees of belonging, make pronouncements on who is inside and outside the stories, and who is central and marginal. This idea is important in unlocking the efficacy of certain forms of political rhetoric in Sri Lanka on ethnic and communal identity and its attendant violence.

Many scholars have focused on the affinity between the narrative form and nationalism (Anderson 1991, Bhabha, ed., 1990). Nationalism is invariably portrayed as the story of a redemptive journey in which redemption is seen as a "self-justifying practice of an idea or mission over time, in a structure that completely encircles and is revered by you, even though you set up the structure in the first place, ironically enough, and no longer study it closely because you take it for granted" (Said 1993, 69). This understanding of the nation as a shared journey from putatively common origins to the recovery of desired futures lends itself to narrative form; conversely, a discourse such as nationalism is rendered as the story of recovery by the logic of narrative itself. Narratives not only discursively ar-

ticulate social reality, but are central to its endless and agonistic rein-
terpretation. Political debate and rhetoric may then be seen as competing narratives of our origin myths and desired futures. In this
context, political leadership becomes a matter of effectively entering
a performative realm in which one attempts to secure social recognition and support for one's preferred narratives. In a Foucauldian
sense, one might argue that the power of an individual leader is attributable less to her agency and more to her socially perceived location within a discourse and to the repertoire of rhetorical roles
that constitute her as a leader at that point in time. Among other
things, this argument ought to at least sensitize us to the importance
of political biography as a genre of analysis that is critical to understanding nationalism. It would not be inaccurate to say that biography in political science has tended to emphasize more the individual as leader on her own terms and less the discursive construction
of political leadership as a receptacle for societal anxieties and hopes.
At the same time, it is important to recognize that abstract qualities
such as leadership and charisma perhaps depend on the ability to
improvise creatively on the available repertoire of narratives and to
articulate and personify anxieties and hopes a step ahead of society
itself.

In an important work, Roland Barthes (1972, 109–59) reminds
us that myth achieves meaning as a lived practice, something that
provides people with a way of being in this world, in contrast to an
epistemic practice such as the writing of history, which gives people
a way of understanding or comprehending their world.[3] One could
argue that narrative, like myth, attains its completion in the realm
of social action beyond the margins of the text. Paul Ricoeur notes
in this regard that "the process of composition, of configuration, is
not completed in the text but in the reader and, under this condition, makes possible the reconfiguration of life by narrative.... [T]he
sense or the significance of a narrative stems from the *intersection
of the world of the text and the world of the reader*. The act of
reading thus becomes the critical moment of the entire analysis. On
it rests the narrative's capacity to transfigure the experience of the
reader" (1991, 26, emphasis original).

Just as one does not interpret *text* narrowly to refer only to written documents, but also sees it as referring to speeches, symbols,

processions, maps, posters, films, and various other forms of political communication, one ought also to interpret *reading* in the widest sense of the term as a societal appropriation of the significance of political texts. In other words, the narratives of the nation obtain their social efficacy and power in terms of the repertoire of actions they make possible: they become real to the extent that they provide a people with a way of living in their time. When such understandings are acted upon, when they enable a people to participate in the "making of the nation," narrative achieves completion. It is thus important to understand Jayewardene's text not merely in its descriptive aspects, but also in terms of the kinds of social actions and collective participation in cathartic violence (for the majority community) that these aspects seem to entail.

A LIFE IN QUEST OF NARRATIVE

It is often the case that political leaders (or, for that matter, the rest of us) are self-conscious about the need to emplot their lives as coherent and redemptive narratives. This was certainly the case with Jayewardene, who in his various writings and speeches is acutely conscious that the manner in which his life is recounted is critical to both his own fashioning of a self-identity and the way he will be judged by history into the next century. One of the more interesting texts authored by Jayewardene is a glossy and slickly produced book titled *Golden Threads* (1984, hereafter cited parenthetically as *GT*). Intended as a history primer, perhaps for middle or high school children, this text is a document in self-fashioning. Below the title on the first page, the audience is clearly defined: "For the Youth of Sri Lanka . . . to whom the torch must pass." The text thus begins by locating the narrator and his audience: the narrator as someone who has, in an Olympian metaphor, led the charge (carried "the torch") of the national journey and is preparing to bestow that responsibility to his young wards. The inside front cover of *Golden Threads* has a remarkable diagram:

_____ Past _____	Present _____	Future_____
544 B.C.–1815 A.D.	1815–1977	1977–

Based on the ancient Pali chronicle *Mahavamsa*, Jayewardene dates the "origin" of Sri Lanka to 544 B.C. and the arrival of King Vijaya and his men from Northern India to the island. The past is thus the period from the founding of the dynasty of Vijaya all the way to the Kandyan Convention of 1815, when the "Sinhala chiefs signed over the Kandyan kingdom to George III of Great Britain" (GT, 4). The present, intriguingly, is the period that spans both the period of British colonial rule (1815–1948) *and* postcolonial Sri Lanka from 1948 to 1977. This configuration effaces the year of independence, something very rare in postcolonial recollections. 1977 is the year the Jayewardene-led United National Party (UNP) defeated the Sri Lanka Freedom Party (SLFP) at the elections and assumed power (with Jayewardene serving as prime minister initially, then as president once the new Gaullist constitution went into effect in 1978). It thus becomes the terminus of the present and the beginning of the future.

This eclectic and fabulist time line accomplishes a number of things, some so obvious that one is sometimes in danger of forgetting them. Chiefly, myth, chronicle, and history have all been thoroughly intermixed. To date the beginning of Sri Lanka on the basis of the *Mahavamsa,* besides forever tying Sri Lanka with Buddhist cosmology (the year 544 B.C. also happens to be the year the Buddha gained Mahanibbana or died), effaces both the prior and the non-Buddhist populations of Sri Lanka. Second, by anchoring the origins of Sri Lanka in a Buddhist, Pali chronicle, Jayewardene pushes to the margins the Tamils and other ethnic and religious communities who have no comparable mythic charter of their presence. Further, it ignores the fact that even if the chronicle is true, according to the *Mahavamsa* itself Vijaya's seven hundred men, including the king himself, populated the "new" space by marrying women from the Tamil, Pandyan kingdom of southern India. Perhaps most important (something we will return to later), this origin myth, as currently disseminated, establishes a hierarchy of authenticity within Sri Lanka, the Sinhala Buddhist perched at the apex and the other ethnic and religious groups reduced to supporting positions, but only if they behave themselves.

In a sense, Jayewardene passes up on an opportunity to inscribe Sri Lanka at the very outset with the miscegenation of its population and thus irrevocably to ambiguate the purity of its origins. This move is suggested by at least three of Sri Lanka's most prominent scholars, Stanley Tambiah, Leslie Gunawardana, and Gananath Obeyesekere,[4] although each stresses different aspects of the issue. Tambiah notes in his analysis of the *Mahavamsa* that

> The Vijaya myth concludes... with his sending a mission to Madhura (Madura) in South India to woo the daughter of the Pandu king for Vijaya himself, and "the daughters of others for the ministers and retainers." The king's daughter, together with another hundred maidens for the ministers of Vijaya, all fitted out, according to their rank and "craftsmen and a thousand families of eighteen guilds" were sent across the sea and they disembarked at Mahatittha. These Pandyan Tamil women as proper spouses for Vijaya and his male followers, and a thousand families of the guilds, men, women and children of fully Pandyan identity, in conjunction with Vijaya and his followers, the core *Sihala,* pose at the very beginning of the "official" chronicle history of the island the problems of counting "descent" and attributing identity. (1992, 133)[5]

As Tambiah goes on to note, first, it is a fairly large concession to state that the so-called founding fathers of Sri Lanka populated the realm with women from the Tamil kingdom of the Pandyans. Now, one could counter that miscegenative act with the principle of patriarchal lineage. That is to say, no matter who the founding mothers were, the fact that lineage is tracked through the male suffices to establish the Sinhala character of the origins of this realm (setting aside, for the moment, the vexing question then of what becomes of the mother tongue). But, as Tambiah elaborates, the Sinhalese, according to this founding myth of the *Mahavamsa,* descend also from the thousand families who accompanied the spouses of Vijaya's men. These people are, to stay momentarily within this artificial discourse of racial purity, "to begin with wholly non-Sinhala" and their "incorporation into the broadened category of Sihala is effected minimally through their learning of the Sihala language. Thus, it is by virtue of linguistic incorporation, and not by descent, that they would have become Sihala" (1992, 133–34).

Tambiah's argument deconstructs the essentialist core of identity (variously sought in some nonexistent holy grail of racial or linguistic purity) and reads the creation and reproduction of identity through a socially acculturative practice, in this instance the learning of a language. And Obeyesekere takes this idea a step further when he notes, in a manner designed to question the separateness of the two

communities at all, "Underlying the linguistic and physical differences . . . are strong cultural and racial similarities. Physically the Sinhalese and Tamils cannot be differentiated. Though the initial Sinhalese migrants were probably Indo-European language speakers
who arrived over 2,500 years ago, practically all later arrivals were
South Indians (mostly Tamil speakers) who were assimilated into
the Sinhalese Buddhist community" (1984, 154).

This important argument has many parallels in the context of
South Asia, especially in dispelling the racist mythography of those
who would point to the 'Aryan' origins of the region's upper castes.
Romila Thapar's (1993) work on the historiography of ancient India demolishes the myth that connects linguistic grammars and structures of the Indo-Aryan and the Dravidian languages with race by
pointing out that languages can and do migrate without correspond-
ing migrations of peoples or races. Even the essentialist status granted
to language momentarily here needs to be thoroughly deconstructed.
As Michael Billig notes in a concise summary, "Humans might have
spoken from the dawn of history, with mutually unintelligible ways
of talking being developed in different places, but this does not mean
that people have thought of themselves as speaking 'a language.'
The concept of 'a language' . . . may itself be an invented permanency,
developed during the age of the nation-state. If this is the case, then
language does not create nationalism, so much as nationalism creates language" (1995, 30).

Besides being historically more plausible, arguments such as those
of Tambiah, Thapar, Obeyesekere, and Billig lend themselves to a
conception of history and of origins that is ab initio adulterated, an
adulteration that can, moreover, only be liberatory in a context dominated by discourses of purity and essence.[6]

Besides positioning Jayewardene himself at the head of this charge
into the future from 1977, the time line in *Golden Threads* has to
be read together with the table of rulers given on its inside back
cover. Titled "Sri Lanka's Rulers: A Chronological List," this table
begins with "Vijaya 544 B.C." and literally lists 193 kings or emperors who ruled "all or parts" of "Sri Lanka" from 544 B.C. to
A.D. 1815. This entry is followed by the "Period under British Rule,"
which takes the chronology from George III to Queen Elizabeth II
(1952–72). Then comes the "President under 1972 Constitution,"

William Gopallawa (1972–78). All these set the stage for the grand entrance of Jayewardene himself: "Elected President under 1978 Constitution" (1978–83) and reelected in November 1982.

The multiple farces of this chronology need enumeration. First, it positions Jayewardene as the anchor of a genealogy that includes the names of Sinhala kings with a wide currency in Sri Lanka's symbolic universe: Vijaya, Devanampiya Tissa, Dutta Gamini, Mahinda, Gajabahu, and Parakramabahu, to mention some. The genealogy lists George III (1815–20), Queen Victoria (1837–1901), and Elizabeth II (1952–72) as his political antecedents.[7] By equating "rulers" with "presidents" only, Jayewardene deftly eliminates from his list all of postcolonial Sri Lanka's prime ministers since 1948. Thus, he shares the spotlight with kings and emperors and queens and has, by a rather brazen technicality, written the likes of S.W.R.D. Bandaranaike, Sirimavo Bandaranaike, the Senanayakes, and Kotelawala out of the story altogether. Only the hapless William Gopallawa (a figurehead president from 1972 to 1978 under Sri Lanka's previous Westminster-style political system), damned both by the absence of royal blood and electoral legitimacy, provides lonely foil to Jayewardene.

Second, in his text, Jayewardene enacts a crucial double move through a chronology that seamlessly combines myth and history. While, at one level, he renders his own persona mythic and places it within a pantheon that has tremendous resonance within Sinhala cosmology, in the same breath he renders the likes of Dutta Gamini and Mahinda and others real by this conflation. The combination, which simultaneously effaces the distinctions between the real and the mythic, characterized many of Jayewardene's actions while he was president. Besides the narrow and utilitarian purpose of rendering Jayewardene royal, this genealogy promotes a popular culture in which acceptance of Sinhala domination of Sri Lanka becomes sanctified by supposedly timeless chronicles. Thus, myth here serves an important function designed to "legitimate an order either by rationalizing the origin of its construction or providing a view that naturalizes it" (Shapiro 1993, 50).

The chronicle of Sri Lanka's rulers is not some inane exercise in deluded grandeur tucked away in a children's book. It was circulated by the Sri Lankan embassy, for example, when Jayewardene visited President Ronald Reagan in Washington, D.C., in 1984. The same genealogy appears in K. M. De Silva's (1981) widely read and authoritative work on Sri Lankan history and politics.

Moreover, in his speeches and other writings, Jayewardene reiterates the theme that he is the lineal successor to 193 kings and emperors of Sri Lanka. The following example is typical:

> *Sri Lankan nation* has stood out as the most wonderful nation in the world because of several unique characteristics. *Sinhala nation* has followed one faith, that is Buddhism for an unbroken period of 2500 years.... [T]here is no other nation that can boast such a heritage.... [T]he language of the King and the people 2100 years ago had been Sinhala which we speak today. It is one of the oldest Aryan languages in the world.... Another unique heritage is the country's history of sovereignty and territorial integrity. No other nation has enjoyed national independence for such a length of time as we have.... We are the most wonderful nation in the world. We must be proud of our history. (Colombo *Daily News*, June 12, 1987, p. 1., emphasis added)

Note the easy slide from "Sri Lankan" nation to "Sinhala nation" at the outset of this excerpt. Such slippages are all too common in the political rhetoric of Sinhalese political leaders and Buddhist clergy. Jayadeva Uyangoda makes an important etymological point in this regard when he notes that "This disjunction [between Sri Lankan nation and Sinhala nation] is acutely evident in an attempt to translate the construction 'nation-building' into Sinhalese in order to convey what it entails. *Jathiya godanegima* in the Sinhala political idiom has only one meaning—the building of the Sinhalese nation, and *not* of the Sri Lankan nation" (1994, 13, emphasis original).

At a social level, the production and dissemination of such a meticulous genealogy of kingship in Sri Lanka that spans 2,500 years is more than the mere aggrandizement of a president. In a telling insight, Etienne Balibar connects such genealogies with the production of the social imaginaire of the nation: "genealogy is no longer either a body of theoretical knowledge or an object of oral memory, nor is it recorded and kept privately: *today it is the state which draws up and keeps the archive of filiations and alliances*"(1991, 101, emphasis original).

Many of Jayewardene's actions after he became president in 1978 display a similar desire to be placed in the pantheon of royalty. He updated the *Mahavamsa* from where Yagirala Pannananda had left off in the 1930s, bringing it up to the moment of his own accession to the presidency; in line with the ancient kings, he gave prominence to the grand irrigation schemes along the Mahavali River; his election promise was to create a *dharmistha* (a neologism signifying a "righteous society" on the lines of the Indian Buddhist king Asoka); he desired to addressed as *utumanan* (Your Excellency); he spent huge amounts of money, estimated at Rs 1,000 million, to restore the Cultural Triangle between Anuradhapura, Polonnaruwa, and Kandy (see Kemper 1991, for details). The new Constitution, although modifying the 1972 Constitution that had declared Buddhism to be a state religion, made clear that Buddhism had pride of place and, moreover, that the state had the duty to protect and foster the Buddhist way of life.

Regarding Jayewardene's lapses between delusion and reality, Valentine Daniel notes that "Within a span of a few days one finds him claiming that he was Asoka, the Prince of Peace, and also that he could, if he wished (and implying that he might choose to), wipe out the Tamils within a few minutes if he only so decided. On another occasion, while claiming to be a vessel of Buddha's compassion, he urged his supporters among the Tea Estate Tamils to use whatever work-instruments were at their disposal as weapons against any outsider who tried to enter the plantations to create trouble" (1990, 230). Similarly, Minister of Lands and Mahavali Development Gamini Dissanayake deeply believed that he "was engaged in the restoration of Sri Lanka to the glorious days of Parakramabahu the Great" (Daniel 1990, 230). In earlier decades, there had occurred a similar self-fashioning on the part of D. S. Senanayake and other Sri Lankan leaders (Kemper 1991, 24).

Although it is tempting to see many of these actions in terms of the short-term political capital they created for Jayewardene, a closer examination indicates more. For example, the updated *Mahavamsa* stayed clear of discussions of the merits or otherwise of recent political leaders, including Jayewardene himself, and became more of a chronicle of modern civil society. Jayewardene's profiting from these forms of religiosity ought not to be calibrated on a narrow utilitarian calculus, but on a more powerful and socially symbolic level: they provided a people with a sense of their place and their time. Steven Kemper (1991) points to Jayewardene's uncanny ability both to argue that politics should be thoroughly imbued with the values and principles of Buddhism and simultaneously to reduce the role that the often troublesome Buddhist clergy played in politics.

In *Golden Threads*, Jayewardene specifies exactly the threads that comprise the "warp and woof of the long, rich tapestry of our island tale": (a) Buddhism, (b) Sri Lanka's "unique hydraulic agriculture" that disappeared in medieval times but is now about to "reappear," (c) an "independence" that lasted from 544 B.C. to A.D. 1815 and was regained in 1948, (d) monarchical rule and the demise of feudalism, (e) Sinhala, "one of the oldest Aryan languages spoken from the beginning of the Sinhala race continuously down to today," and finally, (f) "life in the new technological world to come." Although perhaps redundant, it is necessary to point out that this cloth is woven exclusively from the golden threads of the Sinhalese: this "island tale" cannot be told in a language other than Sinhala.

Throughout this text, the Tamil presence serves as a whetstone for the delineation of Sinhala–Sri Lankan identity (and, as we have seen, the two are often the same in Jayewardene's rhetoric), a presence that is always in need of qualification. Thus, the Tamil King Elara is described as "an intruder" and someone who "legend has it...was just" (*GT,* 4). The syncretism of Buddhism, which like any living faith was influenced by other religions and practices, is effaced, and the effort to produce purity is reflected in Jayewardene's descriptions: "*despite* Cholan, Pandyan and Pallavan intrusions, there was sufficient stability down this long era to ensure the continuity of the Anuradhapura civilization. *Despite* strong Mahayanist and Hindu influences the Theravada retained its integrity" (*GT,* 6, emphasis added). The two "despites" in the quote serve as qualifiers that reduce the Tamils to intrusions, to impure influences that have compromised the integrity of a posited unity. In contrast to Jayewardene's pejorative reading of such intrusions, John Holt suggests that with regard to the influence of Pallavan culture from southern India on Sri Lankan religious and sculptural traditions during the early medieval period, "artistic similarities between insular Southeast Asia and Sri Lanka point to a common source of religious and cultural inspiration: South Indian Pallava culture.... Of greatest cultural importance to the period from the seventh to the tenth centuries was the political link established between the fortunes of the Pallava Empire and Sri Lanka" (1991, 80–82). In this manner, the

Tamil presence serves as the means to produce a Sri Lanka that is unambiguously Sinhala and Buddhist. At a more general level, what the quoted passages from *Golden Threads* attempt to accomplish is an anachronistic rendering of a plural and assimilative history into a closed, singular, and pure narrative that lineally connects the myth of the origin to the present-day division between the ethnic groups that populate Sri Lanka.

The glorious Theravada Buddhist civilization of Anuradhapura ended, according to Jayewardene, with the conquest by the miasmic forces from southern India and the beginning of a medieval dark age in the Rajarata (the abode of kings). Staying within the Edenic narrative structure, Jayewardene depicts a spatialization of Sri Lanka, girded on the sacred and profane. He avers: "In the first quarter of the thirteenth century from South India came Magha—the Tiger. The wasteland he created became the kingdom of malaria, the domain of the anopheles, breeding prodigiously in the dark stagnant waters of the great irrigation works. The legitimate kings and their subjects began that long trek southward" (*GT,* 7). This passage makes a series of familiar moves in the narrative genre of chosen peoples and their promised lands. Thus, the South Indian presence (in Sri Lankan rhetoric quite often conflated with Tamil, although historically Magha would be from contemporary Orissa) is bestialized as the Tiger, and from the days of culture and civilization we descend into a dark wasteland. The image of the sexual profligacy of the hated other contained in the phrase "breeding prodigiously" is by now a familiar one in racist literature. And for those who would aver that connecting Jayewardene's allusion to the breeding mosquitoes with the Tamils of Sri Lanka is far-fetched, consider his 1985 statement: "It is essential that we completely destroy the (militant) movement. . . . Like destroying the breeding places of mosquitoes to wipe them out, we should find where the militants are and destroy them" (quoted in Swamy 1994, 167). *Golden Threads* continues, the "legitimate" kings and subjects, which in this context can mean only the Sinhalese, are banished southward and begin that other staple of such narratives: a purifying and strengthening exile until the recovery of the kingdom.

After a rough and ready summary of the intervening centuries, notable for its brazenly selective vision of Sri Lanka as a land of Sinhala Buddhists, Jayewardene summarizes the period since independence: "Democracy on the whole worked smoothly.... With the return of the UNP in mid-1977 this island enjoys a kind of political freedom which it had never known in all its 2500 years of storied history. Religion, race, caste, and family are no longer passports to advancement or obstructions to individual progress" (GT, 20). Needless to add, no Tamil in post-1948 Sri Lanka can recognize her own experience in this "history." In fact, Jayewardene's interpretation of the entire issue of postcolonial Tamil-Sinhala ethnic relations is boiled down to the following, his only reference to the issue in the book: "Terrorism, a World phenomenon raised its ugly head in the North and East, and some Tamils joined them to press for separation. In 1980 these activities increased and the killing of Sinhala security forces in the North in 1983 were followed by Sinhala-Tamil riots throughout the island" (GT, 22). Any rational agency on the part of the Tamil and the possibility that Tamil grievances may be genuine — based on discrimination and violent exclusion at the hands of the Sinhalese majority — are eliminated here.[8] Instead, so-called terrorism is naturalized through a metaphor of unpredictable and irrational bestiality ("raised its ugly head"). It is estimated that in the pogrom of July 1983 anywhere between 2,000 and 3,000 Tamils were killed (Spencer 1990a, 616; government estimates put the figure at 350), property worth about $300 million was looted or destroyed, and more than 100,000 were rendered homeless and became refugees in their own land. The pogrom is justified by Jayewardene, however, as a response to this insensate "phenomenon." Overwhelmingly directed against innocent civilians, systematically organized by individuals high in the ruling political party, and often conducted in the presence of the Sinhala-dominated police and armed forces, the pogrom is further justified as a response to "the killing of security forces in the North."[9]

Having diminished the ethnic question to a problem of terrorism, one further reduced as a nonparticular "world phenomenon," and having homogenized the nation into a supportive realm, Jayewardene can turn his attention in the last part of Golden Threads to the question of his country's tryst with the future: its moment of arrival as an ersatz Singapore. Following dazzling full-page color pictures of the New Parliamentary Complex in Sri Jayawardhanapura and the Victoria Reservoir in Kandy (both serving as monuments to Sri Lanka's entry into modernity) the final section begins, titled "The

New Scientific Technological Age." The frontispiece here is a digitized reproduction of a personal computer, radiating a rainbow of colors from its monitor.

Jayewardene has never made a secret of his admiration for Lee Kuan Yew, the architect of Singapore's success and its father, patriarch, prime minister, senior minister through its transformation in recent decades. The choice of Singapore as a model to emulate is worthy of some attention. Of all the societies in the world today, I would argue, Singapore symbolizes best both the energy of global capitalism and its voracious drive for consumption. It is a place that has been literally annihilated by the acceleration of time: its definition is as a momentary platform, a fleeting node in the circuits of world capital. Akin to its location as a node in global communications, capital, and electronic circuits, most visitors to Singapore are transients who change planes at Changi Airport, touted by the government as the Asian Airtropolis (the greatest shopping mall in the sky where you are duty bound to shop duty-free). They invariably duck into the city for a frantic spin to sample not only its various simulacra of nature—the Sentosa theme park with its Underwater World and the world's largest aviary in the Jurong Bird Park, the zoo—but also glitzy shopping arcades and third-world ethnic food made according to first-world standards of sanitation. With its rigidly ordered society leavened only by the frenzy of acquiring and trading commodities, Singapore is a quintessentially ersatz product of late capitalism. In attempting to emulate it, Jayewardene has set for himself and his society the eternal postcolonial task of mimicking an original that is spurious to begin with.

Jayewardene's desire to become the patriarch of such a society is also understandable on a different register. Singapore is a society that has supposedly solved its ethnic question successfully. By enforcing an ethnic hierarchy with Chinese at the top and all others (Malays, Tamils, Eurasians) positioned at various levels of assigned inferiority, Singapore has been able to give its undivided attention to accumulation. Jayewardene is surely seduced by the vision of a society in which everyone knows their place.

The concluding lines of *Golden Threads* complete the circle that began with the metaphor of passing on the torch to the youth of tomorrow. Jayewardene notes, "We have no time to waste. The future urgently beckons. . . . We must participate in this revolution [of technology and information] if we ever hope to catch up with the developed world. We need to know all about it before we can participate or catch up. The quest for that knowledge—that is the odyssey on which we must now embark" (6). Time is embodied with content in typically postcolonial fashion: it is seen as an evanescent resource not to be wasted so that "we can...catch up" with those far ahead in the race.

In its entirety, *Golden Threads* illustrates how a complex social reality is modulated and rendered comprehensible by narrative. At various points, it resembles one or the other genres available—namely, tragedy, epic, romance, and even farcical comedy. After its glorious beginning with its consecration as Dhammadipa, the island was plunged into a series of dark ages due to conquests from without. At each point, redemption arrived in the form of a Sinhalese king who reunited the realm and recovered the promised land. Jayewardene fashions himself as the culmination of a long genealogy of such successful kings and emperors (the great "unifiers"). The mythographic foundations of the narrative are socially powerful: their epistemic authority is an ancient Pali text. Most importantly, the entire narrative, from beginning to end, is achingly exclusionist. Its ecumene is built upon an exclusion by blood. There is simply no way a child of Tamil, Burgher, or Moor can see herself in the unfolding of this land.

Golden Threads ultimately evokes a pastoral vision: under a Bo tree, with the tank, the temple, and the paddy fields in the background, a gentle patriarch instructs a group of wide-eyed children about their glorious heritage and the beckoning future. Like most idyllic visions in soft-focus, this one too shatters upon closer examination. In the words of the poet Sivaramani, all of twenty-three years old when she killed herself in Jaffna in May 1991, there are some other children in Sri Lanka as well:

A burst of gunfire
shatters the stillness
of a star-filled sky
destroying the meaning
of children's stories...
like sheep
they have learned
all of this
To tear off

the wings of insects
make guns
from sticks and logs
kill friends
thinking them enemies
these are the games
our children play.
In a night
full of pressure
during war
our young have grown up. (Sivaramani 1992)

A HIERARCHY OF AUTHENTICITY

At a certain level, Jayewardene's text has one redeeming quality: it is frankly, almost artlessly open about his vision of Sri Lanka as primarily the abode of the Sinhalese Buddhists. In many of his writings and speeches, he is oblivious as to whether his vision is too sectarian and partial to be inclusively national. To put it baldly, the idea that there are many who may be Sri Lankan and not Sinhalese or Buddhist genuinely does not seem to occur to him. Jayewardene, like so many others in Sri Lankan society, "continues to confuse routes with roots" (Carter 1987, xviii).

Such a rendering of national space into exclusively Sinhala territory is evident at the highest levels of society, not just among the political elite. In a work on Sri Lankan politics of the 1980s, one of the country's high-ranking diplomats—educated at the exclusive Royal College, the University of Ceylon, and Harvard University, the youngest ambassador, and one-time emissary to the European Union—had this to say about the pogrom of 1983: "As explained in detail...the Tamil people in general and those in Jaffna in particular, have systematically provoked the Sinhalese. A backlash against the Tamils, especially the bigoted amongst them, was indeed inevitable" (Dissanayaka 1993, 1). In a self-contradictory mixture of faith in meritocratic fairness, on the one hand, and numerically proportionate ethnic representation, on the other, T. D. S. A. Dissanayaka went on to observe the following:

> For generations the Tamils have yearned to join Government service and since 1956 all manner of obstacles have been placed in their path. Now, under President R. Premadasa the interests of all com-

munities have been safeguarded in admission to the Government service. Recruitment is strictly on the basis of ethnic ratio.... [T]he prestigious firm Hayleys is known for its excellent management. However even as recently as 1983, a vast preponderance of their accountants were Tamils, so was their Finance Director. *That anomaly has now been rectified.* Even more recently the Hatton National Bank had a Tamil Managing Director and somehow 5 out of 6 of his Assistant General Managers were Tamils. In turn they recruited all manner of Tamils. I too have an account in that Bank and wondered why they did not change their name to the Jaffna National Bank. *That defect has now been rectified.* ... Of course the Tamils are free citizens living in a free country. They can patronize whomever they want and recruit whomever they want. However, a separate issue is that their predilections are clear to anybody except the Tamils themselves. It has been truly said that wise people learn from the mistakes of others, fools not even from their own. The Tamils are anything but fools, they are just incorrigible. For that they pay a heavy price and during racial riots some pay the supreme price. (1993, 123–24, emphasis added to highlight the chilling repetition)[10]

Running through this paragraph is a tension between a belief in a Sri Lanka as exclusively for Sinhalese and a belief in liberal values of equal citizenship and the democratic rights of minorities. There are, if you will, contradictory epistemes of fairness and entitlements running through Dissanayaka's rendition of national space. This tension between a view of the nation as a realm populated by putatively equal citizens, irrespective of any other markers, and a view that sees the nation as a realm in which the majority community is privileged over all others is a tension that goes to the very heart of postcolonial nationalism and the incredible violence that it has unleashed. It is resolved on this occasion in favor of a crude majoritarianism and done so from a self-assured standpoint that can be the privilege of only those in the mainstream. According to this standpoint, any indication that the Tamil occupies a space "disproportionate" to their numerical presence in society must arise either from mendacity or clannishness, is either an anomaly or a defect, and must, moreover, be violently "rectified."

Where does this sense of entitlement regarding a mainstream come from? It is certainly quite recent in that the consciousness of various groups and collectivities in Sri Lanka was not always inscribed within such enumerated, nationwide and clearly defined ethnic categories. Perhaps the answer lies in the unique ways in which modernity arrived in the colony, mediated by a colonial state, and the ways in which it has interacted in the postcolonial period with the exigencies of winning elections and acquiring one's rightful share of the national pie. It was during the late-colonial period that societies such as India and Sri Lanka were for the first time brought under the regime of censuses, national agricultural yield and land-revenue data collection, trigonometric surveys of territory, fixed and demarcated political boundaries, and, increasingly, the classification of the population into definable groups such as castes, races, languages, religions, and the like. Building on a number of important works (notably those of Cohn 1987a, Kaviraj 1992, Anderson 1991, and Ludden 1993), Arjun Appadurai (1993) makes an important argument regarding the legacy such colonial enumerative practices constitute in regard to the contemporary politics of nation building and the contradictory definitions of fairness and equity they imply. He points out that the practices of enumeration had opposite effects on the colonizer and the colonies: in the former, serving to unify and produce an imagination of putatively equal citizens, and in the latter, supporting the idea of exotic, eternally differentiated and fragmented caste, tribe, communal, and other group-oriented identities.

At one level, such enumeration "unyoked social groups from the complex and localized structures and agrarian practices in which they had been previously embedded" (Appadurai 1993, 327), a process perhaps characteristic of modernization and capitalism everywhere. But where these unmoored and alienated identities coalesced into a new imaginaire called the individualistic, national citizen in the post-feudal west, the dictates of empire produced different consequences in the colonies. First, by quantifying and codifying previously localized and lived classifications (notably that of caste), British colonial enumeration promoted and stimulated far wider ecumenes of such self-identifications. Second, in the colony there was an important difference that regarded political representation not in terms of putatively equal citizens but rather in terms of the sectarian rights of special groups—religion-based electorates, to mention one prominent example. Such state-sponsored fragmentation constituted an important part of colonial policies of divide and rule, and its carryover into postcolonial democratic politics based on suffrage has been devastating.

The fragmenting of an incipient Indian or Sri Lankan populaire into these eternally divided groups changed the character of politics in a fundamental way: it moved the idea of *representation* from within a realm of equal citizens to one of numerically proportionate *representativeness* of these fragmented groups. To put it differently, it was now argued that political and economic power, in order to be fairly and equitably distributed, ought to match closely the numerical *proportions* that various minority communities and the majority community comprised in the nation-at-large. This difference between representation (as a liberal-democratic ideal) and representativeness (in the postcolonial reality) is critical to understanding the tensions in the quote from Dissanayaka above. And it is on the basis of the idea of representativeness that he can argue that the Tamil minority was *overrepresented* in the professions, civil service employment, mercantile trade, and the educated sections of the populace, whereas correspondingly the Sinhala majority was *underrepresented* in the same offices.

Once the rhetoric of politics came to be coded within this modernist and enumerative regime, it was a short step to make the argument that the Sinhalese were a deprived and discriminated majority, while the Tamils were a pampered and uppity minority. The interaction between categories such as Sinhala Buddhist or Tamil Hindu (which may be said to have acquired such a numerical valence only in recent times) and the requirements of competitive, electoral politics based on universal suffrage in the postcolonial period has been predictably explosive and violent, which ought to indicate that Sri Lanka's ethnic strife is not born out of any atavistic and primordial attachment to traditions, one that would go away if it was force fed modernity in ever-increasing doses. The ethnic violence that wracks the country today is the definitive indication that Sri Lanka has arrived as a modern nation.

Ultimately, the Tamil is not so much seen as inferior by Jayewardene or Dissanayaka as he is seen as being out of his place. In other words, it is not a matter of who is more deserving or meritorious (attributes susceptible to socially accepted standards of verification), but rather that an entire community is given, ab initio, the status of those who don't belong "here." The limits of Sinhala ecumene in this regard was best expressed by the former industries minister Cyril Mathew when he said in December 1983, addressing the annual conference of the ruling United National Party, that "Sri Lanka is Sin-hala history and nothing else" (Wilson 1988, 222).

Like most other Sinhala politicians in postcolonial Sri Lanka, Jayewardene built his political career upon intransigent opposition to any concessions to the Tamil minority when he was trying to gain power and upon stonewalling, dissembling, and complicity with annihilatory violence against them when he was in power. I offer one illustration of such dissembling and stonewalling in an interview I had with him in 1992.[11] The context was a discussion of the riots of July 1983:

SK: One of the watershed events that is often mentioned in the lit-erature, a watershed event in the history of your country, is July 1983 ... (interrupted)

JRJ: You are talking about the violence.

SK: Exactly, that is what I am referring to. The July 1983 riots. A lot of authors have argued that was the turning point because by the end of three days, 60 percent of Colombo's Tamils were in refugee camps.

JRJ: Yes, quite right.

SK: That's an incredible degree of violence and what seemed un-canny was ... (interrupted)

JRJ: Nobody said that it was done by the government.

SK: No, I am not saying it was done by government. But what seemed uncanny was for the rioters to know which store was Tamilian and which was not ... (interrupted)

JRJ: Quite right.

SK: ... and picking only the Tamil stores for looting and ... (inter-rupted)

JRJ: I thought it was all planned.

SK: By whom?

JRJ: By ... by the JVP. (Long pause). You see, I got a commission into it. And they said it is difficult to come to a conclusion that it was planned by JVP and nobody else.

SK: (quoting JRJ): "it was difficult to come to the conclusion that it was planned by JVP and nobody else"?

JRJ: (quoting himself) "And nobody else."

SK: But that sentence doesn't put the blame on the JVP.

JRJ: No, but they didn't put the blame. I am saying I think so.

SK: So your Commission of Inquiry came to an opposite finding from what you believe.

JRJ: Not opposite, they couldn't. No evidence.

SK: They couldn't confirm it. (Pause). What struck a number of people was the long delay between the rioting and your coming on national television to address the nation.

JRJ: (laughs) Everybody is raising that (said between laughs — and then, firmly). That you must leave to the leader to decide when.

Although this exchange exemplifies the oft-repeated charge made against Jayewardene of dissembling and entangling his adversaries in minute, legalistic non sequiturs, one is still faced here with a fact that demands explanation. Jayewardene (unlike someone such as Cyril Mathew) is an extremely well-read man, conversant in ideas of secularism, liberalism, multiethnic societies, nation building in plural societies, and the like. Moreover, as he and many another Sinhala political leader would hasten to add, not only do they count many Tamils, Burghers, and Muslims as close friends, but their own families have married into these communities. How does this cosmopolitan image of Jayewardene mesh with the president who chose not to appear on national television for more than four days after the July 1983 pogrom?[12] And when he did, besides ignoring completely the plight of the Tamils, suggested that the minorities had been pandered to for too long and the riots were the spontaneous (and hence legitimate) reactions of an enraged Sinhalese people?

This disjunction between the personal and the political among many South Asian elites (often revealed in an overarticulate defense of tolerance and liberal democratic ideals of equality, on the one hand, but participation in or condoning of violence against the minorities, on the other) is a question worth exploring further. One can perhaps find the beginnings of an answer in an idea articulated by Jayadeva Uyangoda regarding majoritarian nationalism and the orientalist heritage that informs it in the postcolonial period. Echoing the distinction between representation and representativeness, Uyangoda argues that one ought to make a distinction between the supposedly dissolving forces of modern nationalism (the creation of citizens all putatively equal) and the assumptions of majority communities regarding their own legitimate rights and opportunities after independence:

> When the colonial rulers left the island, it was easy to imagine the state as the main instrument to be utilized for correcting the historical injustices that the Sinhalese-Buddhist majority community was thought to have suffered under the colonial state. With this instrumentalist view of the state, the nationalist enterprise soon after independence was to re-define and reconstruct political relations of the state in such a way that ethnic relations would be reordered in a new hierarchical pantheon. In the new order, the Sinhalese-Buddhist community was to occupy the apex of the pantheon, with all other communities, ethnic as well as religious, to be relegated to the bottom. It is in this reordering of ethnic relations of the postcolonial state that the realization of the full and real meaning of "independence" was sought. (1994, 13)

Read in this context, *Golden Threads* represents a story that crystallizes the sense of an originary hierarchy of authenticity: there are some to whom this island is home; the others are permanent guests who live in Sri Lanka at the behest of the majority community. They can continue to live here provided they remember their place. As Uyangoda elaborates, "What is the 'proper' political behavior expected from the minorities? When we look at Sinhalese politics we notice that both Sinhala nationalist ideology and the state has had a remarkable answer to this question: the establishment of an ethnic hierarchy in which the majority community is assured of its 'legitimate' place and the minorities of their 'proper' place" (1994, 14). Viewed against this hierarchy, the periodic pogroms and explosions of violence against the Tamils (1956, 1958, 1977, 1981, 1983) in Sri Lanka represent efforts to put them back in their place on grounds that they have become too assertive and need to be taught a lesson, according to an oft-used phrase. It is hardly coincidental that the bouts of collective violence in recent times have all occurred immediately after or during efforts to open a dialogue on redressing minority grievances in Sri Lanka. The fear that such redressal may go "too far" and "appease" minorities is a critical part of the communal violence (see Bastian 1990 for a careful empirical demonstration of this fact).

The hierarchy of authenticity also enables one to explain the attitudes (both overt support and studied indifference) of urbane, well-educated, and cosmopolitan leaders such as Gamini Dissanayake, Lalith Athylathmudali, and Jayewardene regarding these violent pogroms against minorities. Having defined the nationalist project in Sri Lanka to be the majority community's recovery of its rightful place, such violence can be explained, even justified, as the supposedly legitimate and spontaneous anger of the apex community against others who have momentarily forgotten their status as a mere supporting cast.[13]

In terms of the distinction made between myth and history at the beginning of this chapter, there comes about a disjuncture between the epistemic status of Tamils, as a people with a tenuous claim to Sri Lanka as decreed by the narratives of history, and their ontic status, that of a "disproportionately" successful group of professionals or bureaucrats or businessmen or, yes, even successful terrorists or militants. The episodes of collective violence can then be interpreted as instances of the majority community forcibly reasserting, by means of the annihilation of the Tamils, the unity of its epistemic and ontic understandings of the created hierarchies.[14] I submit that this point goes some way toward explaining not only the disjuncture between the intellectual understandings of the national project held by and actual political action taken by someone like Jayewardene, but also the disjuncture between everyday instances of camaraderie between the two communities and the episodes of mass violence in civil society.

I am, of course, fully aware of the politicians' careful orchestration of these so-called spontaneous bursts of Sinhala anger and the collusion of law enforcement agencies in the pogroms. But evidence of orchestration by itself does not demonstrate that ethnic violence in Sri Lanka is exclusively the handiwork of evil politicians or that with the elimination or transformation of some of these politicians the problem will disappear. If the actions of chauvinistic leaders are the spark, we are still left with the reality that there is plenty of combustible tinder in civil society. In other words, we have to explain why, even as they help neighbors to escape or provide succor to victims, significant sections of the majority community feel the violence against the minority community is, at a certain level, both understandable and necessary. In this, the majority community's attitude in Sri Lanka is no different from that of many middle-class Hindu toward Muslims or Sikhs in India, or from that of the Muslim majority toward Hindus in Bangladesh. Again and again, we can see a distinction made between, on the one hand, the concern and affection for one's (minority community) neighbor and, on the other, the support for or condonation of the lesson being taught to the minority community at large.

Golden Threads and other narratives in its genre acquire social efficacy because they provide the moral and mythic charter that redeems and encourages antiminority violence. Violence becomes a form of tough love for the majority community, a cathartic experience that reasserts the nation. Indeed, one could argue that a concept such as tough love (used initially to describe the combination of gruesome violence and a form of paternalistic love exhibited by some slave owners in the American South toward their black slaves) does capture significant elements of majority/minority relations in much of South Asia. The flavor of such tough love is chillingly captured in the following statement made by Gamini Dissanayake, minister of lands and irrigation under Jayewardene, on September 5, 1983, barely a month after the July pogrom: "They [the Tamils] are bringing an army from India. It will take 14 hours to come from India. In 14 minutes, the blood of every Tamil in the country can be sacrificed to the land by us. Who attacked you [Tamils]? Sinhalese. Who protected you? Sinhalese. It is we who can attack you and protect you" (quoted in Wilson 1988, 222). Perhaps most importantly, these narratives provide people with a sense of being in the politics of their time. Participation in collective violence, either physically or epistemically, becomes a ritual that renews their commitment to the making of the nation, to redressing the dissonance between the putative versus the actual order of things.

CONCLUSION

The effort to produce Sri Lanka from a space called Ceylon concisely showcases the physical and epistemic violence that accompanies postcolonial nation building. In contrast to works that regard such violence either as an atavistic aberration in the otherwise justifiable and progressive process of modernization (the primordialist argument) or as a necessary step in the creation of nation-states (the argument mainstream international relations scholars make by modulating the history of Europe), I argue that the problem of postcolonial nationalism is not that it is insufficiently modernist, but rather that it may have learned the lessons of modernity all too well. The violence is a product of an enumerated consciousness framed in terms of majority and minority communities as well as the just desserts that ought to accrue to them. This enumerated self-consciousness is a legacy of a dialectical encounter between the colony and the metropole, and it has produced a colonial version of modernity that marks it as both similar to and different from the experiences of the west.

The Sinhalese majority regards the new nation as a space that properly belongs to itself, one in which purportedly various but lesser outsiders ought to know their place. An argument that conflates the idea of representation with that of numerically proportionate representativeness lies at the heart of their feeling of being discriminated against in terms of economic power and status. The colonial legacy is seen as critical in this elevation of outsider minorities to a disproportionately large presence in the economy, the bureaucracy, and other positions of power and prestige. Hence, the very raison d'état of the postcolonial nation is to reverse such historical discriminations—that is, help the majority community gain its rightful place in the hierarchy of things and put various minorities in their proper places. This tendency is powerfully augmented by the politics of an electoral democracy as the notion of majority and minority is extended to the national space. As William Connolly notes in a context different from but very relevant to the point being made here, "Electoral politics contains powerful pressures to become a closed circuit for the dogmatism of identity through the translation of difference into threat and threat into energy for the dogmatization of identity" (1991, 210–11). For the various minority communities, such a majoritarian view of the national project is not merely alienating, but also energizing to their vision of separate homelands and self-determination.

In the next chapter, I take up the issue of the minority community's reactions to the overbearing embrace of the majority in postcolonial nationalisms. It is important to stress that the cycle of majoritarian discrimination and minority ethnonationalism in postcolonial space is neither inevitable nor inescapable. I offer two contrasting modes of center-periphery relations to demonstrate precisely this point. I argue that the case of Tamil nationalism in Sri Lanka illustrates how Sinhala majoritarianism produced a violent movement for secession, whereas the case of Tamil Nadu in India illustrates how a potentially secessionist Dravidian movement reconciled itself to a role as a unit within a larger polity when the majoritarian embrace was not quite so overbearing. The political lessons to be drawn from these two contrasting examples are critical in any discussion of postcolonial nationalism.

3

Essentially Tamil:
The Divergent Narratives
of Eelam and Dravidinadu

Forgetting, I would even go so far as to say historical error, is a crucial factor in the creation of a nation, which is why progress in historical studies often constitutes a danger for the principle of nationality.
— ERNEST RENAN, "WHAT IS A NATION?"

Ethnicity is not. Any more than the nation. I begin this chapter by evoking Frantz Fanon's famous quote, "The Negro is not. Any more than the white man" (1967, 231), to indicate the dialectical and mutually constitutive character of ethnicity and nation under the regimes of modernity. Neither nation nor ethnicity is an immanent force, an essence within history, destined for eventual recuperation. Rather, they have to be understood in a relational framework, one that highlights their mutual indispensability and the hierarchizing effects of their interaction (Comaroff 1991). The intellectual and political privileging of the nation-state and its univocal discourse of sovereignty has produced a tendency to regard each and every assertion of ethnicity as retrogressive, antinational, incipiently secessionist—an inferior variation on the grander theme of nationhood. The history of modern times in the postcolony is written exclusively in terms of how the nation came (or ought to come) into its own, and every detour on the way is regarded only as a violent, cleansing, and strengthening encounter between the nation and subnational or antinational atavisms.

This history deliberately forgets the unredeemable debt that nation building owes to ethnicity and vice versa. Far from a detour on the way to arrival as a nation-state, so-called particularistic identities such as ethnicity, language, religion, and region constitute the principle of difference against which national identity is sought to be constructed and reproduced. Conversely, the effort to force diverse places into the uniform space of the nation engenders ethnic identity and ethnonationalism in its wake. As a succinct formulation has it, all across the world "state and nation are at each other's throats, and the hyphen that links them is now less an icon of conjuncture than an index of disjuncture" (Appadurai 1996, 39).

In this chapter, I look at the play of identity and difference in two theaters: Tamil nationalism in Sri Lanka and Dravidian nationalism in the southern state of Tamil Nadu in India. My purpose here is two fold. First, I wish to demonstrate that ethnic identity is not an essentialist force lying latent within every society, waiting to erupt into violent secessionism. There is no ethnic group inherently prone to separatism or secession: whether it moves in that direction is in large part dependent on the degree of centralization and majoritarianism that accompanies the nation-building effort and on the degree to which diverse cultures within a national space are accorded autonomy and recognition. Looked at in this way, Sri Lankan Tamil nationalism and Dravidian nationalism offer a useful contrast. Sri Lankan Tamils regard their nationalism as the story of a people driven from moderation and desired accommodation to secessionism because of Sinhalese chauvinism. In contrast, Dravidian nationalism began as a potentially secessionist movement in the 1930s and 1940s but became accommodationist once it realized the political dispensation of independent India offered it an opportunity to come to power at the state level and accorded it a degree of autonomy on questions of language and culture. The degree of such autonomy was never, to be sure, enough to fully satisfy Dravidian aspirations, yet it proved sufficient to deflect that movement from secessionism. Wittingly or otherwise, the example of Dravidianism demonstrates the efficacy of even the limited federal imaginaire that underwrote nation building in India in contrast to the unitary model that informed Sri Lanka. The contrasting histories of Eelam and Dravidian nationalisms powerfully support my argument for reimagining South Asia as a space marked by decentralized nation-states with high degrees of provincial autonomy.

Second, I suggest that the tendency in mainstream scholarship that sees Dravidian and Sri Lankan Tamil nationalisms as being intimately related to and energizing each other is more a reflection of the anxieties of nation building in postcolonial societies and of the strongly ingrained suspicion of movements that seek to loosen the tight embrace of majoritarian nationalism, rather than of any persuasive historical evidence as such. This hermeneutic of suspicion vis-à-vis ethnicity is buttressed by electoral and geopolitical calculations, in both countries, that encourage an opportunistic twinning of the two Tamil nationalisms. Both this suspicion of ethnicity and the twinning of the two Tamil nationalisms are powerfully supported by an international relations discourse that avers that the ideal nation-state is a homogenized, uniform, and sovereign space in which sectarian loyalties, especially those that may cross national boundaries, have no place. I begin by examining such instances of essentializing Tamil ethnicity in recent literatures.

ESSENTIALIZING ETHNICITY IN SCHOLARSHIP AND STATECRAFT

In a speech delivered to the Armed Services Institute of India in New Delhi on March 10, 1989 (when the Indian Peace Keeping Force was still in northeastern Sri Lanka) the Indian high commissioner in Sri Lanka, Jyotindra Nath Dixit, outlined three reasons for India's high-profile diplomatic and military intervention into Sri Lanka's ethnic struggle during the 1980s. Central to his first and third reasons for Indian intervention was a singular notion of "Tamil ethnicity" (his second reason, having to do with Indian geopolitical compulsions, need not detain us here).[1] As his first reason, he cited the danger to nation building emanating from such ethnic identity, claiming that the "first voice of secessionism in the Indian Republic was raised in Tamil Nadu in the mid-sixties. *This was exactly the same principle of Tamil ethnicity, Tamil language.* So, in a manner, our interest in the Tamil issue in Sri Lanka, Tamil aspirations in Sri Lanka was based on maintaining our own unity, our own integrity, our own identity, in the manner in which we have been trying to build our society (Dixit 1989, 249, emphasis added).

What is critical in this statement is the conflation of Tamil here (in India) and Tamil there (in Sri Lanka) through a singular discourse that avers they were "exactly the same principle of Tamil ethnicity, Tamil language." The conflation is further strengthened and then interestingly nuanced in Dixit's third reason for Indian intervention: the suggestion that the Indian government had to go to the aid of the Sri Lankan Tamils because if they did not, it would cause the Tamils of India to feel that "we are not standing by our own Tamils; and if that is so, then in *the Tamil psyche, Tamil subconscious,* the question arose: is there any relevance or validity of our being part of a larger political identity, if our deeply felt sentiments are not respected? So, it was a compulsion... which could not be avoided by any *elected* government in this country (1989, 250–51, emphases added).

Two aspects of Dixit's statements are worth further investigation. First, they suggest that the link between Tamil Nadu and the Sri Lankan Tamils was so strong that the former's "deeply felt sentiments" needed to be respected on pain of a resurgence of Tamil Nadu's secessionist proclivities. By arguing that the movement for Eelam by Sri Lankan Tamils could promote instability and (possibly) secession in Tamil Nadu, Dixit was making an explicit link between the two nationalisms. *For Dixit, and for a number of others within the universe of Indian foreign policy studies, making this link is critical: the entire justificatory edifice for Indian presence in Sri Lanka came to hinge on the putative unity between the two Tamil nationalisms. In its absence, Indian actions would constitute a military intervention that violated Sri Lankan sovereignty; its presence, conversely, rendered the Indian army a peacekeeping force committed not merely to help Sri Lanka solve its ethnic problem, but more importantly to secure the principle of nationalism and sovereignty from the ravages of primordial ethnicity in South Asia at large. The link constitutes the difference between an authoritarian bully, on the one hand, and, on the other, a hegemon whose leadership is necessary for the survival of the system of sovereign states in South Asia.*

Second, there is a crucial tension on the issue of Tamil ethnicity in the two quotes from Dixit that goes to the very heart of postcolonial nationalisms. In the first quote, the ethnonationalism of Sri Lankan Tamils is posited as a threat to the Indian nation and the whole enterprise of pluralist nation building in India or Sri Lanka. In the second quote, however, Dixit argues that no *elected* Indian government could afford *not* to demonstrate its support of the Tamil cause in Sri Lanka because otherwise it might alienate the Tamils of Tamil Nadu. In other words, the ethnic struggle in Sri Lanka becomes an unpassable opportunity for the ruling party in India to appeal to and acquire support within Tamil Nadu and recover a state that had been lost to the Congress Party for two decades, as well as to appear to the rest of India as the defender of kindred ethnic minorities in neighbor countries. Thus, although Dixit decried ethnicity as divisive, parochial and separatist, he was also compelled to note that pandering to the self-same ethnicity afforded an opportunity for the ruling party to show itself to be a protector of minority rights of various ethnic groups and to produce and reproduce the nation itself. Ethnicity thus constitutes both the dangerous oppositional force against which the nation is sought to be constructed and something that could be cynically manipulated or utilized by political parties in their efforts to gain followings and win elections. Once again, the locus of nation/ethnicity is constitutive of power because it creates the enunciative spaces that allow for the production of identity through the deployment of difference.

At a more general level, Dixit's views on this supposedly intimate connection between the two nationalisms are representative of a wide cross-section of both Indian and Sri Lankan politicians, policy makers, media, and academic authors who have written on the subject, even though their reasons for subscribing to such views differ. In an emblematic passage, P. R. Chari makes the following observation: "No doubt, these [separatist] sentiments were strengthened by the historical, cultural, linguistic, familial and similar linkages existing between Tamil Nadu and Sri Lankan Tamils. . . . It is, therefore, quite explicable that a vociferous section of the Tamil Nadu leadership began pressing the Union leadership to intervene vigorously in Sri Lankan affairs and secure the rights of the Sri Lankan Tamils, despite the Union government's initial reluctance to enlarge its extra-territoral responsibilities" (1994, 3).

Why historical, cultural, and other linkages should be automatically translated into Tamil Nadu's support for the political rights of the Sri Lankan Tamils is not elaborated upon, but assumed to be the case. Given the ingrained suspicion of ethnicity as the always already subversive of nationalism, P. R. Chari need do no more than assert the putative commonality of Tamil ethnicity across the Palk Straits and its consequent dangers. In particular, I would like to draw attention to the last phrase in the quote from Chari—namely, the suggestion (in which he echoes Dixit) that the union government was initially "reluctant" to expand its extraterritorial responsibilities but was forced to do so under pressure from the politics of Tamil Nadu. As the rest of this book documents (and as the first chapter detailing the emergence and content of the Indira doctrine after 1971 has already indicated), one can more convincingly argue the opposite: namely, it was the union government in Delhi that was keen to use the imputed connections between the two Tamil communities as an alibi to intervene in Sri Lanka in order to assert its regional hegemony. Other influential authors who echo the arguments made by Dixit and Chari that the two Tamil ethnicities were joined somehow and that Tamil Nadu led the center in its Sri Lankan policy are S. D. Muni (1993, 65), Dagmar Hellmann-Rajanayagam (1994, 131–32), and Mick Moore (1993, 600).

For a different set of reasons, one finds a similar pattern replicated among Sri Lankan scholars. Kingsley De Silva, often meticulous in presenting the weak linkages between Sri Lankan Tamil nationalism and Dravidianism in Tamil Nadu (see, for instance, 1981, 551, and 1986, 220–21), more generally echoes the view that the two nationalisms were intertwined and that, together, they represented a serious threat to Sri Lankan unity. Thus, describing the situation of the 1970s, he notes that "the increasingly turbulent politics of the Jaffna peninsula *began to be treated as an integral part of the internal politics of Tamilnadu*. The DMK [Dravida Munnetra Kazhagam], effectively checked from pursuing its separatist goal in India, took vicarious pleasure in giving encouragement and support to separatist tendencies among the Tamils of Sri Lanka" (1986, 272, emphasis added).[2] In a later part of the same book, De Silva is more unequivocal when he avers, "Once a separatist movement emerged among the Tamils of Sri Lanka, *it was fostered, nurtured and protected in Tamilnadu*" (1986, 324, emphasis added). A number of other Sri Lankan authors similarly echo De Silva's contention that Tamil nationalism in Sri Lanka was "fostered, nurtured and protected" by the Dravidian movement in Tamil Nadu (Dissanayaka 1993, Kodikara 1992b, and Sivarajah 1992a).

Linking the Sri Lankan Tamil movement to external forces such as the Dravidian movement was a critical step in both diminishing and exaggerating it as far as Sri Lankan society was concerned. It diminished Sri Lankan Tamil nationalism by: (a) portraying it as externally inspired and therefore traitorous; (b) indicating a primordial sentiment among the Tamils, thus minimizing Sinhalese responsibility for Tamil grievances; and (c) denying Sri Lankan Tamils cultural originality and autonomy by seeing them as derivative appendages of a larger cultural and intellecutal formation in Tamil Nadu. It simultaneously exaggerated Tamil nationalism in that the threat posed by the eleven million Sri Lankan Tamils could now be alloyed with the fifty-five million Tamils of Tamil Nadu, justifying a violent and intransigent response by the state.

Mainstream scholarship in India and Sri Lanka thus winds up first combining and then essentializing Tamil ethnicity in the two societies. The predictable last step in this process—namely, "discovering" historically enduring mindsets, static characteristics, ancient dispositions (for example, toward militarism and suicide) common to "the Tamil" in both societies—has been taken in recent essays by D. P. Sivaram (1992) and Michael Roberts (1996). In ancient and medieval Tamil kingdoms, literature, poetry, martial castes, and militarist culture, they seek the origins of Tamil discourses of self-determination, methods of armed struggle, the LTTE's cyanide culture, and other aspects of their movement. Imputing unchanging characteristics and continuity to "the Tamil" across centuries marked by dramatic transformations is a violently reductive and essentializing argument that Edward Said (1978) describes as orientalism. In the contemporary context, the argument suffers from two more failings: first, it misunderstands the uniquely modern transnational and global forces that inform the tactics and strategy of a guerrilla outfit like the LTTE. And second, the imputing of such unchanging essence to "the Tamil" denies any sense of politics as an open-ended, agentive process in which a negotiation with, not an effacement of, difference is possible. To understand the tactics, strategy, and ideology of a late-modern guerrilla group such as the LTTE, one may be better served by authors who locate terrorism in a quintessentially modernist and disenchanted secular frame (Der Derian 1992 or Nandy 1990b), than by authors who discern enduring Tamil martial traditions (Sivaram 1992) or some inherent penchant for self-immolation and suicide going back centuries (Roberts 1996).

The depiction of an essentialist Tamil identity in both societies emerges and gains currency because of its utility in a discursive framework that unites scholarship with the Indian and Sri Lankan states in the suspicion of ethnicity. In the next section, I suggest that this same history can be read very differently from a perspective that sees identity as dialectically related to the production of otherness. I argue that it is an open political and historical question whether ethnicity necessarily takes the trajectory of ethnonationalism. Such a view is neither complicitous with singular notions of national sovereignty nor convinced that Tamil "here" was ever and always the same as Tamil "there."

THE NARRATIVE OF TAMIL NATIONALISM:
FROM ACCOMMODATION TO SECESSION IN SRI LANKA

Said discusses the relationship between narrative and a veridical reality "out there" by reminding us that orientalism was neither a tissue of lies nor a distortion of some discernible truth. Rather, it has endured as a body of knowledge and has commanded an epistemic stature because it is, at a multiplicity of levels, effective and productive of both power and knowledge. As he notes, representations, to be effective, require a discursive consistency, a consistency that is "a form of cultural praxis, a system of opportunities for making statements.... (they) operate as representations usually do, for a purpose, according to a tendency, in a specific historical, intellectual and even economic setting.... [R]epresentations have purposes, they are effective much of the time, they accomplish one or many tasks" (1978, 273).

In the pages that follow, I summarize how Sri Lankan Tamils narrate their experiences in postcolonial Sri Lanka. I do this largely by abstracting from a number of historical and political tracts written in recent years.[3] In doing so, like Said, I am aware that the truth or otherwise of these representations is impossible to establish in some final sense. What is important is that significant numbers of Sri Lankan Tamils recognize their lives in this narrative. It describes for them how they have come to be where they are now and may be in the future. The narrative is intensely political as it socially constructs their past, present, and possible futures.

Sri Lankan Tamils see theirs as a reluctant transition from a politics of desired accommodation to violent secessionism. In their view, this transition has occurred on account of the majority's view of Sri Lanka as primarily the abode of Sinhala Buddhists, with other communities (especially Tamils) playing, at best, a supporting role. This majoritarian vision has been translated into reality in the decades since independence by the steady political, economic, and sociocultural marginalization of the Tamils. During the British colonial regime, Sri Lankan Tamils came to occupy a large share of civil service positions and acquired a considerable degree of economic clout (Roberts 1979, Tambiah 1955). Whatever the origins of such "disproportionate" success in the colonial period, the decades since independence have seen a sharp swing in the opposite direction in terms of both economic and political power (Committee for Rational Development 1984, Wilson 1988, Arasaratnam 1986). Moreover, this diminution has been punctuated by bouts of annihilatory violence, often called pogroms, directed against Tamils in 1956, 1958, 1977, 1981, and 1983.

At independence, Ceylon was a polity dominated by "an isolated cosmopolitan, English-educated, westernised Sinhalese-Tamil bourgeoisie [which] provided the underpinning for the island's stable set-up" (Wilson 1994a, 133). Just prior to independence, the British set up the Soulbury Commission on the Constitution to assess the question of ethnic ratios in the new Parliament. The leader of the All-Ceylon Tamil Congress (ACTC), G. G. Ponnambalam, argued for an equal division of power, with the country as a whole being divided into a hundred territorial units, fifty of which would be earmarked as "general" and fifty for the various minorities together (the "fifty-fifty proposal" as it came to be called). To argue for equal representation for minorities in a context where nearly three-quarters of the country was Sinhala-Buddhist seems audacious in retrospect. Yet such was the climate of the times that not only was this possibility entertained seriously, but at one point, with the support of the Sinhalese political elite, a compromise that awarded fifty-seven units to the Sinhalese (under the rubric of "general") and forty-three to all the minorities was actually offered. Clearly, ethnicity had not yet overpowered alternative forms of identity at this time. More importantly, the fifty-fifty episode reflects a political culture still centered in the anglicized and westernized elites. In retrospect, the Tamils' sticking to their guns on fifty-fifty and not grabbing the offer of fifty-seven to forty-three made by the Soulbury Commission was seen as a "tactical error"on their part (Arasaratnam 1979, 505; also see Russell 1982). This error was reflected in the first elections to the new Parliament when the Sinhalese captured 67 percent of the seats, a share that would increase and stay around 80 percent in later decades.

Once acquiring political power became a matter of numbers, party competition in mass elections on the basis of universal adult suffrage, with no special provisions for minority or communal representation, forces were set in motion that would make the genteel politics of Colombo's Cinnamon Garden elites forever obsolete. The temptation to rally three-quarters of the population under the rubric of Sinhala-Buddhist identity by the "invention of enmity" (Little 1994) against Tamils was impossible to resist. Sri Lankan politics entered a phase in which the mobilization of Sinhala ethnic identity around the triad of the race, the land, the faith became the norm. The two main political parties, the United National Party (UNP) and the Sri Lanka Freedom Party (SLFP), were thereafter locked in a battle for the allegiance of the majority, and the appeal to ethnic chauvinism became a staple of everyday politics. As Eric Meyer notes, "From 1948 to 1977, despite the fact that successive Sinhalese governments toyed with the idea of concessions, all promises came to nothing since the opposition party of the moment, either UNP or SLFP, constantly raised the communalist bidding, whilst the constant attitude of the Tamil leaders was to turn in on themselves" (1984, 145).

Almost upon independence, the UNP regime disenfranchised nine hundred thousand Estate Tamils through legislation passed in 1948 and 1949. In fact, the preceding two decades had witnessed the steady erosion of their voting rights, an erosion that Sri Lankan Tamils supported every bit as much as the Sinhalese and the British did. The disenfranchisement of the Estate Tamils was one of the reasons for a split in Ponnambalam's ACTC, which had acquiesced with UNP's actions in exchange for a ministerial portfolio for Ponnambalam. This exchange was opposed by a faction within the party, and their exit led to the emergence of the Ilangai Tamil Arasu Kadchi (or, as it came to be known, the Federal Party) under the leadership of S. J. V. Chelvanayagam (Wilson 1994a).[4]

On its formation, the Federal Party began to voice its disquiet on a number of matters, including the changing demographic balance between Tamils and Sinhalese in regions that the former regarded as their traditional homelands (the northern and eastern provinces) largely on account of state-sponsored settlement of Sinhalese there through irrigation schemes. The issue of the traditional homelands of Tamils perfectly showcases the tensions underlying postcolonial nationalism and the ways in which modernity is translated into the vernacular in that space. On the one hand, historians such as Kingsley De Silva regard the Tamil claim on traditional homelands as a "theory of dubious historical validity" and "a potent and divisive myth" (1986, 212; also see De Silva 1987). He points out that if the whole nation were properly regarded as the domain of all Sri Lankans, as any progressive modern ought to, it makes little sense to carve out special areas as traditional homelands of certain ethnic groups. Moreover, Sri Lankan Tamils have settled in large numbers in and around Colombo, while nearly a third of the Tamil-speaking Muslims have been an itinerant, mercantile community spread all across the country. In other words, migrations and dispersion of communities is the norm in any country. What sense does it then make to talk of traditional homelands?

Underlying De Silva's argument is an understanding of national space as uniform and populated by identical citizens. For Tamils, increasingly aware of their status as a precarious minority, the aforementioned demographic changes would be akin to a colonization of their areas of habitation. In this regard, they would find the following recent history ominous for their society: "The areas of large Sri Lanka Tamil majorities have been contracting over the years, leaving by 1981 only Jaffna and Mullaitivu...in the far North and Batticaloa in the East as districts of large Tamil numerical preponderance. Sri Lanka Tamils in 1911 formed a majority of the populations of all districts in the Northern and Eastern provinces. Since this is no longer the case, the territories of the 'Tamil homeland' may be thought of as shrinking" (Kearney and Miller 1987, 115). From the Tamil perspective, both their claim to an antiquity in Sri Lanka equal to that of the Sinhalese and their ultimate bargaining chip in the event of a complete breakdown of relations with the majority community rested on preserving their majority in areas they considered traditional homelands. In the context of this insecurity, De Silva's theoretical demolition of their claims, premised on a modernist definition of national space as abstractly equal, would be unconvincing to them, to put it mildly.

In making the case for a modernist conception of national space, De Silva significantly elides the fact that other crucial aspects of politics in postcolonial Sri Lanka hardly show the same unremitting commitment to modernity. For example, what sense does the idea of abstract and equal national space make in a country that has declared itself constitutionally committed to giving Buddhism "the foremost place" and assigned the state the duty to "protect and foster Buddhism," as the Constitution of 1972 did? Such a theological conception of national space hardly jibes with the secular-nationalist critique of traditional homelands. Given such departures, De Silva's critique of the Tamil claim to a traditional homeland is no different from the supposedly polemical and pseudo-historical claims of the likes of Satchi Ponnambalam (1983). That De Silva writes in the impeccable prose of a British-trained historian and has the venerable narrative of modernist nation building on his side does not change the fact that his version of national space is every bit as contestable and representational as Ponnambalam's.

The contending poetics of space between De Silva and Sri Lankan Tamil nationalists can be read along a register that is critical to understanding both modernity and postcoloniality. In this instance, as in so many others, the encounter between the local and the modern does not produce a replica of the latter in the former. Rather, the supposedly progressive and rational need for uniform national space (in other words, the modern) is used as the bludgeon with which to subdue the local and the particular by deeming them retrogressive. Modernity is not merely a weapon in the hands of state builders and their academic accomplices, but more: it insinuates itself through the world by the violent and steady transformation of alternative definitions and embodiments of space and time — a transformation, however, that can never quite efface the particularities of the premodern contexts it encounters. Modernity thus ought to be unmoored from its specific origin location in the west and regarded as an idea that is realized only in its vernacular manifestations all over the nonwest. Various authors (Spivak 1988a, King 1995, Said 1993) have consequently argued against the self-contained versions of (western) modernity that inform much of the scholarship of the metropole, for it is in the colony and the postcolony that modernity attains completion. The idea is summarized by Homi Bhabha when he notes that "each repetition of the sign of modernity is different, specific to its historical and cultural conditions of enunciation" (1991, 207). In the debate over traditional homelands in Sri Lanka, one sees the clear nexus between power and what passes for modern knowledge in postcolonial space.

This debate ought to sensitize us to the idea that land and territory are not inert, abstract, and natural. Each effort at creating a national space is resisted by various local recalcitrances hostile to the principles around which such unification is attempted. As Henri Lefebvre reminds us about the production of national space, "Each state claims to produce a space wherein something is accomplished — a space, even, where something is brought to perfection: namely, a unified and hence homogeneous society.... What then is the state?... [I]t is a framework . . . to ensure that the interests of certain minorities, of certain classes, of fractions of classes, are imposed on society — so effectively imposed, in fact, that they become indistinguishable from the general interest" (1991, 280–81). For the settlement of Sinhalas in Tamil majority areas to be viewed without suspicion, the Tamil would have to feel she is an equal and full member of the Sri Lankan family. Suffice it to say, this feeling has hardly been approximated in contemporary Sri Lanka.

As early as 1950, the Federal Party was articulating the demand for a separate Tamil majority region with a high degree of provincial autonomy in a federal rather than a unitary order. On the issue of what exactly the Federal Party desired at this stage, there is an interesting difference of opinion that, once again, pertains to the unique forms in which modernity enters and is domesticated in postcolonial space. De Silva (1986, 207–26) argues that the Federal Party was ambiguous about its position on secessionism even at this early stage, and in giving their speeches in Tamil, the leaders of the party were openly secessionist. In contrast, when they spoke in English in Parliament for example, they stayed clear of such secessionist talk. This difference left their "real" position on regional autonomy dangerously ambiguous, in De Silva's view.

We might aver that the Tamil minority was being held to a standard that the majority community would itself fail resoundingly. In the previous chapter, we observed that even urbane and articulate exponents of the English language, such as Jayewardene, routinely used the terms *Sri Lankan* and *Sinhala* interchangeably. The tendency to equate Sri Lankan with Sinhala was even more pronounced when such leaders spoke in Sinhalese (Uyangoda 1994). If their vision of Sri Lanka was exclusively Sinhala, were the Tamil leaders all that different? It is all the more ironic that De Silva's discussion of the political rhetoric of the Federal Party is unleavened by the recognition he displays regarding the nature of majoritarian nationalism in post-colonial Sri Lanka: "In Sinhala, the words for 'nation,' 'race,' and 'people' are practically synonymous, and a multi-ethnic or multi-communal nation or state is incomprehensible to the popular mind.... [T]he abandonment of the concept of a poly-ethnic polity was justi-fied by laying stress on the Western concept of a democratic sanc-tion deriving its validity from the clear numerical superiority of the Sinhala-speaking group.... [T]he focus continued to be all-island one, and Sinhala nationalism was consciously or unconsciously treated as being identical with a Sri Lankan nationalism" (1988, 73).

The entry of modern nationalism into the postcolonial realm has to face a discomfiting question: Is it possible that in countries such as Sri Lanka and India a liberal-democratic idea of the nation, with equal and individual rights for all citizens, had a very limited ambit and that for most people the nation evoked more particularistic af-filiations? In other words, were secessionist tendencies imputed to Sri Lankan Tamils even though the meaning of the nation itself was interpreted in the vernacular through identities that were sectarian and particularisitic, in a western sense of such terms? In an insight-ful essay on the paradox between democracy and participation in a postcolonial order, Sudipta Kaviraj makes an important point: "The idea of vernacularisation indicates the near impossible paradoxical-ity of what we must attempt: when the western idea really enters the vernacular it must change its meaning; but we have to try to capture that fugitive meaning in English, precisely the language from which it is trying to escape" (Kaviraj, n.d., 1). He goes on to note that whatever the origins and intent in the west of ideas such as democ-racy, individual rights, and equality of all citizens, their postcolonial vernacularization often means their translation into majoritarian domination and the jostling of enumerated, group identities for pro-portionate shares in assets.

Rather than read the rhetoric of the Federal Party through a lens that sees ethnicity as always already secessionist, I would submit that a more nuanced understanding of politics in the postcolony would lead us to appreciate the ways in which nation and ethnicity are im-bricated and the paradoxes that emerge in the course of a vernacularization of the political idiom in such societies. In other words, as modernity spreads through the postcolonial world, it does not so much clone its western originals as translate them into a domestic idiom whose meanings and import depart considerably from the originals and are embedded in distinctively different nexuses of power and knowledge. Yet the desire to see the postcolonial experience replicate the putative experience of the west in nation building, when it suits the interests of the majority community, underlies De Silva's characterization of the Tamil as provincial and secessionist. In this characterization, the postcolonial anxiety to emulate western originals operates to hierarchize the mainstream over the marginal.

The rest of the narrative of Tamil nationalism in Sri Lanka can be summarized in short order: the Tamils see the 1950s and 1960s as a period of repeated betrayals by the Sinhalese political leadership. In the movement toward secession, June 1956 came to be regarded as a critical turning point. In that month, Parliament under the new prime minister, Solomon Bandaranaike of the SLFP, passed the Official Language Act declaring Sinhala to be the sole language of administration. Tamil nonviolent protest and satyagraha were met with violence from the Sinhalese, many of whom felt the act did not go far enough in ensuring Sinhala domination over Tamil in official discourse. As a response to Sinhala Only, the Federal Party upped its demands: from self-governing districts based on a Swiss cantonal model to a model that would eventually weld the Tamil-speaking areas of the north and east into larger, provincial or regional units. However, even such limited demands for regional autonomy consistently ran against a newly self-aware majority that regarded such demands as the entering wedge of the breakup of Sri Lanka and as occasions for a violent response.

In an effort to take some of the sting out of the Sinhala Only Act, on July 26, 1957, the prime minister, who was evidently more moderate than the rank-and-file supporters of the SLFP (Manor 1989), signed an agreement with the leader of the Federal Party, Chelvanayagam. This agreement, which came to be known as the Bandaranaike-Chelvanayagam Pact (or the B-C Pact), marked the next critical milestone in the narrative self-understanding of the Tamils of Sri Lanka. The B-C Pact tried to accomplish four things: first, it gave Tamil official status for administration in the northern and eastern provinces; second, it implicitly recognized the principle that some portions of Sri Lanka constituted a traditional habitat or homeland of the Tamils by its proposal to set limits on the settling of Sinhalese peasants in newly irrigated areas of the North and East so that the existing Tamil majorities stayed intact; third, it promised to reexamine the question of the disenfranchisement of the Estate Tamils that had occurred in 1948–49; and finally, in discussions of autonomy, it implicitly escalated the territorial unit from that of districts to that of regions or provinces. By mid-1958, the pact lay in shambles, however. From the Tamil perspective, Bandaranaike reneged on his promises as he was unable to resist the wave of Sinhalese opposition to the pact.[5] Save for the milquetoast passage of an amendement to the Sinhala Only Act of 1956 that resurrected a clause on "reasonable use of the Tamil language," it seemed a complete betrayal to the Tamils. Moreover, Federal Party members who launched a nonviolent movement for the implementation of the pact were attacked, and in May of 1958 the country exploded in communal riots that made the violence of 1956 look insignificant (Vittachi 1958). The prime minister had been completely outflanked by Jayewardene and UNP supporters, who embarked on a march to Kandy to register their opposition to the pact, as well as by extremists within the SLFP and the Buddhist clergy. (In the next year, a monk would assassinate Bandaranaike for his betrayal of the Sinhalese.) Bandaranaike had supposedly given away one-third of the land and two-thirds of the coastline to one-tenth the population — a phrase that would become common currency in later years.

Fresh elections in 1960 saw the SLFP acquire a sizable majority in Parliament, allowing them to ignore promises made to the Federal Party before the elections. In March 1965, just prior to the next round of general elections, Chelvanayagam entered into another pact, this time with Dudley Senanayake, the UNP leader. As it turned out, for the UNP to form the government and for Senanayake to become prime minister, they needed the support of the Federal Party. Although this need was leveraged by the Federal Party into a promise that the Senanayake-Chelvanayagam Pact would meet a different fate from the B-C pact, events transpired otherwise. Although the Tamil-proposed district councils saw their autonomy sharply curtailed by direct central government oversight, the pact implicitly recognized the northern and eastern provinces as Tamil-speaking areas. It moreover agreed in principle that Tamil-speaking people should be given preference in allotments made for new lands that came under irrigation (in other words, to reverse or at least stabilize the incidence of Sinhalese colonization of Tamil territory). Further, Tamil was to be made a language of administration on a par with Sinhala, and both languages were to be used in administration as well as in court proceedings.

The government ran into serious and violent opposition led by the SLFP during parliamentary sessions in early 1966 as it debated the Senanayake-Chelvanayagam Pact. The wheel now turned full circle with the SLFP in opposition, turning the heat on the UNP regime for violating the sanctity of Sinhala Only and for other envisaged amendments to implement the pact. By October 1966, the UNP had lost three by-elections to the SLFP, and by the middle of 1968, faced with a Sinhalese backlash to the proposed devolution in the District Councils Bill, Senanayake admitted defeat and unilaterally abrogated his pact with Chelvanayagam. From the Tamil perspective, it was obvious that, individuals aside, the very structure of postcolonial politics in a unitary state militated against any solution to their problems. The Federal Party quit its participation in government.[6]

The tremendous victory of the SLFP in the parliamentary elections of 1970 (with its allies, it won 125 seats in a house of 151) and the prime ministership of Mrs. Sirima Bandaranaike (1970–77) pushed the Sinhala-Tamil divide to unbridgeable proportions. The SLFP quickly enacted into law what had become a reality for most Tamils: the Sinhalese regarded the island as exclusively theirs. Ceylon was renamed Sri Lanka, and by a fiat the new Parliament was deemed a Constituent Assembly for the task of writing for Sri Lanka a constitution of its own to replace the colonial period's Soulbury Constitution in operation until then. Besides reinscribing Sinhala as the sole official language of the country, the Constitution of 1972 abolished Section 29 of the previous document, which served as a protector of minority rights. Section 6 of Chapter II of the new Constitution removed any ambiguity regarding the second-class citizenship of those who were not Buddhist: "The Republic of Sri Lanka shall give to Buddhism the foremost place and accordingly it shall be the duty of the State to protect and foster Buddhism while assuring to all religions the rights granted by Section 18 (1)(d)" (quoted in Wilson 1988, 53). Further, the regime enacted a policy of 'standardisation' of marks obtained by students in high school examinations, which resulted in Tamil students having to excel their Sinhalese counterparts by wide margins to gain access to much sought after degrees in medicine, engineering, and sciences. The disastrous results of standardization begun in 1970 were compounded by another policy, enacted in 1973, by which admissions to universities were to be based on the population of the area or province. Thus, the "overeducated" northern province (with an overwhelmingly Tamil population) saw its share of admissions into science programs drop from 27.5 percent to 7 percent between 1969 and 1974 (Wilson 1988, 47; also see Chandra De Silva 1977 and 1984). By the mid-1970s, with the vast majority of high school graduates in the northern province seeing their access to university education choked off and unemployment at 43 percent for Tamil youth, the socioeconomic underpinnings of a militant guerrilla movement had been laid (Arasaratnam 1986, 70–73).

In a protest against the decisions to arbitrarily declare Parliament a Constituent Assembly, Sinhala the sole official language, and Buddhism the state religion, and against the revocation of sections that had provided minorities with some protection, Chelvanayagam resigned his parliamentary seat on October 2, 1972, to coincide with the birthday of Mahatma Gandhi. He then proclaimed his reelection to Parliament to be a referendum on whether Sri Lankan Tamils wished to live under the Constitution of 1972 or to secede. Put simply, if he won reelection, it would be interpreted as a definitive statement that Sri Lankan Tamils wished to secede and form a separate nation. Despite attempts to delay the election on various pretenses, when it was eventually held on February 6, 1975, Chelvanayagam won with the largest majority his constituency, Kankesuntarai, had ever seen.

In May 1972, the various Tamil parties now coalesced under the Tamil United Front (TUF), which was renamed the Tamil United Liberation Front (TULF) in 1975 to indicate its explicitly secessionist aim. This aim was buttressed in the Vaddukoddai resolution of May 14, 1976, when the TULF called on the Tamils of Sri Lanka to "throw themselves fully in the sacred fight for freedom and to flinch not till the goal of a sovereign socialist state of Tamil Eelam is reached" (Wilson 1994a, 128). The formation of the TULF marked the first time in nearly three decades that the various factions of the Sri Lankan Tamils stood united, as it combined the ACTC and the Federal Party. It also marked a period in which the Sri Lankan Tamils arrived at an understanding with the Estate Tamils, though on most issues their interests were still divergent.

In the very next year (1977), the three leading Tamil figures of this moderate phase—Ponnambalam, Murugeysen Tiruchelvam, and Chelvanayagam—passed away. Over the next few years, faced with escalating Sinhala violence and a history of betrayals of and paltry rewards for moderate Tamil leaders, Tamils would turn to a new brand of politicians: armed, militant rebel youth. The youth had witnessed firsthand what they considered the bankruptcy of moderate Tamil politics in preceding decades. With the exception of Chelvanayagam, their leaders seemed ready to sell the Tamil people down the river in exchange for petty ministerial perks in Sinhala-dominated regimes. On the other hand, Sinhalese politicians, even the best of them, were incapable of making and politically delivering any concession to Tamil cultural, political, and economic autonomy. Faced with this narration of recent history, Tamil militant groups regarded moderation and compromise with the political establishment as options that had been tried repeatedly and had conclusively failed. By the early 1980s, the LTTE and other militant groups—even Chelvanayagam himself at the end of his life—had arrived at the position that to settle for anything less than a sovereign Tamil Eelam would be sheer folly.

Postcolonial Sri Lanka perfectly showcases the ineffable debt that identity owes to difference. While the Sinhalese used Tamils as a whetstone for producing a sense of self-identity, the Tamils became conscious of themselves as an ethnic minority as a consequence of the process of majoritarian nation building. That is, the building of the nation along majoritarian lines served as the impetus for the emergence of ethnonationalism. Here, as elsewhere, making the nation is coeval with its violent unmaking. In retrospect, it is sobering to remember that this journey from Ceylon's independence to the Vaddukoddai resolution calling for secession took less than three decades (1948–76). To deflect the journey from that desired future will require a fundamental reimagination of national space in Sri Lanka. At a minimum, as I argue, this reimagination has to be a pluralist and decentralized vision of the nation.

THE DRAVIDIAN MOVEMENT: FROM SECESSION TO POPULISM IN TAMIL NADU

If Sri Lankan Tamil nationalism went from moderation to secession, the Dravidian movement followed a trajectory that is precisely opposite. A close look at the Dravidian movement indicates that (a) their secessionist tendencies, both historically and in recent years, were grossly exaggerated, and (b) their connections with Sri Lankan Tamils were nowhere near as intimate as Indian and Sri Lankan governments or mainstream scholarship would have it. A number of works have examined the rise of a form of Tamil nationalism from the late–nineteenth century onward (Arooran 1980, Baker 1976, Baker and Washbrook 1975, Barnett 1976, Hardgrave Jr. 1965, Irschick 1969 and 1986, Washbrook 1976 and 1989). Most histories of the Dravidian movement follow a similar chronology: after an initial focus on the renaissance of Tamil literature at the turn of the nineteenth century, they examine the emergence of the Justice Party and the non-Brahmin movement from 1917; the Self-Respect Movement of "Periyar" E. V. Ramaswami Naicker and the anti-Hindi agitations of the late 1930s and early 1940s; the emergence of the Dravida Kazhagam (DK) in the mid-1940s and the Dravida Munnetra Kazhagam (DMK) under C. N. Annadurai in the late 1940s; the victory of the DMK in elections to the state legislature in 1967, which ended two decades of Congress Party rule in Tamil Nadu; and the period from 1967 to 1997, which has seen the dominance of the DMK and its splinter party, the (All-India Anna Dravida Munnetra Kazhagam (AIADMK), formed in 1972, in the politics of Tamil Nadu.

In the genealogy of Dravidianism, the Justice Party (its official name, rarely used, was South Indian Liberal Federation) is notable for its coinage and use of the category *non-Brahmin.* The Justice Party was a party of the elite, in fact of the petty royalty that had been the mainstay of native support for the colonial regime. Formed in 1916, they were a product of the limited electoral franchise of the time, the growing enumeration of group identities, and the selective favors bestowed on such groups by the colonial regime. As the census and other classifying and data-gathering efforts of the Madras administration revealed, Brahmins were vastly overrepresented in the educated sections of the populace and the civil service bureaucracy, as well as among professional elites (doctors, lawyers, media professionals, teachers, and salaried classes generally). The Justice Party sought a redressal of Brahmin overrepresentation in favor of non-Brahmin castes by petitioning the colonial state (see Baker 1976, 322, and Washbrook 1976, 286, for details).

However, the ostensibly progressive and radical aspect of Justice's political program—that is, anti-Brahmin or non-Brahmin ideology—did not expand into an anticasteist critique of Tamil society or of the wider Sanskritic culture of the Brahmins. Instead, it preferred to restrict itself to the parameters of an intra-elite competition for spoils of colonial office. (The leader of the later DMK, C. N. Annadurai, would often sarcastically refer to the Justicites as a "party of laced *veshties* and silk *jibbas*" [Sivathamby 1993, 13–47.])[7] In that competition, the category non-Brahmin served the Justice Party in good stead, given the tremendous overrepresentation of Brahmins in middle-class professions in turn-of-century Madras. That non-Brahmin upper castes represented by Justice were similarly (if not equally) overrepresented compared to the vast majority of the populace of the Madras presidency was a matter left delicately alone (Radhakrishnan 1993).

When Justice made its first demand for secession in June 1940, it was on its last legs. The structure of political and economic opportunity that underwrote its rise in the earlier period had long passed. The electoral franchise had greatly expanded beyond the limited realm of the 1910s because of a series of concessions made by the British, culminating with the Government of India Act of 1935, allowing for self-government at the provincial level. Congress, by now a mass-based political party, had made tremendous inroads in the Madras presidency in 1920s and 1930s and had come to power with huge majorities in the elections to the provincial government of the Madras presidency in 1937, elections in which the Justice Party was routed.

More importantly, the rise of "Periyar" E. V. Ramaswami Naicker's Self-Respect Movement in the 1930s had outflanked the non-Brahmin platform of Justicites. Not only had Periyar's movement expanded anti-Brahminism into a much wider anticasteist and rationalist ideology, it also brought into mass politics the castes and classes of people with whom Justicites did not associate. It was in this context of being literally rendered irrelevant that the Justice Party, which had a history of collaboration with the colonial regime, made a last ditch effort to throw a spanner in the wheels of Congress and curry favor with the colonial regime by its demand for a separate and loyalist state of Dravidanad.

At this time, Periyar united the Self-Respect Movement with Justice and joined in the demand for Dravidanad. His own motivations for demanding Dravidanad were vastly different from that of Justice and thus merit close attention. Periyar had been elected president of the Justice Party in 1939, when he was in jail because of his actions during the anti-Hindi language agitations of the preceding year. He joined in the demand for a separate state not out of any programmatic attraction to the Justice Party's policies and platform (such as they were) but rather as the culmination of a far-reaching social and ideological critique of mainstream Indian nationalism represented by the Congress. He had cut his political spurs in Congress in the mid-1910s but had left it because of principled objections to its consistent refusal to give prominence to issues of social reform, especially regarding caste, in its movement to unite the nation (see Visswanathan 1983 for details on a series of episodes that show how Congress's idea of nationalism dismissed social reform as detracting from the "primary contradiction"—namely, colonial rule). Especially in the Madras presidency, Congress was dominated by Brahmins, most of whom, for all their democratic and equalitarian rhetoric, remained incurably bigoted and casteist in their personal, professional, and political lives.[8] Their vision of independence for all Indians rang hollow, given their deeply ingrained notions on caste and their belief in the innate superiority of Brahmanic and Sanskritic culture over the rest of India.

Based on a wide-ranging critique of Congress's hegemonic mainstream nationalism, one that relied heavily on a symbology of politics both North Indian and Sanskritic in its inspiration, Periyar left the Congress Party and started the Self-Respect Movement that dominated the Madras presidency in the 1930s. At its peak, the movement launched a determined assault against caste, Sanskritic culture, imposition of Hindi language, and North Indian domination of Indian society. Periyar's was an eclectic attack, occasionally inspired by rationalism, at other times by a version of socialism or communism, and at still others by an iconoclastic atheism. The high point of the Self-Respect Movement was reached during Congress rule over the Madras presidency in 1937–39. At that time, Congress declared Hindi the national language, and Periyar's Self-Respecters led the fight against its imposition in Madras. Periyar argued that peninsular India, especially Tamil society, had once been an egalitarian and progressive Dravidian civilization in which caste was unknown. It was the North Indian, in the form of the Brahmin, who brought into the South the pernicious institutions of caste and many another objectionable practices characteristic of the North's Sanskritic culture. Consequently, his anti-Hindi language agitation was part of a more thoroughgoing critique of northern Indian hegemony, Sanskritic culture, and their local representatives, the Brahmins.[9] His argument for a separate Dravidanad had an underlying cosmology and a degree of societal support that were quite different from the narrowly instrumental calculations of the Justice Party.

The first Dravidanad Separation Conference was held in June 1940 in Kanchipuram, about a hundred miles out of Madras. A map of the desired country revealed, to put it mildly, a rather expansive cartographic imagination. It included the entirety of peninsular India, all of the eastern coastline, and, incredibly, parts of Bengal (Arooran 1980, 245). The striking aspect of this representation of desired space is that at no time did Periyar or the Justice Party ever consider including Jaffna or any portion of Tamil majority provinces in Sri Lanka, which were as little as twenty miles away, even as they included those who showed no affinity for the political cause of the Tamils: namely, other so-called Dravidian peoples of Karnataka, Kerala, and Andhra, as well as those even farther afield, such as in Bengal. In the first chapter, I argued that despite the invocations of a divine cartography, the geographical imaginaire of the nationalist movement in India coincided with the administrative boundaries of the erstwhile Raj. Just as the nationalist elite never seriously considered including Nepal or Ceylon within its ambit (because they weren't part of the British Indian adminstration governed from the viceroy's office in New Delhi), it would appear that the movement for a Dravidanad was unable to shake off this colonial legacy. Despite the proximity of Jaffna, it was not considered part of the envisaged Tamil state, even though provinces such as Bengal were.

In 1944, at its annual conference, the Justice Party dissolved into the newly formed Dravida Kazhagam.[10] The DK espoused Periyar's ideology and was variously committed to anticasteism, rationalism, anti-Brahminism, atheism, anti–North Indian hegemony, non-Sanskritic culture, socialism, and opposition to the Hindi language. All of these commitments were combined into an overarching ideology of Dravidianism that became the main rhetorical trope in Tamil politics for decades to come. At the point of its formation, the DK was both secessionist (from the rapidly approaching nation called India) and loyalist (to an equally rapidly retreating British Raj).

The next months would see the disappearance of the idea of secession and a similarly rapid distancing of the Dravidian movement from its loyalist lineage in the Justice Party and in Periyar himself. At the outset, many of the younger political leaders were concerned that the loyalist history of Justice would delegitimate the DK. In fact, one of the reasons for renaming the new organization was to distance itself from this history. By mid-1947, a faction within DK, led by C. N. Annadurai, was already arguing for a revision of the party line on Indian independence. A public split soon occurred with Periyar declaring August 15, 1947, independence day, to be a day of mourning, but Annadurai and others in DK celebrated it as a day of freedom and rejoicing. In October 1947, significantly, Annadurai and his followers boycotted the Dravida Kazhagam conference on the separation of Dravidanadu. Matters between Periyar and Annadurai came to a head, and on September 17, 1949, DK split into two parties, and the newly formed Dravida Munnetra Kazhagam (DMK), led by Annadurai, left the fold with more than 75 percent of the total membership of DK.

Ostensibly, the reasons for the split up of DK was the decision Periyar (who was by now in his early seventies) made to marry a woman of twenty-nine, but an examination of the politics of this period reveals other, more important factors. First was the desire of many in DK, led by Annadurai, to convert the social movement into a political party and fight for office in the postcolonial order. The mass base of the Self-Respect Movement, the anti-Hindi agitations of the late 1930s, and the possibility of translating the ideology of Dravidianism into a politics of Tamil identity were alluring. The second reason involved a desire on part of DMK to disown its (weak) secessionist and (somewhat stronger) loyalist heritage and plunge into the political process as a regional party, one untainted by ideas of secession (Barnett 1976, 56–86). But it is equally important to remember that the emerging political dispensation of India, namely a federal state (albeit an overcentralized one), allowed DMK to envisage an autonomous future for itself within the national fold, which would not have been possible in a unitary state or one in which the center ran roughshod over state's rights.

Washbrook argues that DMK, especially after it gained power in Tamil Nadu in 1967, went about the task of revising its loyalist history with a vengeance. He then proceeds to suggest that this revisionism was proof of the fact that the Dravidian movement was bereft of ideology from its very beginnings and little more than an opportunistic product of the factional politics of the early twentieth century:

> There is, however, no clearer example of the extreme flexibility of history, culture and identity in Tamil consciousness than the amazing *volte face* performed by the Tamil nationalist movement after 1967. Having gained state power in Tamil Nadu and developed new relationships of clientage with the Congress government in New Delhi, the Dravidian ideology promptly began to re-write the history books.... Dravidian ideologues "discovered" that Tamil Nadu, rather than being a backwater of the anti-colonial freedom struggle which had created the Indian nation, had been its leading sector.... Tamil Nadu could parade a contingent of heroes and martyrs to the national cause who... being more ancient than the heroes of "the North," were regarded as being venerable. In the matter of a few years, the changed context of relationship with New Delhi had managed to produce a fundamental re-interpretation of the meaning of modern Tamil history and of the values which that history expressed. A sub-nationalist movement originally created for separatist ends began to see itself as having "liberated" the very nation from which it had wanted to separate. (1989, 229–30)

To Washbrook, such revisionism indicates the vacuous character of the Dravidian movement and the parties that emerged from it. However, in his trenchant critique of the "flexibility" of Dravidian ideology, Washbrook misses out on much that is important about such a rewriting of history. First, folding the separatist history of the Dravidians into the grand narrative of Indian nationalism is not so much an instance of hypocrisy as it is a reflection of the hegemony of nationalist ideology. Tamil society is hardly unique in discerning post facto that it had been nationalist all along. The "Indian national movement" is often a post facto narration of various nineteenth-century peasant struggles, revolts by soldiers of the British Indian army, civil servant petitions, and the like—all of which were later seamlessly woven into the story of a gradually emergent Indian national identity. The history of nationalism everywhere is simply rife with retrospective illusions that render the ornery tendencies of local recalcitrances into a progressive narrative of how the nation gradually awoke to a consciousness of its nationality. Rather than see this rendering as an instance of the hypocrisy of such local recalcitrances, we ought to be sensitized to the hegemonic power of the nation and, as Prasenjit Duara (1995) has recently argued, of the need to rescue history from the overarching writ of the nation.[11]

Second, the desire of DMK to write Dravidianism into the larger national family came from the realization that independent India offered a federal space within which Tamil linguistic, cultural, and regional autonomy could be fostered. This space was never quite federal enough to fully satisfy DMK, and even this limited degree of federalism was eroded in later decades under Mrs. Gandhi, yet it was not so trivial that secession seemed a legitimate or necessary political choice. The contrasting experience of Sri Lankan Tamils at this same time ought to serve as a poignant reminder that the alternative to the so-called revisionism that Washbrook excoriates in the DMK is often violent secession.

Third, it is worth suggesting that as a political party, DMK was doing to the mass campaigns that drove the Self-Respect, anti-Hindi, and anti-Brahmin agitations of the 1930s what the subaltern school of historians have suggested Indian nationalism did with the various peasant jacqueries, tribal millenarian movements, and antilandlord and antirent campaigns in the Indian countryside: namely, integrating movements that arose from different provocations and along tangential trajectories under the principle of nationalist hegemony.[12] Institutionalized politics may always be a matter of *both capitalizing on and reining in* such subaltern energies, and in that respect, the Dravidian movement's reconciliation with the larger narrative of Indian nationalism was a variation on a larger theme perfected by nationalisms elsewhere. Once again, the more interesting question may be one that analyzes the surplus of such subaltern energy

(Pandian 1994) that drove the politics of Dravidian nationalism, rather than one that offers a normative dismissal of the movement as revisionist history.

Finally, just as Indian nationalism decried ethnicity as a parochial and inferior variation on a larger theme, so ethnicity often used pan-Indian nationalism as the oppositional principle by which to define itself. In this respect, Dravidian nationalism never wrote itself completely into the narrative of the Indian nation as Washbrook implies, but constantly reiterated its difference and particularity (Ramaswamy 1994) in a number of ways, but perhaps most significantly in the claim of the Dravidian movement to represent the interests of Tamils everywhere in the world. In reality, the target audience of this often grotesquely exaggerated worldview of the Dravidian movement was the domestic constituency within Tamil Nadu to whom DMK had to distinguish itself from Congress in order to secure its electoral and political support. This last aspect of the Dravidian movement — namely, its self-anointed role as the leader of a world *thamilakam* — would predictably increase as its own secessionist character decreased in the decades after the 1940s. Moreover, its overblown rhetoric in this regard would be useful for those interested in tainting the DMK with the secessionist charge long after its bite had ceased to be anywhere near as effective as its bark.

Such nuances escape the rather crude lenses through which Washbrook analyses the Dravidian movement. At one level, the progressive ideology and content of the anti-Brahmin movement are discounted as being no more than a product of factional rivalries among the elite classes of early twentieth-century Madras (see Pandian 1995 for a critique), and, at another, the later revisionism of DMK is moralistically critiqued for its eternally demagogic and spurious character. I would prefer to see the reconciliation of Dravidian ideology as an instance of how a potentially secessionist movement based on ethnicity enters the fold of nationalism when it finds a pluralist space that respects its autonomy and offers it the opportunity to partake of political power and office.

If, for Washbrook, DMK's move away from secession is an instance of expedient revisionism, for many others in India it is an instance of noble patriotism triumphing over primordial regional chauvinism. According to this story, the Dravidian was tamed from his secessionist proclivities by the Chinese invasion of 1962. Tamil Nadu was supposedly an incorrigibly secessionist space until that event. Following it, in a surge of patriotism, DMK is supposed to have discovered the error of its ways and disavowed secession thereafter. (Although there are many exemplars of this narrative, the clearest and most popular version can be found in Akbar 1986.) An additional factor that supposedly spurred DMK to give up on Dravidanad was the passage of the sixteenth Amendment to the Indian Constitution (in October 1963), which proscribed speech questioning the sovereignty and integrity of India, and required all candidates for political office to take an oath reaffirming the sovereignty of the nation.

As we have already seen, DMK had given up on secession long before the Chinese invasion or the sixteenth Amendment to the Constitution; indeed, the very split of DMK from DK in 1949 arose from the desire to distance itself from the secessionist genealogy. Additionally, in a series of meetings between 1958 and 1960, the de jure status of the party on secession was discussed threadbare and by November 1960, there emerged a "consensus" that "the Dravida Nadu demand should be publicly abandoned" (Barnett 1976, 109–10). It is important to realize why many in India prefer to explain DMK's veering away from secession in terms of the war of 1962 rather than with the more mundane story of successful federalism. Explaining it in terms of the former narrative sees the nation-building process as one sanctified and tempered by war and violence. The bond that ties Tamil Nadu to India becomes one of blood and sacrifice rather than a matter of successful, if mundane, political engineering. Unfortunately for those committed to blood-and-soil explanations of nationalism, both chronology and historical evidence indicate the DMK had veered away from secession even before 1962 and for less inspiring reasons.

My argument that Dravidian nationalism lost its secessionist character even before the early 1960s on account of federal accommodation and the opportunities contained therein is buttressed by the events that followed soon after. Forgetting the lessons they ought to have learned from the earlier abortive attempt to impose Hindi on Tamil Nadu (in the late 1930s), the central government decided to give it another shot in the mid-1960s. Tamil Nadu was immediately wracked by violent anti-Hindi protests and a resurgence of both anti–North Indian sentiment and renewed talk of secession. Rather than regard this resurgence as a sign of the ineradicable secessionism of the Tamil, I think we ought to frame it within a discussion of majoritarian nationalism and the rights of peripheral, minority cultures. Given the powerful linkages made in Tamil society between the imposition of the Hindi language and the issue of North Indian hegemony, Sanskritic culture versus local practice, caste and Brahmin domination, and Aryan versus Dravidian civilization, the issue quickly went beyond language and spread to the emotive issue of majoritarianism versus the rights of peripheral minorities. Language became the metaphor for the relationship that ought to govern center and state, and the violent anti-Hindi agitations in Tamil Nadu at this time (mid-1960s) are indicative of the fact that ethnonationalism is not an essentialist force so much as it is a response to forced unification on some principle of majoritarianism.

The experiences of Tamil Nadu in the mid-1960s indicate further that subaltern feelings against majoritarian nationalism were effectively neutered by institutionalized politics and DMK. Most works on Dravidianism suggest that the anti-Hindi agitations weren't so much led or abetted by DMK as they were instances of its leadership's (only partially successful) efforts to check the violence and radicalism of the movement. For instance, Barnett notes, "By 1965, the DMK had become 'responsible' and predictable, and their activities could be calculated and anticipated. Had the DMK remained in control, the agitation would no doubt have remained nonviolent, limited and largely symbolic" (1976, 133). As in the late 1930s, Congress gave up on the idea of making Hindi the national language and deferred it, once again, to an uncertain date in the future.

The growing moderation of DMK was completed once it came to power in the state assembly elections of 1967. Since then, DMK (and AIADMK after 1972) has been loyal to central governments almost to a fault, which is also indicated by the changing pattern of electoral alignments in the state. After coming to power in 1967, DMK supported the Congress regime of Mrs. Gandhi in Parliament, and her minority government survived two years (1969–71) because of the support extended by the twenty-five DMK members. In the various electoral understandings between DMK, AIADMK, and Congress (I) in the elections of 1977, 1980, 1984, 1989, and 1991, some patterns emerge clearly.

First, neither regional party has shown any reluctance to enter into such understandings with the ruling party in New Delhi. Even though Mrs. Gandhi's regimes proved to be excessively centralized and very loathe to conceding any autonomy to states, DMK and AIADMK have competed with each other to curry its favor. Second, whereas DMK has at least retained faint echoes of its secessionist tradition by its consistent and well-articulated demands for greater state autonomy and federalism, AIADMK, as early as October 1973, explicitly disavowed any demand for state autonomy in its party manifesto and preferred to state blandly that it wanted neither dependence nor independence, but interdependence. Third, in terms of seat adjustments, a division of labor has emerged since 1980. Congress (I) has been given the lion's share of parliamentary seats (two-thirds usually), while the regional party gets the dominant share of Assembly seats (again, usually two-thirds). More than anything else, this pattern of electoral adjustments reveal that DMK and AIADMK have become comfortably ensconced as regional parties within a larger nation, decidedly junior partners to the center, quite content to consolidate their hold on the levers of power at the level of state government.

This situation is a far cry from the days of the Self-Respect Movement and the general attacks on caste and religion socially and North Indian dominance politically. Jacob Pandian avers that the Dravidian movement managed to attack and demolish caste privilege based on the Sanskritic authority of the Brahmin, even while it simultaneously strengthened the institution of caste itself in Tamil society and was co-opted by a society still obsessed by notions of ritual pollution and purity (1987, 134–35). This argument is supported by Marguerite Barnett's contention that, on the one hand, the Dravidian movement has done little to ameliorate the worsening conditions of those at the lowest end of the caste ladder, while on the other, "the fissure between Brahmin and non-Brahmin is being healed at the top under the aegis of Tamil nationalism" (1976, 300).

From the early 1970s on, as any real threat of secession receded, the DMK and AIADMK's rhetorical espousing of the cause of Tamil peoples (in Tamil Nadu, elsewhere in the country, and in the world) increased for two important reasons: first, both parties desired to distinguish themselves from their main political rival at the state level—namely, the Congress Party; and second, once the AIADMK emerged as a breakaway party of considerable following, the two

Dravidian parties competed with each other to lay claims to Tamil heritage and distinctiveness with increasingly overblown rhetoric. Ironically, the two Dravidian parties' self-anointed role as spokesmen for a worldwide *thamilakam,* their sponsorship of gaudy pseudo-historical conferences that rewrote world history from a Tamil-centric perspective, their espousal of the causes of Tamil peoples everywhere, including Sri Lanka, are all better understood as reflecting this diminution of their actual secessionist threat, rather than as continuing their proclivity toward secession, as mainstream scholarship would aver.

In summary, the argument of this section has been to suggest that the trajectory and development of the Dravidian movment in Tamil Nadu was opposite that of the Sri Lankan Tamils. In large part, the movement away from secession toward accommodation was enabled by the federal political dispensation of India, centralized and increasingly authoritarian though it was. At the very least, the history of Dravidianism ought to indicate that the Sri Lankan Tamils may well have similarly settled well short of secession had the Sri Lankan state been less unitary and majoritarian in its character.

DIVERGENT NATIONALISMS

At the beginning of this chapter, I indicated a powerful set of reasons that impelled both scholars and state elites in India and Sri Lanka to suggest that the two Tamil movements were inextricably linked to each other. This putative linkage was used to justify the Sinhalese state's annihilatory response to the issue of Tamil nationalism in Sri Lanka; and in the case of India, it was used as the perfect alibi to adopt an interventionist posture regarding Sri Lankan domestic affairs. In this section, I offer an explanation as to why this putative unity between the two nationalisms is disingenuous when one closely examines the actual histories and trajectories of the two movements.

I would like to enter the discussion by directly addressing the discourse of danger that underlies mainstream analyses of the two Tamil nationalist movements. There is nothing objectionable about Tamils in India expressing concern about the treatment of Tamils in Sri Lanka. In fact, the multiple violences and discriminations visited upon Tamils by the Sri Lankan state since independence have merited condemnation on humanitarian grounds, and if such protests came from Tamil Nadu, well, so much the better for that state. It might be more worthwhile, however, to ponder why the expression of concern by Tamil "here" about the welfare of a Tamil "there" produces acute suspicion and discomfort among state elites and many scholars in both India and Sri Lanka, and why such expressions of concern are immediately interepreted as evidence of the primordial and dangerously essentialist Tamil character underlying both movements.

One of the most noticeable aspects of the Dravidian movement, as we saw in the previous section, was its material and ideological basis in anti-Brahminism. In contrast, Brahmins, who constituted less than one percent of Sri Lankan Tamils, were nowhere near as important in Jaffna or Ceylon's Tamil community as their counterparts were in Tamil Nadu. The impact of colonial rule had led to a different political economy, one in which the Brahmin stayed predominantly within the religious fold, while the agricultural caste of the Vellalars came to dominate both the professional, educated classes and the agrarian sector. Unlike in Tamil society in Tamil Nadu, the impact of Christianity was far greater in Tamil society in Sri Lanka, and the Vellalar variety of Hinduism was one that was considerably intermixed with Christianity. In a forceful rebuttal of the claim that Sri Lankan Tamil nationalism had close cultural and political ties to the Dravidian movement in Tamil Nadu, R. Perinbanayagam notes, "Jaffna Tamil leaders of the early twentieth century did not typically dwell on their Dravidian roots. Many of them may have gone back and forth between Jaffna and South India, participating in political life in both places, but their two-way access was a result more of colonial ties between South India and Sri Lanka than of a common culture. Moreover, the early founders of separatist ideology were not Hindus at all, but good Jaffna Christians" (summarized in Little 1994, 45). In Tamil Nadu, the attack against "local" Brahminism could be coupled with a powerful critique of Sanskritic culture and North Indian hegemony, which gave a powerful fillip to a regional or separatist ideology. None of these factors were germane to the Sri Lankan case.

Beginning with non-Brahminism, the Dravidian movement at its apex expanded into a full-scale critique of caste. Although Barnett and Washbrook, among many others, are correct that the Dravidian movement was often long on anticasteist rhetoric and short on improving the lives of those at the bottom, it is a fact that some of the most egregious and overt aspects of caste discrimination had largely disappeared from Tamil society in India by the 1960s. For example, the exclusion of lower castes from entering temples was one of the first things to go in Tamil Nadu, almost with independence itself. Yet, in Sri Lankan Tamil society, not only was the domination of the Vellalars overwhelming, but most such overtly exclusionary aspects remained intact. Bryan Pfaffenberger has commented that Jaffna was "the most conservative of Tamil societies anywhere" (1982, 33) in the matter of caste. The ban on lower castes entering temples remained in place in Sri Lankan Tamil society into the 1970s. Even as late as that, the renowned Vellalar Tamil nationalist leader, one time cabinet minister, and professor of mathematics (no less!) C. Suntheralingam found it politically feasible to lead a movement against temple entry for lower-caste Tamils in Sri Lanka. Indeed, after 1956, the pressure to present a united front against Sinhalese ought to have given great impetus to Tamils to cross such caste barriers, but this was not so. It was mainly the Marxists among Tamils who initiated such moves, and the Federal Party "joined in this enterprise especially after 1956 but as the mainstream political party of the Tamil minority and dependent on vellala votes it was much more circumspect in dealing with these issues" (De Silva 1986, 219).

It would be 1977 before a so-called lower-caste person would be elected from Sri Lankan Tamil society to Parliament, in the fifth general elections of independent Sri Lanka. In Tamil Nadu, not only had the Nadar leader K. Kamaraj served a stint as Tamil Nadu's chief minister (in the 1950s), but he had also brokered the succession of two prime ministers and acquired the sobriquet "kingmaker" by then. The deferential, casteist, and conservative Tamil society of Jaffna must have regarded the anticaste rhetoric and program of the Self-Respect Movement and Dravidian ideology with some degree of alarm and certainly with considerable distaste. This reaction was further reflected in the superior and aloof attitude they adopted toward the Estate Tamils of Indian origin, largely on account of the lower caste and class position these Tamils occupied, in their view.

There were important political reasons for the two Tamil movements to stay aloof. To secure redress as a minority, Sri Lankan Tamil elites focused their attention on Colombo in the decades immediately before and after independence. There was little or nothing to be gained and much to be lost by making common cause with Tamils in Madras at this time. In an effort to assert their claims to the Sinhalese majority, it was logical for them to prove their antiquity in Sri Lanka and their distance from the Tamils of India. As Sinnappah Arasaratnam notes,

> A second source of Ceylon Tamil nationalism is the emphatic assertion of Sri Lanka as the legitimate and ancient home of the Tamils and of Tamil institutions. Nothing annoys the Tamils of Sri Lanka more than the argument, used by Sinhalese to placate Tamil opinion, that their culture and language are preserved adequately and are flourishing in South India and there was, therefore, no need to make a special provision in Sri Lanka. The Tamils react to this by emphasising their separateness from India, the longevity of the Tamil tradition in Sri Lanka, and by asserting, with dubious historical arguments, their contemporaneity with Sinhalese settlements in Sri Lanka. (1979, 511)

For a DMK interested in revising its genealogy of collaboration and distancing itself from secessionist history, there seemed little point in supporting the cause of Sri Lankan Tamils in any material fashion, overtly or covertly. During the critical turning points in the narrative of Sri Lankan Tamil nationalism in the 1950s and 1960s (the enactment of Sinhala Only in 1956, the anti-Tamil riots of 1958, the betrayals of the Bandaranaike-Chelvanayagam Pact, and the Senanayake-Chelvanayagam Pact), DMK politicians, who were then in the opposition in the state legislature and central Parliament, encouraged the Indian government to take an active stance and pressure the Sri Lankan regime to alter its policies toward the Tamils. They were even more outspoken in their comments on the betrayal of the Estate Tamils in the legislation of 1948–49 and in the Sirima-Shastri Pact of October 1964, which envisaged the repatriation of half a million Estate Tamils to India within fifteen years. As I noted earlier, the discourse of danger that regards every expression of ethnic solidarity as suspicious ought not to blind us to the fact that, on this occasion, the DMK was expressing humanitarian concerns that were eminently worthy of support. At the same time, it is important to recognize that the DMK concern for the welfare of the Sri Lankan Tamil or the Estate Tamil rarely proceeded beyond rhetoric.[13] Speeches in the Indian Parliament and in the state legislative assembly in Madras were directed at target audiences within the electorate of Tamil Nadu. When it came to support for the cause of the

Tamils in Sri Lanka, the story was depressingly familiar: the DMK found little reason in the 1950s and 1960s to do anything more than pay lip service to it.

In the 1970s, the rewriting of the Constitution, standardization, and the anti-Tamil riots of 1977 were occasions in which the DMK and AIADMK tried to outdo one another in party competition by vociferously espousing the cause of the Sri Lankan Tamils. Yet, it is easy to exaggerate the degree of such support: for all their speeches in Parliament and processions taken out by the opposition party, there is little evidence of any material or other form of overt or even covert support by the Dravidian parties for Sri Lankan Tamils. Arasaratnam buttresses this point when he notes that in the period from independence to about 1970, "(T)hough there was considerable cultural links with Tamil revivalism across the Palk Straits, there was no hint of extra-national political links with South Indian Dravidian groups. The Sinhalese fear of such links were always there, but these were unrealistic—being founded on ancient historical memories rather than hard contemporaneous data" (1979, 515; see also Cheran 1992).

Immediately after independence, Sri Lankan Tamil leaders occasionally made references to the desirability of joining in a federation with India. Such references were, in fact, made not only by Tamil politicians in Sri Lanka, but by a number of parties and individuals at this time all across South Asia. The nation-states created in 1947–48 had not yet begun to exercise a complete thrall over the imaginations of everyone in the region. But even at this time, leaders such as Chelvanayagam found their overtures to Tamil politicians across the Straits unwelcome. Referring to this period (1947–48), Alfred Wilson notes that "Given the nearness of the South Indian mainland, it was to be expected that when Chelvanayagam conceived of the idea of federalism, he would think of a relationship with Tamil Nad in India, and of the Tamil areas of Ceylon forming a unit of the Union Republic of the Indian federation. However, he withdrew from this position as soon as politicians from Tamil Nad, when questioned on the subject by the pro-government press, expressed disapproval" (1994a, 3).

In the 1970s, a series of significant events demonstrate the "correctness" of DMK regimes when it came to matters involving Indo-Lankan relations. In 1973, when M. Karunanidhi of DMK was chief minister, a Sri Lankan Tamil militant, Kuttimani, was captured in Tamil Nadu. He was wanted by Colombo for attempting to smuggle dynamite into Sri Lanka. Karunanidhi had Kuttimani arrested and deported to Sri Lanka to serve his prison term (Swamy 1994, 28). In November 1973, the same DMK regime arrested three Sri Lankan Tamils for violating the Indian Passport Act, and they too were handed over to the Sri Lankan government (Palanithurai and Mohanasundaram 1993, 74). It was around this time (1972) that the leader of the Sri Lankan Tamils, Chelvanayagam, visited Tamil Nadu and New Delhi in an effort to rouse support for the Tamil cause in Sri Lanka. Although he received a warm welcome in Madras, "he did not get the expected response. Despite the expression of sympathy it had been made clear to him by the DMK leaders, that Federal Party's cause was an internal matter of Sri Lanka" (Palanithurai and Mohanasundaram 1993, 73). Efforts by other Sri Lankan Tamil leaders in New Delhi proved similarly fruitless. Given the close friendship that existed at this time between the two prime ministers, Sirima Bandaranaike and Indira Gandhi, India's reluctance to enter this Sri Lankan domestic issue was perhaps not unexpected.[14]

Later on in the same decade, in 1977, when anti-Tamil riots of unprecedented severity rocked Sri Lanka, the response from Tamil Nadu was more vociferous, but still nowhere near as strong or outraged as befitting a party and a state supposedly sympathetic to the idea of Tamil pan-nationalism. The opposition DMK took out processions against the riots and organized a general strike in support of Tamils in Sri Lanka. In contrast, the Indian government (led at this time by Morarji Desai of the Janata Party) and the AIADMK regime in Tamil Nadu both expressed their concern regarding the safety of "Indian nationals" in Sri Lanka but stayed clear of commenting on the issue in any significant way. Overall, these protests in Tamil Nadu were described as being "mild" (Palanithurai and Mohanasundaram 1993, 52).

In January 1981, during the Fifth International Tamil Research Conference held in Madurai, Tamil Nadu, the leader of the TULF, Appapillai Amirthalingam (successor to Chelvanayagam) spoke in the course of his address about the problems of Sri Lankan Tamils and the discrimination and violence of the Sinhalese. The chief minister of Tamil Nadu, M. G. Ramachandran (usually referred to as

MGR) of AIADMK, responded that the Tamil conference was an inappropriate place to advocate the political ideologies of individuals or movements. He further noted that Tamil Nadu wished to retain a cordial relationship with neighboring countries and governments. The timing of this event merits attention: January 1981 would be the last time the chief minister of Tamil Nadu needed to take such a diplomatically correct stance on Sri Lankan affairs for some time to come. Soon after, there would be a sharp change in policy on Sri Lanka and the Tamil question there at the level of the central government in New Delhi, producing in its wake a new set of opportunities and enunciative spaces for both the Tamil parties in Tamil Nadu and Jaffna, as well as for the central governments in Delhi and Colombo. It was in this dramatically altered context that the pogrom of July 1983 against the Sri Lankan Tamils (examined in the next chapter) would explode, inaugurating a different era in relations between the two Tamil ethnicities.

In this section, I have suggested that an examination of the historical, political, and cultural backgrounds of the two Tamil nationalisms offer compelling reasons as to why they stayed, in the main, relatively aloof from each other. In contrast with a mainstream historiography (in both Sri Lanka and India) bent on suggesting that Tamil ethnicity was a common essentialist force underlying both Sri Lankan Tamil nationalism and Dravidianism, I argue that they arose from distinctly different social formations and moved along opposite political trajectories. Although the logic of electoral politics and competition (between Congress and DMK before 1972 and between DMK and AIADMK after that year) often meant that the Dravidian parties tried to outdo the other in rhetorically espousing the causes of various Tamil diaspora, this rhetoric never translated into any form of material support for the Sri Lankan Tamil cause. In that sense, the Dravidian parties remained firmly within the parameters of Indian foreign policy as set by New Delhi.

Yet the discourse of a mainstream, realist international relations scholarship has narrated the history of these two Tamil movements as intertwined and closely related. The suspicion of ethnicity and the valorization of a univocally sovereign model of the nation has together produced a tendency to essentialize Tamil "there" and "here" and to combine them into a primordial threat to the principle of the nation-state. A more detailed examination of the history of these two movements seems to indicate that the facile commingling of the two Tamil nationalisms is one more instance of the amnesia that produces the nation and of the politics of anxiety that reproduces it, rather than historical fact as such.

MODULATING 1971 IN JAFFNA

In chapter 1, I discussed the modulation of the events of 1971 leading up to the emergence of Bangladesh. Within India, 1971 was an important step in the ongoing self-fashioning of the nation. First, it signified the emergence of India as a country to be reckoned with, a regional power of significance, one adept at the Machiavellian game of realpolitik. Second, it gave a tremendous fillip to incipient notions of India's historical destiny as the regional hegemon of South Asia and induced a strong aversion to the presence of any extraregional interference therein. Third, it inaugurated the idea that India had a legitimate interest in the fate of so-called kindred ethnic minorities in neighboring countries, on whose behalf it may intervene if circumstances so dictated. And finally, it set in motion what I have described as a twin-track policy for the central government of dealing both with neighbor countries and with states domestically: a combination of overt diplomatic pressure and covert, intelligence-based destabilization of hostile regimes. In this section, I briefly consider how 1971 came to be modulated within the universe of the Sri Lankan Tamils.

The emergence of Bangladesh pushed certain sections among the Sri Lankan Tamils further along the road to Eelam and created expectations regarding the possible role that the central government in India might play in helping them achieve it. Chelvanayagam's biographer dwells at some length on the deep impact 1971 made on the Tamil leader: "Chelvanayagam . . . pondered the questions which the emergence of Bangladesh inevitably raised, namely that they should give up the federal demand and declare a Tamil state. If they did so, it meant separation. He added that this question would be submitted to the forthcoming Annual Convention [of the Federal Party], for it demanded 'very deep and serious thinking.' More critical and significant was his journey to Madras, the capital city of Tamil Nad, on 20 February 1972, an event which marked a turning away from Colombo" (Wilson 1994a, 117–18). Although I would hardly go as far as to suggest that Bangladesh was the decisive or even a very important reason for the Tamils to decide on secession (the intransigence of the Sinhalese majority deserves sole credit for that), I am suggesting that its emergence may well have pushed Tamils over the brink on explicitly declaring Eelam to be their goal.

Later that year, the newly formed TUF came up with a Six-Point Demands list that echoed the six-point formula used by Mujibur Rahman and the Awami League in the months leading up to the secession of Bangladesh. These demands were: give the Tamil language official status; make Sri Lanka a secular state; decentralize administrative structures; write the fundamental rights of minorities into the Constitution; abolish the caste system; and give citizenship to all those who seek it. This list was presented to Mrs. Bandaranaike's self-proclaimed Constituent Assembly only to be ignored. In the last years of his life, Chelvanayagam (and TULF) increasingly turned to India and Tamil Nadu for help in regard to Sri Lankan Tamil affairs. We have already seen that at this time the Tamil political parties in Tamil Nadu played it by the book in responding to such overtures. TULF emissaries contacted Mrs. Gandhi at this time, but because of her excellent relations with Mrs. Bandaranaike the meeting had no results.

Yet Bangladesh had laid the grounds for something different to emerge when conditions were "right." For some Sri Lankan Tamils, it whetted hopes for Indian help and intervention on their side against the Sinhalese. And in India, it had created a mindset that the fate of ethnic minorities in neighbor countries was a legitimate area of interest. After the abortive initial contacts between TULF and the Indian government in 1972, Mrs. Gandhi was preoccupied with political turmoil in 1973–74, followed by the Emergency (June 1975 to March 1977). She then spent nearly three years out of power, having been defeated by the Janata Party. It would be January 1980 before she returned to power and once again picked up the threads of her policy toward Sri Lanka and South Asia. This time around, in a strange sort of way, one could say that conditions were right for Sri Lankan Tamil hopes for Indian intervention. Mrs. Bandaranaike was now out of power, and Jayewardene's regime seemed to go out of its way to antagonize India and certainly did not kowtow to Indian pretensions as regional hegemon. Soon, the Tamil issue would appear as the perfect theater for Mrs. Gandhi to assert Indian hegemony and bring around the recalcitrant regime of Jayewardene.

CONCLUSION

Mainstream scholarship would have it that Sri Lankan Tamil nationalism and Dravidian nationalism were both instances of an essentialist, primordial ethnic identity that represented a danger to the project of constructing sovereign nation-states. Such a view fails to recognize the debt that identity owes to difference: in South Asia, as elsewhere, the production of the nation is in counterpoise to various, eternally inferior and dangerous others. Intent as it is on demonstrating the reactionary and atavistic character of ethnonationalism, such scholarship generally fails to realize that dangerous ethnicity is a discourse that provides diverse enunciative opportunities: it allows parties and leaders to portray themselves as nationalists, patriots, self-sacrificing heroes, regional hegemons interested in protecting beleaguered minorities in neighboring countries, and so on. The dialectics of inside/outside and identity/difference operate as ever to create and reproduce the very categories that are supposedly the foundational realities that animate discourses such as nationalism and ethnicity. These enunciative opportunities allow for the making of careers, winning elections, shaping political ideologies, acquiring followings, endowing nations with content and meaning, and acquiring and retaining power.

Proceeding from an understanding of social reality that is not premised on a hermeneutic of suspicion and that does not seek to uncover some deeper, infallible truth or foundational essence underlying identity, I have tried to show how the histories of Sri Lankan Tamil nationalism and Dravidian nationalism can be read instead as narratives. Sri Lankan Tamil nationalists see themselves as a people who had tried in every way to seek accommodation and a fair deal from the Sinhalese majority. It was after the repeated failures of such attempts and because of the growing violence of the Sinhalese that they turned to Eelam as the only alternative. In the case of Tamil Nadu, existing historiography on the Dravidian movement can be more plausibly interpreted to suggest that after a brief and not serious flirtation with secession, it developed along lines that reinforced its connections to the Indian union. By the 1970s, the Dravidian political parties were, if anything, remarkable for the pliancy they exhibited to the center rather than for any secessionist ideology. This same historiography would suggest that for important socioeconomic and political reasons, the two Tamil nationalisms emerged from different provocations and moved along divergent trajectories.

I submit that there is a crucial political lesson contained in the divergent experiences of the two Tamil nationalisms: the importance of state structures that are federal in their imagination and that respect and recognize the need for a pluralist ethos. If the Dravidian movement veered away from its incipient secessionism, in large part it could do so because of the political dispensation of postcolonial India, which offered them an opportunity to come to power at the state level. Indian federalism no doubt remained overcentralized and fell far short of the demands of various state-level regimes, but it was nevertheless sufficient to co-opt the Dravidian movement. In Sri Lanka, a unitary state and the rapid growth of a chauvinistic, majoritarian nationalist ideology produced precisely the opposite result: the Tamils, who desired accommodation were inexorably driven toward secessionism by the exclusivist and singular conception of a Sinhala-Buddhist nationalism that deemed them eternally second-class subjects. In terms of the overall argument of this book, there could be no better illustration of the importance of a pluralist and federal political imaginaire for postcolonial nationalisms than the divergent histories of the two Tamil nationalisms.

By the late 1970s, the DMK and AIADMK were comfortably ensconced as regional parties with their secessionist history a mere memory. At this same time, Sri Lankan Tamil nationalism was hardening to a secessionist view led by militant youth. In this context, the change in Indian policy toward Sri Lanka occurred in the early 1980s under Mrs. Gandhi. From regarding the ethnic struggle in that country as a domestic matter, India now ostensibly considered the Tamil struggle there to have grave implications for the security and integrity of India. In this shift, it was almost predictable that Indian state elites and many in the academy and media would immediately latch on to the "secessionist history" of Tamil Nadu: this history would serve as the perfect alibi for an expanded Indian role in Sri Lankan affairs. Although at one level this cynical use of Tamil ethnic identity can be seen as a direct legacy of the way in which Bangladesh had come to be modulated in Indian self-fashioning, at another it represented a genuine tragedy. One of the few success stories of Indian federalism, reflected in the experience of the Dravidian parties, would now be thoroughly besmirched. The shift in Indian policy would begin by essentializing "the Tamil" and his ethnicity as always already and incurably secessionist.

II

Delusions of Grandeur:
India, Tamil Nadu, and Sri Lanka

4

Modulating Bangladesh: India and Sri Lanka, 1980–84

Foreign policy demands scarcely any of those qualities which are pe-culiar to a democracy. They require, on the contrary, the perfect use of almost all those in which it is deficient.
— ALEXIS DE TOCQUEVILLE, DEMOCRACY IN AMERICA

The preceding chapters examined the social constructions of India, Sri Lanka, and the two Tamil nationalist movements as contested narratives. Throughout, the focus was trained on the interaction between ethnicity/nation, self/other, minority/majority, inside/outside, and various other antinomies in the production and reproduction of these selfsame identities. Rather than proceeding from a standpoint of epistemic realism (the notion that "the world comprises objects the existence of which is independent of ideas or beliefs about them" [Campbell 1992, 4]) oriented toward discovering *the* underlying truth of the matter, I have argued for the following: a social and repre-sentational view of reality; the essential contestability of such repre-sentations; and the absence of any foundational (or primordial) an-chors that govern the form and content of the central categories that animate the discourse of international relations.

Inevitably accompanying a view of reality as socially produced and representational is an understanding of the intertwined nature of power and knowledge. Every interpretive act is also necessarily reflective of a will to power and dominance, of the desire to impose an understanding on a reality that is in no way an accomplice in our knowledge-seeking practices. As Foucault notes in this regard, "interpretation is the violent or surreptitious appropriation of a system of rules, which in itself has no essential meaning, in order to impose a direction, to bend it to a new will, to force its participation in a different game, and to subject it to secondary rules" (1977, 151–52). This view of power is radically different from those that emphasize only the constraints exercised by it and instead shifts the terrain of power to a discursive realm sensitive to its productive and enunciative capacities. Once again, Foucault: "power... doesn't only weigh on us as a force that says no, but... it traverses and produces things, it induces pleasure, forms knowlege, produces discourse. It needs to be considered as a productive network which runs through the whole social body, much more than as a negative instance whose function is repression" (1980a, 119).

A central idea emerging from this discussion of power and knowledge is that discourses create enunciative spaces for actors to enter talking. The interplay of nation and ethnicity, as seen in the second chapter, allowed Jayewardene to fashion himself as a patriot, a leader of the Sinhalese people bent on recovering a distant golden age. Similarly, a certain worlding of India and the region secured the Nehruvian state as a secular, scientific modernizer of a society condemned to play catch up, and the narrative of repeated betrayals by Sinhalese constituted the discursive space for an ethnonationalist movement of the Sri Lankan Tamils. In each instance, the narrative creates a sense of being in the world, of making sense of it, of knowing what to do: it is in this sense that I see the interaction of power and knowledge as productive of enunciative spaces that allow each of us to occupy social roles with varying contents and agencies.

In the next three chapters, I analyze Indian political and military intervention in Sri Lanka during the 1980s in terms of the way various actors constituted these events, rather than from the vantage viewpoint of an objective and impartial authority on the outside. I suggest that various actors involved in Indo-Lankan relations in the 1980s were embedded in different constructions of events and engaged in different modes of self-fashioning, and that they availed themselves of rhetorical opportunities available within these distinct narratives.[1] The interaction of these often divergent constructions of social reality led to a military intervention that was disastrous for nearly everyone concerned. Yet, such an intervention and its tragic aftermath were almost inevitable given the narratives that animate postcolonial nationalism, and they created opportunity structures for politicians, militant groups, academic and media elites, military personnel, and bureaucrats to fashion selves, make careers, build nations, and leave their mark on history.

HEGEMONY AS COERCION

Antonio Gramsci (1971) argues that the effective hegemony of a given political order rests more on a societal consensus on the legitimacy of that order than it does on the state's coercive ability to bludgeon its citizens into submission. To the extent that a state constantly and egregiously demonstrates its power as enforcer, it reveals not so much a strong state as a weak one, Gramsci famously argues in his analysis of why the first socialist-communist revolution occurred in backward, semifeudal tsarist Russia than in the more industrialized, capitalist, and liberal-democratic states of Europe. Indian pretensions toward regional hegemony in South Asia, by this definition, would certainly fall much closer to the coercive than the consensual end of the spectrum. And even this rather eviscerated notion of hegemony (which reduces to mere dominance) was perhaps true only with regard to the smaller states in the region (Sri Lanka, Nepal, Bhutan, the Maldives) and did not apply to either Pakistan or (after 1971) Bangladesh.

Until the late 1970s, Sri Lanka had by and large escaped the overbearing attention of its neighbor to the north. Indeed, regarding a number of occasions (the Sirima-Shastri Pact of 1964 on repatriation of Estate Tamils to India and the concession of the disputed Kachathivu Island to Sri Lanka in the early 1970s), one could argue that the Indians even acted in ways that went against their own short-term interests in order to keep relations with Sri Lanka on an even keel. This period of cordial relations continued after Mrs. Gandhi's defeat at the polls in March 1977 and in the ensuing Janata coalition regime under Morarji Desai. Although Jayewardene sharply departed from the foreign policy previously followed by Sri Lanka (which basically was in line with Indian preferences on most matters) and moved in a strongly pro-western and pro-market direction, India was not too concerned. After describing relations between India and Sri Lanka in the Desai regime as reaching the "high water mark," the Indian high commissioner in Colombo at the time, Thomas Abraham Sr., noted that Desai was "not really concerned about the Tamil problem there because, from his point of view, it was not central to the security and well-being of the Indian Republic. He therefore did not want to build the problem too much."[2]

This attitude changed very quickly after Mrs. Gandhi's return to the prime ministership in January 1980. The Congress had campaigned on the slogan that it was the only party that could provide a government that worked, and that important matters of national security, both domestic and foreign, had been allowed to run dangerously adrift under the Janata regime. In contrast to a number of academic works that regard regional foreign policy as one of the few areas of notable success under Janata (see, for example, Ali 1993, 244, Bradnock 1990, 37, and Thomas 1986), Mrs. Gandhi and the Congress Party averred that during the Janata interlude, neighboring regimes had become too uppity and Indian hegemony acquired with much effort in 1971 had been squandered. Moreover, they alleged, extraregional powers were meddling in the Indian ocean region with impunity.

With Mrs. Gandhi's return to power the lessons of Bangaldesh as understood by Indian state elites came to be applied in a number of contexts, both domestically and regionally. On the regional front, as Mahmud Ali notes in an emblematic quote, "Mrs Gandhi's return to power in 1980 ended the 'Janata Spring' of South Asian accord. All along India's frontiers, Delhi's security men renewed destabilization campaigns against recalcitrant neighbors. RAW [Research and Analysis Wing, India's external intelligence agency] operatives set up larger camps to provide useful training to separatist groups" (1993, 288).[3] Within the country, as noted earlier, Mrs. Gandhi's return was marked by the discrediting of legitimately elected state governments by encouraging extremist forces in such states, imposing President's Rule, and then calling for new elections.

Soon after Mrs. Gandhi was ousted in 1977, some extremely critical remarks about her and her son Sanjay were made in the Sri Lankan Parliament, including some by Prime Minister Ranasinghe Premadasa. When Jayewardene came to New Delhi as a guest of the Janata regime in 1978, he declined to visit the former prime minister and made gratuitous references to recent periods of darkness and tyranny both India and Sri Lanka had endured (under the regimes of Mrs. Gandhi and Mrs. Bandaranaike). Whatever the excellence of (or perhaps because of) the equation established between India and Sri Lanka during the Janata interlude, Mrs. Gandhi was determined that there would be a settling of accounts with Jayewardene and the UNP regime once she returned to power.

It was the meshing of these two factors — (1) a perceived need to reassert Indian regional hegemony after the Janata interlude, and (2) the view that Sri Lanka, especially Jayewardene, was getting out of line and needed a lesson in realpolitik — that set the parameters for Indian policy toward Sri Lanka during Mrs. Gandhi's second regime. It bears reiteration that both these factors spoke directly to a certain self-fashioning of India as a regional hegemon, the belief that it was the rightful legatee of the Raj's role as the strategic center of South Asia. Predictably, from the very outset a series of differences emerged between the two regimes. Sri Lanka's opposition to the Soviet invasion of Afghanistan in late 1979, support for Britain on the Malvinas or Falkland Islands war of 1982, proposed membership in the Association of South East Asian Nations (ASEAN) in the early 1980s (interpreted by New Delhi as another instance of a desire to escape Indian influence), and tendency to strike an independent stance in various fora (the United Nations and the Non-Aligned Movement, for instance) put the country in opposition to India. In addition, the Indian government held Sri Lanka accountable for a related set of what it considered provocations: the provision of broadcast facilities to the Voice of America for transmission from Sri Lankan soil and the selection of U.S. consortium of companies to refurbish the Oil Tank farm in Trincomalee harbor. In the bidding for this contract, an Indian company's offer was rejected. At this time, RAW alleged that Jayewardene intended to provide a base to the United States Navy in Trincomalee.[4] Mrs. Gandhi did not miss any opportunity to comment gratuitously on the internal affairs of Sri Lanka, most prominently on the treatment meted out to her friend and erstwhile prime minister, Mrs. Bandaranaike (who was stripped of her civil rights at this time and faced with a number of court cases on abuse of power during her term as prime minister) and increasingly on the treatment of the Tamil minority in Sri Lanka.

If the Indians were proceeding on a path set for them by the narrative of regional hegemon, Jayewardene's actions were productively constrained by the need to appear as a leader capable of standing up to his dominant neighbor to the north and of putting the Tamil minority in its place. The more Mrs. Gandhi commented on the ethnic situation in Sri Lanka—namely, on the plight of the Tamils there—the harder it was for Jayewardene to contemplate any concession on that issue. On the contrary, a hard-line stance on the ethnic issue domestically and a position against India regionally dovetailed neatly. Both were key elements in an enduring Sinhala cosmology (which often alloyed Sri Lankan Tamils with the Tamils of Tamil Nadu and sometimes even posited that all of India was Tamil), and both inevitably put Jayewardene on a collision course with the Indians.

"TAMIL" ETHNICITY AND THE POLITICS OF REGIONAL HEGEMONY

In the period 1977–81, Sinhala-Tamil relations in Sri Lanka took a turn for the worse. Notwithstanding promises made to Tamils in its Election Manifesto of 1977 and minor ameliorations in university admission procedures and the constitutional status of the Tamil language and Buddhism, the UNP regime of Jayewardene continued the history of discrimination against them. Ironically enough, the TULF was the main opposition party in Parliament, the UNP's rout of the SLFP having been so complete in the parliamentary elections of 1977. This new-found status of TULF as the main opposition in Parliament translated into precious little as far as improving the lot of the Tamils were concerned. Violent anti-Tamil riots in 1977 and 1981 marked deteriorating relations between the two communities. In May-June 1981, during elections to the newly formed District Development Councils (DDC),[5] the overwhelmingly Sinhala police forces rioted in Jaffna, killing a number of Tamils and looting property. In the course of this riot, they destroyed the Jaffna Public Library, a repository of ancient Tamil literature and priceless collections of materials pertinent to their culture, identity, and antiquity. The presence of two ministers well known for their Sinhala chauvinism, Cyril Mathew and Gamini Dissanayake, in Jaffna at the time and evidence of involvement of state machinery and personnel in these riots further convinced Sri Lankan Tamils of the "apogean barbarity of Sinhalese vindictiveness that seeks physical as well as cultural obliteration" (Tambiah 1986, 19–20).[6]

The end of the 1970s saw a decisive shift in the center of gravity of Sri Lankan Tamil politics: from middle-class, professional leaders of TULF to the militant youths who were the detritus of standard-ization and lowered employment prospects. Often coming from castes lower down the hierarchy than the Vellalars who dominated TULF, these educated youth had witnessed nothing but majoritarian discrim-ination in their lifetimes. The riots of 1977 and 1981 furthered their alienation from the unsuccessful politics of accommodation of the Tamil leadership for more than three decades. At least two emerg-ing militant groups, the LTTE and the Marxist-inspired Eelam Peo-ples Revolutionary Liberation Front (EPRLF) were led by individu-als from non-Vellalar lower castes such as the Karayars and included large numbers from such castes in their cadres. The veritable alpha-bet soup of other militant outfits — including the Tamil Eelam Lib-eration Organization (TELO), the Peoples Liberation Organization for Tamil Eelam (PLOTE), and the Eelam Revolutionary Organiza-tion (EROS) — were often led by youth of upper-caste origins, but their social base comprised large numbers of nondominant castes of the northern and eastern provinces.[7]

From the late 1970s, many Tamil militants in Jaffna were respon-sible for the assassinations of purportedly collaborationist Tamil politicians affiliated with either of the two major national parties (UNP and SLFP) and of army and police personnel. They were also involved in a series of bank robberies and attacks on government property and institutions (see Swamy 1994, 1–91, for details). The porous coastal border with Tamil Nadu meant they could literally disappear across the Palk Straits after commiting these acts. The in-cidence of such armed robberies and political assassinations, fol-lowed by escape to Tamil Nadu, began to climb steeply after 1980 (Swamy 1994, 63–91). On May 19, 1982, two Tamil militants (who would later become very prominent), Velupillai Prabhakaran of the LTTE and Uma Maheswaran of LTTE at this time but soon the leader of the newly formed PLOTE, were arrested by Tamil Nadu police after a shoot-out in the crowded Panagal park area in Madras city. The aftermath of their arrest would indicate a shift in policy on Sri Lanka in Mrs. Gandhi's regime. Prabhakaran and Maheswaran were wanted by the Sri Lankan government on a number of charges: the former for eighteen murders and two bank robberies, the latter for nine murders and a bank robbery. The Sri Lankan government did not even have photographs of the two men, and sizable monetary rewards had been announced for their capture. An elated minister in Sri Lanka announced an award of one million rupees to Tamil Nadu police for apprehending the two men.

Unlike previous occasions of arrest, this time the two militants were not deported. The ostensible reason given was that they had been arrested and were awaiting trial in India for attempted murder and transgression of the Indian Explosives and Firearms Act, among other crimes. (The speciousness of this argument is obvious when contrasted with Kuttimani's arrest in May 1973, as noted in the previous chapter. He too was charged under the Explosives Act and the Passports Act of India, but was nevertheless extradited to Colombo.) Although some fringe opposition parties (initially not including DMK) drummed up a campaign of sorts against their extradition, the presence of Sri Lankan Tamil militants in India was not yet open knowledge, and there was little public support for their cause in Tamil Nadu. Had the central government wished it, Prabhakaran and Maheswaran could have been sent to Colombo within hours, with no political repercussions worth the name in Tamil Nadu.

The decision against deportation was the first clear indication that the Indian government under Mrs. Gandhi had decided to use the Tamil issue in Sri Lanka as a means of exercising leverage on Jayewardene. The inspector-general of police (Intelligence Branch [IB]) in Tamil Nadu at the time, K. Mohandas, who was resposible for arresting the two men, connects this event with a shift in central policy:

> At that stage, I had premonitions of the shape of things to come. There were some straws in the wind which indicated that New Delhi had some grandiose schemes (in the thinking and planning stage) to take advantage of the situation. Some of my Delhi sources told me that there was some vague talk of "another Bangladesh" in Sri Lanka. Some others conveyed to me that New Delhi was anxious to have its presence in Trincomalee which had the potential of becoming the most important harbour in the Indian Ocean. I conveyed these bits of fairly reliable information to MGR [the chief minister of Tamil Nadu]. The reaction was a stoic silence.... MGR did not apparently wish to annoy Indira Gandhi just when they were coming closer politically. (Mohandas 1992, 68)[8]

By the end of 1982 a number of separate events had come together in a way that primed Sri Lanka to be the perfect theater for a demonstration of Indian hegemony. Sri Lanka was led by a president disinclined to kowtow to Indian delusions of grandeur, and it had a vociferous ethnic minority that could point to a long history of legitimate grievances that had gone unaddressed. This same ethnic minority could be portrayed as having intimate connections with a kindred minority within India, thus justifying Indian interest in Sri Lanka's domestic affairs. There was a rapidly growing militant movement among Sri Lankan Tamil youth who crossed the Palk Straits with ease. Finally, Indian pressure on Jayewardene to solve his ethnic problem by devolving power to the Tamils put a benign and progressive face on Indian intervention: the hallmark of a true hegemon. Indian intervention could have both regional and domestic payoffs. Regionally, it could serve as a reminder to neighbors on the costs of alienating India. Domestically, it could heighten the image of Mrs. Gandhi and Congress as protectors of ethnic minorities both within and without the country, and it could improve the electoral fortunes of Congress in Tamil Nadu, a state lost to that party since 1967. Also, as demonstrated by the nationwide Assembly elections of 1972 after the success in Bangladesh, foreign policy successes had a happy knack of transmuting themselves into greater popularity for the ruling party at home.

The combination of reasons indicates that, as argued at the beginning of this chapter, ethnicity was not merely the dangerous other of nationhood, but was also locked in a dialectical and mutually constitutive relationship with it, a relationship pregnant with all sorts of political opportunities. As ever, acquisition and retention of state power was a matter of effectively mediating the relationship between inside and outside. Further, as noted in earlier chapters, this form of capitalizing on the dialectic between ethnicity and the nation was hardly confined to Indo-Lankan relations. Rather, a common pattern of first creating a discourse of danger to the nation via ethnicity was articulated, followed thereafter by an authoritarian intervention by the central government in order to save the nation. Kashmir, Punjab, and Assam (among others) indicated this pattern within the country, and Sri Lanka was rapidly emerging as the regional exemplar of this modulation of the events of 1971.

TRAINING THE MILITANTS:
THE BEGINNINGS OF THE TWIN-TRACK POLICY

In an analysis of collective violence in South Asia, Gyanendra Pandey, an historian of the subaltern school, relates an interesting anecdote. As far back as 1931, during an enquiry into the reasons for a communal riot between Hindus and Muslims in the city of Kanpur in British India, various Hindus and Muslims were asked if they really hated each other so deeply and if they were acting on their own volition. Many replied, "Khufyawalon ne larwana hai" ("Intelligence Branch people have caused us to fight" in Pandey's [1994, 202] translation from Hindi). As far back as 1930, it was evidently standard practice to blame identarian violence on the machinations of intelligence agencies acting out imperial policies of divide and rule.

In the early 1990s, as I was conducting my own research into Indo-Lankan relations, it seemed that India's RAW was involved everywhere in domestic and regional politics. The agency had been created by Mrs. Gandhi in 1968, although its very existence remained a secret until after the Emergency ended in 1977. In the decade 1968–77, RAW's "successes" were legion: it was accorded a large share of praise for the Bangladesh operation, especially for its role in infiltrating the Mukti Bahini and ensuring that extremist, leftist factions within that group were marginalized by pro-Indian factions (Ahmad 1993, 254–55). RAW was credited with coordinating various scientific and other agencies leading to India's highly secret and successful Peaceful Nuclear Explosion in the Pokhran Desert in 1974, which caught the world by surprise. It is supposed to have played a key role in India's takeover of Sikkim in 1974 and is praised for its infiltration of insurgent groups in Mizoram, Nagaland, and other states in the Northeast (Hazarika 1994).

RAW, along with IB (the Intelligence Bureau, the putatively domestic arm of Indian intelligence gathering), was held responsible for some of the worst excesses of the Emergency period, including the tracking down and imprisonment in June 1975 of thousands opposed to Mrs. Gandhi's regime. The series of coups and countercoups in Bangladesh in 1975–76 was also supposedly in part due to RAW's activities in that country (Rose 1987, 3–33, Ahmad 1993). The close identity between RAW and Mrs. Gandhi led to the organization's having its budgets slashed and its wings severely clipped during the Janata interlude (see Raina 1981, 80–83, for details). In more recent years, RAW has become everyone's alibi in both the Indian and regional contexts, with opposition parties and state-level regimes, dissident factions within Congress, various militant groups all over the country and in the region, regimes in neighboring countries, all tracing their woes to a seemingly omniscient and rogue agency.

More generally, at least since 1971, South Asia has seen the continuous proxy war between the various nation-states in the region largely conducted through the intelligence agencies of the governments. Thus, in Kashmir and Punjab insurgencies, the Indian government discerns the hand of the Inter-Services Institute (ISI) of Pakistan, and the latter alleges RAW is behind similar movements in Sind, Baluchistan, and the North-West Frontier Provinces and among the Mohajirs (Pakistanis who were originally migrants from India during the Partition). Bangladesh alleges RAW's support for the Chakma tribal insurgents in the Chittagong Hill Tract regions of its country, and the Indians attribute many of the problems they face in the northeastern states to the intelligence agencies of Pakistan, China, Bangladesh, and Myanmar. It ought to be evident that the absence of war as defined by the conventional security studies literature is small comfort in South Asia as large-scale conflict continues to thrive through such so-called low-intensity measures orchestrated by intelligence agencies. The body counts alone indicate this: it is estimated that the insurgency in Punjab resulted in more than fifty thousand deaths, and similar figures are touted for Kashmir and in the northeast as well. We need a radical redefinition of our understandings of war and intelligence generally. Der Derian supplies this alternative: "I offer at the outset a definition that is openly hermeneutic rather than comprehensively hermetic: *intelligence is the continuation of war by the clandestine interference of one power into the affairs of another power* (1992, 21; emphasis original).

The precise beginning of Indian training of Sri Lankan Tamil militants is difficult to date. According to Indian central government officials, any camps prior to July 1983 must have been set up either by the militants themselves in remote rural areas of Tamil Nadu or with the connivance of sympathizers there. The central government certainly had no involvement in this beginning. Police officials in Tamil Nadu concur with this view regarding the pre–July 1983 training and suggest that local former servicemen may have been hired by militant groups to provide basic training. Some of the militant leaders had received training in Libya and other Middle Eastern countries and may have been imparting this training to the rest of the militants at this time. In other words, any training camps prior to July 1983 did not have the explicit support or involvement of either the central government in New Delhi or the state government

in Tamil Nadu, and in any event, they did not amount to anything
on a significant scale. At worst, from the Indian viewpoint, India
could be accused of negligence, not of seriously attempting to un-
dermine and destabilize Sri Lanka.[9]

The view from Colombo regarding these same pre–July 1983
camps, however, was quite different. First, the Sri Lankans found it
highly objectionable that Tamil militants were being provided with
any sanctuary at all in Tamil Nadu. The refusal to extradite Maheswaran and Prabhakaran (who was wanted for, among other things,
the 1975 assassination of Alfred Duraiappa, the mayor of Jaffna)
and the easy to-and-fro movement of militants across the Palk Straits
seemed to indicate Delhi's complicity in the matter. Second, many
in Sri Lanka were convinced that the pre–July 1983 training had the
support of the Tamil Nadu government or the Indian government or
both, which constituted official policy oriented toward destabilizing
Sri Lanka through the Tamil militants. To the suggestion that the
training of Tamil militants on Indian soil by the Indians began after
the riots of July 1983 Lalith Athulathmudali, a prominent cabinet
minister in these years responded by saying: "No, not true. We had
arrested certain people in Sri Lanka long before July 1983 who had
been trained in camps in India." Echoing the same point was Gamini
Dissanayake, then minister of lands and development: "I think it
[the training] started before July 1983 with the active collaboration
of the M. G. Ramachandran regime in Tamil Nadu and perhaps with
the connivance of some groups in Delhi."[10] It is worth stressing that
depicting the Tamil militants as having received training in India prior
to July 1983 was important for both of these ministers; in a small
way, it justifies the pogrom that followed.

Resisting the impulse to impose my own reading of what really
happened in the emerging situation, I prefer to highlight its enunciative possibilities. Attributing Sri Lankan Tamil militancy exclusively
to Indian or Tamil Nadu machinations served Jayewardene well in
that it diminished Tamil grievances to an externally inspired terrorist problem. Dismissing the training camps as the misguided actions
of Eelamist sympathizers in Tamil Nadu allowed the Indian government regime in Delhi to distance itself from such actions, even if it
had actively connived in them. And divining Mrs. Gandhi's intentions
on this matter became a priority for MGR, Tamil Nadu chief minister, who wished to ingratiate himself with her at this time. There

emerged a circle of plausible deniabilities that served everyone rather well, while individual responsibility was clouded. Soon, events on the ground would provide Mrs. Gandhi with an opportunity for more brazen intervention in Sri Lanka to secure recognition of Indian hegemony in the region.

THE POGROM OF JULY 1983 AND INDIA'S TWIN-TRACK POLICY

In the months preceding July 1983, Sri Lanka was rocked by a series of attacks and counterattacks by security forces and Tamil militant groups in the North. Supported by the Prevention of Terrorism Act, which virtually gave the security forces a free hand in arrest, torture, and disposal of bodies, the Jayewardene regime hammered away at the militant groups (Hoole et al. 1990, 52–62). On July 18, 1983, in an interview to the *Daily Telegraph* of London, Jayewardene revealed his state of mind regarding the situation: "I am not worried about the opinion of the Jaffna people now.... We cannot think of them. Not about their lives or of their opinion about us." To a considerable extent, Jayewardene was cornered by the steadily increasing anti-Tamil rhetoric and pro-Sinhala chauvinism that he and other leading politicians in Sri Lanka had done so much to foment. Now, two additional factors had entered the picture: (1) the Tamil youth were hitting back hard in what he described as "terrorism" and they as an armed struggle for liberation; and (2) the Indian government was moving from a position of neutrality to one of providing, at minimum, sanctuary to the militants.

On July 23, 1983, a truck carrying soldiers of the Sri Lankan army exploded over a landmine on Palaly Road in Thirunelvely, Jaffna. Thirteen soldiers, all Sinhalese, were killed. Their bodies were to be flown back to Colombo the following day (July 24) for a ceremonial burial at the Borella Cemetery in the heart of the city. The bodies were expected to arrive at the cemetery by midafternoon. It took much longer than expected to bring them from Jaffna, and by 6:00 P.M. a huge crowd had gathered and had been worked up by the impassioned speeches of Sinhala politicians. Suddenly, it was announced that there would be no funeral and that the bodies of the soldiers would be sent directly to their villages for the last rites. That evening, the pogrom of July 1983 began as the crowd wound its way home, attacking Tamils, their stores, and houses, burning automobiles, and looting property.

Over the next four days, beginning in the early hours of July 25, anywhere from 2,000 to 3,000 Tamils were killed, but according to government estimates, only about 350 people were murdered (Spencer 1990a, 616). The loss of property from looting and arson, almost exclusively Tamil property, was estimated at $300 million, and the commercial center of Colombo, the Pettah, dominated by Tamils, was devastated. At the end of the four days, nearly 70 percent of Colombo's Tamils would be in refugee camps, and in the weeks to follow, more than 160,000 Sri Lankan Tamils would cross over into Tamil Nadu, India.[11] On July 25 and 27, fifty-three Tamil prisoners, most charged with political offences and including some prominent leaders of the Tamil militant movement, were massacred in Colombo's Welikade Prison. According to the government, the massacre was the work of Sinhalese prisoners. Given that these prisoners were armed with deadly weapons, obtained ready access to the Tamil prisoners, and were not restrained by their guards until they had completed the killings, and that Jayewardene's regime was reluctant to conduct an inquiry into the riots, the claim sounds specious. (For a chilling account of the Welikade massacre, see Parthasarathy 1985.)

Many works cite anecdotal as well as other forms of evidence that indicate the involvement of some prominent UNP politicians and branches of the state machinery in conducting the pogrom against the Tamils. Far from being a spontaneous riot, it seemed to have been orchestrated by some in the ruling party and by segments of the state apparatus. As Tamils were being herded into refugee camps, carrying literally nothing but the clothes they wore, President Jayewardene was conspicuously absent for four days. In their biography of the president, Kingsley De Silva and Howard Wriggins describe his slow reaction (it took him more than twenty-four hours to declare a curfew, three days to ensure the curfew was effective, and four days to address the nation) as a "loss of nerve." However, his speech on television four days into the pogrom is perhaps a better indicator of his frame of mind. Jayewardene, always one to blur the difference between Sri Lankan and Sinhalese, did not sound like a man afflicted by any loss of nerve. He described the pogrom as a consequence of a "mass movement by the generality of the Sinhalese people.... The time has come to accede to the clamour and national respect of the Sinhalese people." Not one word in the president's speech referred to the murders of the Tamils or to the fact that more than two-thirds of Colombo's Tamils were in refugee camps. Appearing after the president on television, the then minister of trade (and later of national security and deputy minister for defense), Lalith Athulathmudali, shed tears, not for the Tamils, but for the Sinhalese who had to undergo the pain of waiting in lines for food due to the dislocations caused by the riots. The minister of lands and development, Gamini Dissanayake, from the hill country constituency of Nuwara Eliya, promised that the soil of Sri Lanka would be drenched with the blood of every Tamil within fourteen hours. He returned to his constituency to ensure that a local politician who was obstructing the actions of the rioters and trying to maintain law and order had been overruled and that the mobs had been given a free hand against the Tamils. Nearly every Tamil-owned shop and property was burned in Nuwara Eliya. Not one Sinhala member of parliament or minister (let alone the president or prime minister) visited the refugee camps or made a single gesture of help or commiseration toward the Tamils.[12]

A number of attempts have been made at explaining the incredible violence of the pogrom of July 1983. Some have cited the character of capitalist development in recent decades in Sri Lanka as a key factor. A dismantling of the welfare safety net and the conversion of large, formerly rural classes into an anomic, urban *lumpenproletariat* created the social base from which the mobs emerged (Tambiah 1986 and 1996). Others have emphasized the criminalization of politics, which is reflected in the recruitment and use of thugs in election campaigns and rallies; in the routinized use of underworld characters in raising money to finance election campaigns and to disrupt election rallies of opponents; in the disappearances of dissidents, human rights activists, prisoners under trial, and political opponents; in the corruption of the police and armed forces, recruitment of which has increasingly become a thoroughly politicized matter; and in the emergence of so-called trade unions, which are little more than the personal armies of Sinhalese politicians with a record of ethnic chauvinism (Abeyesekera and Gunasinghe, eds., 1987). Some others have focused on the education system and the media, which produce and reproduce the ethnic divide and contain the worst manner of stereotyping of the other community (Nissan 1984), and still others see it as a problem of "managing" ethnic conflict in plural societies (De Silva 1986). An important, if sometimes underemphasized, thread running through all these explanations is that the pogrom is indissociable from the very process of modernist nation building in a multiethnic society. As highlighted in the second chapter, the collective violence of the Sinhalese against the Tamils was not so much an atavistic holdover from primordial reservoirs of hatred but quintessentially modernist, utilitarian, and often chillingly rational in its calculus. The pogrom did much to support statements such as the following: "[I]t is evident that one of the most difficult points for commentators to grasp—and for large numbers of Tamils also—is that the Sinhalese...have no intention whatsoever of reaching a negotiated settlement with the Tamils...and, above all, [the Sinhalese have] the insatiable urge to *punish* the Tamils for their past and present 'misconduct'" (David Selbourne, quoted in Wilson 1988, 184, emphasis original).

In the context of the present discussion, the pogrom of July 1983 presented the Indian government with the perfect opportunity to escalate their involvement in Sri Lankan affairs. First, 160,000 refugees were crossing the Straits and into camps in Tamil Nadu. Second, the sheer scale of violence and the resultant murders, looting, arson and economic destruction came as a shock to most in Tamil Nadu, provoking a widespread sense of outrage. Third, the riots of July 1983 created a new class of victims and refugees: articulate, middle-class, educated professionals were evicted from their homes and had become indistinguishable from Tamils who lived in areas such as Wellawatte and other rough neighborhoods and who were also fleeing the violence. The access people from such upper-class backgrounds had to the media and to the political establishment was greater than is the usual case with refugees. The pogrom of July 1983 became an indefensible act that put the Sri Lankan regime on the ropes for years to come.

Besides a one-day general strike called for by all political parties, which effectively shut down Madras city, the leader of the opposition, Karunanidhi, resigned his seat in the state legislature. While mass processions were taken out in various parts of Tamil Nadu in solidarity with Sri Lankan Tamils, Karunanidhi and a few others demanded a Bangladesh-type or a Cyprus-type operation by the Indian army in Sri Lanka. A petition with more than twenty million signatures collected in Tamil Nadu was presented to the United Nations in protest over the pogrom. Although undoubtedly the sheer scale of violence and numbers of refugees explain the strong pro–Sri Lankan Tamil reaction in Tamil Nadu, there was an important additional factor in 1983, compared to the situations in 1981 or 1977. The ruling party at the center (Congress) had already indicated a shift in policy toward active interest in Sri Lankan affairs, and it was perhaps predictable that the two leading parties at the state level (AIADMK and DMK) were now vying with each other (and, it must be remembered, with Congress) to stake their claim to be the defenders and protectors of Sri Lankan Tamils.

The widespread outrage about the pogrom could have been channeled by the Indian government in a variety of ways. For instance, they could have interpreted it as discourses on minority rights or as a more general issue of human rights; they could have mobilized the United Nations or the Non-Aligned Movement or the emerging South Asian Association for Regional Cooperation (SAARC) to pressure the Sri Lankan regime. Instead, the government of India, although it no doubt gave lip service to the above options, accorded primacy to a line of argument that emphasized ethnicity and its dangers to the nation-state: the pogrom of Tamils in Sri Lanka could stir the embers of a long-simmering secessionist tendency among the Tamils of Tamil Nadu. In order to contain the dangers of such tendencies, which supposedly would directly impact the security, integrity, and sovereignty of India, the Indian government had a legitimate interest in the domestic affairs of the Sri Lankans. Indian "mediation" was vital to ensure the Sinhalese cut the Tamils a fair deal within Sri Lanka. This decision marked the initiation of India's twin-track policy in India's dealing with Sri Lanka. On the one hand, it became directly and overtly involved as self-appointed intermediary between the Sri Lankan government and Tamil representatives. On the other, the arming and training of militants now involved the central government (through RAW) and exceeded anything that may have gone on before July 1983.

The first track, mediation by the Indians, was ostensibly taken up at the invitation of the Sri Lankan government, but coercion was palpable. As early as July 26, at a time when Jayewardene was conspicuously silent about the pogrom, the Sri Lankan government found the time to express its displeasure at Indian interference in its internal affairs. By August 2, Jayewardene had made frantic requests for aid or support to the United States, Britain, Pakistan, and Bangladesh. By the middle of August, he had explicitly rejected Indian "good offices" in what he considered "my own problem," and his cabinet had rejected G. Parthasarathi's mission as special envoy from India (Muni 1993, 186–87). Moreover, in the immediate aftermath of the riots, the Jayewardene regime expelled all the TULF members of parliament by passing the Sixth Amendment to the 1972 Constitution, which outlawed the largest opposition party on grounds of its being secessionist (because they all swore by the Vaddukoddai resolution described in the previous chapter).

Jayewardene has since made it clear he had little choice in the matter of Indian mediation. His feelers to western countries were usually met with responses to the effect that he ought to use India's help in settling matters with the Tamils (De Silva and Wriggins 1994, 580–81). When rebuffed by the United States and Britain, Jayewardene turned to Pakistan and China for help, limited though it might be. In addition, he sought out the help of a certain mercenary group in Britain and from the Israeli secret service in training the Sri Lankan army to fight the militants, which played into Indian hands because they could now plausibly allege Jayewardene was bringing groups and forces hostile to Indian interests into the region, justifying a hard-line Indian policy toward his regime.

By October 1983, Sri Lanka had reluctantly agreed to India's role as a mediator—to use her "good offices," as it was commonly put, to help Sri Lanka resolve its ethnic crisis. It was, however, obvious that Jayewardene was going to use every opportunity to settle the issue on his own terms and wriggle out of any commitments made to India, as he saw it, under duress. The military option, headed by the newly appointed minister for national security, Lalith Athulathmudali, continued alive and well into 1984, as the Sri Lankan armed forces hammered away at civilian and militant alike in the Tamil provinces. An additional factor operating on Jayewardene at this time, according to the Sri Lankan journalist Merwyn De Silva, was his obsessive fear that India was intent on toppling him from the presidency and on reinstalling Mrs. Bandaranaike.[13]

In India, the official line was that they would work with the Jayewardene regime in coming up with a solution to the ethnic problem that fit within the framework of Sri Lanka's Constitution and that was acceptable to both Sinhalese and Tamils. Represented by the shuttle diplomacy of G. Parthasarathi (a close adviser to Mrs. Gandhi and a bureaucrat originally from Tamil Nadu) in his talks with Jayewardene and TULF between October and December of 1983, this track culminated in the writing up of a document referred to as Annexure C. Using the District Development Councils' idea mooted by Jayewardene after he came to power in 1978, Parthasarathi attempted to arrive at a via media between the Sinhalese and Tamils. The central thrust of Annexure C was that it expanded the level of devolution from the district to the point where it approximated that of a province, in spirit if not in letter. It also significantly increased the powers devolved to the provincial administration compared to the DDC scheme.

Negotiations between Parthasarathi and Jayewardene captured, in a microcosm, all the tensions and mutual suspicions between the two regimes. Indians believed moderate Tamils (represented by the TULF) might be persuaded to settle for Annexure C, but would balk at anything short of the concessions contained therein. They were of the view that something substantial had to be conceded by the Sinhalese to bring the Tamils back into the national fold after the pogrom. The Sinhalese perceived the situation quite differently. As had been the pattern in previous decades, they could not stomach the idea of conceding either a merged northeastern province or any genuine devolution of powers to provincial councils. Even if there were any groups inclined toward such moderation, doing so under Indian pressure was unthinkable. Throughout 1984, Jayewardene stalled on progress on Annexure C, using as his excuse an All-Parties Conference (APC), to which he had invited the hard-line Buddhist clergy or *bhikkus*. De Silva and Wriggins emphasize that Jayewardene was faced with an intransigent Sinhala civil society and serious opposition from within his cabinet and from his own prime minister (1994, 577–93).[14] But TULF politicians who had been influential in the deliberations on Annexure C felt that Jayewardene, as was his wont, had begun to dissemble and distance himself from a document he had helped create.[15] Mrs. Gandhi's assassination on October 31, 1984, removed the pressure on Jayewardene to reach a settlement with the Tamils. He immediately postponed by a month the plenary session of the APC scheduled for November 15. Soon thereafter, on December 26, 1984, Annexure C was abandoned (although many of the proposals contained within it would resurface in later documents, most prominently the Indo–Sri Lanka Agreement of July 1987). Although Jayewardene cited the backing out of TULF (on December 23) as a primary reason for abandoning the proposal, TULF felt the negotiations in the APC were a charade that diluted the proposals to a point where it was simply unacceptable.

The second track of Indian policy was represented by the covert arming, training, and attempted infiltration of various Tamil militant groups by RAW. This track of Indian policy was supposed to complement the overt track by strengthening the hands of Parthasarathi in his attempts to extract meaningful concessions from the Sri Lankan government in constitutional matters on the ethnic issue. The wave of Tamil refugees into Tamil Nadu after July 1983 provided the Indian government a cover under which to train the militants while maintaining that India was home only to refugee camps and no more. Around August 14, 1983, TULF leader Appapillai Amirthalingam had a meeting with Mrs. Gandhi, and the change in policy on the Sri Lankan issue seems to have emerged after this meeting—a point of view expressed by the former Indian high commissioner in Sri Lanka, Thomas Abraham Sr.[16] Abraham was then in Geneva and was called back to New Delhi in early August 1983 for "urgent discussions" on the Sri Lankan issue. Although Mrs. Gandhi may have decided then that the Sri Lankan Tamil issue was the perfect one with which to bring Jayewardene into line with Indian policy, Amirthalingam himself seems to have left this series of meetings with a vastly exaggerated belief in the extent to which India was willing to go in helping TULF and the Tamil cause in Sri Lanka. Put simply, Amirthalingam began to believe that India under Mrs. Gandhi was willing to intervene militarily on behalf of the Sri Lankan Tamils. His thinking at this time is summarized by A. J. Wilson as follows: "The TULF leaders expected Mrs. Gandhi to intervene militarily in Ceylon, emulating the Turkish invasion of northern Cyprus in 1974—Amirthalingam was positive that there would be such an intervention despite Mrs. Gandhi's official disclaimers.... Amirthalingam and the TULF leadership had fervently hoped for an Indian military intervention...and [Amirthalingam] said that Mrs. Gandhi had assured him that the Indian army was poised for an assault if any further anti-Tamil pogrom took place" (1988, 202–3).[17]

However, the effects of the change in Indian policy were immediate and palpable. Police officers in Tamil Nadu began to notice that the quantity and sophistication of arms carried by militants had improved sharply after the pogrom, to the point where the local police, armed often with little more than a *lathi* (wooden stick) and occasionally with a .303 rifle of World War II vintage, would have a difficult time controlling the militants.[18] Moreover, the numbers of militants and training camps began to mushroom all across Tamil Nadu. One estimate has it that between September 1983 and July 29, 1987 (when the Indo–Sri Lanka Agreement was signed in Colombo), about twelve hundred Tamil militants were trained on Indian soil (Swamy 1994, 110). Camps were established in at least thirty-one different locations within the state of Tamil Nadu (including Madras city and in districts such as Chengalpattu, Salem, Tiruchi, Pudukottai, South Arcot, Ramanathapuram, and Madurai, among others) as well as outside the state (the places commonly mentioned are Dehra Dun and Chakrata and some sites in Madhya Pradesh and Karnataka). The training was supposedly done by army officers on deputation to RAW and included use of "automatic and semi-automatic weapons, self-loading rifles, 84 mm rocket launchers, heavy weapons, and in laying mines, map reading, guerilla war, mountaineering, demolitions and anti-tank warfare while selected cadres from some groups were given training in diving and underwater sabotage" (Swamy 1994, 110).

The first of the groups of militants selected for training were 350 'boys' from TELO, chosen because that organization was regarded as the most pliable and pro-Indian of the various groups. The boys were also marked as being untainted by any ideological orientations, especially of a Marxist hue. The groups that were not selected for training at this initial stage included PLOTE and EPRLF (both of which were explicitly Marxist in ideology), as well as LTTE, which was already beginning to reveal an autonomous streak. Within weeks, however, on account of RAW's intent to penetrate and keep the various militant groups under the influence of India, training was expanded to include all of them. Approximately two hundred militants from EROS, one hundred from EPRLF, and seventy from PLOTE were part of this initial round of training (Subramanium 1992, 84–89). Soon thereafter LTTE was trained, separately on its own request, at a site near Bangalore. Besides training, India supplied weapons to the militant groups from 1984 until the very eve of the signing of the Indo–Sri Lanka Agreement of July 1987. It also looked the other way when "imports" of armaments by Tamil militants reached Indian airports or ports.

The Indian government maintained that there were only refugee camps housing Sri Lankan Tamils and denied the existence of any camps for training and arming militants. These denials became barefaced lies as evidence of the presence of the training began to mount.[19] Armed with photographs of such camps, Sri Lankan government officials protested to the Indian government, which steadfastly denied their existence. (In 1992–94, many Indian officials, especially those who had retired, gave up their pretense about these camps. Among those who agreed, off the record, that such camps existed and were run by RAW to train and arm militants were a former foreign secretary, a former high commissioner to Sri Lanka, advisers to both Indira Gandhi and Rajiv Gandhi, besides members of Parliament and police officials from the state of Tamil Nadu. Predictably, the one person who doggedly maintained that such camps never existed was a former chief of RAW.)

The central government could deflect Sri Lankan and regional protests about such camps by offering denials or, failing that, by passing the buck to Tamil Nadu's alleged secessionist proclivities. In this context, the following quote from Rohan Gunaratna strikes me as capturing the essence of the Indian position at this time: "Each and every official, including Sri Lanka's Indian High Commissioner Chhatwal [he means India's high commissioner in Sri Lanka], was thoroughly briefed to deny the centre's direct involvement in the Sri Lankan crisis. If they were forced to admit by showing them photographs of training camps and confessions of captured militants they were supposed to say that Sri Lankan Tamil militancy was supported only by sections of the Tamil Nadu public" (1993, 104). The utility of ethnicity in the actions of state elites ought to be obvious here.

In the meantime, within Tamil Nadu the militant groups were soon embroiled in the rivalry between DMK and AIADMK. Karunanidhi supported TELO, which was reason enough for MGR to develop a strong antipathy to that group and to begin to look for one that would be more faithful to him. Soon, he would pick the LTTE as the group that he most favored. Between late 1983 and July 1987, he would develop a close relationship with Prabhakaran and would publicly support the LTTE and even provide them with crores of rupees for their cause.[20] By mid-1984, however, the militant groups were already becoming more than a nuisance in Tamil Nadu. Besides committing various minor infractions such as shoplifting, harassing women, parading around in military regalia, and openly displaying their weapons, they began rapidly to dissipate their welcome with actions of a more serious nature.[21] Perhaps the worst in this period occurred on August 2, 1984, when two bombs designed to explode in midair on two separate Air Lanka flights to Paris and to London were accidentally detonated in Meenambakkam Airport in Madras. The explosion brought down a part of the concrete ceiling of the terminal and killed more than thirty people, twenty-four of them Sri Lankans. Tamil Nadu police uncovered sufficient evidence that the blasts were the work of Sri Lankan Tamil militants then resident in Madras. K. Mohandas recalls the aftermath of the investigations thus:

> the inevitable call came from Delhi, summoning me for a "discussion" of the case....I presented myself before a senior policy maker and his constitutional adviser in New Delhi the next day. It was the latter who did most of the talking. Beating around the bush, he indirectly indicated that we had a duty to protect the Sri Lankan militants and that, if we continued along the known line of investigation in the airport blast case, the Sri Lankan government would take advantage of it and proclaim to the world the existence of militant training camps in India which had "officially been denied" by New Delhi. He added that there was also the danger of Tamil chauvinist political parties in Tamil Nadu taking advantage of the situation and joining hands with the militants with the objective of establishing a bigger Eelam, including Tamil Nadu. (1992, 118–19)[22]

The Indian government's policy seemed superficially contradictory. On the one hand, it had initiated a diplomatic process to resolve the ethnic problem in Sri Lanka through devolution and provincial autonomy for the Tamils. On the other, it was undermining this process by arming the militant groups. Members of at least one of these groups, namely the LTTE, was explicit that they would settle for nothing short of a separate country. I argue, however, that Indian actions in 1983–84 seem contradictory only to those disposed to think of policy as a set of actions oriented toward solving problems—that is, toward achieving a desired outcome or conclusion in a finite period of time. I believe Mrs. Gandhi initiated a twin-track policy with regard to Sri Lanka without any expectation that she would be able or even want to solve the ethnic problem there. She wanted neither the Tamil militants to achieve Eelam nor the Sri Lankan state to defeat the militants decisively. She did not consider it likely that Jayewardene would speedily resolve the Tamil issue by a devolution of powers to the minority, nor was it on the cards that he would bow down to all of India's demands on geopolitical and other matters. The twin tracks were not so much oriented toward a speedy resolution of problems as designed to keep India's neighbors in a continuous state of destabilization. The gains of the policy were to be found in the process, not in the destination. It kept Jayewardene's regime off balance and curtailed its efforts to bring hostile forces into India's backyard; it afforded an opportunity for Congress to portray itself as the defender of a kindred ethnic minority, a portrait that could someday be parlayed into votes and maybe even power in Tamil Nadu; it served as a constant reminder to all the smaller neighbors that the costs of alienating India were not negligible. In other words, the twin tracks were about the continuous acquisition and retention of political power. If and when, in the course of the working out of the policy, a clear opportunity to fashion a dramatic foreign policy success presented itself (as had happened in mid-1971 with the case of Bangladesh), India would act decisively. But until then Mrs. Gandhi was perfectly content to let the two tracks proceed, sparing little thought on where and how they could be made to meet.

This strategy of maintaining one's neighbor in a steady-state disequilibrium (to coin an oxymoron) rested upon the unstated assumption that the Tamil militant groups would remain ever pliable and always under Indian control. In 1983–84, RAW was telling the militant groups that India was for the creation of Eelam but could not state this publicly on account of international opprobrium (Swamy 1994, 114). Although such double-talk may have fooled some of the more naive militant outfits, LTTE was different. They knew that the Indians were not behind their ultimate aim of Eelam and that they merely wished to use the outfits to pressure the Sri Lankan government to kowtow to their hegemonic designs. At best, India might be intent on solving the ethnic question through devolution. Consequently, as early as 1984, LTTE decided that it would not tie its future prospects, funding, training, and so on too closely to the apron strings of India. In other words, RAW's plans to infiltrate and control the various Tamil militant groups had already run into a serious adversary: LTTE.[23]

CONCLUSION

What is striking about the enunciative stations occupied by various individuals and institutions in Indo-Lankan relations in the early 1980s is their productive and fertile character: these stations were embedded in scripts that commanded empathetic audiences and allowed for endless iterations. Indian pressure allowed Jayewardene to fashion himself as a resolute Sinhalese leader standing up to both the despised Tamil within his country and their external supporters. In Tamil Nadu, the DMK and AIADMK, who had in the 1970s been diplomatically correct in their stance on the Sri Lankan Tamil question, now followed the central government lead in brazenly advocating the Sri Lankan Tamils' cause. To Sri Lankan Tamils, the shift in Indian policy appeared to be a godsend. On the one hand, it exaggerated the hopes held by members of TULF regarding India's likely role in their struggle for autonomy and equality. On the other, it converted a group of ragtag, impoverished militant outfits into well-armed freedom fighters. Although some of these militants believed the Indian government to be supportive of their quest for Eelam, LTTE had already divined that Indian actions had less to do with the well-being of Sri Lankan Tamils than with securing its hegemony in the region. In India, the return of Mrs. Gandhi to power in 1980 reinaugurated the twin-track policy in a number of different settings. By playing ethnicity against the nation, Mrs. Gandhi sought to retain power both domestically and regionally. The constant refrain was that the nation was in danger due to the fissiparous and atavistic forces of ethnicity and religious extremism. Yet, in many instances, it was evident that these putatively dangerous forces were locked in a mutually constitutive and productive relationship with national identity and were actively fomented by the central government itself.

In October 1984, the difficulties of operationalizing the twin tracks were brought home by the assassination of Mrs. Gandhi. As an extensive literature has by now documented, the Congress had indulged in dangerous brinkmanship in Punjab at least since the late 1970s. They discredited moderate elements in the Akali Party by boosting the stock of extremist groups, especially that of Sant Bhindranwale, a rabble-rousing priest with a small band of violent and committed followers. If the idea was to "use" Bhindranwale first to discredit the Akalis and then allow Congress to step into the power vaccuum thus created, the strategy backfired. By mid-1984, Bhindranwale and his movement had acquired a momentum and a degree of autonomy from his erstwhile sponsors that made him a serious threat and Punjab a state rocked with an extremist insurgency. In July 1984, the Indian government sent the army into the Golden Temple at Amritsar to flush out Bhindranwale and the rest of his armed followers. In the assault, hundreds if not thousands of soldiers, Sikh militants, and civilians were killed, and the sanctum sanctorum of the Sikh's holiest shrine itself was badly damaged. Barely four months after the assault on the Golden Temple, two of Mrs. Gandhi's Sikh bodyguards assassinated her. The assassination was a direct result of the twin-track policy adopted by Mrs. Gandhi in relation to Punjab. It was this same combination of overt diplomatic pressure on Jayewardene's regime and covert assistance to Tamil militant groups that Rajiv Gandhi inherited when he was sworn in as prime minister on October 31, 1984. As we see in the next chapter, under Rajiv the basis of Indian hegemony over Sri Lanka would shift from coercion to attempted consensus, but paradoxically with results that were even worse than those engendered under his mother's second regime.

5

Hegemony as Spectacle: The Theater of Postcolonial Politics

*I believe you can reach the point where there is no longer any differ-
ence between developing the habit of pretending to believe and developing the habit of believing.*
— UMBERTO ECO, FOUCAULT'S PENDULUM

In the previous chapter, I argued that the primary means employed
by India to exercise its dominance in South Asia and specifically in
Sri Lanka was a twin-track policy that combined overt diplomatic
pressure with covert destabilization. This twin-track policy came to
be regarded as the optimal way of conducting regional relations due
to its purported success in 1971, which culminated in the breakup
of Pakistan and the creation of Bangladesh. In this chapter, I suggest
that although the twin tracks remained the core of Indian policy on
Sri Lanka, under Rajiv Gandhi the quest for Indian hegemony in
South Asia shifted from coercion not merely to consensus (to use a
simplified Gramscian spectrum) but to hegemony as spectacle. Although as enamored of an aggrandized notion of India in the region as the previous regime and of its centrality on some imagined
world stage, his administration sought to achieve hegemony by the
orchestration of grand spectacles in which India already appeared
to be what it sought to become: the consensual leader of the subcontinent, a state committed to the peaceful resolution of ethnic
and other identarian conflicts through dialogue, and a fast-rising

economic and military power in the international community. The overriding self-image of the Indian state under Rajiv Gandhi was that of a highly efficient, managerially competent, and apolitical problem solver. The "computer boys," as Rajiv and his coterie were often called, were to carry India into the twenty-first century through their managerial and technological acumen. There was a strong element of paternalism, if not hubris, in the self-image of an India assisting her neighbors in resolving both their domestic and their bilateral problems with India in a progressive and democratic direction.

The theatricality of the Indian state under Rajiv was by no means exceptional or unique. As Clifford Geertz reminds us in his brilliant exegesis on Negara, the theater state of Bali in the nineteenth century, etymologically *the state* condenses within itself at least three layers of meaning: status, pomp, and governance (1980, 121). Under modernity, Geertz observes, the meaning of the state in political theory came to be overwhelmed by the last and most recent of these three valences, that of governance, whereas the other two — namely, status and pomp — seemed to have receded from our horizon of meaning. Yet, the recession in meaning of the state as pomp and status, the symbolic dimensions of state power, is not so much a reflection of the altered basis of statist authority under modernity or of the lessened importance of its performative or symbolic dimensions, as it is a legacy of nineteenth-century social science, which has rendered the study of such notions unscientific, metaphysical, or epiphenomenal. In other words, the diminished attention to pomp and status is already one of the prominent signs of the modern. This has led us to underestimate, among other things, the eschatological character of most state-building projects; the affinities between a religious imagination and patriotism; the sublimation of individual and societal anxieties in the performance of "our" nation on various international playing/killing fields; the orchestration of legitimacy by grand statist, developmental projects; and the role of state-sponsored memorials and monuments in producing a sense of belonging. As Geertz notes in regard to the Balinese state,

> It was a theatre state in which the kings and princes were the impresarios, the priests the directors, and the peasants the supporting cast, stage crew, and audience. The stupendous cremations, tooth filings, temple dedications, pilgrimages and blood sacrifices, mobilizing hun-

dreds, even thousands of people and great quantities of wealth, *were not means to political ends: they were the ends themselves, they were what the state was for.* Court ceremonialism was the driving force of court politics; and mass ritual was not a device to shore up the state, but rather the state, even in its final gasp, was a device for the enactment of mass ritual. Power served pomp, not pomp power. (1980, 13, emphasis added)

I suggest in this chapter that India under Rajiv Gandhi was a theater state in Geertz's sense: the spectacles of power were not merely *means* to achieve certain ends of the state, but *were* the state itself. In suggesting this, I do not imply that the Indian state in its previous incarnations was necessarily devoid of such symbolic elements. Indeed, it could be argued that one of the hallmarks of the so-called developmental state is the extraordinary importance attached to symbolic signifiers such as science, technology, and industrialization as sources of legitimacy (see Abraham 1998). In the first chapter, in the sections on the Nehruvian state, I remarked on the centrality of icons such as the Bhakra-Nangal Dam or the steel mill at Rourkela in securing the legitimacy of the new state. Similarly, historians such as Bernard Cohn (1987b) remind us of the extraordinary importance of pomp, splendor, and ritual in the representations of the late-colonial state.

In the staging of a series of spectacles, the ambition of the Indian state under Rajiv Gandhi was to act, to appear, and consequently to become a hegemonic power in the South Asian region. The audiences of these theatrics were multiple: they included the domestic, the regional, and certainly an international audience whose ecumene, upon closer examination, invariably turned out to be the west. As with any discursive regime, spectacular politics was rife with opportunities for the crafting of political careers, winning elections, making money, securing power, displaying authority, and commanding allegiances. The orchestration and utilization of such opportunities were not the monopoly of any one individual or group of persons. Rather, spectacular politics, like politics everywhere, set in motion a process whose outcomes were neither predictable nor amenable to control or orchestration. In the pages that follow, through a close analysis of four different episodes in Indo-Lankan relations in the mid-1980s, I show that the Indian state continued its quest to be seen as the dominant power in South Asia. Ironically, the overweening Indian desire to be recognized as regional hegemon provided the Sri Lankan state with a unique opportunity to trap India within its own rhetorical web: by late 1987, they inveigled the Indians into a war against their erstwhile wards, the Sri Lankan Tamil militants.

THE THIMPU TALKS

When Rajiv Gandhi inherited power on October 31, 1984, the media emphasized certain aspects of his persona that would presciently indicate the predominance of image as substance in the years to follow. First was his reputation as Mr. Clean: in a society where politics had come to be regarded as the first refuge of scoundrels, his initial reluctance to enter public life in 1981 was regarded as a positive sign. However, by the time he became prime minister, he had already shown signs of having imbibed what is politely called "Congress culture" in India. He was part of the decision-making coterie that had unseated the democratically elected government in Andhra Pradesh and, as Congress Party president, was witness to the destabilization campaigns launched by the party in Punjab and Kashmir. Although he may not have agreed with the policies therein, he did not (or could not) do anything to alter their course. Despite his involvement in such affairs, his reputation as Mr. Clean remained unsullied. Second, his main claim to political office was the organizational skills he supposedly displayed in staging two of the most egregiously wasteful and pompous spectacles of the early 1980s: the Asian Games of 1982 and the Seventh Non-Aligned Summit of 1983, both held in India's capital New Delhi. In many ways, his brief political apprenticeship seemed ideal to equip him for presiding over the theater state to follow.

The reality of his limitations in an increasingly criminalized political structure was evident all around the capital city even as he was being sworn in. New Delhi conducted its own pogrom on the Sikh minority in the four days following Mrs. Gandhi's assassination (November 1–4, 1984). The involvement of some Congress Party leaders and their goon squads, the use of state machinery, and the overt and covert participation of some police forces in the orchestrated murders of more than two thousand Sikhs and in the looting of their property are well documented in India.[1] Though Rajiv Gandhi was prime minister for the next five years, with the largest parliamentary majority of any regime since independence, not a single person was brought to justice for the massacre of the Sikhs.[2] On the contrary, in an aside both flippant and chilling, he seemed to justify the pogrom a few weeks after it happened by saying at an election rally that "when a great tree falls the earth shakes."[3] Mr. Clean's regime began with some of the most bloodstained hands India's history has known.

On Sri Lanka, there was a subtle shift in emphases, although Rajiv Gandhi did little or nothing to alter the twin-track policy he had inherited. Unlike his predecessor, who seemed more intent on letting the ethnic conflict there simmer, he felt that India ought to help Sri Lanka solve its ethnic problem by getting directly involved, putting pressure on all parties, and pushing them toward a solution. In this effort, he is supposed to have charged his new foreign secretary, Romesh Bhandari, with the "task of sorting out the Sri Lankan crisis in thirty days" (Bradnock 1990, 73). This unrealistic brief perfectly captures the breathlessness of the early months of the new regime and sets the stage for an era of politics as spectacle.

Many were underwhelmed by Bhandari, who fancied himself a South Asian Kissinger. They thought he had an exaggerated faith in shuttle diplomacy and was often foggy on crucial details. As one former foreign secretary acidly observed, "the man flew to more capitals and countries in his first weeks in office than I did in my entire term." Another noted that every trip of his was a "resounding success" or a "stunning breakthrough," even if little had actually been accomplished, earning him the name "no-problem Bhandari." In one instance, he was to initiate a new neighborhood policy, one that emphasized cordial and supportive relations in the region rather than fear or suspicion. He recalled his brief thus: "it is India's responsibility to try and convince its neighbors that we wish nothing else but their welfare, their prosperity, their unity, their development, their progress...a good strong stable mature India is in their interest and not inimical to their interest. With this viewpoint, I was directed to go and visit all these places and that is why...I went on a whirlwind tour around the neighborhood with this message."[4] What is striking is the flavor of a self-anointed, benevolent hegemon. Indian officials seemed genuinely incapable of understanding that their assumption of centrality in the region, whether revealed by covert interference in neighbor's affairs or in such extravagant interest in their well-being and progress, was simply not shared by these countries themselves.

Although Bhandari's "whirlwind" tour of the region drew mixed reviews, it was quite reflective of the way the new regime approached problems. By mid-1985, Rajiv had signed a series of accords on a number of fronts, including India's most pressing problems in Punjab, Assam, and Tripura. On Sri Lanka, the desire to see a spectacular and dramatic solution to the ethnic conflict was first symbolized by what came to be called the Thimpu talks. These talks between a delegation from Jayewardene's regime and representatives from various Tamil militant groups and TULF were held in two rounds in the capital of neighboring Bhutan, in mid-July 1985 and again in mid-August. The Indian government accorded a lot of prominence to these talks, held under its sponsorship, as inaugurating a new era of South Asian cooperation.

Yet, events in the period immediately preceding the proposed talks revealed that this was a particularly inopportune moment for such an exercise. In the months January–May 1985, a series of attacks and counterattacks occurred between various Tamil militant groups and state security forces in the north and east of Sri Lanka. On May 14, 1985, Tamil militants killed 146 civilians in Anuradhapura, ostensibly in retaliation for the killing of 70 civilians by Sri Lankan security forces in Velvettithurai. A day later, Sri Lankan security forces killed 48 more Tamil civilians. These killings were followed by further rounds of provocations and reprisals, all involving large numbers of civilian casualties.

A year earlier, in April 1984, as part of its plan to coordinate, infiltrate, and use the Tamil militant groups as part of its strategy in Sri Lanka, RAW had sponsored the creation of a new umbrella organization called the Eelam National Liberation Front (ENLF), which was made up of TELO, EROS, and EPRLF (LTTE refused to join initially). Now, in April 1985, as a prelude to Thimpu and under RAW pressure, LTTE also was made to join ENLF. Indicative of the degree to which RAW was underestimating the militants, even as it formed ENLF as a way of controlling them, the four leaders of the groups signed their own pact at this time, resolving to stop at nothing short of Eelam.

It was in the midst of these massacres and virtually full-blown war between Tamil militants and Sri Lankan security forces that the Indian government decided talks in Thimpu must proceed. At the outset, it inexplicably seemed to retreat from positions adopted in Annexure C, alienating the militants and TULF. In March 1985, Bhandari announced in Colombo that the militants would first have to give up violence before talks could proceed, an announcement seen by the militants as a stunning reversal of India's previous position. Just prior to that, Rajiv Gandhi announced a volte face on the issue of merger: now, it transpired, India was not in favor of merging the North and East into a single political unit (never mind that no Tamil group, not even TULF, was ready to give up on the demand for merger). This was followed by the announcement that India did not favor a devolution of power to the district level exceeding that of states within the strongly centralized Indian Union.

At the very least, the series of incidents leading up to Thimpu indicated two things: one, the Indian government was back-tracking from positions adopted earlier, with the new positions revealing a tendency to be taken in by Sri Lankan government perspectives on matters; and two, rather than reflecting any conscious change in policy, Indian reversals revealed a lack of coordination at the top and a cavalier disregard for the details and history of prior negotiations on these issues. It seemed that the prime motivation driving the Indians was to have a conference at Thimpu under their aegis. Jayewardene predictably sent to the talks a second-string team comprised of jurists and constitutional experts with no direct political authority to negotiate anything. India, through RAW, literally forced the Tamil militants, in the form of ENLF, to come to the negotiating table along with TULF and PLOTE.

The "talks" rapidly descended into a shouting match between the two sides. Whereas the militants wanted as a first step the acceptance of their four demands or principles (recognition of the Tamils as a nation, the right to their traditional homelands, the right to self-determination, and the rights of all Tamils to citizenship), the Sri Lankan delegation queried the legitimacy of these groups to speak for Sri Lankan Tamils at all and pointed out that conceding to the four demands was tantamount to a concession to Eelam. They further alienated the Tamils by tabling a diluted version of the district development scheme that had already been rejected by the latter in the preceding year's All-Parties Conference.[5]

Between the first and second round of talks, the cease-fire between the militants and the Jayewardene regime was shattered with more killings and reprisals in northern Sri Lanka. On the day the second round of talks resumed, Sri Lankan security forces massacred nearly two hundred civilians in the town of Vavuniya, triggering a walkout by the militants. As a penalty for the failure at Thimpu, which they blamed entirely on the militants' intransigence, the Indian government ordered the deportation of two Sri Lankan Tamils, Anton Balasingham, the chief spokesman for LTTE, and C. Chandrahasan, son of Chelvanayagam and at this time close to TELO. Although Sri Lankan politicians enjoyed the spectacle immensely (seeing it as a payoff for wooing Bhandari so assiduously), those familiar with the details and history of the negotiations were baffled at this bizarre turn in Indian policy. It was evident that neither the Sri Lankan government nor the Tamil militants were ready for negotiations and had come to Thimpu largely to indulge India's desire to host a meeting between the two groups and to appear as the region's peacemaker and moral leader. In addition to other factors, Jayewardene desperately needed to demonstrate to various western aid agencies and donors that he was pursuing something more than a military option against the Tamils. Yet the hastily set up conference had crucial consequences, some perhaps intended and others that became clear only post facto. It further marginalized TULF among Tamils as the militants now moved to center stage. It indicated to the more canny among the militant groups (especially LTTE) and to some in the Jayewardene regime that Indian policy making revealed an overweening desire for enacting such spectacles that might be worth exploiting.

The year following the collapse of the talks saw the various Tamil militant groups settling their internecine rivalries through murder, while the Sri Lankan government, momentarily spared the close attention of New Delhi, attacked their strongholds in the North and East, often in the midst of dense civilian populations. The new minister of national security (and deputy minister of defense), Lalith Athulathmudali, went after the militants with scant regard for civilian casualties. Based on its experiences in ENLF and Thimpu, the LTTE decided it was time to establish its supremacy over the other Tamil groups and to ensure that Indian efforts to control the militant movement did not come to pass. In February 1986, it withdrew from the RAW-sponsored ENLF. Then, in a dramatic escalation between April 28 and May 4, 1986, it virtually decimated TELO. Hundreds of TELO cadres were killed in Sri Lanka, including its leader, Sri Sabaratnam. The two reasons given by the LTTE for the massacre of TELO cadres were: first, they were a group of criminals and robbers, and second, they "were acting as the agent of Indian imperialism" (Hoole et al. 1990, 83). While RAW's protégé was being massacred, the agency remained curiously indifferent.

If the decimation of TELO indicated LTTE's desire to become independent of Indian influence, the timing of the attack confirmed it. The attack occurred one day before the two new Indian emissaries charged with responsibility for Sri Lankan affairs, P. Chidambaram (a minister and Congress MP from Tamil Nadu) and Natwar Singh (former foreign service officer and Congress MP), arrived in Colombo for talks with the Sri Lankan goverment and TULF. On May 3, with Chidambaram and Singh still in Colombo, an Air Lanka Tristar plane was blown up at Katunayake Airport, killing seventeen and injuring forty. This was followed by a bomb explosion at the Central Telegraph Office, which killed a dozen people and injured more than a hundred.

Chidambaram's approach was quite different from Bhandari's. A lawyer by training and with some expertise in constitutional matters, he focused on details involving devolution of powers, drafts of proposed amendments to the Constitution, drafts of proposals to set up provincial councils, the nature of elections to the government, the distribution of police and security forces between the center and the regions, land settlements, and other matters. The first draft of proposals between Chidambaram and the Sri Lankan government, numbering more than fifty pages, called for provincial councils instead of district councils, but stayed clear of a merged northeastern province (which meant none of the militant groups would have any truck with the proposals). Jayewardene then called a Political Parties Conference in June 1986, this time excluding the Bhikkhus, to discuss the Chidambaram proposals. The SLFP boycotted the meetings this time, ensuring no consensus of Sri Lankan opinion.

Then, Jayewardene typically began to waffle on key elements in the proposals. First, he introduced references to local bodies with powers that would whittle away what had been secured for the chief minister and the legislature of the provincial governments. Then he added a long and complex statistical note on land settlements that sought to deny the principle that the North and East constituted the traditional homelands of Tamils. In this section, he introduced new concepts into the equation, such as the National Settlement Schemes and the National Ethnic Ratios. TULF felt that these new schemes, if implemented, would result in "a further influx of Sinhalese colonists and the erosion of the demographic composition of the Tamil and Muslim populations (both Tamil-speaking and constituting about 65 per cent of the total) in the Eastern Province" (Wilson 1988, 198). After first promising that, unlike in the APC of 1984, this time he was not going to wait for a consensus but push the necessary legislation through Parliament, Jayewardene began to backtrack by August 1986, suddenly insisting that nothing would be enacted until the militants lay down all their arms. Finally, the retreat was completed when he decreed that executive powers in a provincial council would rest with the president-appointed governor of the council and not with the chief minister or legislature of the province. This last stipulation rendered farcical the entire exercise in devolving power to provincial councils. As always with Jayewardene on the question of devolution of power to Tamils, it was a case of one step forward and two steps back.[6] It was also obvious that Jayewardene had discounted neither the military option (which was proceeding apace) nor waiting out India or capitalizing on weaknesses and divisions on the Indian side, as he had done at Thimpu.

Meanwhile, LTTE appeared to have widened the sources of its finances and arms, besides becoming more sophisticated in propaganda and organizational matters. It now had offices for publicity in a number of world capitals, including London, Geneva, and Paris, besides a visible presence in Malaysia, the United States, Canada, and Australia. It was hardly recognizable as one of the innumerable outfits that had been picked up by RAW for training a few years before and was by now quite independent of its Indian sponsors, besides being the most dominant militant group. In October 1986, under pressure from the Indian goverment to accept the proposed Provincial Councils Bill being mooted as a follow-up to the Chidambaram proposals, LTTE virtually declared Eelam. Prabhakaran announced his intention to return to Jaffna and take over civil administration of the northern province in January 1987. They would then establish their own system of courts, police, and justice, and issue their own currency. For some time now, LTTE had been collecting "taxes" from the people of Jaffna to conduct its war.

As LTTE loomed as a threat to Indian plans vis-à-vis Sri Lanka, the central government still had one last card to play: MGR, the chief minister of Tamil Nadu. The latter had favored LTTE ever since August 1984 and had maintained close contacts with its leadership (for his possible motivations in doing this, see the previous chapter). It was now up to him to deliver LTTE to the negotiating table and get them to settle for something less than Eelam, perhaps some variation of the Chidambaram-Singh proposals. Besides demonstrating his importance and loyalty to the government in Delhi, delivering LTTE to the negotiating table could further his image as a champion of Tamils vis-à-vis Karunanidhi and DMK. The LTTE, of course, wooed MGR because he was in power and in a position to help them. At the same time, they were quite realistic that his support for them had more to do with his desire to stay on the right side of New Delhi and to score points against Karunanidhi than with any desire to help create Eelam.

THE SAARC SUMMIT OF 1986

After the debacle at Thimpu, the Indians decided that the SAARC summit to be held in Bangalore in November 1986 would be an ideal stage on which to announce a settlement to the ethnic conflict in Sri Lanka under their sponsorship. The fact that Jayewardene and the Tamil militants seemed as far apart as ever didn't seem to matter very much to the Indians. Rather, they expected MGR to deliver the LTTE and were confident that they would be able to cajole Jayewardene into agreeing to some version of the Chidambaram-Singh proposals worked out earlier that year in July. The militants were in a particularly weak position at this time.

Since their large-scale exodus to Tamil Nadu after July 1983, the militants had done much to squander the initial hospitality and sympathy of their hosts. Besides the blast at Meenambakkam Airport, there had been many occasions when locals and militants had clashed—for example, in the coastal town of Vedaranyam in December 1985. In May 1986, a militant shot at locals in Saligramam, Madras; villagers in Pudukottai District had petitioned that the

PLOTE camp be moved from their midst on account of looting and robberies; and there had been clashes between fishermen and militants on fishing rights in the waters off Tamil Nadu.[7] On November 1, 1986, two incidents further contributed to local alienation from the militants. A lawyer was shot dead by an EPRLF militant in the Choolaimedu area of Madras city, and on the same day, in protest against the repeated depredations made by a PLOTE camp, the people of Orathanadu in Thanjavur District had a violent altercation with the militants. Unlike in July 1983, when sympathy for the Sri Lankan Tamils was at its peak, these actions revealed a growing sense of alienation from the militants and even strong opposition to them in Tamil Nadu.

These circumstances seemed to be ideal for the Indian government to pressure the militants to come to the bargaining table and accept a deal based on the July proposals (or some variation thereof) negotiated between Chidambaram and Jayewardene. But in a significant change in policy, one that lacked a discernible rationale, the Indian government picked only LTTE to talk with Jayewardene at the SAARC summit. Although this decision may have been an accurate recognition of ground realities in Jaffna, where LTTE called the shots, one has to wonder about its wisdom, especially given that LTTE had repeatedly declared its intention to settle for nothing short of Eelam. At the very least, it set a dangerous precedent by further reinforcing LTTE's belief that it alone spoke for the Tamils of Sri Lanka. It reversed the entire logic of A. P. Venkateswaran (the foreign secretary who had replaced Bhandari) and the line of the Ministry of External Affairs, which involved pushing TULF to negotiate with Jayewardene in Colombo over the Chidambaram proposals. Finally, it negated the prevailing rationale wherein RAW was supposed to keep the various militant groups in some sort of a balance of power and combine them with the moderate TULF to pressure the Sri Lankan government. Now, suddenly, it appeared as if the Indian government was putting all its eggs in one basket, the LTTE.

As at Thimpu, the need to have an ostentatious and spectacular breakthrough on the ethnic conflict in Sri Lanka and to announce this breakthrough during the SAARC summit on Indian soil weighed more heavily on Indian decision making than any other considerations. The summit came four years after the regional organization had first been mooted and was deemed to be the perfect occasion to coronate India as regional hegemon by its sponsorship of a peace accord between the LTTE and the president of Sri Lanka.

However, before any such vision of doing a Camp David in Bangalore could become reality, LTTE had to be softened up, and Jayewardene had to be convinced of India's new tough stance against the militants. In order to accomplish both, the government of Tamil Nadu was ordered to disarm the Tamil militants summarily and place them under a close watch. The militants had been given virtually a free hand for the preceding three years and had far more sophisticated weapons than the police in the state of Tamil Nadu, where there were about thirty-one camps spread throughout ten districts. Despite the scale of the task, the disarming of the militants was successfully completed in predawn raids orchestrated by K. Mohandas, the state's director general of police. Mohandas estimates the arms seized that day to have been worth Rs. 40 crores and included "Surface-to-Air Missiles, AK 47 rifles, rocket launchers, two-inch mortars, hand grenades, rifles and pistols and a very large quantity of ammunition including long-range cartridges, apart from powerful explosives" (1992, 146).

Immediately after disarming the militants, Mohandas received word that Prabhakaran was to accompany MGR to Bangalore for the SAARC summit. What was on offer was a modified version of Chidambaram's July 1986 proposals. That is, the package on the table did not provide for merger and contained provisions that would continue Sinhala settlement in the eastern province, steadily changing the ethnic balance there. There was no way this offer was going to be acceptable to Prabhakaran: he flatly refused even to meet Jayewardene, let alone enter negotiations on such a package. The anticipated plans to announce a breakthrough in Bangalore in the form of a peace pact between Jayewardene and Prabhakaran, brokered by India, collapsed in a heap.

Prabhakaran returned to Madras. By all accounts, MGR was furious with his "intransigence" especially because it had caused him to lose face with New Delhi. A journalist who had access to Prabhakaran at this time remembered the fiasco at SAARC as marking the end of MGR's cordial relations with Prabhakaran. MGR felt that he had put his personal prestige on the line and promised to deliver Prabhakaran's agreement to New Delhi and that Prabhakaran had let him down. He called Prabhakaran on the telephone and spoke to him "like a schoolmaster," informing him that after this "you should be conducting the struggle from your own land."[8] Barely weeks after this conversation, in January 1987, Prabhakaran packed up and left Tamil Nadu for Jaffna.

In November 1986, the Indians seemed baffled by LTTE's decision not to play along at SAARC. They were unsure whether to push for a tough line and threaten to expel the group from India (hardly a threat because LTTE had already announced their intent to return to Jaffna) or whether to try and bring them into line through inducements (which wouldn't work because it seemed the group would settle for nothing short of Eelam). Clearly, the center had overestimated MGR's (and possibly RAW's)[9] leverage over Prabhakaran, just as it had probably underestimated the resolve of the latter. Nor was it convinced of Jayewardene's bona fides in settling the issue through negotiations. His actions after the SAARC summit showed a desire to capitalize on the estrangement between LTTE and the Indians by pursuing a military solution to the ethnic conflict.

On December 18, 1986, almost immediately after the summit, LTTE killed more than one hundred members of the EPRLF, including prominent leaders. The reason given for this massacre was the same as that given for the TELO massacre: EPRLF had moved too close to India and RAW (Swamy 1994, 218). The massacre of the cadres of two groups regarded as close to RAW ought to have indicated at least a couple of things to the Indians: first, LTTE and RAW were already in a proxy war, reiterating the fact that modern conflict in South Asia is more pervasive and likely between intelligence agencies and covert outfits than it is between the uniformed personnel of national armies; and second, RAW's claims regarding its ability to control the militant groups, including the LTTE, were totally off the mark.

In a desperate attempt to salvage something in the aftermath of the SAARC summit, Chidambaram and Singh returned to Colombo for one more round of talks on the July 1986 proposals. The December 1986 proposals, as they came to be called, tried to push the idea of excising the Sinhalese-majority Amparai District from the eastern province and merging the latter with the North. At the end of the year, the Muslims still did not agree to this proposal, TULF had already left the talks, the Sinhalese would not countenance merger, and LTTE would settle for nothing short of Eelam.

By this time, it was obvious the Indians had moved along a strange trajectory: from being a party to the ethnic conflict in Sri Lanka by providing sanctuary and training to the militants in 1983 to becoming mediators who were more keen on "solving" the problem than the protagonists to the conflict themselves were. At both Thimpu and Bangalore, the Indian desire to broker a spectacular breakthrough on the ethnic conflict in Sri Lanka seemed to outweigh all other considerations. Having failed to pull this off by negotiations, the Indians turned to alternative methods to demonstrate their hegemonic leadership in the region.

OF BRASSTACKS AND BLOODING MIRAGES

In late 1986 and early 1987, the Indian army embarked on an extraordinarily ambitious military exercise called Brasstacks.[10] One indication of the scale of the exercise is that it was not merely the largest military exercise ever conducted in South Asia, but among the largest mobilizations of any armed force in the world since World War II and comparable to the largest conducted by NATO and Warsaw Pact forces. The exercise was conducted east of the Indira Gandhi Canal in the state of Rajasthan and along a north-south axis: both meant to reassure Pakistan that the exercise was not in any way a camouflaged operation designed to invade that country. The presence of the canal between the troops and the Indo-Pakistan border meant any rapid movement of men and materiel across the canal would involve the use of gigantic water-crossing equipment: something not easily hidden from the other side. The north-south axis of the exercise meant any sudden westward move into Pakistan could be discounted, as the repositioning of troops would be a slow and lugubrious affair, again not likely if the exercise was a cover for something else.

Appealing to the sense of grandeur and gigantism that animated both Rajiv Gandhi and his army chief of staff, General Krishnaswamy Sundarji, as well as the rest of the regime, Brasstacks involved the coordinated action of the army, the different wings of the Indian government, Indian Railways, Indian Airlines, and various port authorities. Indeed the "bigness" of the exercise seemed to be its main propellant. As Kanti Bajpai and colleagues note, "The 'bigness' of the Exercise seems to have fascinated him [Rajiv Gandhi], because he wanted it to be larger than any other held earlier in the South Asian subcontinent. It would seem that he had no larger political or strategic objective in mind although it was believed by some that he wished to strike a heroic posture and impress the neighbors" (1995, 20). Due to a series of perceptions and misperceptions, information and disinformation, signals and crossed signals—all built on a four-decade long history punctuated by enmity and warfare—at one stage (circa January 23, 1987) it appeared as if a war between India and Pakistan was imminent, almost unavoidable. With more than a million troops massed along the border, the situation was poised on a hair trigger. After direct conversations at the highest levels, the face-off gradually subsided and the crisis slowly died down by the end of February 1987.

Although the full details surrounding Brasstacks would take us too far afield, two aspects of it are worthy of elaboration. First, decision making on the Indian side was obviously vitiated by poor coordination between various institutions and agencies, but also by a seeming incapacity to fathom what these actions must look like to counterparts in Pakistan. Second, the momentum driving the exercise seemed to be a sense of grandeur and arrogance, an almost juvenile fascination for gigantism and high technology, with little or no thought attached to the consequences or the larger national purpose (such as that may be) of the exercise itself. In a trenchant comment on the entire episode, one observer noted that "we are left with an overriding and unfortunate impression—our prime minister is unable to command his own brief and, what is even more distressing, he is no longer able to conceal his incomprehension of it either" (Jaswant Singh, quoted in Bajpai et al. 1995, 29).

One of the fall-outs of the exercise was that it soured relations between the prime minister and his chief of staff, General Sundarji. Apparently, the prime minister felt that General Sundarji and the minister of state for defense, Arun Singh, had not kept him fully informed on exactly how things were building up during the exercise. This was especially true for a short period when the prime minister was on vacation on an offshore island and was stunned on his return to discover how close to war the two countries were. Further, nearly all circumstantial evidence pointed to General Sundarji and

Arun Singh having overstepped their own authority to the point where they could be accused, whatever their actual intent, of usurping the authority of the prime minister and indeed of acting as de facto prime ministers.

Brasstacks had been preceded by an exercise of similarly gargantuan scale vis-à-vis the Chinese, which was called Operation Checkerboard. It was evident theatrical politics had become the main modus operandi of the Rajiv administration at this time. Yet, although Brasstacks revealed a ship of state that was seriously adrift, it is important that the denouement of the entire exercise was not grand or worthy of a hegemon: it ended with a whimper rather than a bang, and at this point Rajiv's government was characterized by "an imperial culture or air... relatively untested... [and] lack[ing] in experienced political leadership" (Bajpai et al. 1995, 69): they were simply spoiling for a chance to display their military might.

In January 1987, Jayewardene decided to jettison talks on the Chidambaram proposals and to switch tracks to the military option. January seemed opportune for a number of reasons. India seemed to have run its course with LTTE and seemed distracted, what with all the furor over Brasstacks and other domestic issues. Jayewardene himself had never ever really given up the military option. In fact, quite the contrary: his actions in 1984–87 are better interpreted as a man wanting to hit the Tamils as hard militarily as he could, but being dragged unwillingly to negotiations by the Indians. The diplomatic interludes seem, at least in retrospect, efforts by him to fob off the Indians (as well as various international aid agencies) and to buy time to arm and train his troops. The militants had been stating this argument all along, and at least one other Sri Lankan observer would agree entirely (see Jayatilleka 1995, 10).

In 1987, Jayewardene had less than two years to serve out as president. Although he did not rule out running for a third term until the latter half of 1988, he was by now an old man, and chances were Sri Lanka would elect a new president in the next elections. There were three obvious contenders for nomination in the UNP: Prime Minister Premadasa, the minister of lands and development, Gamini Dissanayake, and the minister of national security, Lalith Athulathmudali. Whereas Dissanayake and Athulathmudali came from privileged backgrounds, the upper caste, and prestigious schools and universities, Premadasa had fought his way from a lower-middle-class background to become heir apparent of the UNP in the era of mass politics. By no stretch a man of privilege, he represented the changing face of Sri Lankan politics as it vernacularized from the *goyigama* (upper castes) to people like himself. Each of these men was positioning himself for a run at the presidency, and his stance on the ethnic question would determine, to a considerable degree, his prospects.

In their respective plays to achieve power, they situated themselves carefully in terms of the narrative of Sinhala identity outlined in previous chapters. A number of enunciative opportunities presented themselves: one was appealing to Sinhala majoritarian chauvinism by attacking the Tamils as fifth columnists who were externally sponsored by India; a second option was splitting the Sri Lankan Tamils from the Indians and currying favor with the latter by pandering to their notions of regional hegemony; yet another position was actually accepting Sri Lanka as a multiethnic and plural society in which Tamils had their place (this last position was best articulated by actor-politician Vijaya Kumaratunge of the United Socialist Alliance at this time). In the months that followed, the three heirs apparent—Premadasa, Athulathmudali, and Dissanayake—jostled with each other, trying to figure which mode of self-fashioning would likely propel them to the presidency.

Premadasa and Athulathmudali made very clear their antipathy toward India and the latter's pretensions on mediating the ethnic question. Given the minority complex of most Sri Lankans vis-à-vis their huge neighbor and Indian provocations through the 1980s, the anti-Indian line could pay rich dividends. Both politicians were perceived as hard-liners who regarded Indian interference as a primary stumbling block to any solution. It is not that either man ruled out cutting a deal with the Tamil ethnic minority (in fact, on that issue they were probably more amenable than Jayewardene), but rather that they set two preconditions at this time: first, Indian noninvolvement, and second, the "terrorists" laying down arms before negotiations.

The difference between the three men in terms of strategy owed more to the positions they came to occupy. As prime minister, Premadasa was already the party's anointed heir, and the nomination was his to lose. By continuing to take a hard line on India and the ethnic question he could, barring unforeseen circumstances, count on that nomination. This meant that Athulathmudali and Dissanayake, if they wished to out-flank Premadasa to the nomination, would have to accomplish something out of the ordinary. The two men adopted differing strategies in this attempt. Athulathmudali figured the conduct of the war against militants was his best bet. Because he was the premier strategist in the war and the minister of national security, the credit for any military victory over the militants would naturally accrue to him. Given the enduring Sinhala cosmology, often described as the "Mahavamsa mindset," a decisive victory over the Tamils, which would mean a victory by proxy over their Indian backers, and the reestablishment of Sinhalese dominion over Jaffna could well be Athulathmudali's ticket to the UNP nomination. He could anoint himself as a modern-day Duttagamini, the mythic Sinhala hero who had once defeated the Tamil king Elara and reunited the realm.

Dissanayake was no less a hard-liner on the ethnic issue, but he differed with the other two men on the role of India.[11] Citing the experience of Finland and the Soviet Union, he suggested Sri Lanka ought to try and establish a better equation with Delhi by showing a greater sensitivity to the latter's geopolitical ambitions and pretensions.[12] In this way, Sri Lanka might be able to isolate the militants by cutting the links with their sponsors. This line of thought, although vastly more risky than the positions held by either Premadasa or Athulathmudali, actually had tremendous potential, as events would reveal. Whether by accident or by a deep insight into the workings of the Indian political system, Dissanayake correctly figured that New Delhi's overwhelming concern was to be seen and recognized as regional hegemon by others in the neighborhood and beyond. The fate of Sri Lankan Tamils was of lesser importance in comparison with Indians' geopolitical ambitions, all their talk about the dangers of Tamil secessionism for India notwithstanding. (Of course, to some degree, this "finlandization" policy had been characteristic of Sri Lanka ever since independence; perhaps Dissanayake was merely seeking to bring Jayewardene's foreign policy back in line with that trajectory.)

A good many Indian demands in this context could be conceded by Sri Lanka with little or no loss to itself: on Trincomalee, on the Voice of America broadcast facilities, on Israeli advisers, on voting in the United Nations and in SAARC, and so on. By apparently kowtowing to the Indians, Sri Lanka could gain either their cooperation or at any rate their indifference on the Tamil question. Either way, the Sinhalese could then sort the Tamils out in their own time and on their own terms. The risk involved in Dissanayake's strategy was that it brought him closer to India at a time when such proximity could mean political suicide. Still, as the youngest of the three contenders, and the one on whom the odds were longest, Dissanayake perhaps had no choice but to try a high-risk strategy to outflank the others. And, in any case, the anti-India/anti-Tamil platform was too crowded already: besides Premadasa and Athulathmudali, SLFP and Mrs. Bandaranaike were prominently ensconced there. Moreover, the ultranationalist Janatha Vimukthi Peramuna was making tremendous headway amongst rural and urban youth, further adding to the size of the anti-India crowd.[13]

On January 8, 1987, under the overall command of Athulathmudali, the Sri Lankan army began operations against the militants in the north. In addition to a ground assault from seventeen camps, there were also air attacks. Casualties began to escalate between January and March, and the Sri Lankan army was gaining territory. In a scattered retreat, LTTE returned to the Jaffna peninsula, abandoning camps and outposts elsewhere. By March 7, Sri Lankan troops were closing in on the peninsula and were soon locked in battle against LTTE. For the first time, the latter was forced to call other militant groups to join the struggle against the Sri Lankan army. Almost just when Athulathmudali's operations began, Dissanayake arrived in New Delhi and announced that Colombo remained committed to some version of the December proposals of Chidambaram, an announcement contrary to what Jayewardene and others were doing and saying at this time. Then on January 22, 1987, Dissanayake stated that "If India has certain geopolitical perspectives about the region and feels that Sri Lanka should support them, we should be willing to look at it and come to an understanding with India on the vital perspectives of their concern" (quoted in Muni 1993, 98). Although this statement must have sounded like music to Indian ears, it also indicated the alternative paths to power being devised by Athulathmudali and Dissanayake at this point in time. As Sri Lankan troops forced the militants into retreat and began to corral them in the Jaffna peninsula, India made repeated protests in the subcontinent and global forums, urging Sri Lankans to desist from the military option and return to the negotiating table. These pleas and threats were either ignored or refuted by the Sri Lankan president.

On Good Friday, April 17, 1987, LTTE massacred 127 civilians. Four days later a bomb exploded in the Pettah bus stand in the heart of Colombo, killing more than a hundred people. The outrage of the Sinhalese can well be imagined. To talk of pursuing negotiations, with or without Indian mediation at this point, seemed ludicrous. The president and the prime minister of Sri Lanka once again expressed their intent to pursue the military option. Premadasa was explicit: "We have listened long enough. We have waited long enough. The time has come to wipe out this cancer from our midst.... Any friend who tells us to find a political solution [in an obvious reference to India] will be considered the biggest enemy" (Swamy 1994, 232).

Despite the attacks in the south, Athulathmudali's campaign proceeded to tighten the noose around the peninsula. The air raids from Sri Lanka's handful of World War II vintage Siai Marchetti and Pucara planes pounded civilians with crude homemade bombs, sometimes just drums of boiling tar or kerosene mixed with shrapnel, which would be lit and rolled out of the aircraft over towns and villages. The impact of the assaults and an embargo on Jaffna resonated in Tamil Nadu on a scale not seen since the pogrom of July 1983. On April 27, MGR announced a grant of Rs. 4 crores to LTTE and other militant groups to resist the economic embargo and military attacks.[14] Not to be outdone, Karunanidhi demanded an armed Indian intervention into Sri Lanka and the creation of a Cyprus-type situation there.

In early May, Indian overtures for reopening talks were rebuffed by both LTTE and the Sri Lankan government. In his May Day message and in the face of the army's assault, Prabhakaran reiterated that "an independent Tamil Eelam state is the only final solution" (see Statesman, June 5, 1987). Athulathmudali's campaign now shifted gears and on May 26, Operation Liberation began. Jayewardene inaugurated it by saying, "This is a fight to the finish. Either we win or they win" (Fernando 1988, 66). In an unexpected shift in the line of attack, the eight thousand–strong Sri Lankan army went for the eastern edge of the peninsula, the Vadamarachi coastline, instead of attacking, as one might have anticipated, the Jaffna or western end of the peninsula. By May 30, Prabhakaran's home town, Velvettithurai, had been overrun, and nearly one-fourth of the peninsula had been captured. On the next day, land's end along the eastern coastline of the peninsula, Point Pedro, fell to the advancing Sri Lankan forces. The next thing to consider was whether or not to take Jaffna.

Situated on the western end of the peninsula, a densely packed town of more than one hundred thousand people, Jaffna was the stronghold of the militants. It was, moreover, the cultural and political capital of the Tamil people, dominated by the centuries-old Dutch fort overlooking the ocean. There was no way an assault on Jaffna could avoid huge civilian casualties. By attacking from the east, Athulathmudali had accomplished something of considerable significance. The army had built up momentum with a series of victories and had gained ground rapidly. Now, with a naval blockade around the western coastline of the peninsula, they could attack Jaffna with a virtually free hand. Whether the army could repeat the success of Velvettithurai in Jaffna—with its thick population, narrow streets, concentration of militants and snipers, and the unavoidable attention of a world media—was an open question, ever to remain so because of Indian intervention in early June.

It became evident the Lankans had underestimated or, at any rate, guessed wrong about Indian intentions. A successful military assault led by Athulathmudali was unacceptable to the Indians: it was regarded as a decisive rejection of their hegemony in the region. After indicating they would not stand by if Jaffna was attacked or if the embargo was not lifted immediately, the Indians sent a Red Cross flotilla of about nineteen fishing boats with kerosene, cooking oil, and food from Rameswaram on the Tamil Nadu coast to Jaffna. The Sri Lankan navy stopped the flotilla from entering its waters and forced it to return to Rameswaram. The flotilla contained more journalists than Red Cross personnel and was intended as a major media spectacle to demonstrate India's new tough stance. In the event, the turnaround of the flotilla was seen by many as a punch in the nose, and the attempt was lampooned as "bumboat diplomacy." In a particularly unkind (because truthful) cut, one Sri Lankan naval officer is reported to have said, "take the supplies to Tamil Nadu where starvation [is] rampant" (Chopra 1987).

Still smarting from the incident, the Indians decided that on the next day (June 4, 1987), at approximately 4:00 P.M., five Antonov-

32 transport planes, escorted by four Mirage 2000 fighter jets of the Indian Air Force, would take off from Bangalore and drop about twenty-five tons of food and supplies over Jaffna a little before 5:00 P.M. The intent to air-drop food was communicated to the Sri Lankan high commissioner in New Delhi, Bernard Tillekeratne, as late as 4:00 P.M. that day when he was summoned to the office of the Indian minister of state for external affairs, Natwar Singh: in other words, Tillekeratne first heard of the operation just as the planes took off on their mission. A shocked Tillekeratne replied that his government was not even aware of the intended airdrop, and in the interests of avoiding any mishap, couldn't it be delayed? The Sri Lankans had, after all, in the aftermath of the returned flotilla, agreed to discuss the logistics of some Indian aid to Jaffna. What, then, was the necessity for such a blatantly aggressive and humiliating act? In the time it would take Tillekeratne to get back to his office and call Colombo, the airdrop would have commenced already. Tillekeratne had to use Natwar Singh's telephone to call and inform Jayewardene about the impending airdrop. The previous night (actually, the early hours of the morning of June 4), in a meeting which lasted from 1:00 A.M. to 4:00 A.M. and was headed by Rajiv Gandhi himself, the Political Affairs Committee of the cabinet met and decided on this course of action. Hence, primary responsibility for the decision to air-drop food supplies and the manner in which it was done has to be borne by the prime minister himself (see *India Today*, June 30, 1987, 24–35).

By midafternoon on June 4, anticipating a violent Sinhalese reaction to the news of the airdrop, Indian High Commissioner Dixit in Colombo had already moved confidential files and documents from his office to a safe place, and Indians resident in the city had been advised to go to Indian-run hotels and stay put in their rooms.[15] Dixit then bluntly conveyed a message to Athulathmudali as he informed the latter: "We will not let you take Jaffna." What transpired next is best left to Dixit himself to describe in an excerpt from my interview with him:

He [Jayewardene] was very angry. "So, Rajiv Gandhi will go to war, will he?" I said, "Sir, he doesn't have to." He said, "So, you're going to carry out air strikes?" I said, "No sir, it is not physically possible to carry out air strikes. If one of our Jaguars or Mirages really takes off on an air attack mission, by the time it reaches combat height it would cross the island of Sri Lanka and it cannot strike" [laughs heartily]. . . . When our AN 32s escorted by Mirages left, there was some noise that they will shoot some of them down, they'll fix them. When I heard this, I went to Lalith. I said, please convey to the president, and I want you to take note of this as national security minister, they will only come and drop this food and go away, and we'll have to protect them. Just so long as you realize that even if a single plane is shot at, these Mirages will fan out and destroy all your air fields. It will be a targeted operation, they will not affect the civilians. We know where all your air fields are, there aren't too many of them. Four or five, they will finish them off so you won't be able to do any more of your air operations. . . . He [Lalith] said, "You are acting like a bully," and I said, "No, I am just conveying to you the seriousness of the government of India. These are policy decisions." . . . I got a bad reputation as a result [laughs heartily].[16]

Of all the things India had done vis-à-vis Sri Lanka through the 1980s, the one act that has left a lasting impression and has continued to rankle most Sri Lankans long afterwards is the airdrop of June 4, 1987. Jayewardene, predictably, crystallized popular sentiment in a narrative that had deep resonance in Sinhala civil society. As Chief Guest at a ceremony on the enshrinement of Buddhist relics in Anuradhapura, a few days after the airdrop, he noted in a meticulous calculation that retrojected the idea of Sri Lanka back over two millenia: "In the long history of relations between India and the Indian states, we have been invaded 16 times from Indian soil and four times by powers from the Far East and the West. . . . [T]he Indian invasion of June 4 was the 21st. We were occupied for 715 years, the whole island or a portion of it, in a history of 2500 years. This [airdrop] has added a few hours to this total" (*Daily News*, Colombo, June 12, 1987).

The reactions of various other ministers in Jayewardene's cabinet echoed the idea that the Dhammadipa had been violated and inscribed the Indian action in a discourse of sacred space profaned by a long-standing historical adversary. Premadasa observed, "although the Portugese, Dutch and British invaded Sri Lanka and ruled us, the darkest period of our country dawned when the Cholas from South India invaded our country. King Dutugemunu . . . chased them away and a bright period dawned thereafter" (quoted in *Daily News,*

Colombo, June 12, 1987). Similarly, the minister of finance and planning, Ronnie De Mel, noted "a terrible calamity has befallen this country, unprecedented in recent history owing to our geographical and strategic proximity to the Indian subcontinent.... [D]espite all these invasions from South India, the Sinhala race, our religion, our culture and literature and our traditions could never be destroyed because of the unremitting efforts of the Mahasangha and the undaunted courage of the Sinhala heroes of yore" (quoted in *Daily News*, June 5, 1987).

Repeatedly, one finds the equation of Sri Lanka with Sinhala and the jettisoning of any pretense toward being a multiethnic or plural society. Besides the retrospective illusion that charts an unbroken genealogy of the "Sinhala nation" over two thousand years, the source of the impure outsider is always South India and the depredations of the (Tamil) Chola dynasty is unfavorably contrasted even with Dutch, Portuguese, and British colonialisms. The interplay of identity and difference within these discourses of the nation in danger are illustrative: Sri Lankan identity is constructed as exclusively Sinhalese in counterpoise to the Indian and (by derivation) Tamil other.

Elsewhere, Premadasa was more earthy and blunt about the latest Indian provocation. He described the airdrop as the act of "dogs that had shat on the Jaffna peninsula" (quoted in *India Today*, June 30, 1987, 27). From a discursive universe of international law and the proper conduct of interstate relations, Foreign Minister A. C. S. Hameed protested against this "naked violation" of Sri Lankan sovereignty and integrity. He noted that "ultimately what we got was a demarche of 35 minutes. Delhi did not give us any explanation while announcing its plan to intrude into our airspace. What added insult to injury was that we were told that any resistance would be met with force. You cannot issue threats like that. You don't conduct bilateral relations like that.... [Y]ou...cannot conduct diplomatic relations in this fashion" (*India Today*, June 30, 1987).

Various Sri Lankan leaders constructed the Indian airdrop in terms of the sacrality of national space and its violation by a long-standing enemy on behalf of a traitorous domestic minority, a construction that allowed them both to fashion the nation in specific forms and to locate themselves in a discursive formation as patriots and defenders of the realm. On the other side, Indian newspapers could

scarcely conceal their pride at this display of machismo. In an editorial, the nation's leading English-language newspaper noted that
"basic issues affecting India's security are also at stake. As it is, too
much rope has been given to the Sri Lankan government allowing it
to vastly strengthen its armed forces with external assistance....
The question now is whether New Delhi should go in for a Cyprus-
type solution. If it decides against this option, then it must decide
what other solution it can live with. And even if New Delhi remains
opposed to direct intervention it cannot allow Mr Jayewardene to
achieve military victory over the militants" ("Firmness at Last," editorial, *Times of India,* June 3, 1987). All agency here is confined to
the Indians: they decide on various options; they evaluate when too
much rope has been given or what outcomes they can live with;
they dispense solutions to the problem and can allow and disallow
various scenarios. Sri Lanka is nothing more than a blank slate on
which Indian policy makers can inscribe their desires. Striking a similar tone of an unquestioned right to dispose of Sri Lankan affairs,
an editorial in New Delhi's leading daily observed that "New Delhi
cannot be faulted for its growing impatience with the involvement
of Israel and Pakistan in Sri Lanka.... India does not need to act as
Big Brother but this factor cannot be deemed a license for smaller
powers in the region for showing the thumb to New Delhi and ignoring its legitimate regional sensibilities" ("A Policy at Last," editorial, *Hindustan Times,* June 5, 1987).

The idea that India was the rightful regional hegemon in South
Asia was best exemplified by the *Hindu,* a newspaper known hitherto
for its relative staidness and sobriety. In two editorials, the newspaper revealed that the latest spectacle enacted in Sri Lanka spoke to
important anxieties regarding a national self-image in an international theater. The *Hindu* editorialized, "Every child in the South
Asian region must be expected to know that the physical, political,
military and logistical capabilities to counter the Sri Lankan ruling
clique's brutal course against innocent Tamil civilians is [*sic*] very
much in the possession of India—that is not the problem at all"
("A Message to Sri Lanka," June 6, 1987). The pronounced anxiety
and fear of being shown up as less than masculine in the hard world
of realpolitik was further reflected when the *Hindu* noted that "The
international ramifications of this will be considerable, but the consequences of being shown up as weak-kneed will be even greater for

India. Today, India is being perceived in the region as a power that cannot assist its friends or influence its neighbors. The failure to take another step after its unprecedented airdrop will certainly lead to the collapse of the Tamil cause and will only serve to confirm India's infirmity in the worst possible manner" (*Hindu,* June 9, 1987). Although a small handful of Indian columnists distinguished themselves by rising above this discourse that saw Indian belligerence toward a smaller neighbor as action befitting a strong and hypermasculine regional power,[17] most were rife with jingoism and full of praise for the government. In perhaps the perfect exclamation point to this testosterone-driven militarism, the correspondent of the *Hindustan Times* observed that the airdrop was the first opportunity to "blood" the newly acquired Mirage 2000s of the Indian Air Force (June 5, 1987).

In the aftermath of the airdrop, Jayewardene was boxed into a corner on the domestic political scene as well. Even prior to the airdrop, Colombo was the site of massive opposition protests and rallies. A month before, on May Day, all the opposition parties and various extremist fringes such as the rapidly reemerging JVP and sections of the Buddhist clergy, held a huge rally in Colombo's Campbell Park. May Day celebrations had been banned by the UNP government, but the defiance of the ban was total. The opposition demanded a general election and refused to participate in upcoming local government polls (scheduled for August 15). This rally was quickly followed by a series of strikes that paralyzed many critical services: students, teachers, nurses, doctors, professionals. More than anything else, Jayewardene was stunned by the lack of worldwide condemnation of India's actions, especially from the United States and Britain. After considering whether to demand that India be reprimanded in the Security Council of the United Nations, he gave up on the idea when it didn't gain much support. A move to censure India in SAARC fell through as well, thwarted by the proviso in its charter that excluded bilateral issues from its purview. Although China and some of the other South Asian nations protested, the silence from the rest of the world was deafening.[18] The message he was receiving from most western powers was that he should settle his differences with the Indians and get them to help him rather than pursue a confrontation with them. In addition to all these factors, there was, finally, Jayewardene's state of mind: he was convinced that the Indians were out to topple him. Although he had entertained such fears ever since Mrs. Gandhi returned to power in 1980, it seemed to preoccupy, almost obsess, him in the period of May–July 1987. He was afraid of an Indian invasion to be followed by Mrs. Bandaranaike's assuming the presidency. He realized that once the Indians ruled out the military option he had pursued under Athulathmudali's initiative, he would need to find a way out. At this point, the line suggested by Dissanayake, which had not seemed all that promising earlier, began to look like his only bet. With a powerful country such as India maintaining the peace in the North, he could turn his attention to fire-fighting operations in the South, where things were rapidly spinning out of control due to the insurgency mounted by the JVP.[19]

THE INDO–SRI LANKA AGREEMENT OF JULY 1987

Of all the instances of spectacular politics examined in this chapter, the signing of the Indo–Sri Lanka Agreement (ISLA) of July 29, 1987, was undoubtedly the most theatrical. Between the airdrop and the signing of the agreement by Rajiv and Jayewardene was a period of less than two months, and yet, within that time, a document that significantly altered Indo-Lankan relations and the ethnic conflict within Sri Lanka was signed. In both its coercive and consensual aspects, the document is a perfect showpiece for Indian notions of regional hegemony. Thus, one part of the agreement reflects complete Sri Lankan capitulation to India's geopolitical requirements and unambiguously recognizes Indian primacy in the region at the expense of its own autonomy and sovereignty. Another part of the document deals with the ethnic struggle in Sri Lanka, and here Indian hegemony in its supposedly benign and progressive dimensions is reflected by the changed vocabulary used to fashion Sri Lankan identity.

Taking up the latter issue first, the ISLA built upon the trail of documents from Annexure C of late 1983 to the proposals of Chidambaram and Natwar Singh of December 19, 1986. In this regard, the relevant portions of the agreement called for the establishment of provincial councils (including the merger of the North and East pending a referendum in the eastern province) to whom powers would be devolved; the explicit recognition that Sri Lanka was a multiethnic, multilingual, multireligious society; and the recognition of Tamil and English as official languages in addition to Sinhalese. The recognition of Sri Lanka's plural character and the establishment of the provincial councils went against the grain of both its unitary Constitution and the discourse of Sinhala majoritarianism that dominated its postcolonial political experience in general. In forcing the Sri Lankans to recognize their plural and multiethnic character, the Indian government was powerfully embellishing its image as a progressive and democratic force in the region, always a critical component of its self-anointed role as hegemon.

Much of the rest of the agreement focused on geopolitical and military issues. Although India would ensure Sri Lanka did not disintegrate (a real possibility were it to fight a two-front war: against the militants in the North and the rapidly growing JVP insurgents in the South), the Lankans had to accept the geopolitical realities of South Asia. They had to realize that pursuing a military solution to the ethnic war was unacceptable to the Indians; that extraregional and other powers hostile to India should not be in Sri Lanka; and that concessions had to be made on issues such as Trincomalee, the Voice of America broadcasting office, Israeli and British mercenaries, and Pakistani and Chinese military training and weapons. In return for Sri Lankan recognition of their pluralist character and these geopolitical realities, the Indians would become a direct participant in a solution to the ethnic crisis: they would "underwrite and guarantee the resolutions, and co-operate in the implementation of these proposals." The Indians agreed to ensure that their territory would not be used in a manner prejudicial to the Sri Lankans and that they would cooperate with the Sri Lankan navy in preventing militant movement across the Straits. Crucially, they would bear the responsibility of getting the Tamils to accept the agreement and to disarm the militants if they did not surrender their arms to representatives of the Red Cross. Further, "an Indian Peace Keeping Contingent may be invited by the President of Sri Lanka to guarantee and enforce the cessation of hostilities, if so required."[20]

This summary of the document reflects its recent genealogy and the circumstances under which its line of thinking gained currency. It clearly represented the line of thought articulated by Gamini Dissanayake: in exchange for Sri Lanka's recognition of India's regional hegemonic pretensions, India was brought in as an underwriter of the agreement itself. It contained the possibility of splitting the Indians from the Sri Lankan Tamils and even of possibly pitting the Indians against the militants, specifically the LTTE. This last point was something that would become clear only as efforts to implement the agreement unfolded, and it is difficult to argue that Jayewardene or Dissanayake envisaged the way things would turn out. However, caught up in the euphoria of getting the Lankans to agree to such far-reaching concessions on their domestic and regional policy, and of having signed an agreement that would resolve the ethnic struggle in Sri Lanka by according greater rights and autonomy to a minority, the Indian government seemed oblivious to this possibility until it was too late. The Indians felt that the Indo–Sri Lanka Agreement of July 1987 would serve as the model for other countries in the region in framing their relations with India. Many who were close to Rajiv Gandhi at this time were convinced that the agreement was a major accomplishment in terms of securing India's paramountcy in the Indian Ocean region (although which countries seriously wished to infringe upon this self-anointed paramountcy were never clearly elaborated). Most of all, such individuals were quite certain that the agreement had made headlines all across the world and had greatly embellished India's image as a regional power and, specifically, Gandhi's image as a daring peacemaker and a statesman of international standing.[21]

One of the most striking aspects of the ISLA is that although it concerned the affairs of three important groups — namely, the Indian and Sri Lankan governments and the Sri Lankan Tamils — only the two governments were involved in its actual drafting in the period between June 4 and mid-July 1987. The Sri Lankan Tamils, to the extent they were represented at all, had their views ventriloquated for them by Indian and Sri Lankan officials, but in no direct way did either the moderate politicians of the TULF or the militants play any role in the drafting of the ISLA. As Prabhakaran would point out, although the ISLA took good care of India's geopolitical demands vis-à-vis the Sri Lankan regime, it dramatically altered the equation between Tamils and Sinhalese in Sri Lanka, something that no one had arrogated the Indians any right to negotiate on their behalf (*India Today*, August 15, 1987).

In the weeks of June and early July, one of the main issues that divided the Indian and Sri Lankan regimes was the question of merger of the northern and eastern provincial councils. Although no Tamil party would agree to a compromise that did not involve merging the North and East, the Sinhalese majority would not accept merger because they regarded it as tantamount to a breakup of the country. Any consensus on merger seemed impossible and continued to defy resolution until mid-July. Its "resolution" would capture in a microcosm all the problems of the impending agreement itself. Jayewardene came up with a suggestion that won the approval of the Indians: temporary merger of the North and East, pending a referendum to be held in the eastern province before December 31, 1988, in which a simple majority opposing the merger could reverse it (De Silva and Wriggins, 1994, 636–38). A clause stating that "The President may, at his discretion, decide to postpone such a Referendum" was then added, which would enable Indians to highlight the fact that merger (albeit one that had to be approved by a referendum, or "merger-minus" as it came to be called in discussions) had been conceded, while simultaneously Jayewardene could sell the agreement to the Sinhalese by saying, yes, we have temporarily conceded on merger, but we can reverse it in the referendum.

The resolution of the merger question was inadequate in that everyone suspected they were the ones who were going to be victimized by it in the course of time and hence were predisposed to preemptively double-cross the others. This predisposition is evident in what happened later. Jayewardene stated his intent to go out and campaign against merger whenever the referendum was held (Muni 1993, 106), and Dissanayake, in his capacity of minister of lands and development, seemed to increase the pace of Sinhala settlements in the river valley projects in the eastern province. Rajiv Gandhi pushed the idea that the proposed referendum would never take place: using his prerogative under the added clause, the Sri Lankan president would indefinitely keep postponing the referendum in the East. In this context, the following exchange between Rajiv Gandhi and a group of Tamil militants is instructive of the diverse understandings of the situation:

> On the question of the merger of the northern and the eastern provinces, the [Tamil] groups raised the objection of why it should be subjected to a referendum. Rajiv Gandhi responded: "The clause saying that the merger will be subjected to a referendum has been inserted into the Accord to sell the proposals to the Sinhalese. *The merger will never take place.* It will be postponed indefinitely." Gandhi

went further in assuring the groups by stating: "President Jayewardene personally gave me his assurance on the matter." ... When this author asked President Jayewardene whether he gave such an assurance to the Prime Minister of India, the latter said: "No, never." (Gunaratna 1993, 191, emphasis added)[22]

Between mid-June and mid-July, discussions on the proposed agreement gained pace despite this ambiguous resolution of the merger issue. In the meantime, hoping to bring matters back on to the track of a military solution, Athulathmudali departed to Pakistan and the United States, while another fast-rising UNP leader, Ranil Wickramasinghe, went to China with similar designs. Nothing tangible by way of support sufficient to counter the Indians was forthcoming from these quarters, further impelling the line pursued by Jayewardene and Dissanayake. Premadasa was in Japan from July 9 to July 25 and was either unaware that an agreement of such magnitude was in the works (which seems highly unlikely) or had judiciously abstained himself from affairs of state at this time.

Before the agreement was actually signed, Jayewardene's cabinet would have to be convinced of its merits. In a rather extraordinary departure from norms, Indian High Commissioner Dixit twice addressed the Sri Lankan cabinet, explaining the agreement. In terms of cabinet procedure, once a decision is put to a vote and carries a majority, a cabinet member either fully supports the decision or resigns from the cabinet. A vote on accepting the agreement was not necessary: there was no opposition. Although both Premadasa and Athulathmudali made critical comments about the agreement to newspapers and at public speeches, and boycotted some of the social functions associated with its signing, they did not record their dissent in the cabinet meetings or resign on this count. (To his credit, one member of the cabinet, Gamini Jayasuria, did resign.)[23]

The Indians now had the more difficult task of carrying the militants, although Gandhi had already made it clear that he was going to sign the agreement, with or without their support. The various militant groups other than LTTE could do little to oppose India: they had been politically marginalized and militarily defeated by LTTE. Although they had signficant objections to various ambiguities in the agreement, they had little choice but to acquiesce. The attitude of the various militant groups (barring LTTE) was perhaps best captured by V. Balakumar of EROS when he noted, "We were informed that India would be going ahead with the agreement which, in any case, is between them and Sri Lanka. Nobody asked us for our approval. Whether we support it or reject the agreement doesn't matter. India is going ahead with it. How can we prevent it?" (quoted in *India Today*, August 15, 1987, 77).

Their reservations about the agreement were by no means negligible and were in fact crucial. On issues such as merger, on the use of the term "historical habitations" instead of "traditional homelands" in the agreement, on the second-class status given to Tamil although it was classified as an "official language," on the real extent of devolution of power to the proposed provincial councils, on the difficulties of such devolution while Sri Lanka remained a unitary state, and on the issue of continued Sinhala colonization of lands in the North and East, the agreement did seem to sell short their interests. Dixit and Foreign Secretary K. P. S. Menon met with representatives of all militant groups and explained the terms of the agreement.[24] TULF had similar reservations, but having been politically marginalized, there was little it could do. It did write a detailed letter to Gandhi containing these reservations about the agreement and handed it over during the meeting, but that was that (TULF 1988, 147).

Now came the thorny question of the LTTE and their coming aboard the proposed agreement. Despite reverses in the Vadamarachi operation, they remained a significant military and political force in Jaffna. Dixit's first secretary (political) Hardeep Singh Puri flew into Jaffna on July 19 to apprise Prabhakaran of the impending agreement. He told him that merger of the North and East had been accepted, as was official status for Tamil. It is not known, however, if Puri conveyed the ambiguous terms in which both these concessions by the Sri Lankans was actually worded in the agreement. Prabhakaran set two preconditions: first, Sri Lankan troops must move back to the pre-Vadamarachi situation, and second, all Tamil refugees must be resettled safely in their homes. Puri flew back to Colombo, and both preconditions were worked into the agreement.

On July 24, Puri returned to Jaffna and persuaded Prabhakaran to come to New Delhi to sort out directly with the prime minister himself any remaining differences. What Prabhakaran expected to happen there, to what extent he was familiar with the details of the proposed agreement, and what actually happened in New Delhi are all matters of controversy. Many in the Indian government were of the view that Prabhakaran, albeit with reservations, had accepted the terms of the agreement, especially after an eleventh-hour personal meeting with Gandhi (lasting nearly ninety minutes) on the night of July 28 in which many of his concerns were addressed. In other words, some argue that prior to its signing, he had accepted the agreement. Some others disagree. They aver that Prabhakaran was kept virtually under house arrest and incommunicado while in New Delhi and subject to tremendous pressure by RAW and others. He was not apprised of the detailed contents of the proposed agreement until he reached New Delhi, and when he saw it, he was shocked. He first said that he had been tricked and that the agreement was a complete sellout of Tamil aspirations. He eventually agreed under duress and to ensure his safe return to Jaffna.[25] Moreover, Gandhi failed to follow up on the personal assurances he gave in the course of his meeting with Prabhakaran and Balasingham: he did not even meet them after his return from Colombo on July 30, although they were forced to remain in Delhi for another couple of days.[26]

Although it would be impossible to sift between these competing versions to come up with something like what really happened, LTTE's reservations about the agreement were substantive and could not be dismissed out of hand. In addition to the concerns voiced by the other Tamil groups, their past experience with Jayewardene and the Sinhalese gave them little reason to trust them. Second, although the agreement secured important geopolitical concerns for India, it left the Tamils in an unprotected situation. After Sri Lankan troops returned to their pre–May 25 positions, the timetable in the agreement stipulated that the twelve-year long militant movement be completely diarmed in seventy-two hours. Third, the committee monitoring the proposed referendum would consist of five members, four of whom were to be presidential nominees and the fifth to be selected from the eastern province, thus leaving the northerners out of any role in overseeing the referendum itself. The requirement of a simple majority, rather than two-thirds, to overturn the merger rendered its reversal almost a fait accompli given the altered demographics of the eastern province from decades of colonization and the troubled equation between the Tamils and Muslims in that province. Finally, while the Sri Lankan army continued to be a presence in the region, the complete disarmament of the militant groups was something LTTE could not countenance: to disarm would mean Tamils were left at the mercy of the Sinhalese and had only India to defend them in the future, a precarious state of affairs to say the least.

As the date for signing neared, the contents of the agreement or versions thereof leaked out in Sri Lanka, evoking mass protests, violent rallies, arson, and looting in Colombo. The banned JVP was a rapidly growing presence, with the SLFP, the bhikkhus, and other oppositional groups also energized by this sellout of national autonomy. Dixit remembers that just days prior to the signing of the agreement, Jayewardene himself had a moment of doubt and began to wonder if he should go through with it: "I took the final draft to him, probably twenty-sixth of July. Riots started on the twenty-seventh. Twenty-eighth he called me and said, 'Are you sure you want to go through with this, can't we wait?' I said, 'Sir, at this stage, after everybody has announced that we are going to sign this, you pull back.... Of course, if you say no, we can't force you, but then the consequences are unpredictable. I don't really know what will happen.' "[27] On the evening of July 28, Jayewardene was not the only one who was having doubts as to whether he should go through with the signing. Many in Rajiv's cabinet and the Political Affairs Committee in New Delhi, reading reports of violence in Colombo, were second-guessing the prime minister's proposed trip. Finally, on grounds that such a late cancellation might precipitate utter chaos in Sri Lanka, it was agreed that Rajiv would fly out the next morning to Colombo. Helicopters then flew the Indian prime minister and his entourage from Katunayake Airport to the president's official residence on Galle Face Green: a motorcade through town from the airport was deemed too dangerous. In any event, the streets were completely deserted, Colombo being under curfew. Seven of the twenty-eight ministers in Jayewardene's cabinet abstained themselves, including Premadasa and Athulathmudali. At 3:30 P.M., the agreement was signed in the audience hall of the presidential palace.

Even before the agreement had been signed, Jayewardene asked Gandhi if they might activate a certain portion of it—the part pertaining to the induction of a peacekeeping force. According to Dixit, about three hours before the signing ceremony (which means about noon, barely an hour after Gandhi had landed in Sri Lanka), Jayewardene requested the latter to induct Indian troops into northern Sri Lanka, which would enable him to move some Sri Lankan army personnel back to the South, especially to Colombo, which looked explosive. Rajiv Gandhi refused to consider the request until (a) the agreement had been signed, and (b) a separate request for inducting Indian troops, as per the agreement, was made by Jayewardene in writing.

The stunning speed with which the portion of the agreement dealing with induction of Indian forces went into operation took most Indians, possibly even the prime minister, by surprise. Among those admitting that they were caught off guard by the rapidity of that development were Dixit himself and Chidambaram. The latter recollected telling the prime minister, even as he accompanied him for the signing ceremony, that there should be no precipitate induction of the Indian army, preferably none at all. Years later, Chidambaram felt that more than anything else, Jayewardene's request was the clearest indication that he was playing a deep endgame by which he would inveigle Indian troops to fight LTTE and literally get them to do their dirty work for him.[28]

Thus, the ink had not dried on the agreement, literally, before the part pertaining to the induction of the Indian Peace Keeping Force was deployed. By the evening of July 30, just hours after Gandhi left Sri Lanka for Delhi, the first of six thousand Indian troops (two brigades) were airlifted to Palaly Air Base in northern Sri Lanka.[29] The same planes that carried the Indian troops were then used to airlift Sri Lankan soldiers in the North to Colombo. Two Leander-class frigates from the Indian navy were stationed off Galle Face Green, visible clearly from the city. On July 30, as Gandhi was about to emplane for his return to India, he walked past a guard of honor. A naval rating suddenly lunged forward and swung his rifle butt at the prime minister. Gandhi instinctively ducked his head and was caught a glancing blow on his shoulder. Had he not reacted quickly, it would have been a serious injury, possibly fatal. In a microcosm, the incident captured the breathless and unreal character of recent events. Gandhi and his advisers were basking in the glory of an agreement that, in their view, represented a spectacular recognition of Indian hegemony in South Asia and something that was making headlines in western capitals. Ironically, perhaps the only aspect that did make the news everywhere was the television footage of the attempt to decapitate the prime minister. Convinced of their position on the world's center stage, however, Rajiv Gandhi and his entourage were too busy congratulating themselves on their latest foreign policy success to take much notice of such annoying details.

CONCLUSION

In analyzing the Indian state under Rajiv Gandhi in this chapter, I have suggested that the quest for recognition of its hegemony was not a means to some other, more tangible or material or fundamental end: rather, the quest defined the state itself. The enactment of various spectacles of politics—at Thimpu, during the SAARC summit at Bangalore, in Exercise Brasstacks, in the airdrop over Jaffna, and finally during the signing of the Indo–Sri Lanka Agreement of July 1987—were not events orchestrated toward the achievement of some other, more substantial ends to which these theatrics were mere accompaniments. These spectacles were the ends themselves; they were the signifiers of a state that saw itself as a regional hegemon, an emerging world power, the cynosure of an international community whose ecumene curiously coincided with what one might call the west. Hegemony was a matter of appearing to be hegemonic and, more importantly, of being recognized by others as such.[30]

As the Indians staged their spectacular politics, some Sri Lankans saw an opening upon which they capitalized. One has to credit the political acuity of Dissanayake and Jayewardene for realizing that the Indian desire to be recognized as a hegemonic regional power contained an opportunity to split the Indians from the group with whom they ostensibly sided: the Sri Lankan Tamils. Yet, to what extent the events that followed (outlined in the next chapter) were anticipated or even intuited by either of these men cannot be determined. What we can say is that every discursive regime is embedded with a multiplicity of locutional spaces, and the outcome of the attempts by various individual desires to impart a specific direction to events is something that may well exceed any one individual's intentions. Certainly as Indian troops landed at Palaly Air Base in northern Sri Lanka, few realized that this was the beginning of India's longest and costliest war.

6

Narratives in Contention:
Interpreting the Agreement of July 1987

It is this that sets apart the thousand million people who inhabit the subcontinent from the rest of the world... the special quality of loneliness that grows out of the fear of the war between oneself and one's image in the mirror.

—AMITAV GHOSH, SHADOW LINES

In a piece that inaugurated the influential subaltern school of historiography, Ranajit Guha (1983) describes the British colonial archive on Indian peasant protest movements as the "prose of counter-insurgency." Written from the perspective of officials saddled with the task of maintaining "law and order," the archive eviscerates any agency or rationality on the part of the peasant as he fought against the multiple discriminations of colonial rule. Instead peasant rebellions are described through metaphors that see them as irrational, incomprehensible, and naturalistic: forest fires, rainstorms, raging rivers, earthquakes, and the like. Throughout, the colonial archive juxtaposes western rationality and respect for property with a nativist, millenarian irrationality that left random destruction in its wake. Guha suggests we might better understand subaltern consciousness by first acknowledging that what passes for conventional history is predominantly a prose of counterinsurgency, then proceed to read that prose against the grain and to augment it with sources deemed outside the ambit of conventional historiography (such as myth, ballads, folk songs, proverbs, stories, and so on).

167

I begin this chapter by suggesting that the dominant narrative that undergirds mainstream international relations is likewise one that seeks to secure the foundations of statist sovereignty by regarding every move that questions it as an insurgent practice worthy of disciplining by force or caricature or both. Just as the colonial archive was animated by a desire to fortify the Raj, the texts of international relations are written to secure and preserve an interstate system premised on the idea of statist sovereignty. This prose commences by taking for granted that which demands explanation — namely, its own origin story or presencing. Its standard narrative assumes an initial contractarian construction of sovereignty, then turns to the latest threat to that sovereignty, and ends with a tale of the arduous recovery of the political kingdom by the triumph of the state over such threats. The encounter between sovereignty and its insurgents allows for a staging of sovereignty itself and of its reproduction through discourses of national security and national interest. As ever, the encounter between identity and its other secures the former in specific ways and disenfranchises alternative imaginings of the received order. Or as Roxanne Doty has it in a recent summarization, "Counterinsurgency aims to restore (or in many cases to create) the status quo, to naturalize the authority of a particular social order, and to make deviant and illegitimate those who seek to disrupt it. At the same time, however, counterinsurgency reveals the contingent and incomplete nature of the representational practices that construct and naturalize social identities and positions of authority" (1996, 77).

The Indo–Sri Lanka Agreement of 1987 sought to inscribe the entry and function of the Indian Peace Keeping Force (IPKF) within a discourse of counterinsurgency. It was there to preserve the sovereignty of the Sri Lankan state: in exchange for the latter's recognition of the legitimate grievances of the Tamil people, the IPKF would ensure the unity and integrity of Sri Lanka by disarming the Tamil militants, enabling their return to democratic politics, and by allowing the Sri Lankan state to give full attention to the JVP insurgency in the South. Problems abounded with this representation of the agreement as an instrument of counterinsurgency designed to restore statist sovereignty. First, the agreement emerged out of Indian efforts to act and be recognized as a regional hegemon, inevitably compromising the very sovereignty of its smaller neighbor, Sri Lanka, that it now sought to restore. The feeling was deep among most Sri Lankans that it was an agreement dictated to them, and its signing gave a tremendous fillip to ultranationalist forces such as the JVP. Second, although the agreement averred that Tamil ethnonationalism was a threat to the sovereignty of Sri Lanka, such ethnonationalism had served as an opportunity and a site for the production of statist authority in both India and Sri Lanka. This was reflected in how the Tamil insurgency was used by Sri Lankan regimes to further strengthen majoritarian ideology and pass draconian laws limiting personal freedoms; in India's ability to destabilize neighbors through the militants; in the Congress Party's efforts to secure support and following among ethnically kindred minorities within India; and in the Dravidian parties' efforts to appear as the spokesmen for a worldwide Tamil community. The Indian state sought to render these multiple motivations into a singular prose of counterinsurgency, even though events on the ground constantly exceeded the representational containments of such a narrow reading of the agreement. This chapter details how various actors sought to interpret the agreement in line with their preferences and how a document ostensibly intended to bring peace to Sri Lanka wound up inaugurating a decade of incredible violence in that country. By the end of the encounter between the Indian army and the LTTE, the principle of statist sovereignty sought to be consolidated by the agreement was more fragile and tenuous than ever.

REPRESENTING THE AGREEMENT OF 1987

The first war that needed to be fought was one of representation. Events in weeks preceding the agreement moved at such a breathtaking speed that no one seemed clear as to what exactly it signified. Accordingly, each of the various groups struggled to impose their interpretive will on that document. A brief examination of these multiple efforts is necessary to understand the outbreak of the later war. The IPKF saw itself as entering a rather routine engagement, one that it had done ad nauseam within India: enter a war-torn zone, separate the adversaries, collect all the weapons surrendered by various militant groups, establish some modicum of peace and order, and help in the reconstruction of damaged roads and infrastructure. A large contingent of troops had landed at Palaly Air Base, and another had been ferried to Trincomalee in the eastern province. Overlooking the incredibly beautiful China Bay, on a verdant hilltop, is a guest house of the Trincomalee Oil Tank farm, where many IPKF officers stayed. Built by the British in the 1920s, it is a lovely structure with a spectacular view of the bay. An entry in the visitor's book reveals the frame of mind of many in the IPKF when they reached Sri Lanka. Squadron leader and helicopter pilot K. J. Bhatt, who stayed there from August 19 to September 15, 1987, had this to say: "It saddens me that for three warring years since the last entry of July 1984 this book has been blank. May the Accord succeed and be a symbol of hope for entire mankind—a living vibrant real symbol that 'yes, we can succeed and hope for a better tomorrow.' Then may this hilltop be once again filled with the sounds of laughter and gaiety, overlooking the tranquil serenity of this thousand year jewel of Sri Lanka—magnificent Trincomalee harbour."[1]

On the night of July 29, the overall force commander of the IPKF, Lt. Gen. Depinder Singh was in Madras, setting up his headquarters there. His initial feelings about the impending operation were, as he recalled, "pure and simple: to stop a conflict that had been going on.... [F]rom a soldier's point of view, it was a ... simple operation of separating two warring factions and making sure that they stayed apart."[2] Even Singh's meeting with Prabhakaran in Madras, on the latter's way home to Jaffna on August 2, did little to dispel his optimism. He recalled Prabhakaran being quite upbeat about the agreement and even telling him that when the disarming began, he would personally hand over the biggest machine gun to the general. The only discordant note occurred when the conversation turned to Prabhakaran's experience in Delhi. Singh recalled "he mentioned that...he felt very humiliated. He felt very let down by the External Affairs Ministry, particularly by the high commissioner.... [T]hey had told him you must come to Delhi and we want to consult you and you will be free to say what you want...and when he reached Delhi he found that...he wasn't consulted, he was just told: Look, we're doing this and you will concur."[3]

Two important aspects about the induction ought to be emphasized at the outset. One was that the actual number of troops inducted initially (about six thousand) was much less than what one might have anticipated with two divisions earmarked for Sri Lanka. Many soldiers were on leave and weren't recalled immediately as would have been the case were it not a peacekeeping operation. Second, Indian forces in Sri Lanka were never able to shrug off the feeling that although they were ostensibly neutral and impartial, they were really to tilt in favor of the Tamils. Afterall, the basis of India's policy in the recent years had been that Tamils were at the receiving end of the actions of an uncaring Sri Lankan army and a chauvinistic Sinhalese majority. It would soon become evident that this tilt in favor the Tamils, which became a softness toward the LTTE, was certainly not shared by the Indian high commissioner in Colombo or by New Delhi, much less by the Jayewardene regime.

Tamil Nadu's politicians had had nothing to do with the terms negotiated in the agreement or its implementation in the weeks that followed its signing. MGR, in a terse eight-minute speech (he had been seriously ill for some time now and very weak) to a crowd estimated at two hundred thousand on Marina Beach in Madras, said, "the militants should have confidence in the efforts of the Prime Minister, extend him all support and respect the agreement." In a speech that lasted fifty-five minutes, Rajiv Gandhi could hardly be accused of understatement when he noted that the agreement had "no precedent in the history of the country, and no parallel in the world" (*Frontline,* August 8–21, 1987, 15). Further, as the newsmagazine noted, "The rally was held in the face of criticism of the Rajiv-JR agreement by the DMK, the Dravida Kazhagam, the Tamil Nadu Kamaraj Congress and a few other parties and [of] a call for a protest demonstration on that day, which, however, went largely unnoticed." The Indian government and the media were ecstatic at the resounding recognition of Indian hegemony in South Asia contained in the agreement: it clearly precluded smaller neighbors seeking extraregional help in solving either their domestic conflicts or bilateral problems with the Indians, and the provisions for devolution of powers and recognition of the pluralist character of nation building powerfully augmented the Indian self-image regarding its progressive and enlightened role in the subcontinent. The agreement was touted as the ideal model for all neighbors in their relations with India and seen as the ideal culmination of more than five years of a judicious blend of coercion and diplomacy in bringing the Sri Lankans around. Reflective of the upbeat mood, Congress parliamentarians moved to get Rajiv Gandhi and Jayewardene nominated for a Nobel Peace prize, revealing the aspirations of some in the prime minister's coterie, if not his own.

The LTTE's efforts to represent the agreement in specific ways merit the most attention. Addressing a huge rally of tens of thousands of people at the Sudumalai Amman Temple just outside Jaffna on August 4, Prabhakaran gave a speech that was no resounding acclamation of the agreement (in fact, quite the contrary), nor did it by any stretch of imagination go back on the commitment to Eelam. (The text of the speech is reproduced in Ram 1989, 147–49.) The narrative structure of his speech focused on a promise belied and a struggle temporarily suspended, to be resumed in due course, rather than on the agreement as an enduring solution to the Tamil question. He began by noting that the agreement had been primarily motivated by India's geopolitical concerns, and despite its important consequences for Sri Lankan Tamils, they had not been consulted in its drafting. He said he had initially refused to support the agreement, especially its provisions for the LTTE's surrender of arms, and had reluctantly agreed to those provisions only after he was given the Indian prime minister's personal assurances of protection. Then, in a deft rhetorical move, Prabhakaran sought to represent the agreement as a document that put the IPKF on the side of the Tamil militants against the Sinhalese and the Sri Lankan army:

> We do believe that India will not allow the racist Sri Lankan state to take once again to the road of genocide against the Tamils. *It is only out of this faith that we decided to hand over our weapons to the Indian Peace-Keeping Force....*[4] In taking from us our weapons — the one means of protection for Eelam Tamils — the Indian government takes over from us the big responsibility of protecting our people. *The handing over of arms only signifies the handing over, the transfer of this responsibility.* Were we not to hand over our weapons, we would be put in the calamitous circumstance of clashing with the Indian Army. We do not want this. We love India. We love the people of India. There is no question of our deploying our arms against Indian soldiers. The soldiers of the Indian Army are taking up the responsibility of safeguarding and protecting us against our enemy. *I wish very firmly to emphasize here that by virtue of our handing over our weapons, the Indian government should assume full responsibility for the life and security of every one of the Eelam Tamils.* (Ram 1989, 148, emphases added)

After having indicated exactly what the LTTE regarded the responsibility of the Indians to be, Prabhakaran proceeded to unequivocally state his commitment to Eelam: "I do not think that as a result of this Agreement, there will be a permanent solution to the problem of the Tamils. The time is not very far off when the monster of Sinhala racism will devour this Agreement. *I have unrelenting faith in the proposition that only a separate state of Tamil Eelam can offer a permanent solution to the problem of the people of Tamil Eelam. Let me make it clear to you here, without a shadow of a doubt, that I will continue to fight for the objective of attaining Tamil Eelam"* (Ram 1989, 148, emphases added).[5] Prabhakaran's speech already reflected a desire to escape the clutches of the agreement, and the first step in doing so was to prepare the ground so that the LTTE would not be held historically culpable. The portions of his speech connecting the surrender of arms by the militants to the takeover of their protection by the IPKF clearly reflect this line of thinking. If the IPKF were found wanting in that regard, LTTE's return to arms could be justified as a resumption of their role as the protectors of the Tamil people of Sri Lanka.

As Prabhakaran's speech was being transmitted live from Jaffna, through Madras to Army Head Quarters and on to the Prime Minister's Office in New Delhi, an incident occurred that is interesting in light of claims that he had accepted the agreement while in Delhi and had gone back on that acceptance later. There was simultaneous translation of Prabhakaran's speech into English (he was speaking in Tamil) as it was beamed to the Prime Minister's Office. Major General Yashwant Deva (retired), Signals, was responsible for the installation and maintenance of the communications hookup between Jaffna and New Delhi via Madras (where he was stationed). He recalled the relay of the speech that day as follows:

> Suddenly, there was an interruption and the interpreter sitting over there [in Jaffna] said, "I cannot hear anything because the crowd has started surging forward, and the crowd is shouting. I can't follow anything." These were moments of anxiety as far as Delhi was concerned. A voice from there [Delhi] said that, "PM wants to know, immediately, he wants to know what is happening, what is happening, what is happening?" Because he [Prabhakaran] had not made an announcement. And then suddenly he said that he was helpless, that he accepted the accord because he could not fight the IPKF. "I cannot fight the Indian army, so I accept the accord." And there was commotion and cheering and things like that. It was an enthusiasm regarding that [in the prime minister's office]. Now, the question is very simple: till that time even the PM was not really sure what kind of game he [Prabhakaran] is going to play. Because I could see the anxiety in that room, I am witness to that anxiety. So, it is only after he clarified that he has accepted the accord that there was a sigh of re-

lief, a sigh of relief in Delhi, a sigh of relief all around the chamber of the PM. So he [Prabhakaran] played his cards close to his chest.[6]

The Sinhalese interpretation of the agreement was predictable. The riots in the days preceding its signing, the curfew on Colombo during those days, the groundswell of public opinion against the agreement — all reflected its unpopularity. While the SLFP described the agreement as a sellout of national sovereignty, Premadasa and Athulathmudali within the ruling party continued their earlier stance of vehemently opposing Indian intervention in Sri Lankan affairs. Dissanayake began the speedy resettlement of Sinhalese peasants in the eastern province without showing similar alacrity on behalf of Tamil refugees. The sites first chosen for such resettlement were politically loaded: the Trincomalee and Amparai districts. It must be remembered that in contrast to Chidambaram's December 19 proposals, which envisaged the excision of the Amparai district (on account of its preponderance of Sinhalese) from the eastern province prior to any merger with the North, the agreement left Amparai within the eastern province. Similarly, resettling the Sinhalese speedily in the Weli Oya regions on the borders of the northern and eastern provinces was something that would arouse LTTE's worst fears because it would have critical implications for the referendum. Immediately after the signing ceremony, Dissanayake went on television and, speaking in Sinhala, reminded his audience of this fact and indicated that the merger was a temporary affair soon to be reversed. (Jayewardene's attitude on merger was examined in the previous chapter.) In the aftermath of the signing, the feeling among Jayewardene, Dissanayake, Ronnie De Mel, and others seemed to be "we have pulled one over the Tamils; we don't really have to bother with them because we have secured the support of Delhi" (Jayatilleka 1995, 9). Thus, although the prime minister and Athulathmudali may be described as actively hostile to the agreement, the others (Dissanayake, De Mel, and Jayewardene himself) regarded it as a coup that would either disarm the LTTE or pit it against the Indians.

The previous chapter detailed the internecine warfare between LTTE and other militant groups. Now, the disarming began to resemble a classic prisoner's dilemma stand-off. LTTE was loath to disarm first, for fear that other militant outfits were waiting to settle past scores with it. The reverse held true as far as the others were concerned: surrendering arms before LTTE did would be suicidal. Neither LTTE nor the other outfits were sure that disarming was a good idea in the first place, given that it would mean their complete dependence on the Indians for their own security in the future. The IPKF's charge was to serve as an impartial referee who would ensure a simultaneous and orderly disarmament. At no point had they been asked to prepare for the possible noncooperation of the militants or for settling armed conflicts between Tamil militant groups. As Depinder Singh states quite simply in his book, "when inter-militant clashes took place, the IPKF came in for some unwarranted criticism for not stepping in and stopping the fighting. Nobody could tell me, incidentally, how to stop an inter-militant group fight in the middle of nowhere" (n.d., 44).

By the middle of August 1987, a new element entered the picture. LTTE now alleged that RAW had begun arming the other groups. The truth of this charge is impossible to verify, and the possibilities are literally infinite. What follows here draws extensively from interviews with the various people involved at this time. Many in the Indian media and a few officials in the Indian Ministry of External Affairs were of the view that RAW may have started rearming groups hostile to LTTE as a way of helping the implementation of the agreement, with or without the sanction of the prime minister. Arming these other groups could lead to the diminution of the LTTE's power, and the latter was perhaps the most important stumbling block in the successful working out of the agreement. The rivalry between RAW and the Ministry of External Affairs was both well known and enduring. The agreement was regarded as a coup for the ministry, but seen as having cut RAW out of the action.[7] Others, including many in the army, media, and militant groups, thought RAW was up to all sorts of tricks in Sri Lanka and would certainly not put it past that organization to try and sabotage the agreement itself. Some among the militant groups alleged that individual officials of RAW were susceptible to corruption and that the continued flow of arms to rival militant groups may have been a product of that corruption. An official of RAW was quite clear that neither the agency nor any of its functionaries would act in a way that controverted the agreement. Some others, in the media and among police officers, felt that the rivalry between RAW and IB (each having its own protégés among the groups) carried on even after the agreement was signed and that such rearming was entirely plausible. Noting the fact that the agreement had no dearth of enemies, still others went farther afield and alleged these other Tamil groups were being armed by dissidents (especially Athulathmudali) within Jayewardene's cabinet or by the Pakistanis or Chinese as a means of sabotaging the agreement. There was the possibility, strongly argued by LTTE itself, that such arming occurred with the full knowledge of both New Delhi and Colombo as a way of corralling, if not annihilating, LTTE because it was the only obstacle to the agreement. Finally, there is the possibility that LTTE was looking for a way out of the agreement, and such an allegation served their purpose rather well.

The "truth" of what really happened was vastly overdetermined in terms of the various plausible scenarios. Although scholars have sought to discipline this ambiguity and impose singular narratives of what must have really happened, I find that task less interesting; moreover, I have no way of divining exactly what may have happened in any case. Rather, I suggest that each of the interpretive possibilities argued for by different participants empowers them in distinctive ways and secures their place in history within exculpatory narratives. Each of them privileges his or her own version on the basis of superior intelligence or a form of oculocentrism ("I was there—I saw it with my own eyes") or on the basis of access to privileged and classified information or of the inherent morality of their position. Given the surfeit of "privileged" sources, it seems to me to be more interesting to chart the various plays of domination over a contested reality rather than to drop anchor in any one of these politically complicit narratives.

A strategy that sought to arm militant groups hostile to LTTE and to promote promote a debilitating internecine war, leaving a force pliant to India at the helm of affairs, had an important precedent in India's relations with neighbors and with insurgent groups. In fact, precisely such a policy had been awaiting use as a backup option in Bangladesh in 1971, though it had not been needed on that occasion. Recollecting that episode, the journalist Mohan Ram notes:

> India, unsure that it would have its way in Dacca when Bangladesh finally became a reality, wanted to ensure that a regime friendly to it would be in power. So emigre leaders, often seen in Calcutta's bars and brothels, virtually rode back to Dacca on Indian tanks to provide the government when Sheikh Mujibur Rehman, the "father of

Bangladesh," was still prisoner in Pakistan. India's contingency plan, in the event the protégé leadership did not make it in Dacca and the Mukti Bahini staked its claim to power, was a surrogate guerrilla force called the Mujib Bahini, armed and trained by it. Since the emigre leadership was installed in Dacca, there was no need to use the shadowy Mujib Bahini for a proxy war. The redundant force of 20,000 Mujib Bahini men was dropped and left to fend for itself. (1989, 66)

If it had been the Indians' plan to use the other Tamil militant groups as an alternative to LTTE, they had underestimated the political acumen of LTTE, which had long harbored suspicions regarding Indian designs. A journalist who had visited Jaffna and maintained contacts with Tamil militant groups through the 1980s knew of the tremendous interest LTTE had shown in Indian intelligence dealings with insurgents in Nagaland, Mizoram, Tripura; in the way the Tibetan refugees had been handled by India; and in RAW's operations in Bangladesh in 1971. He recalled conversations with LTTE leaders in which they would say that the last situation they wanted to wind up in was that of the Tibetans, whose struggle would gain the attention of the Indian state or fall by the wayside depending on whether the latter wanted to pressure the Chinese or have a rapprochement with them.[8] At any rate, as the previous chapter has shown, the LTTE had already twice massacred the cadres of two outfits regarded as moving too close to RAW—namely, TELO and the EPRLF. In other words, it wasn't just the Indians who were modulating Bangladesh: LTTE were learning from that affair, too.

In the middle of August 1987, fights between LTTE and other groups broke out, leading to more than a hundred casualties. The disarming, which had been halting and of dubious sincerity to begin with, now slowed to a trickle. Indian military intelligence revealed that LTTE and other militant groups were continuing to receive fresh supplies of armaments and ammunition from outside and were stockpiling and storing them in various locations, as the sudden shortage of grease and polythene in Jaffna indicated. Soon another round of killings and reprisals broke out, now between Muslims in the eastern province and LTTE, specifically in Trincomalee, Batticaloa, Kalmunai, and Eravur. LTTE alleged that the Muslims had been massacred by Sinhalese police or army in an effort to alienate the Muslims as a prelude to wrecking the merger when the referendum was held; the Muslims saw the massacres as definitive proof of the folly of making common cause with Tamils in a separate, merged north-eastern province.

In retrospect, the weeks following the signing of the agreement seemed to catch LTTE a trifle off balance. They were faced with the evident euphoria of the IPKF's arrival in Jaffna and the palpable desire of the civilian population for a negotiated solution. At the same time, they were very unsure of their own prospects in any elections to provincial councils. Already, the canny Jaffna Tamil could be heard saying things such as, "We would like TULF and LTTE to share power. TULF has experience and LTTE has idealism. A combination would be in our best interests" (*India Today,* September 15, 1987, 128). To a group by now accustomed to regarding itself as the sole voice for and custodian of the Tamil cause, such sentiments sounded like the beginning of the end. Looming after the elections was a referendum in which the odds seemed stacked in favor of a reversal of merger. The ambiguities of the agreement on key issues such as the powers of the provincial councils, resettlement, and the colonization of lands made the future uncertain. Capping all this, the sorry track record of past Sri Lankan governments and the contradictory actions of various institutions and individuals comprising India were there to be reckoned with. In this situation, one could argue that sometime in mid-August, if not earlier, the LTTE began to think that they had to wriggle out of an agreement that sought to cage them, even if it meant taking on the IPKF. In less than two months, LTTE broke the back of the agreement through three separate incidents: the fast unto death by a prominent militant, Thileepan; the question of membership of the Interim Administrative Council to run the province until the provincial council elections; and, finally, the suicide of thirteen LTTE cadre at Palaly Air Base. In each of these incidents, LTTE sought to portray itself as a committed and principled organization and, conversely, the Indian and Sri Lankan governments as untrustworthy from the perspective of Tamil interests. The two governments, on the other hand, tried everything they could to pin LTTE down to the terms of the agreement and to commit itself to functioning within a sovereign and unitary Sri Lankan state. A brief analysis of these episodes reveals how LTTE tried to control the war of representations and emerge as a group with valid reasons to break the agreement, whereas the two governments tried to show that the LTTE had all along been an intransigently secessionist force, one that would not accede even after all its demands (short of Eelam) had been met.

Rasaiah Parthipan, alias Thileepan, was twenty-three years old and the Jaffna chief of LTTE's political wing. On September 15 Thileepan began a fast unto death on a platform in front of the Nallur Kandasami Temple in Jaffna. His five demands were: a halt to Sinhalese colonization of Tamil areas; stoppage of the opening of new police stations in Tamil areas until an interim adminstration was formed; stoppage of rehabilitation work by IPKF until the formation of the Interim Council; the disarming of Sinhalese home guards; and immediate release of all Tamil prisoners detained under the Prevention of Terrorism Act. LTTE orchestrated a macabre spectacle around his imminent martyrdom. The temple was a historic site and drew thousands to its precincts everyday. Posters of the fast and the list of demands were plastered all over Jaffna. Thileepan lay on a raised platform with the huge insignia of LTTE's flag, with its roaring tiger, as a backdrop. His parents were seated in the inner circle around the platform. As soon as the fast began, All-India Radio, with thinly veiled sarcasm directed at Prabhakaran, noted that Mahatma Gandhi himself used to fast rather than passing that privilege on to his lieutenants. This comment was followed by an allegation that LTTE was using the fast to direct attention away from its massacre of other militant groups. Prabhakaran now came out publicly with his charge that RAW was "training and arming antisocial elements against the unarmed cadres of the LTTE.... [T]hese groups were sent to Tamil Eelam at a crucial time when we were cooperating with India in the process of disarmament." To which the Indian government replied, on September 20, that the killings of Tamil militants were "engineered by LTTE" (*Frontline*, October 3–16, 1987, 118).

On September 24, Dixit spoke to Jayewardene, who responded he would accept the five demands if LTTE publicly announced its support for the agreement. By September 25, Thileepan was sinking fast and unconscious. For days now, crowds had been ferried and bused to the temple, and violent slogans were raised promising dire consequences were he to die. Prabhakaran rejected pleas by community leaders that he step in and call off the fast. He replied that the fast had been voluntarily undertaken by Thileepan, and his five demands were posed against India; if he died, the responsibility was solely India's. The intent clearly was to tie Thileepan's death to the Indians and thus delegitimize their presence in Sri Lanka. Across the peninsula, Tamils were incited to throw stones and harrass IPKF soldiers to provoke an atrocity.

Thileepan died on September 26. All through the previous day and that morning, negotiations had been going on between LTTE and Dixit on a matter slightly tangential to the five demands—namely, membership of the Interim Council to govern the province until elections. In a signficant concession to LTTE, the Indians got Jayewardene to agree that the Interim Council would now consist of twelve members, seven of whom would be LTTE, including one Muslim nominee (giving them a clear majority), two would be from TULF, two would be Sinhalese, and one would be a Muslim not appointed by LTTE. In addition, the chairman of the Interim Council would also be an LTTE nominee. This concession represented a stunning victory for LTTE: the Indians had blown a lot of their capital with Jayewardene in order to get him to agree, and they had, yet again, alienated other militant groups who were now completely cut out of the action. More importantly, they had swallowed their pride in conceding to LTTE's demands on the Interim Council. All these were now incorporated into an agreement between the LTTE and the Indian government, signed by Prabhakaran's second-in-command Mahendra Raja, alias Mahattya, and Hardeep Puri on the morning of September 28. This same document settled a number of LTTE's reservations about the July agreement on the extent of devolved powers, on colonization of lands, and on the composition of police forces in the North and East. Further, it agreed to use its provisions to address Thileepan's five demands. In exchange, LTTE agreed to cooperate fully with the Indians on implementing the agreement of July 29, 1987, to surrender all arms barring those for personal protection of the leaders themselves, and to avoid mutual criticism in the interim.

As far as the Indians were concerned, with the Interim Council dominated by LTTE (it had a majority of members and the chairmanship) and with IPKF in charge of the northeast when elections to provincial council would be held, the LTTE was on an excellent wicket. They found it difficult to see what more could be conceded to LTTE under a democratic framework in terms of regional autonomy. LTTE had everything going for them at this moment except, it would seem in retrospect, the only thing they really wanted: a separate nation-state of Tamil Eelam. The breakthrough on the question of membership in the Interim Council was made hours before Thileepan died on September 26. Announcing that as a major concession, his fast could have been called off and his death possibly averted. Prabhakaran's refusal to do so indicated he was more interested in making a martyr of Thileepan and painting the two governments in the worst light possible than he was in saving the life of his comrade. Dixit revealed his take on the way it all ended:

> He [Prabhakaran] said, "You must come and tell Thileepan to break the fast." I said gladly, because I know the young man. "But," I said, "I must have a guarantee that when I offer him a glass of orange juice to break the fast, he should not strike it out of my hand in the presence of two thousand people. Personally I have no ego problem, but I have an ego problem as the high commissioner for eight hundred million people. Are you sure [he won't knock it out of my hand]? Because I know how volatile you chaps are." He said, "No, I can't guarantee anything." I said, "Forget it, . . . I didn't ask him to go on a fast. I will not go unless you assure me . . . that assurance I need."[9]

Within hours of agreeing to the revised composition of the Interim Council, LTTE went back to its tactic of objecting and renegotiating earlier agreements. Although the details need not detain us (they had to do with the selection of the chief administrator of the Interim Council of the northeastern province), as in Thileepan's fast, the pattern was the two governments conceding to nearly all demands of the LTTE and the latter, perhaps taken off guard by these concessions, upping the ante at every turn in an effort to break out of the agreement. As September ended, the two sides were still deadlocked on negotiations on the leadership of the Interim Adminstrative Council.

Meanwhile, pressure on Jayewardene to take a hard line against the Tamils and the Indians had been mounting ever since a grenade attack in Parliament.[10] The IPKF had been in Sri Lanka for two whole months (August and September) even though the agreement called for the disarmament to be completed in seventy-two hours. Instead, not only had it dragged on inconclusively, but fights between Tamil groups, between Tamils and Muslims, between Sinhalese settlers and Tamils, between IPKF and LTTE, and between straggling Sri Lankan army soldiers and IPKF were becoming frequent. It was obvious that weapons continued to move uninterrupted into the North. Sinhala impatience with the stuttering efforts of IPKF was rising. Meanwhile, the president seemed to be bending over backwards, making one concession after another to the demands of LTTE, under the advice of the Indians. Sinhala fears that IPKF was not only a permanent occupationary force but moreover one designed to carve out an Eelam for the Tamils seemed worryingly plausible. The legislation to establish provincial councils (through the Thirteenth Amendment to the Sri Lankan Constitution) was moving fast, adding more fuel to the majority's disenchantment with Jayewardene. All this proved fertile ground for the JVP, whose chauvinistic pro-Sinhala and anti-Tamil rhetoric was now powerfully augmented by the presence of more than six thousand troops from a foreign country, India no less, on Sri Lankan soil.

LTTE's efforts to break the agreement through Thileepan's fast and the wrangles over Interim Council had failed because the two governments were more pliable than the group had anticipated. Now, it would seem, LTTE decided to orchestrate something of such magnitude that it would decisively wrest public support in Jaffna back to their side and completely discredit both governments. Their opportunity came soon enough. On October 2, a Sri Lankan navy patrol intercepted a boat crossing the Palk Straits off Point Pedro. Seventeen LTTE members were aboard, including two regional commanders, Kumarappa (Batticaloa) and K. Pulendran (Trincomalee). It is not clear exactly how much the boat had by way of armaments or what its mission was. The men offered no resistance as they were transported to Palaly Air Base, where they were placed in the custody of the Sri Lankan army. IPKF too had a presence on the base. LTTE claimed that there were no arms on the boat and that it was merely transporting documents and furniture from Tamil Nadu to Jaffna as they had wound up operations there. Whatever weapons they had in the boat were for the personal protection of Kumarappa and Pulendran, as allowed by the agreement. The Sri Lankan government, including Jayewardene himself on television, claimed the boat was full of weapons.

Immediately, LTTE began to pressure IPKF for the release of the seventeen men. The Sri Lankan army's position was that they had been arrested for violating at least two laws: they had left Sri Lanka without passports or visas, and they were carrying arms. The argument that the Indo–Sri Lanka Agreement of 1987 provided them with amnesty would not hold water: that covered the period prior to its signing; this was October. The agreement also dealt with political offenses, whereas this was clearly a penal offence. Moreover, one of the men, Pulendran, had been identified as being responsible for the Good Friday massacre of 127 civilians in April 1987 in Habarana, outside the zone for which the agreement granted amnesty — namely, the Northeast. The IPKF's man on the spot, sensing that the situation could spin out of control, insisted to his Sri Lankan counterpart, Brigadier Jayantha Jayaratne, that IPKF should have custody of the men. But the brigadier, by now in telephonic contact with Athulathmudali, the minister of national security, had orders to do no such thing. Athulathmudali ordered the brigadier to transport the men to Colombo, where they would be interrogated and shown on television. Meanwhile, LTTE had organized a huge crowd outside the gates of Palaly Air Base, shouting slogans demanding the release of the prisoners.

General Depinder Singh flew into Colombo and pleaded directly with the president himself, who claimed he had to accede to the demands of his minister of national security and his service chiefs. All General Singh could extract from the president was a promise that the men would neither be tortured nor shown on television. He conveyed this promise to the LTTE leaders back in Jaffna, and they said it was not enough. All this time, Dixit had been out of the loop as he was in New Delhi on a social function. As soon as he heard of the situation, he rushed back to Colombo and got in touch with General Harkirat Singh, the operational commander in Jaffna. He ordered the general to take the men into IPKF's custody. What followed was a classic vignette of Indian bureaucratese as the general read out of the procedure book to Dixit: "And that foolish man said, 'No, you are not in my chain of command. You send this message to your minister, your minister must send this to defense minister; defense ministry will send this to Army Headquarters; Army Headquarters will send it to Headquarters, Southern Command, Pune; Pune will send it to Tactical Headquarters, Madras, and when I get orders from Madras, I'll act.' I said, 'We don't have the time. This could take three hours or twelve or...I am telling you I will take full responsibility.' 'No.'"[11]

Dixit then turned to Jayewardene and tried pleading with the president. According to Dixit, Jayewardene agreed finally to hand the men over to IPKF. But before Jayewardene could step in and do this, Athulathmudali acted. He ordered Brigadier Jayaratne to load the men onto an aircraft he had sent and dispatch them to Colombo forthwith. Brigadier Jayaratne hesitated as the situation outside the camp was explosive. Besides, he wasn't sure how the prisoners would react if he attempted to move them forcibly. Athulathmudali then told him either to send the prisoners right away or to hand over command to his deputy, fly back to Colombo immediately, be sacked, and face court martial for insubordination. Brigadier Jayaratne collected thirty-five of his bigger soldiers and walked toward the hangar housing the seventeen men.

Earlier that day, LTTE leaders Mahattya and Balasingham had requested a meeting with the prisoners. Under pressure from the Indians, Brigadier Jayaratne had let this meeting take place at about two in the afternoon. Mahattya supposedly communicated Prabhakaran's orders to the men: if an attempt was made to transport them to Colombo, they should kill themselves by consuming cyanide. He is also supposed to have given cyanide capsules to any of the men who weren't carrying them. At about five in the evening, as the soldiers tried to drag them to the airplane, all seventeen men swallowed the cyanide. Thirteen, including Pulendran and Kumarappa, died, but four survived.

In my interview with him, Athulathmudali flatly denied the role of saboteur attributed to him: he claimed that on the said day he was still in the hospital recovering from injuries sustained in the grenade attack in August.[12] Brigadier Jayaratne was killed a year later. Dixit is clear that it was Athulathmudali's intransigence that led to the suicide; if only the Indians had gained custody of the men, a face-saving way out could have been found. There is yet another line of thought: around 4:30 that evening, a message supposedly came from New Delhi to Dixit and IPKF, telling them to stop trying to avert the deportation of the men to Colombo (Hoole et al. 1990, 189) and to let matters take their course.[13]

Although LTTE members' tremendous dedication to their cause was well known, symbolized by the cyanide capsule every member wore around his or her neck, everyone was astounded by the seventeen men's unquestioning attempt to kill themselves on an order from their leader. Following on the heels of Thileepan's fast unto death, the mass suicide made many realize that even as nationalist guerrilla organizations went, LTTE was exceptional. Prabhakaran may have decided that trying to subvert the agreement by hairsplitting and other methods had about run its course: it was time to engineer something of such magnitude that war would be inevitable. Moreover, this demonstration had to be made in such a way that it would show India and Sri Lanka in the worst light, stay within the LTTE's macabre narrative of a suicidal commitment to Eelam, rally the support of Jaffna's population for LTTE, and split them away from their newfound enthusiasm for the Indians and their soldiers. The suicide of the thirteen men, in a way, fit all these requirements: it proved to be the proverbial last straw as far as breaking the agreement was concerned. (The innermost calculations of Prabhakaran in eliminating such a large number of his cadre, including two top regional commanders, will remain a mystery. There were supposedly deep tensions within LTTE between the northern and eastern Tamils. The elimination of Pulendran and Kumarappa, both prominent leaders from the East, may not have been an entirely accidental consequence of the mass suicide.)

The realization that a point of no return had been crossed was evident to all parties: the Indian and Sri Lankan governments began immediately to push for a strong response to LTTE. Prabhakaran himself disappeared, and the swift and murderous attacks on the remaining Sinhalese in the North, including some Sri Lankan soldiers held captive by the LTTE, and soon on the IPKF indicated his strategy. Jayewardene had been pushing for a more aggressive Indian attitude against LTTE for some time now, in part because of the pressures he was under in the South and in part because he sensed a growing impatience in both Rajiv Gandhi and Dixit regarding LTTE's intransigence to the agreement. Besides, a scenario that had seemed vaguely possible in mid-July now seemed almost tantalizingly close—namely, the Indian army taking on the LTTE and completing a task that the Sri Lankans had not been able to accomplish.

Ironically, the one group most reluctant to begin hostilities was the IPKF. Depinder Singh has recounted in his book the degree of sympathy and affection the Indian army officers had for LTTE in the early days after the induction. Depinder Singh and Harkirat Singh were also aware the actual numbers of troops inducted left them too thin on the ground for an immediate onset of war against LTTE. A rapid escalation of troops had begun in the second week of October, but it would be well into the month before the requisite men and matériel would reach Jaffna and Trincomalee. Their efforts to convey this to the army chief of staff and through him to the prime minister were either ignored or dismissed as irrelevant: the prevalent view seemed to be that LTTE could be mopped up even with the relatively smaller force they had on the ground. General Sundarji and Defense Minister K. C. Pant flew into Colombo to announce the commencement of hostilities against LTTE. Sundarji, the army chief of staff, had already expressed his views that the Indian army would need no more than a few days to put LTTE in its place. In a desperate and last attempt to stave off the inevitable, Depinder and Harkirat flew to LTTE headquarters on the campus of Jaffna University and met Mahattya. The meeting left them convinced that war was imminent. The two reluctant warriors repaired to devise an opening salvo.

From early August to mid-October, an intricate war of representation had been ongoing. The two governments had attempted to cage the LTTE within the confines of the agreement, especially on the question of surrendering their arms, by making a series of concessions to their demands. The LTTE — sensing that the agreement could defer the possibility of Eelam by decades and afraid that their disarming was a prelude to a planned annihilation of the organization itself — focused on the alleged arming of rival Tamil groups by RAW as its reason for not cooperating. It first tried to wriggle free by hairsplitting and making increasingly unreasonable demands, then when those tactics failed, by orchestrating spectacles that resonated with the narrative of a suicidal nationalist guerrilla force and portrayed the two governments in the worst light possible. After the mass suicide at Palaly, the LTTE thought it had created a decisive rift between the Indians and the populace of Jaffna. The war of representation could now give way to a real war.

FROM PEACEKEEPERS TO WARRIORS

The first encounter in the hot war between the IPKF and LTTE would set the tone for the rest of the conflict. Worried that the Indian army was a sitting duck for a suicide bomber and aware that reinforcements in the form of more men and matériel were possibly at least two weeks away, General Depinder Singh decided that going straight for the operational headquarters of the LTTE, believed to be in a building at Kokuvil near the campus of Jaffna University, would be a perfect opening move. As he remembered it, the decision was based in part on the attitude that attack was the best form of defense in a context like this. (It could also have reflected the overall tendency to underestimate the LTTE as a fighting force at this time.) A heli-landing operation would deliver 103 paracommandos to the soccer field at the university. The first wave of commandos would secure the landing site for further sorties from the helicopters that would bring in soldiers from the Thirteenth Sikh Light Infantry. The latter would free up the paracommandos, whose mission was to destroy LTTE headquarters. They were then to reconnoitre with soldiers from the Seventy-second and Ninety-first Infantry brigades and return to base.

The heli-landings commenced at 1:00 A.M. on October 12. In the five landings that were completed, the 103 paracommandos were delivered, but about only 30, instead of the planned 130, soldiers from the Thirteenth Sikh got there. From the very first landing, the helicopters came under tremendous fire from the ground, and the soldiers failed in their efforts to secure the heli-landing site. In part, they failed because in their haste to reach the operational headquarters of LTTE, the main target, enough of them did not stay back and ensure the securing of the heli-landing site, the first and indispensable step in the entire operation. Three of the four MI-8 Hind helicopters available for the operation were hit by bullets the first time around, and the decision was made back in Palaly Air Base that there would be no more sorties that night. But this decision from headquarters could not be conveyed to the thirty soldiers of the Thirteenth Sikh already at the landing site because their radio was out of commission due to the attacks and the death of its operator.[14]

The paracommandos suggested to the Thirteenth Sikh that they accompany them on the mission because they were by now under heavy fire. The company commader of the Thirteenth Sikh, Major Birendra Singh, had a difficult decision to make. He could not be sure that there would be no further attempts to heli-land reinforcements, and his primary task had been to secure the landing site. He declined the offer to accompany the paracommandos and chose to stay back on the soccer field and await help that never came. This decision left the thirty men (or those that survived the initial landing) of the Thirteenth Sikh dangerously undermanned and in the heart of enemy territory. After a night spent exchanging fire with snipers, the remaining men faced the break of dawn with rapidly depleting ammunition. At around 11:30 A.M. on October 13, the ammunition ran out, and the last three men charged the enemy with bayonets: two were killed, and one was injured but survived. He was the only one out of thirty who escaped death.

Meanwhile, the paracommandos who had left on their mission to destroy the operational headquarters of the LTTE had an equally sorry tale to tell. As General Singh recounts it: "in their enthusiasm and anxiety to do things quickly, the paratroopers left the spot. By then, of course, they were under fire also. And so they thought that the more time they give to the LTTE, the more cause for concern, so they pushed off. But the second mistake they made was that instead of going where they were supposed to go, and they had the compass bearings and they had been...charts had been made for everyone of them. They got hold of a local boy, and he led them astray. He said, 'I know where they are.' So, he took them somewhere else."[15] The paracommandos never got to the operational headquarters of LTTE. Instead, they were led on a wild goose chase through the night. They spent the next day fighting for their lives and eventually trickled home to base after dark. Nearly thirty paracommandos, a newly formed and elite corps, did not make it back.

India's opening gambit in the war against LTTE, designed to destroy its headquarters and maybe even some of its top leadership, was a disaster. It ended with the Indians losing more than sixty soldiers but with no losses on the side of the militants. The IPKF was excoriated in the media for its failure to maintain secrecy (it appeared as if LTTE had been lying in wait, knowing the exact spot and timing of the heliborne operation) and the lack of any element of surprise (IPKF had spent the previous two days rounding up more than a hundred militants from various groups and attacking and closing down two newspapers and a television station in Jaffna run by LTTE, and their helicopters had made a number of reconnaissance runs over Jaffna university campus). One of the reasons why the paracommandos apprehended a local boy and sought his help to find the headquarters of LTTE lay in a startling fact. More than two months after arriving in Jaffna and five months after contingency planning on Sri Lankan operations had ostensibly begun, Indian forces did not have even the most rudimentary maps of the areas they were in. Some of the maps they used were fifty years out of date, having been made in 1937, during colonial times.[16]

To make matters worse, in the media and even among Indian bureaucrats, the heli-landing operation was used to paint a picture of a bumbling army with incompetent leadership. For example, it was put out that the paracommandos had been air-dropped (as distinct from heli-landed), using white parachutes, over the university campus on a full-moon night. The story went that most of the paracommandos were picked off by waiting LTTE snipers even before they hit the ground.[17] The problem clearly exceeded one of tactics. Whereas LTTE was clear that they wanted to break the agreement and oust the IPKF, the latter was confused about its mission. They had entered Sri Lanka ostensibly as a peacekeeping force with a fairly minimal and easy set of responsibilities. Now, it appeared that they were being asked to conduct a counterinsurgency operation in a foreign country about which (notwithstanding its proximity) they had little knowledge or experience.

Once the operation to go after the LTTE headquarters had failed, the next order to come down the pipeline reflected a desire to retreat into the familiar territory of the last war and to escape the complexities of such a counterinsurgency operation: the IPKF was ordered to "take Jaffna." And this the Indian army proceeded to do over the next two weeks through a five-column, ground troop–intensive, massively armored operation that took twice as long as anticipated. Throughout the laborious conquest of Jaffna, the IPKF came under tremendous attack from LTTE snipers, improvised land mines, booby traps, and other devices in a town with narrow streets and a high population density. Predictably, the IPKF incurred enormous casualties and caused an incredible amount of destruction to the town and its civilian population. It would do in the second half of October 1987 precisely what the Indians had prevented the Sri Lankan state from trying to do during the Vadamarachi operation earlier in the year: take Jaffna by sheer force of arms and numbers, making little distinction between civilian and guerrilla. On October 26, a week later than expected, and with vastly greater resistance than envisaged, the five columns of Indian troops converged in Jaffna town, and it was officially under the control of the Indian army.

It was a Pyrrhic victory as the leadership of LTTE and much of its cadre melted away across the lagoons and into the jungles of the

Vanni. They would regroup outside the narrow band of control exercised by the IPKF (in the towns and along the arterial roads) and would bleed the IPKF white. According to official Indian figures, in the assault on Jaffna alone, 262 of their soldiers died and nearly a thousand were injured, and they had killed between 700 and 800 LTTE (Kadian 1990, 50). One of the most reliable accounts, written by a group of human rights activists in Sri Lanka, had this to say about the Indian assault on the town in October and the month thereafter:

> During the months of October and November, 1987, Jaffna witnessed death and destruction on a scale unprecedented in its history.... The so called Operation Liberation, in the middle of 1987 in the Vadamaratchi area brought the action into the heartland of the Tamils in Sri Lanka. A similar fate for the rest of Jaffna peninsula had been in the offing and frequently threatened. It is a tragic irony that it was left to the Indians who had all along been championing the Tamil cause and had been looked upon as their saviours and protectors, to complete this task.... [I]n terms of the agony, destruction, terror and mayhem of complete war and the duration of continued action, the Indian military action far surpassed anything Jaffna had ever experienced. (Hoole et al., 1990, 281)

The authors had well-substantiated reasons for calling the Indian destruction of Jaffna "unprecedented" even in that city's tragic history. Although facts and figures seem inadequate to convey the violence, perhaps two vignettes may do so. On October 21, 1987, Deepavali Day,[18] the Indian army assaulted Jaffna Hospital on suspicion it harbored some LTTE militants. At the end of a siege lasting more than twenty-four hours, seventy civilians had been killed, all of them either doctors and staff or ailing patients. Here is an account of what happened:

> The Indian Army entered through the out gate, came up along the corridor and fired indiscriminately. They fired into the Overseer's office, and into other offices. I saw many of my fellow workers die.... Another worker whispered to me: Keep lying down and do not move. So we lay down quietly, under one of the dead bodies, throughout the night. One of the overseers had a cough and he groaned and coughed once in a way in the night. One Indian soldier threw a grenade at this man killing some more persons.... In another spot one man got up with his hand up and cried out: We are innocent. We are sup-

porters of Indira Gandhi. A grenade was thrown at him. He and his brother next to him died. The night passed by, and the morning dawned. Still, it was absolutely tense. At about 8:30 am, Dr. Sivapathasundaram, the Paediatrician, came walking along the corridor with 3 nurses. He had convinced them that they should identify themselves and surrender. They were walking with their hands up shouting: We surrender, we are innocent doctors and nurses. Dr. Sivapathasundaram was gunned down point blank and the nurses injured. He was a man who had come to save the lives of the children and neonates marooned in the hospital. (Hoole et al. 1990, 267–68)

The quoted section above was written by Dr. Rajini Thiranagama, senior lecturer in anatomy at the University of Jaffna and a human rights activist. Dr. Thiranagama would be killed at the age of thirty-five by LTTE a couple of years later in Jaffna.

As in many counterinsurgency situations, the army stopped trying to distinguish between combatant and civilian, and the latter often paid a huge price. The psychological destruction that came in the wake is illustrated in this experience of a man and his wife:

A middle-aged engineer whose 3 children and mother-in-law had been pulled out of their home and shot dead on the street for no apparent reason, developed a severe grief reaction with secondary alcoholism. He spent his days in deep sorrow with attacks of crying spells, the pangs of grief buffeting him like waves. His mind was preoccupied with thoughts of his children. He complained of loss of purpose in life with suicidal ruminations. His nights were particularly bad with recurrent nightmares about his daughter. The soldier had lifted up her frock and shot her through the groin. She could not walk and had to drag herself along the road and finally bled to death for lack of adequate medical attention. This picture kept recurring in his mind. He would say: "She was deeply loved and I brought her up without a care. And now she had to suffer like this. . . . It is unbearable," and break into sobs. Hostility, a feature typical of grief reaction, was apparent in his accusations of medical mismanagement, wanting revenge ("I'll personally kill these soldiers") and his filing a case. His wife too was inconsolable and he expressed a fear that she would cry herself to death. They felt that without their children, life had lost its meaning. Previously an occasional drinker, he had now started drinking heavily and was in a state of intoxication most of the day and night. (Hoole et al. 1990, 293)

And thus did the Indian Peace Keeping Force subdue Jaffna.

A POLITICAL AND MILITARY QUAGMIRE

General Depinder Singh had long maintained it would be a thankless and endless task for IPKF to get embroiled in a counterinsurgency war. Yet, that was precisely what happened from October 1987 until March 1990, when the last Indian soldier left Sri Lankan soil. India's longest war lasted thirty-two months, and would end with 1,155 soldiers dead and almost 3,000 wounded. Many among the wounded lost their limbs as they stepped on the home-made "Johnny" mines perfected by LTTE. Civilian casualties are estimated at anywhere between 3,000 and 4,000. Although sources claim LTTE lost 2,220 cadres and had 1,220 wounded, LTTE itself claims it lost less than 600. On average, India spent about Rs. 5 crores a day during the IPKF's operations in Sri Lanka (see Gunaratna 1993, 315, for details).

The folly of acquiring territory was apparent after the fall of Jaffna. Although it gave the impression of the Indians gaining control in the war against the LTTE, the reality was that the latter's writ ran in the northern and the eastern provinces. The IPKF was able neither to disarm the militants (as envisaged in the agreement) nor to wreak a decisive military defeat on them. As the IPKF's presence in Sri Lanka continued, its popularity and its reputation eroded, not to speak of the continuous drain on it in terms of casualties. The incoherence of Indian policy vis-à-vis the militants was confounded by the fact that talks between RAW and LTTE representatives in Madras continued openly until October 1988 and clandestinely thereafter. The ostensible reasoning behind the two approaches was that the IPKF was supposed to soften the LTTE militarily, while the supposedly diplomatic channel remained open through the talks. Whatever the intent, the effect of such talks was to further demoralize the IPKF, which could not fathom its purpose in Sri Lanka.

General Ashok Mehta, who commanded the Fifty-seventh Mountain Division in Sri Lanka (responsible for the Batticaloa and Amparai districts) trenchantly summarized the incoherence of Indian actions:

> The task kept changing as the political situation kept changing. I cannot recall any specific briefing such as, for example, the task is to destroy the LTTE. I don't think there was ever such a task because the

word 'destroy' I don't think was used in relation to the LTTE.... [T]hroughout my little less than 2 years, I really got nothing from people above me either in terms of intelligence or political guidance or military directions.... [I]t was terribly frustrating to be in charge of an operation situation where the flow of information, or the flow of intelligence from outside was so little and the directions in which to move, either politically or militarily, were so fuzzy.[19]

To such statements from the army generals, someone like Dixit could well respond, "The Army was not able to fully comprehend the political terms of reference of the directive given to them."[20] This response sounds self-serving, a disingenuous attempt to pass off confusion as complexity. The tension between regarding ethnonationalism as hostile to pluralist nationhood, on the one hand, and seeing a neighbor's ethnic problem as an opportunity to destabilize it, on the other, had never been faced up to with regard to Indian actions in Sri Lanka from the early 1980s. Consequently, they simply muddled on, hoping for some magical resolution to appear suddenly from somewhere. After all, as detailed in the previous chapter, the original impetus had been the desire to have a spectacular display of statesmanship and sign the agreement: the devilish details of its implementation seemed a lesser concern. Now that Jaffna had fallen, the hope seemed to be that it would be just a matter of time before the LTTE buckled under and saw things India's way. Even if it didn't, at the top there wasn't much interest in reevaluating options. For nearly two and a half years after the fall of Jaffna, the Indian army continued "jungle bashing" and both suffering and inflicting casualties.

Jayewardene, for his part, commenced delivering the constitutional side of issues—namely, the Provincial Councils Bill and the Thirteenth Amendment to the Sri Lankan Constitution—which he did in the context of the full-blown insurgency of the JVP. The Supreme Court had adjudicated favorably on the constitutionality of both bills (by the slimmest margin possible, five to four) and ruled that a two-thirds majority in Parliament would suffice, a countrywide referendum not being needed. On November 13, Premadasa moved both bills in Parliament, as he was constitutionally obligated to, where they were approved by a resounding majority. Whereas Jayewardene could rightly regard this approval as an indication of the degree to which he continued to call the shots, the Tamil parties regarded the Provincial Councils Bill and the Thirteenth Amendment as inadequate and a virtual reneging on promises made in the agreement of 1987.

It was, as always, left to TULF to spell out its objections. It did so in the form of a letter addressed to Rajiv Gandhi, after failing to convince anyone in the Jayewardene administration on the merits of its case. These objections centered on the issue of single administrative unit, legislative and executive power in the provincial councils, the list of devolved subjects, land and land settlement, Trincomalee port, the Provincial Public Service, and the issue of Tamil as an official language. TULF's objections concluded with the following: "we earnestly request you to ask President Jayewardene not to proceed with the two Bills in Parliament in the present form till the matters referred to herein are discussed and resolved to the satisfaction of the Tamil people" (TULF 1988, 153–56). There was no response from New Delhi.

By the end of 1987, the most significant aspects of the agreement lay in tatters. The disarming of the militants had not occurred; the Indian army had been unable to defeat the LTTE militarily or get them to cooperate with the agreement; and, although significant changes had been made to the Sri Lankan Constitution and provincial councils had been established, per the agreement, many of these changes commanded little credibility with any of the Tamil groups or the Sinhalese, though for opposite reasons. As an instance of counterinsurgency, the document had failed completely. In addition to the war in the North, the rest of Sri Lanka was wracked with violence as the JVP commenced to assassinate hundreds of civilians and a number of leaders identified as cooperating with the agreement. In response, the security forces countered the insurgency in the South with undocumented arrests, imprisonment without trial, and the deaths of JVP cadres in encounters. The number of disappearances engineered by both the JVP and the security forces increased dramatically over these months.

THE AGREEMENT UNRAVELS

The following two years (1989 and 1990) saw the various parties trying to carve out their political fortunes by locating themselves relative to the agreement. On December 25, 1987, after a prolonged illness, the chief minister of Tamil Nadu, M. G. Ramachandran died.

For the next month, Tamil Nadu became a theater of the absurd as his widow, Janaki Ramachandran, and Jayalalitha Jayaraman (a former cinema star and MGR's erstwhile assistant) battled each other for succession. As AIADMK split into irreconcilable factions, President's Rule was imposed on January 30, 1988. For the next year, until January 1989, Tamil Nadu would be under the direct rule of New Delhi. The supply of arms, ammunition, medicines, fuel, foodstuffs, and various other goods moved easily between Tamil Nadu and Jaffna, and Tamil militants injured by IPKF in Sri Lanka routinely obtained treatment from doctors in coastal Tamil Nadu. These details are commonly cited as proof of the reservoir of sympathy for the LTTE's cause in Tamil Nadu.

Yet some facts merit mention in this regard. First, this cross-border traffic was hardly news; it had gone on unimpeded through the entire 1980s, with the central government choosing to look the other way or even abetting it, as seen in earlier chapters. Second, for an entire year (January 1988 to January 1989), the state was under the thumb of New Delhi in the form of President's Rule. Yet the period is conspicuous for the absence of any sustained effort by the central government to monitor the coastlines and ensure that such traffic ceased. As noted, for much of 1988, RAW was actively holding talks with LTTE in Madras to see if a political solution was on the cards. It was, in fact, tacitly agreed between the center and LTTE that injured cadres could be treated in Madras hospitals. Further, the Indian navy and coast guard could not effectively monitor the shorelines even if they had wanted to: it was simply too vast (the Tamil Nadu coastline alone is 1,600 kilometers). Moreover, as every journalist who covered this beat would attest, LTTE paid good money in return for such services. Officials of the government were no more immune to such seductions than ordinary people in Tamil Nadu.

Although the Indian army was at war with LTTE in Jaffna, as far as public opinion in Tamil Nadu was concerned, there were hardly any repercussions. At one level, this was indicated by the fact that both factions of AIADMK in January 1988, tried to outdo one another in braying their loyalty to the central government, including to its policy on Sri Lanka, in an effort to get recognition as the ruling party. Once the Assembly was dissolved, the two factions of AIADMK competed with DMK to gain the affections of the Congress and Rajiv Gandhi. As had been the pattern in Tamil Nadu since the mid-

1970s, the electoral arithmetic dictated that in a polity dominated by three parties, an alliance — or a seat adjustment, to be precise — was the easier way to come to power at the state level (see chapter 3). Throughout the period October 1987 to the end of 1988, while IPKF conducted its war against LTTE, the political scene in Tamil Nadu was marked by the absence of any sustained popular or organized opposition to the central government's Sri Lanka policy. Surveys taken by the newspaper *Hindu* at this time indicated, if anything, that Tamil Nadu supported the IPKF's presence in Sri Lanka to an extent that equalled or exceeded that the support of other places in India.[21]

One important reason for the prolonged spell of central rule in Tamil Nadu at this time can be gleaned by examining what was actually going on in the state at this time. Congress (I) under Rajiv Gandhi had decided that its twenty-year absence from Fort St. George in Madras ought to be brought to an end. Sensing disarray in the AIADMK, Congress attempted throughout the year after MGR's death to win the affections of people and to try to come to power in the state without allying with either Dravidian party. Consider the following excerpt detailing the efforts of Rajiv Gandhi and Congress in the year 1988 in this regard:

> Perhaps no Prime Minister or Congress (I) president before Rajiv Gandhi had spent so much time and energy in Tamil Nadu. In fact, he has set a record for the time spent by any head of the Union Government in a State. Beginning April 1988 . . . Rajiv made seven trips to the State in eight months, covering all the districts and parliamentary constituencies. . . . [T]he Congress (I) seems to be in no mood to cast away what it sees as its first chance in 21 years to regain power in Tamil Nadu. . . . The party considers the State a foothold in the South, because it has lost power in all the other southern States. . . . With the general elections due before the end of 1989, the party intends to make Tamil Nadu a launching pad for its forays into the South. (*Frontline*, December 10–23, 1988, 4–9)

Throughout the year, Congress kept DMK and the two factions of AIADMK guessing about whether or not it would seek an alliance with any of them. In the effort to present themselves as worthy electoral partners, these Dravidian parties did not question the central government's policies on the Tamil issue in Sri Lanka, nor did they mobilize any opposition to IPKF's presence there or about reports of IPKF atrocities in Sri Lanka. It was only after the Congress decided that it was going it alone this time in Tamil Nadu that DMK tried to make some capital out of criticizing India's policy on the Tamil question in Sri Lanka. Even the latter ought not to be exaggerated, as Dagmar Hellmann-Rajanayagam notes:

> the Sri Lanka issue figured only in a very minor way in news and propoganda. There were far more pressing domestic problems to be tackled. . . . *If the Sri Lanka issue came in, it came in via the Congress which tried to gain a new foothold in Tamilnadu politics after 20 years out in the cold, and could do this only by playing the Tamil and Sri Lanka card.* For all other parties, this was an important, but not a life-and-death issue. They had enough "Dravidian" credibility not to need the Sri Lankan Tamils to prove it. . . . In the same vein, they [Congress] emphasised what they had achieved in the Sri Lankan problem by concluding the Accord, which was Congress' work. (1994, 131–32, emphasis added)[22]

In fact, the quote indicates an enduring reality about Indian intervention in Sri Lanka all through the 1980s: if anything, it was motivated to a greater extent by the desire of Congress (I) to reemerge as a political party of substance in Tamil Nadu than by any pressure exerted by so-called secessionist Dravidian parties and ideology on the central government.

When assembly elections were finally held in January 1989, Congress did go it alone in the hopes of carrying the state. As events turned out, Congress miscalculated badly. They wound up with only 20 percent of the popular vote in Tamil Nadu and a paltry number of seats, 26. DMK, which obtained a third of the popular vote (33.44 percent), emerged as easily the largest party in the legislature, garnering 146 seats in a house of 232. Karunanidhi was back as chief minister of the state after a gap of thirteen years. Congress's efforts to parlay the signing of the agreement into electoral success in Tamil Nadu, on the basis of supporting kindred ethnic minorities in neighboring countries, had come a cropper. Befitting their utterly marginal status in Tamil Nadu's politics, the small handful of politicians who had made the Sri Lankan Tamil cause their main platform (such as P. Nedumaran and D. Somasundaram) were routed in the polls. If they could gain no support based on this platform at the height of the Indian army's operations against Sri Lankan Tamils, with the media rife with reports of IPKF atrocities and excesses there, one can well surmise that the real extent of support for the Eelamist cause in Tamil Nadu was negligible.

This detour through the assembly elections in Tamil Nadu is important: it strongly supports my argument that ethnicity is not something primordial and essentialist, always representing a threat to the principle of nationality. For all the efforts of people in Delhi and in Sri Lanka to link the Sri Lankan Tamils and the Tamils of Tamil Nadu through the putative links of their common ethnicity, in general the Tamils within India showed no more affinity for the cause of the Sri Lankan Tamils than people elsewhere. The attribution of a common ethnicity to these two Tamil communities ought to be understood not in terms of a primordial essence that united them, but in terms of the opportunities presented by such a conflation. Although these opportunities were differentially availed of by all parties concerned, the evidence seems overwhelming that the main impetus of the conflation came from the desire of the Congress regime in New Delhi, first, to use ethnicity as an alibi for its intervention in Sri Lanka and, second, to use this intervention as a means to gain the support of Tamils in Tamil Nadu by outdravidianizing the Dravidian parties there.

In Sri Lanka, elections to seven provincial councils, barring the Northeast, were held between April and June 1988. SLFP chose to boycott these elections on the grounds that the provincial councils had been dictated to the Sri Lankans through the agreement. Consequently, most of the elections were won easily by UNP. The turnouts were abysmal on account of both SLFP's boycott and JVP's threat to eliminate anyone who dared take part. On July 31, 1988, a year after the agreement had been signed, Jayewardene announced that elections to the Northeastern Provincial Council (NEPC) would be held in November, with or without the participation of LTTE. And in September of the same year, he announced that the North and East were now merged, pending a referendum to be held at a later date. By this time, Jayewardene had finally decided that he was not going to be a contender for the presidency and that Premadasa would be the nominee for the presidential elections to be held in December 1988. Soon after, in February 1989, elections to the Sri Lankan Parliament were to be held: the country was to go in for three important elections in quick succession.

The provincial council elections in the Northeast were a farce, although both governments tried to paint them as an important step forward in implementing the agreement. LTTE boycotted the elections and threatened anyone who took part in them with eventual retribution. In the North, the boycott was complete, and the candidates of the only party in the fray, EPRLF, were returned uncontested. In the East, both the number of contestants and turnouts were high; indeed, the latter were sometimes suspiciously high. EPRLF and others toeing a pro-India line did well once again. TULF refused to contest the elections on grounds that the provincial councils and Thirteenth Amendment did not go far enough in making the concessions promised to the Tamils. Thus, an election of dubious integrity was held under complete supervision of IPKF, and the EPRLF, a militant group that was now close to India, came to power (De Silva and Wriggins 1994, 699, state that the elections were rigged by the IPKF; I see little reason to doubt them). But the reality in the North was that even though EPRLF controlled the Northeastern Provincial Council, LTTE's writ still ran in that part of the country.

In the presidential elections held on December 19, 1988, neither of the two main presidential candidates (who would get more than 95 percent of the vote between them) supported the agreement, and both explicitly committed themselves to the speedy repatriation of IPKF from Sri Lanka. Mrs. Bandaranaike, the SLFP candidate, promised that she would undo the provincial councils, demerge the North and East, and revisit the Thirteenth Amendment. Premadasa was committed to the provincial councils and the devolution of powers but made it evident that his priorities were the exit of the IPKF and the replacement of the agreement of 1987 with a more evenhanded treaty between the two governments. Premadasa eventually won one of the narrowest elections in Sri Lanka's history, prevailing over Bandaranaike by a wafer-thin margin. The one candidate who supported the agreement, Ossie Abeygunasekara, representing the United Socialist Alliance, received less than 5 percent of the votes cast.[23]

In February, during the parliamentary elections, UNP returned with a majority, albeit a greatly diminished one in comparison with their four-fifths majority in the "long parliament" (1977–89) of Jayewardene's time. In the northeastern province, EPRLF won seven seats, and EROS (a militant group whose political adeptness is best captured by the fact that at this time they were both trusted by LTTE and supported the Indo–Sri Lanka Agreement) won twelve seats. In a sad indication of TULF's marginality, Amirthalingam himself was defeated in Batticaloa and V. Yogeswaran in Jaffna. Once Premadasa and UNP won a majority in the parliament, their attitude toward the Northeastern Provincial Council and the ruling EPRLF there turned actively hostile. They began to do everything to ensure that the EPRLF regime had neither resources nor any assistance from Colombo to work the provincial council system effectively. The EPRLF-led Northeastern Provincial Council survived in power entirely on monetary and other aid from India.[24]

When the presidential and parliamentary elections were over, February 1989, Premadasa began publicly to demand the immediate withdrawal of the IPKF. The months thereafter saw some of the most acrimonious exchanges of letters and messages between any two heads of state as Premadasa and Rajiv Gandhi each tried to salvage their careers out of the agreement. For Premadasa, faced with the JVP insurgency in the South, the first task was to win Sinhala public opinion over from the chauvinists, and the best way of doing this was to demand the immediate ouster of India. However, for Rajiv Gandhi, who had cloudy prospects in the parliamentary elections due that year, a face-saving exit from Sri Lanka was a minimal requirement. Finally, after acrimonious talks, the Indians and Sri Lankans arrived at an understanding whereby the IPKF would return to India in December 1989.

Premadasa then worked out a cease-fire with LTTE in mid-April 1989 and, in a development that stunned everyone, began negotiations with them in Colombo himself. A common interest drove Premadasa and the LTTE together at this point: the rapid withdrawal of IPKF from Sri Lanka. It was around this time that evidence emerged that Premadasa was actually arming the LTTE in its fight against the IPFK as well as in its internecine battles against other Tamil groups. The situation was bizarre: while IPKF was in the North and East ostensibly battling LTTE to implement an agreement that underwrote Sri Lankan sovereignty, the president of Sri Lanka (who possibly owed his election to the Indians) was holding talks with LTTE in Colombo and arming them to kill Indian soldiers! For scholars still enamored of maintaining a clear distinction between the state and the terrorist, such an expedient relationship between the president and the LTTE ought to give pause. Just as the Indians had cynically used the various Tamil militant groups to pressure Jayewardene's regime since 1983, Premadasa demonstrated that he could just as effectively use the LTTE to do the reverse. Once again, ethnonationalism, far from being a threat to statist sovereignty, was used as an opportunity to produce sovereignty itself.[25]

As a retaliation for Premadasa's arming LTTE, RAW was assigned to create a new entity, something called the Tamil National Army (TNA), which would ostensibly protect the Tamils and the EPRLF regime in the Northeast against both the LTTE and the Sri Lankan armed forces once the Indians left the scene. Given the realities of the situation, the TNA could only be forcibly conscripted in the North and the East. RAW relied on militants from the EPRLF, ENDLF (Eelam National Democratic Liberation Front), and TELO to help them "recruit" members for the TNA. They literally kidnapped boys of no more than twelve or thirteen years of age and took them to the training camps. Such abductions occurred from schools, playgrounds, and even homes. Often boys in this age group had to remain indoors and hidden for months on end to escape being captured and conscripted in this manner. Once captured and in camp, the first order of business was to shave off the hair from their heads and even their eyebrows to ensure that if they escaped they could be easily idenitified. These boys, variously estimated at a few thousand, were then given some rough and ready training, put into uniforms, armed with deadly weapons such as assault rifles, and sent out to do battle with the LTTE. For each boy conscripted in this fashion, RAW paid a certain amount of money or weapons to the militants who had done the recruiting. Even this system of recruitment was thoroughly vitiated by corruption. Often, a young boy would be kidnapped by EPRLF or some other group, which would then collect payment from RAW. Soon, the boy's parents would come to these same groups and plead with them for the release of their child. In exchange for a few thousand rupees, tantamount to a ransom, the kidnappers would spring the boy from camp back to his parents.

In my conversations with Sri Lankan human rights activists in Trincomalee and Batticaloa in 1994, one theme was repeated over and over again: the conscription and massacre of the TNA boys at India's behest was simply unforgivable. It had devastated many families, and the senseless slaughter of so many young children was appalling. The human rights activists were also clear that the recruiting for the TNA and the slaughter that followed were not the IPKF's doing so much as RAW's. (In an ironic comment on the "secrecy" of the Indian intelligence agency, just about everyone knew that RAW was headquartered in the Batticaloa guest house.) In the months that followed, hundreds if not thousands of such boys would be massacred by LTTE, which would come into possession of all their weapons as well.

In the Indian parliamentary elections of November 1989, the National Front led by V. P. Singh replaced Congress and Rajiv Gandhi at the center, cobbling together enough seats to form a coalition government. In the state of Tamil Nadu, however, the Congress-AIADMK combination swept the polls, the former winning twenty-four of the twenty-five seats it contested, and the latter winning all eleven it entered. DMK drew a complete blank. Coming less than a year after its victory in state elections, the rout of DMK was mainly a result of the seat adjustment negotiated between Congress and AIADMK. The argument that the state assembly should be dissolved and fresh elections called in accordance with the "new" sentiments of the public was inevitable. As a constituent in V. P. Singh's National Front, DMK was saved from any such immediate fate. However, it would become the sole mission of Congress and AIADMK in Tamil Nadu to create conditions whereby Karunanidhi's regime would be destabilized and toppled so that new state elections could be called.

In searching for a compelling reason to discredit the DMK regime and to prepare the ground for its dismissal, Congress and AIADMK inevitably hit upon the activities of LTTE in Tamil Nadu as a convenient issue. As seen earlier, given the porous boundary between India and Sri Lanka, and the thriving political economy of corruption along the coastline, such charges could always be substantiated with "evidence." In addition, Karunanidhi seemed to play into their hands to a certain degree. First, DMK's rhetoric on the Tamil question in Sri Lanka had always been far ahead of its policies or politics, and some of these flourishes could always be selectively used to indicate their supposedly anti-national inclinations. Second, when the last troops of the Indian Peace Keeping Force left Sri Lanka and arrived at Madras harbor on March 24, 1990, the chief minister was unwisely a notable absentee at the ceremonies to welcome them.

He remarked that he was not about to welcome back troops responsible for the killing of more than five thousand Tamil "brethren." Blaming the IPKF for the follies of the previous regime seemed, at the very least, tactless.

Back in Sri Lanka, the LTTE was in command. The IPKF had been forced out of the country by March 1990, and almost within hours of their withdrawal, the TNA in its various guises was mopped up by LTTE. The puppet regime of the EPRLF collapsed like a house of cards, and its leaders and cadre fled to India. Without a single shot being fired, the entire Northeast had fallen into the LTTE's hands. Jayewardene, for one, was utterly disgusted with this turn of events. He recollected Ranjan Wijeratne (the popular and fast-rising defense minister under Premadasa) coming to his house to discuss the issue with him and the two of them being unable to fathom the logic of Premadasa's actions. They felt the withdrawal of the IPKF should have been done in such a way that once the JVP insurgency had been quelled in the South, the Sri Lankan army could have taken over territory from the Indian army in a phased deinduction. In his haste to get the IPFK out and believing LTTE could be won over by concessions short of Eelam, Premadasa was handing over the North and East on a platter to the LTTE. In fact, the former president revealed rather enviable command over unparliamentary language in his off-the-record comments about Premadasa's folly in trusting the LTTE at this time and the hasty manner in which the IPKF was deinducted.[26] Militarily, in mid-1990, LTTE had no adversaries left in the region they called Tamil Eelam. They were well rested thanks to IPKF's halting of operations against them in September 1989. The TNA had not put up any fight worth the name. The Sri Lankan state had its hands full with the JVP insurgency all over the South, which had now been on for more than two years. In India, the V. P. Singh regime seemed determined to reverse all its predecessor's policies in Sri Lanka. Any decline in Indian interest in Sri Lankan affairs at this point seemed ideal from LTTE's point of view.

In July 1987, the IPKF had entered Jaffna to a euphoric and tumultuous welcome. The Tamil population seemed convinced that peace was at hand, that the Indians would do them no wrong. Three years later, they were the forgotten soldiers of a forgotten war. The EPRLF-led Northeastern Provincial Council, however, still had one trick left to play. Even as that puppet regime packed its bags to abandon Jaffna for exile in India as the LTTE closed in, the EPRLF, a militant group favored by RAW because of their supposed fealty to India, did something that went against everything that India was ostensibly trying to do in Sri Lanka. It inexplicably and unilaterally declared an independent state of Eelam. This futile and soon forgotten quixotic gesture captured, in its own tragicomic way, the confused and contradictory mess that was Indian policy in Sri Lanka.

CONCLUSION

The Indian government tried to portray the Indo–Sri Lanka Agreement of 1987 and the related induction of the Indian Peace Keeping Force, primarily as an act of counterinsurgency. The IPKF's task, ostensibly, was to separate the warring ethnic groups, disarm the militants, oversee the establishment of the provincial councils, and enable Jayewardene to give his undivided attention to crush the JVP uprising in the South. From the very beginning, this representation of the agreement was contested, in both Sri Lanka and India. As previous chapters detailed, Indian motivations in pressuring Sri Lanka to enter into such an agreement exceeded the need for counterinsurgency. There was the desire to appear as a regional power capable of imposing its writ on a smaller neighbor. Some motivation no doubt came from a desire to see Sri Lanka solve its ethnic conflict not just by using the military, but by recognizing itself as a multiethnic society. In addition, there was the ruling Congress Party's keenness to be seen as the defender of kindred ethnic minorities within and outside the country — and, on that score, to win elections in Tamil Nadu and elsewhere.

This genealogy fractured Indian understandings of the agreement, pitting various institutions and individuals against each other and rendering the overall policy incoherent. The IPKF clearly entered Sri Lanka with a rather limited view of their outlined task and with the belief that, if anything, they ought to tilt in favor of the Tamils. The Indian government, especially once hostilities commenced in October 1987, seemed unable to decide whether or not it sought the elimination of the LTTE (assuming that was ever possible). Once Jaffna was taken, but the LTTE refused to go under, the IPKF's mission in Sri Lanka became more and more confused. From there on, Indian policy became mere drift, muddling along in the hope that somehow, somewhere, a face-saving denouement could be found: it never did.

Most people in Sri Lanka saw the agreement as dictated to them by India and at a grave diminution of their own sovereignty. It was thus seen not as an instrument of counterinsurgency but rather as a symbol of Indian hegemony. A halting and halfhearted process of constitutional reform commenced, alienating both the majority community and the Tamil minority, albeit for opposite reasons. Once it failed to solve the ethnic conflict speedily, opposing the agreement became something every aspiring Sinhalese leader used as a springboard for his own political career. The agreement was heaven-sent for the extreme right-wing Sinhala chauvinist group, the JVP, which found the presence of the IPKF on Sri Lankan soil an issue like none other to launch a violent struggle to capture state power. The LTTE recognized very quickly that the "success" (however defined) of the agreement represented the end of their quest for Eelam. From then on, their sole motivation lay in wrecking the agreement. In this latter quest, they were no doubt helped enormously by both the disarray among the Indians and the sizable numbers among the Sinhalese who bore nothing but ill will toward the agreement.

The collision of these multiple, contending narratives on the agreement produced a brutal conflict. At the end of the IPKF's stint in Sri Lanka, matters were as intractable as ever. It is befitting that the last words on this inglorious chapter in Indian regional hegemony be reserved for General Depinder Singh, who poses a crucial question. Ironically, the problem is not that there isn't an answer to this question but rather that there are too many answers to it: "Why did we end up fighting the LTTE? ... [E]ven today, three years after the event, I am not sure whether the LTTE duped us or, perceiving that we were trying to dupe them, they turned the tables on us. Also what role did the Sri Lanka Government perform in muddying an increasingly murky situation?" (n.d., 65).

7

Postcolonial Aporias:
Nationalism, Ethnicity, and Violence

Shiva and Saleem, victor and victim; understand our rivalry and you
will gain an understanding of the age in which you live. (The reverse
of this statement is also true.)
— SALMAN RUSHDIE, MIDNIGHT'S CHILDREN

If an aporia is defined as a problem or difficulty arising from an awareness of opposing or incompatible views on the same theoretic matter, it seems to me that we have reached an aporetic stage in the postcolonial quest for nation building. The very practices that produce the nation are coeval with its simultaneous fragmentation or unraveling. Although the supposedly progressive and universal idea of the nation is expected to eventually triumph over the reactionary and particularist idea denoted as ethnicity, a close look at the practices of nation building reveal that both nation and ethnicity share a logic that seeks to align territory with identity (the belief that every territory is ideally inhabitable by a singular identity); moreover, both nation and ethnicity opportunistically feed off each other as they seek to define themselves in contradistinction. A clear instance of the dialectical, mutually constitutive and productive relationship that connects nation and ethnicity can be found in the reasons for and the eventual failure of Indian intervention into Sri Lankan affairs in the 1980s.

Although it would be tempting to regard the Indo–Sri Lanka Agreement of 1987 as something that could have succeeded if only

the various institutions that made up the Indian state had cooper-
ated, or if the LTTE had played ball, or if the IPKF had been more
efficient, or if the Sinhalese had had the political will, and so on, I
suggest the failure of the agreement to work as an instrument of
counterinsurgency is better read as a sign of a pervasive and deep-
seated crisis of sovereignty as it is presently conceived in South Asia.
One of the most important signifiers of conventional notions of sovereignty, the state's monopoly over the means of legitimate coercion, has now come to be shared not only with insurgent movements of various hues, but also with intelligence agencies under the
imperfect control of the state. In the last two decades, the numbers
of dead from so-called low-intensity interstate and intrastate conflicts vastly exceed by many orders of magnitude the numbers of
those killed as a consequence of more traditionally defined wars.[1]
The continuous and egregious resort to violence, by the state and
various oppositional movements, is itself a signifier of the eroding
sovereignty of these regimes. Each of the countries in South Asia is
home to violent insurgencies that control swathes of territory; command (to varying degrees) the allegiance of peoples within such territories; are plugged into global networks of diasporic support, armaments, and capital; and, in some instances, have acquired a degree
of autonomy from the state that has made them credible alternatives to the state itself. The LTTE, for example, has a diplomatic
presence in a number of western capitals; it simultaneously has relations with a large number of other, similar insurgent movements
in many countries; it has a fleet of ships (registered under various
pseudonyms) for its "foreign trade"; it has repeatedly stunned Indian and Sri Lankan armies by upping the technological ante of
weapon systems used in war; it possesses a mobile communications
network that is much more sophisticated than any in the possession
of the government; at one point, it had established its own courts
and system of jurisprudence in the areas it controlled; it runs a radio and television station and a newspaper; it delivers the mail; it
issues (or denies) visas for people entering its territory; and it col-
lects taxes — from both its domestic constituency (in Jaffna) and its
diasporic constituency all over the world (indeed, its knowledge of
the bank accounts and other financial details of people under its
control would be the envy of any conventional government).

Moreover, insurgent movements are now thoroughly enmeshed within the everyday politics of South Asia and are integral to the state's attempt to produce its own sovereignty and security. This phenomenon is indicated by the multiple roles insurgencies play in the politics of the region. Many receive support from neighboring regimes in their destabilization campaigns against regional adversaries (India encourages Sindhi extremist groups in Pakistan, and Pakistan bankrolls Kashmiri separatists in India). They are used in domestic politics as a means to discredit opposition-led regimes (extremist Khalistani groups were used to dismiss the moderate Akali regime in Punjab). They serve important symbolic functions in the quest for political power (the use made by both the Congress Party and the Dravidian parties of their support for the Sri Lankan Tamil militants at various points in the 1980s is a good case in point). They are used for military purposes by the states in the region (Premadasa's arming of the LTTE in 1989 to help oust the IPKF from Sri Lanka is one instance). And the putative access or control that politicians or intelligence agencies have over such militants can make them important players in political affairs (note, for example, the relationship of Tamil Nadu's chief minister, MGR, and the intelligence agency RAW with the Tamil militants in the 1980s). In other words, the dialectic between the nation and its various ethnonationalist fragments is critical to the production and reproduction of both entities. The quest to "secure" the nation is premised on practices that generate the multiple insecurities that unravel the nation even as it is being made. The debt that a politics of security owes to its ineradicable twin, the politics of insecurity, is captured by Michael Dillon when he observes, "there is a fundamental belonging together of security and insecurity: an indissoluble connection. The radical ambivalence of (in)security is therefore not a paradox. Neither is it a contradiction to be resolved through more careful securing. This ambivalence is inescapable and it provides the very dynamic behind the way in which security operates as a generative principle of formation for the production of political order. It is only because it insecures that security can secure" (1995, 162).

I see the problems of nation building encountered by India and Sri Lanka since their respective formations (in 1947 and 1948) not as instances of inadequate or flawed modernization, but as the very form modernity has taken in these countries. The rise of Sinhalese majoritarian ideology and of Tamil secessionism in Sri Lanka are not a resurgence of primordial or premodern affinities. Rather, the modernist requirements of electoral politics, party competition, access to educational opportunities, employment in state-controlled agencies, and the like have been the proximate forces that have engendered identity politics in their present forms in that country. Similarly, the multiple ethnonationalist crises in India are not departures from modernity, but rather constitutive of it. To regard the experiences of India and Sri Lanka since independence as aberrations from the normal form of modernization is to abstract eclectically a pacified, unambiguated history from Europe (a process I have called modulation) and to reify that process as "normal." As the philosopher of science Georges Canguilhem notes regarding the violent and contested process of producing normality, "The normal is not a static and peaceful term, but a dynamic and polemic one. . . . To normalize means: To force upon a being or a given a claim which makes appear the multiplicity of that given not only a strange, but a hostile indetermined. The concept is polemic in that it disqualifies that which is not submitted to its authority and at the same time insists on its incorporation" (translated and quoted by Wagner 1995, 183–84).[2]

In chapter 1, I argued that a normalized narrative of Europe stood above the postcolony as the arbiter of morality and the model to be replicated. To suggest that the experiences of nation building in India and Sri Lanka are lacking in that they are incompletely modern is to misrepresent both South Asia and the history of Europe. It is reflective of a failure to understand that modernity, from its very inception, emerged in the encounter between the west and the rest. Hence, the contemporary crisis of state sovereignty in South Asia is neither an instance of the incomplete modernization of that zone nor an aberration from some hermetically sealed and authentic narrative of modernization found elsewhere. Indeed, the crisis of sovereignty in South Asia is the most prominent sign of the specific form of modernity in that space at this point in time.

In this chapter, I attempt primarily to accomplish two things. First, I analyze the crisis of sovereignty in South Asia by focusing on an aspect of contemporary politics that reflects this aporia: assassinations. I suggest that an important shift has occurred in the discursive regimes governing assassinations. In the late-colonial period and in the immediate aftermath of decolonization, an assassination reflected the breakdown of an implicit moral contract between a leader and civil society (the assassinations of colonial officials by the so-called Bengal and Punjab terrorists in the early twentieth century and of Mohandas Gandhi in early 1948 are relevant exemplars). In more recent decades, assassinations in South Asia have become secular and amoral events, informed by the utilitarian calculations of political rivalries in an overall context of eroding sovereignty and legitimacy of regimes generally. They have moved from being moral statements (however misguided the morality in question may be) to criminal acts, from being public events to anonymous acts, from having a proud assassin demanding his day in court to a faceless perpetrator intent on escape after the deed or a mute suicide bomber who perishes in the act. I argue that assassinations are an apt theater to depict the organic crisis of sovereignty in postcolonial South Asia.

Second, I analyze the fiction of homogeneity that underlies both the nation and various insurgent, ethnonationalist fragments: the belief that ultimately territory and identity must be aligned, brought into conformity, and that each territory is inhabitable exclusively by a singular "authentic" identity. It is this anxiety to achieve a national space occupied by a singular identity—one underlain by a specific understanding of the history of the last few centuries and of the ascendance of the west—that animates and redeems contemporary violences. Deconstructing this fiction of homogeneity is a critical component of any attempt to envisage a world outside this impoverishing historicist script.

A DISENCHANTED SEASON OF ASSASSINATIONS

One of the most striking aspects of Don DeLillo's story on the assassination of John F. Kennedy in *Libra* (1988) is the meticulous detailing of the construction of Lee Harvey Oswald by a menagerie of individuals with varying degrees of attachment to an entity called the U.S. government. More than a patsy, Oswald is a pastiche put together by these people: a photograph from a high school yearbook here, a signed leaflet demanding U.S. noninterference in Cuba there, a document about his less-than-honorable discharge from the U.S. army, a news report about his defection to the Soviet Union, some Communist Party literature from his collection, and so on. These artifacts are not, in and of themselves, spurious or falsified (indeed, in their own way they are the signposts of a life of quiet desperation in underclass America). Yet their seemingly careless assemblage in one place and time would, after the assassination, allow for the construction of a coherent and recognizable narrative implicating "Oswald" as the sole assassin of the president.

The colossal industry that constitutes the Kennedy assassination today is proof that efforts to contain its representation within the confines of "Oswald" have failed resoundingly. However, I would like to draw attention to something else: DeLillo's depiction of the various individuals working in different parts of the United States, often without any knowledge of the others, who together produced Oswald. DeLillo delineates them as an assorted bunch: disaffected intelligence agency types, underemployed mercenaries itching to get their rocks off after the Bay of Pigs debacle, Cuban emigres with an axe to grind, and various others who knew their way around the seamy underbelly of the state. Despite their diverse backgrounds, they had one thing in common: in terms of their present or past institutional affiliations, most could plausibly be regarded as being part of the "government of the United States." They possessed skills and attributes that made them useful to that entity, especially for what are termed covert operations. DeLillo deftly muddies the distinction between "the state" and "the assassin" as *Libra* progresses inexorably to its climax. This distinction is central to narratives that seek to inscribe an assassination within a moralistic genre: an event beyond the pale of civilized politics. In DeLillo's hands, however, the event becomes something always already possible within the domain of statist politics. The men responsible for killing the president of the United States were, to this way of seeing things, not an unpatriotic, immoral, and venal bunch alienated from the state. They were quite the opposite: they cared deeply about the state and the nation and saw themselves as an indispensable, if also invisible, component of the very state whose executive they would decapitate.

DeLillo's blurring of the distinction between the state and the assassin is important as I turn to recent political assassinations in South Asia. Contrary to those who would narrate these assassinations as the tragic deaths of self-sacrificing statesmen at the hands of anti-national subversives, I am interested in shifts in the larger political culture that have made assassinations an integral part of conducting politics in present-day South Asia and of the multiplex pacts that unite both politician and assassin. In the pages that follow, I weave between a chronology of assassinations in Indo-Lanka and a theoretical discussion of the political culture that has banalized them.

Talks between LTTE and the Premadasa government collapsed in June 1990, barely two months after the IPFK left Sri Lanka. The proximate reasons given for this collapse were all too familiar in Sinhala-Tamil relations. The government insisted LTTE disarm completely prior to contesting elections in the Northeastern Provincial Council, whereas LTTE ruled out any such disarming prior to concessions on crucial issues that underwrote Tamil demands for autonomy. Chief among these demands was the repeal of the Sixth Amendment to the Constitution, which mandated all contestants for electoral office swear, under oath, their allegiance to Sri Lanka's unitary state. Given his party's vastly reduced presence in Parliament, Premadasa could not even begin to address this issue, which needed a two-thirds majority. LTTE had used its year-long talks with the Premadasa administration to eliminate physically a number of important rivals within the Tamil parties, just as the president used that same period to kill tens of thousands of suspected JVP insurgents. In July 1989, while talks with Premadasa were proceeding in Colombo, LTTE killed the TULF's Amirthalingam and Yogeswaran. The assassination of two prominent, moderate leaders of the Tamils, one a former leader of the opposition in the Sri Lankan Parliament, was evidently not sufficient for Premadasa to rethink his decision to conduct talks with the LTTE. Three days after these murders, Prabhakaran's long-time adversary and leader of PLOTE, Uma Maheswaran, was killed. A year later, just prior to the breakdown of talks with Premadasa, LTTE killed another TULF member of Parliament, Sam Thambimuttu, in Colombo. And in June 1990, just as what is widely called the Second Eelam War between LTTE and the Sri Lankan army began, LTTE massacred fifteen members of EPRLF, including its leader, K. Padmanabha, in Madras. In the course of a year, LTTE had physically eliminated a whole slew of potential rivals to its claim of being the sole spokesman for the Sri Lankan Tamil cause. In this reliance upon assassination as a means to achieve political consolidation, the group was hardly an exception, as events would soon demonstrate.[3]

The murders of the EPRLF men created a storm of controversy in Tamil Nadu, both for normative reasons and because it was an expedient occasion to discredit the DMK regime of Karunanidhi. Congress and AIADMK predictably attributed the murders to the allegedly cozy relationship that had developed between LTTE and Karunanidhi. The latter immediately listed a series of crimes and misdemeanours committed by Sri Lankan militants in Tamil Nadu going back to the shoot out between Prabhakaran and Maheswaran in 1982, all committed under AIADMK and Congress auspices and hardly any of which had resulted in arrests and convictions. The massacre of the EPRLF leadership was rapidly domesticated in Tamil Nadu and Indian politics, and its import was determined by inter-party rivalries of the time, a rivalry in which no one could occupy the high ground.

In November 1990, the coalition government of V. P. Singh in New Delhi collapsed and was replaced by a minority government, led by Chandrashekar, that survived on Congress support in Parliament. In addition, AIADMK's contingent of members was crucial to its continuance in office. Rajiv Gandhi could decide exactly when the next elections to Parliament would be held by withdrawing his support to Chandrashekar's regime accordingly. Barely two months after the latter took office, Karunanidhi's regime in Tamil Nadu was ousted as a result of pressure by Jayalalitha and Rajiv Gandhi on Chandrashekar, and President's Rule was declared again in Tamil Nadu. The primary reason given for the overthrow was the "deteriorating law and order situation" caused by LTTE's activities and indicated by the intelligence reports of the IB and RAW. The state remained under President's Rule from January 31, 1991, until new elections in May–June 1991. Most observers in Tamil Nadu, although agreeing that law and order under Karunanidhi were nothing to write home about, would also aver they were not all that different from what had obtained either under President's Rule (all of 1988) or, before that, under MGR (1977–87). On any comparative yardstick, Tamil Nadu in 1990–91 was more peaceful and stable than the vast majority of other states in the Indian union. The fact is that the minute V. P. Singh's government collapsed in New Delhi, Karunanidhi's days as chief minister in Tamil Nadu were numbered: the presence of LTTE in Tamil Nadu and the assassinations of the EPRLF leaders were no more than a fig leaf to provide this overthrow of a democratically elected state government with legitimacy.

On March 2, 1991, Sri Lanka's defense minister and architect of the latest war against LTTE, Ranjan Wijeratne, was blown up in Colombo, allegedly by LTTE. Soon thereafter, on the night of May 21, 1991, Rajiv Gandhi was killed by a sucide bomber at an election rally in Sriperumbudur, a town forty kilometers outside of Madras. In the days following that event, accumulating evidence clearly indicated the involvement of LTTE. Largely on account of the sympathy the assassination elicited for the Congress Party, it returned to power at the center, albeit just short of a majority in the Parliament. In Tamil Nadu, a seat adjustment ensured the AIADMK-Congress combination would romp home in both parliamentary and Assembly elections. Exactly a month after Rajiv Gandhi's assassination, a bomb destroyed the headquarters of the Joint Operations Command of the Sri Lankan Armed Forces in Colombo. On August 8, 1992, nearly the entire top leadership of the Sri Lankan army was killed when their Jeep exploded over a land mine on Kayts Island off Jaffna. Besides General Denzil Kobbekaduwa, others killed in the explosion included Commodore Mohan Jayamaha (naval officer commanding the North), Brigadier Wijaya Wimalaratne (who had led the battle at Elephant Pass the previous year, along with Kobbekaduwa), and seven other senior officers. A couple of months later, on November 16, 1992, an LTTE suicide bomber on a motorcycle killed Vice Admiral Clancy Fernando of the Sri Lankan navy. On April 23, 1993, at a rally for the provincial council elections held in the outskirts of Colombo in Kirillapone, the Democratic United National Front (DUNF, a party formed by a faction that broke away from the UNP after Premadasa became president) leader Lalith Athulathmudali was assassinated by a gunman. A week later, as Premadasa led a May Day rally in the streets of Colombo, a suicide bomber on a bicycle rammed into the president, killing him along with many others. More than a year later, in October 1994, as Sri Lanka prepared for a presidential election, the UNP candidate, Gamini Dissanayake (who had returned to the party, leaving the DUNF), was assassinated along with fifty-three others in a bomb blast at a rally in Thotalanga outside Colombo. LTTE was the main suspect in the assassinations of Premadasa and Dissanayake: the modus operandi, suicide bombers perishing in the assassinations, strongly indicated their hand.

If we analyze this spate of assassinations, certain aspects stand out. Firstly, pace *Libra,* it is difficult to sustain a clear demarcation between the state and the assassins in these murders. Consider, for instance, the deaths of both Indira Gandhi and Rajiv Gandhi. The latter's assassination by LTTE was in many ways a direct consequence of the twin-track policy initiated in Sri Lanka by the former in 1981. Despite efforts by the central and Tamil Nadu state governments after May 1991 to portray the LTTE as a fascistic outfit beyond the pale of civilization, the fact is that for much of the 1980s both had done business with that group. From at least 1983 to 1987 (and even after), such business formed a critical component of the twin-track strategy of pressuring the Sri Lankan regime to recognize India's hegemony in the region and various political parties' riding the putative sympathy of Tamil Nadu for the Sri Lankan Tamil cause. By 1987, the LTTE had spun out of RAW's control and had become a powerful player in its own right. Whether or not LTTE eliminated Rajiv Gandhi because it feared he might return to power or as revenge for the induction of the IPKF into Sri Lanka, the governments of Mrs. Gandhi and Rajiv Gandhi cannot escape responsibility for assisting that organization in its early years. Similarly, it is by now widely recognized that Mrs. Gandhi's policy in Punjab of discrediting the moderate Akalis by supporting extremist Khalistani factions proved literally suicidal. In both instances, the short-term and expedient logic of politics dictated actions that culminated in assassinations, as the insurgents spun out of the control of the state and its intelligence agencies. The larger point, however, is that the distinction between state and assassin is clouded: details of earlier collaboration render difficult, if not impossible, any efforts to inscribe the assassinations in an unambiguously sacrificial narrative.

The blurring of lines between the state and assassins is revealed in the inconclusive character of investigations into the assassinations. Commissions of inquiry, collection of evidence, depositions by witnesses have gone on for years, and yet there appears to be little chance of arriving at a definitive conclusion that commands any social credibility. The nub of the problem regarding the inquiries into these assassinations was revealed in a controversy in India regarding the temporal focus of one of the two commissions of inquiry into Rajiv Gandhi's assassination (the Jain Commission). Whereas the Congress Party wanted to limit the time period under review to 1987 and thereafter, DMK wanted the investigations to go all the way back to 1983, if not before. Congress was obviously loath to include the entire period under the purview of the commission because that would have forced a discussion of why, how, where, and to what extent Indian central government officials and intelligence agencies were responsible for supporting, arming, and training Sri Lankan Tamil militants, especially LTTE. By confining the terms of reference to the post-1987 period, Congress could accuse Karunanidhi's DMK regime of being responsible for Rajiv Gandhi's assassination because it was unable to control LTTE activities in that state. In turn, DMK portrayed the assassination as a consequence not of the allegedly lax law-and-order situation on its watch (January 1989– March 1991), but of central government relations with the militants going back to the early 1980s. To put it briefly, the inquiry into the assassination becomes less a matter of uncovering something called the "truth" or what really happened on May 21, 1991, and more a matter of selectively concealing the twin-track policy of the 1980s with regard to Sri Lanka, which had produced, at one time, a dense network of communications between branches of the Indian government and the people who later assassinated its executive. In this context, efforts to sustain a clear distinction between state and assassin run afoul of a history replete with their intertwined character.[4] Predictably, too, the public release of the report on the assassination of the leader becomes an occasion to try and pin the blame for his death on rivals — both within one's own political party and from other parties — and to try and capitalize on a rapidly dwindling reservoir called the "sympathy vote."

Second, the acquisition and retention of political power have become an extraordinarily violent process in South Asia, one in which the state and its managers have developed relations of intimacy with organizations of dubious legality. For instance, Premadasa's successful annihilation of the JVP in 1988–89 was accomplished by the creation of a shadowy parastatist organization called the Black Cats, a virtual praetorian guard of the president. They were given a carte blanche regarding methods and targets, and were used not only to kill the JVP but to intimidate political rivals and other dissidents. Their very existence and modus operandi were closely guarded secrets, and they were accountable to no one but the president him-self. This extralegislative and extrajudicial organization, it is alleged, gradually expanded its responsibilities to eliminate not merely the JVP cadre, but also suspected sympathizers and their families as well as, soon after, human rights activists, journalists who did not toe the regime's line, and political rivals of the president. A promi-nent analyst of contemporary Sri Lankan politics observes:

> Having failed in his sincere attempts to reach a political accomodation with the JVP, Premadasa presided over the crushing of the movement in mid and late 1989. This was achieved through improved military intelligence and the slaughter of most of those suspected of involve-ment. There are no accurate figures, but 40,000 is probably the right order of magnitude. This was followed by a period when open criti-cism of the government would sometimes evoke gruesome threats. In early 1990, a prominent journalist known to be at odds with the gov-ernment was abducted in broad daylight and killed. Allegations that this was on the orders from the highest levels of government are be-lieved by most Sri Lankans. "Fear" was the term most commonly used to describe the political situation at this time. (Moore 1992, 74–75)

What Mick Moore describes as superior "military intelligence" is nothing other than the growing surveillance of the state over civil society, given that the JVP was (and is) thoroughly intermeshed with the fabric of Sri Lankan society. In quelling an insurrection, the state's punitive reach into civil society was extended considerably, with the paradoxical result that the later assassination of prominent political leaders became difficult to disentangle from the pervasive national-security state itself.

Unsurprisingly, given his access to and control over (how com-plete is something we will never know) such a praetorian guard, Pre-madasa himself was suspected in the assassinations not only of his long-time rival Athulathmudali, but also of Defense Minister Ran-jan Wijeratne (who was rapidly emerging as a popular and charis-matic leader within the UNP) and General Denzil Kobbekaduwa (the war hero came with impeccable *goyigama* credentials and was ru-mored to entertain political ambitions).[5] Where the insecurity of lead-ers has created various coercive agencies personally beholden to them, the routinized use of violence to settle differences has become en-demic. Such organizations (and in this category I would include intelligence agencies, criminal gangs, private armies, and special task forces) are, by their very nature and purpose, not amenable to close control and surveillance from the top: there has to be a degree of plausible deniability between the leader and such forces that preclude micromanagement. From annihilating the JVP to settling scores with sundry other real and imagined adversaries through personalized security forces is but a short and tempting step. As rivals within the state and in society respond with violence of their own, assassinations come to be regarded, like war, as little more than the pursuit of politics by other means.

Third, it is clear that a qualitative shift has taken place in postcolonial politics. The capacity to mobilize and unleash annihilatory violence when needed (during elections or pogroms against ethnic minorities) has become an indispensable requirement for anyone in democratic politics. This requirement, in turn, has produced a nexus between the political system and underworld gangs, their dons, goon squads, police and security apparatuses beholden to certain leaders, and private armies. It is tempting to characterize Premadasa's election itself as marking this transition in Sri Lanka. He was, after all, the first president who came from a non-*goyigama* background, cut his spurs in the tough world of Colombo's slums and working-class neighborhoods, had not been to schools such as St. Thomas or Royal, and was not part of the anglicized elite represented by Jayewardene, the Senanayakes, or the Bandaranaikes. But such a characterization would ignore the propensity for and the actual use of violence in politics by the erstwhile anglicized elites themselves. For instance, Jayewardene's biographers (who can hardly be accused of lacking empathy for their protagonist) are compelled to note that

> there was his ambiguous attitude to political violence.... [A]s a man who often spoke of ahimsa and non-violence, praised Gandhi and admired Asoka, he was as ready to tolerate the use of violence in trade union organization and agitation as had some left parties and the SLFP who had already set the pace before. Some prominent but bold critics were beaten up. To be sure, his direct role in these was never clear, but it is widely believed that he was "not uninformed" about them and did not stop them. At such times some wondered why he was not more strict, indeed whether he was really the man in charge. (De Silva and Wriggins 1994, 726)

As the pogrom of July 1983 revealed, suave and urbane leaders such as Dissanayake or Jayewardene were hardly above such means to their ends, even if their ability to fine-tune them was a matter of doubt. As an observer notes in this regard:

> It was during President Jayewardene's early days of power that criminal elements were given open political patronage and recognition. Underworld elements from Colombo's urban slums and the suburbs were called into service by the UNP leaders to intimidate and terrorize trade union and student activists and opposition workers. When one of these gangsters met his death in a fracas...in 1978, his funeral ceremony was graced by the then President and the Minister for Youth Affairs. When another mobster from a suburb of Colombo, with ruling party connections, was killed in 1989 by unidentified gunmen, his powerful patrons in the cabinet were among the mourners at the funeral.[6]

In India, evidence of connections between the political system, including those at the very top, and various underworld characters and dons has been documented by civil liberties groups, human rights organizations, journalists, and academics.[7] Today this nexus has become routine journalistic fare and very much the common wisdom. Much of the literature argues that an acceleration in the criminalization of politics in India occurred in the mid-1970s, specifically during the period immediately before and during the Emergency (June 1975 to March 1977). Primary responsibility is attributed to Mrs. Gandhi and the entry of her son Sanjay Gandhi with his coterie of thugs into the Congress Party. Once again, it has to be emphasized that it was not the spread of democratic politics and wider circles of political participation that inaugurated the turn to criminals and organized intimidation in India, but the actions of those at the very top, especially those born with silver spoons in their mouths. Contemporary violence, unlike in the past, is marked by a very calculated, utilitarian, secular, and, it must be said, modernist ethos.

Finally, state and insurgent outfits have come to resemble each other increasingly as the latter develop their own bureaucracies and organizations and the former construct rapid deployment forces, swat teams, commando cells, special task forces, and other aspects of a decentralized form of guerrilla warfare. A spiral of mimesis is the result, as Allen Feldman notes in his incisive study of Northern Ireland's troubles:

The emergence of local paramilitary forces presupposed the fragmentation, inversion, and internalization of the social rhetoric of populist aggression historically promoted and centralized by the state. These groups emulated the state's function of repressive and ideological apparatuses and implemented programs of somatic regimentation and aggression anticipated by state militarism. Today the mimesis between paramilitary groups and the state is still evident, though it has shifted to the paramilitary emulation of the manner in which violence is bureaucratized and rationalized by the state's counterinsurgency apparatus. (1991, 41)

Some years ago, Ashis Nandy began his insightful essay on the assassination of Mohandas Gandhi by observing, "Every political assassination is a joint communique. It is a statement which the assassin and his victim jointly work on and co-author" (1980, 70). Nandy implies here not only that a leader gets the kind of assassin he or she desires and deserves, but also that the nature of assassinations are a commentary on the prevailing political culture of a society. In analogous fashion, I suggest the recent season of assassinations in South Asia is a sign of the aporia of postcolonial politics, the definitive sign that sovereignty of the state system is in a deep crisis. An assassination has become a brief and pulsating event that captures and compresses into a dramatic moment the more enduring realities of political life in South Asia. Despite strenuous efforts by the party, family, and associates of fallen leaders to endow their deaths with apocalyptic meaning and significance, as acts of parricide to be redeemed by the eventual coalescence of the national family, I suspect over time they will be rewritten into a seamless narrative of just desserts by an increasingly cynical and irreverent public. Or, as Malcolm X once put it, as a case of the chickens having come home to roost.

THE FICTION OF HOMOGENEITY

Underlying both modern nation-states in South Asia and the various ethnonationalist insurgencies is the belief that territory and identity must somehow be made to coincide, that arrival as a nation-state is coterminous with the exorcisation of all forms of identity barring the unitary sense of nation. In this regard, what is striking about various ethnonationalist movements in South Asia is that they replicate the homogenizing logic of the nation-state to the point where, far from being progressive alternatives to the nation, they constitute its reductio ad absurdum.[8] In a tragic irony of history, the LTTE (the "boys" who first emerged as protectors of Tamils from the Sri Lankan army) has the dubious distinction of killing more Tamils than the Sri Lankan army and the Indian Peace Keeping Force combined. Its dispensation in Jaffna has been violent and capricious, and it has murdered a number of Tamil human rights and community activists in its self-anointed capacity as the sole spokesman for the Tamils. Although some scholars discern progressive aspects in Tiger ideology on issues of caste or gender (Schalk 1994), these aspects pale in comparison to the group's authoritarian, patriarchal, and fundamentally antidemocratic form of functioning (Manikkalingam 1992, UTHR Reports).

It will not do to argue that these insurgent movements partake of a (Leninist) notion of a vanguard party under state repression, and that a respect for democracy and pluralism will surface once the revolution is won. First, that argument replicates the logic of deferrence that characterizes the enterprise of nation building and will prove to be as hollow a claim for insurgencies as it has for the nation-state. Second, many insurgent movements in South Asia are driven by singular and essentialist ideas of puritanical identity. In Sri Lanka, a small but growing literature has documented the intransigently fascist character of LTTE, which has attempted its own form of ethnic cleansing in the northern province with regard both to the miniscule Sinhalese populations there and more prominently to the Muslims.

However, although the LTTE (along with other such insurgent movements) is rightly criticized for its Pol Potist traits, it behooves us to understand a reality of our time: majoritarian nationalism and ethnic cleansing are two points along the same continuum. Both are based on an exclusionary vision of national space; both regard national identity and membership as an ineradicable and unchanging matter of blood and belonging; and both would attempt to carry the fiction of homogeneity to its logical conclusion: the permanent effacement of minorities either through genocide or by according them an eternal second-class status as "guests."[9] To put it simply, the LTTE is both the child of Sinhala nationalism and the macabre future of all of South Asia if majoritarian nationalism is allowed to dominate this space.

The discourse of nation building in postcolonial societies is one that is riven with an anxiety to approximate the historical original of Europe or the west, configured as a space that has forever resolved the question of aligning territory with identity. Never mind that this attempted alignment has proceeded everywhere with egregious violence, that it is a task never destined for completion, that its momentary resolution in many contexts, including Europe, may come just as rapidly undone. In the postcolonial script, these stubborn realities are seamlessly woven into the story of a transition. By revisiting J. N. Dixit's effort to encrypt India's role in Sri Lanka into the nationalist narrative, I offer yet another take on the postcolonial anxiety to approximate ersatz originals: the story of the emergence of India and the discourse of danger central to its continued survival.

Dixit lists three reasons for India's decision to intervene in Sri Lanka. These reasons predictably have more to do with India than with Sri Lanka because his objective may be described as an ontological desire to produce India rather than engage in a narrow, justificatory exercise on intervention. His first reason is as follows:

> in 1978, the politically aware Tamils had come to the conclusion that their future lies only in the creation of a separate State, which can be carved out of Sri Lanka, where they can have Tamil as a language and Hinduism as a religion.... [W]e went through the trauma of the same doctrine being applied to our country in 1945–46, as a result of which we were partitioned. Since then, our effort and experiment has been to build a society which rejected the theory that the territorial nation-state does always have to depend on language and religion. That thesis we have rejected. We, in India, have been trying to build a polity based on terms of reference which say that despite its multi-lingual, multi-ethnic nature, an integrated nation can be created; based on principles of secularism and rational precepts of political and social organisations.... So, the first reason we went into Sri Lanka was the interest to preserve our own unity; to ensure the success of a very difficult experiment that we have been carrying out ourselves.... And what the Tamils in Sri Lanka were being compelled to follow, in terms of their life, which would have affected out polity. Because let us not forget that the first voice of secessionism in the Indian Republic was raised in Tamil Nadu in the mid-sixties. This was exactly the same principle of Tamil ethnicity, Tamil language. So, in a manner, our interest in the Tamil issue in Sri Lanka, Tamil

aspirations in Sri Lanka was based on maintaining our own unity, our own integrity, our own identity in the manner in which we have been trying to build our society. (1989, 249)

Contained within this passage are at least three themes that jostle for attention: first, the idea that India as a nation is founded on pluralist principles that are morally, ethically, and rationally superior to alternative, monological spatial imaginaires; second, despite its superiority on such compelling grounds, this experiment called India is in reality a difficult and fragile one, always tempted by the seductive dangers inherent in singular discourses of religion, ethnicity, and language; and, third, Sri Lanka is particularly troubling for India because Tamil "there" is the same as Tamil "here," and the latter has already proven his susceptibility to the allure of such a narrow linguistic and ethnic vision of nationality.

Dixit's second reason for Indian intervention has to do with the Sri Lankan government's enlisting the help of those outside the subcontinent and others "with whom our relations have been difficult" (1989, 250) in the struggle against the minority Tamils. Embedded in this reason is the view that the entire region of South Asia is properly the domain of India, and the invitation of forces hostile to India into the area is a gravely provocative act. The proximate historical origins of this belief are easily traceable to the pre-1947 British colonial regime, which regarded the Indian Ocean as its eminent domain. This view, too, is inscribed with a discourse of danger as Dixit observes, in classically geopolitical tones that invoke the spirit (though not name) of K. M. Panikkar, "let us not forget that since 1498 the external intrusions into India, the disruptions of the Indian power structure, have not been through the Khyber Pass as much as through the southern coasts of India. This is something which we must not forget. With the rise of sea power, with the rise of air power, with the increase in capacity for communications, free of limitations of land, our strategic thinking has to take into account potential danger which a country can face" (1989, 253). He renders subcontinental space exclusively in terms of the danger of conquest and the possibility of invasions—never in terms of the movement of ideas, cultures, peoples and the enrichment that inevitably accompanies such migrations. It marks both an effort to colonize space decisively through a geopolitical imaginaire and the consequent empowerment of the national-security manager.

The third reason harkens back to the Tamil factor contained in the first. Fleshing out the difficulties of the Indian experiment, Dixit ventriloquizes the feelings of an archetypal Tamil from Tamil Nadu: "They felt that if we did not rise in support of the Tamil cause in Sri Lanka, we are not standing by our own Tamils; and if that is so, then in the Tamil psyche, Tamil subconscious, the question arose: is there any relevance or validity of our being part of a larger Indian political identity, if our deeply felt sentiments are not respected? So, it was a compulsion...which could not be avoided by any elected Government in this country (1989, 250–51).

The first and third reasons succinctly capture the multivalent enunciative space offered by the dyad nation-ethnicity. In the third, Dixit argues that India had to go to the defense of Sri Lankan Tamils because it would prove to the Tamils of India that they lived in a country that would not stand idly by and watch the discriminations visited on their ethnic soul mates across the Straits. Yet, in the first reason he gives for Indian intervention, he argues that India could not allow Sri Lankan Tamils to achieve Eelam because of its implications for the Tamils of India and the Indian experiment in general. If the first reason regards ethnicity as a dangerous counterpoint to the nation, the third reason brings the same ethnicity back into the equation, this time as an opportunity to demonstrate that the Indian nation cares for the various ethnicities that constitute it. The question, "Which of these two reasons really undergirded Indian policy?" is fundamentally misguided, I would submit, because the answer is that both did. Ethnicity is simultaneously opposed to the nation *and* critical to its ongoing production and reproduction; it is always both threat to and an opportunity for making the nation. The Indian government was never able to calibrate exactly where the desire to appease (or more accurately, to profit from) Tamil sentiments ended and where opposition to the creation of Eelam began. There was a clear tension between these two principles, and where precisely the line was to be drawn never emerged with any clarity within the multiple institutions representing the Indian state.

There is an important historical reason why this was so, and it harkens back to the creation of Bangladesh. Once that event occurred, 1971 was rapidly modulated, post facto, as an instance of the skill of Indian realpolitik, of what could happen to neighbors who didn't "behave themselves," and of India's unquestionable suzerainty in the region. Bangladesh came to be modulated into a narrative of Indian geopolitical acumen and success. The troubling question of what the creation of this new nation represented in terms of the Indian experiment (or generally in terms of the principle of pluralist nation building) faded into the background or, more accurately, was brushed under the carpet. The dominant consequence of 1971 was its modulation into a nostrum of effective policy making: overt diplomatic pressure combined with covert destabilization. Did Bangladesh (a nation whose very name attests its basis in linguistic particularity) really represent a success in terms of India's experiment with plurality? Did it imply that India now stood behind various ethnonational movements by discriminated minorities within and outside India? The euphoria of military success and of seeing an adversary cut to size swamped any serious discussion of these issues. These contradictions in the discourse of Indian foreign policy making/self-fashioning (and I have said enough to indicate that the two are the same thing) as they unfolded in Sri Lanka were papered over by harking back to the "success" of 1971. The idea that combining overt, diplomatic pressure on neighboring regimes with covert destabilization through dissident ethnic, linguistic or religious minorities would produce further successes became an article of faith, like a magic formula or mantra, rather than reasoned policy. The twin tracks would meet somewhere, somehow. Well, they didn't. Sri Lanka captured all the contradictions of this policy in a way that 1971 did not.

If India had genuinely desired helping Sri Lanka solve its ethnic problem, a first step would have been the recognition that Tamil ethnicity was not some essentialist, singular force immune to history. As chapter 3 argued at length, due to distinctive administrative, sociocultural, economic, and political traditions, the Sri Lankan Tamils and the Tamils of Tamil Nadu had moved along divergent trajectories. If Indian interest in Sri Lanka's domestic affairs had been dissociated from its largely chimerical implications for Tamil Nadu, Indian advice to Sri Lanka to resolve its affairs through greater devolution of power to minorities, the establishment of provincial councils, and its recognition of itself as a plural society may have found a more receptive audience among both the Sinhalese and the Tamils. Of course, the truth of the matter is that India was never such a dis-interested well-wisher of Sri Lanka, at least not after 1980. Sri Lanka was regarded throughout the 1980s as a space of opportunity: to demonstrate Indian regional hegemony, to help the Congress Party regain a foothold in Tamil Nadu politics, and to parlay this idea of being a defender of kindred ethnic minorities in neighboring coun-tries into continued electoral success in the rest of the nation. Fur-thermore, it would be naive to underestimate either Sinhalese reluc-tance to refashion themselves along such a pluralist image (especially on any advice, disinterested or not, from the Indians) or, increas-ingly, the militant Tamil desire to opt out of the Sri Lankan nation altogether.

Indian self-fashioning in Sri Lanka in the 1980s is ultimately in-dissociable from the experience of creating Bangladesh. Resisting the lure to play the great game is nothing less than an important moment in decolonization, for contained within Dixit's antinomous reasoning for intervention in Sri Lanka is an anxiety, an originary anxiety, regarding the birth and potential demise of this space called India. It is an inescapable anxiety for every modern Indian that has us ever trying to approximate a historical original that is itself spu-rious to begin with. It marks the postcolonial as a person always looking over his shoulder, fearing not so much the lack of approba-tion as the lack of attention by an imagined western audience; it saddles us with a narcissistic obsession about whether we matter in the world out there. The anxiety is about a statement that hovers like a specter behind the strenuous effort at constructing India: "There is not, and never was an India, or even any country of India...no Indian nation, no people of India, but only a conglomeration of dif-ferent and mutually antagonistic native groups."[10] Or, to put it as that imperial wordsmith Winston Churchill did when he cut the very ground from under our feet: "India is a geographical term. It is no more a united nation than the Equator."[11]

The effort to prove ourselves the equals of erstwhile masters has taken its toll. It is time to give up on quests in which the ultimate victory is also the ultimate defeat and in which becoming is a nega-tion of being. To be genuinely decolonized, I suppose, would be effortlessly to inhabit a space that Nandy once described as "not non-West" (1983, 73). But then again, knowing what I know, I wouldn't know.

CONCLUSION

Postcolonial nationalism in South Asia lies at an impasse. What is common to the narratives of national identity as presently constituted in their dominant forms is a desire to escape the politics of our time and place, and to seek refuge in the transcendence of immaculate conceptions, pure belongings, and unambiguated identity. These narratives are premised on the illusion that "there is a there there" — a space of homogeneous citizenship either where everyone is the same or where difference has been ordered along an accepted hierarchy of authenticity, the majority is accorded its due, the various minorities know their place, and sovereignty is either-or. For those who view politics to be the endless, agonistic negotiation of difference in search of fairness and justice, such narratives represents a desire for the perpetual peace of an asocial and apolitical dead end. In the next and concluding chapter of this book, I outline a view on postcolonial agency that resists the seductions of identity and respects the politics of difference.

8

Decolonizing the Future in South Asia

To solve political problems becomes difficult for those who allow anxiety alone to pose them.

— GEORGES BATAILLE, THE ACCURSED SHARE

This book arose from a conviction that the present violence in South Asia, by both states and various insurgent movements, is unconscionable and has to be opposed. The commonly offered *salvatore clausii* (violence is an inevitable and indispensable part of nation building; once economic development reverses centuries of colonial distortion, such political problems will fall by the wayside; ethnic and other forms of false consciousness will one day be replaced by the singular pellucidity of class; and so on) have rung increasingly hollow, at least to my ears. The problems of nation building in South Asia are not so much detours from modernity as they are constitutive of it. To struggle against the aporia of postcolonial nationalism as if either modernity can be wished away or some prelapsarian ethos recovered seems fraught with all sorts of political problems. A useful way of conceptualizing the postcolonial position is to see it as a standpoint from which one simultaneously engages in two crucial tasks: a metacritique of modernity and (an ever) skeptical participation in a pragmatic and progressive politics in our time and space, one that engages modernity and its institutions even as it struggles for a world beyond them.

In articulating such an engagement with the political institutions and struggles immersed in modernity, I am informed by this insight from William Connolly:

> To practice this mode of interpretation, you project ontopolitical presumptions explicitly into detailed interpretations of actuality, acknowledging that your implicit projections surely exceed your explicit formulation of them and that your formulations exceed your capacity to demonstrate the truth. You challenge closure...by affirming the contestable character of your own projections, by offering readings of contemporary life that compete with alternative accounts, and by moving back and forth between these two levels.... The idea is to interpret actively, specifically, and comparatively, without praying for the day (or deferring until the time) when the indispensability of interepretation is matched by the solidity of its grounds. (1995, 36–37)

In contemporary scholarship on South Asia, the disenchantment with the enterprise of nation building is deep even if the envisaged alternative order remains cloudy at best.[1] The powerful coalescence of scientific rationality, an interstate system hierarchized on the principles of social Darwinism, the belief that territory and identity must somehow be aligned, and the modulation of history into a script that demands replication has eviscerated our imaginations of all but the nation. Thus, although Arjun Appadurai observes, "we are in the process of moving to a global order in which the nation-state has become obsolete and other forms of allegiance and identity have taken its place," he is further compelled to note that nothing as yet "implies that the nation-state in its classical territorial form is as yet out of business" (1996, 169). Similarly, Partha Chatterjee (1993) avers in the context of India that "autonomous forms of imagination of the community were, and continue to be, overwhelmed and swamped by the history of the postcolonial state. Here lies the root of our postcolonial misery: not in our inability to think out new forms of the modern community but in our surrender to old forms of the modern state" (1993, 11).

Disenchantment with the idea of the nation is invariably accompanied by a realization of the difficulties involved in reimagining global and local spaces along different and less violent trajectories. The complexity grows as one realizes that in South Asia and elsewhere, we have seen a simultaneous and paradoxical strengthening of the nationalist imaginary in recent years even as certain aspects of territorial nationality are being eroded by the mobility of international capital, armaments, communications and information systems, and diasporic communities. In India, for example, ever newer segments of the population are coming under the ambit of a national media, are realizing they belong to an entity that has a presence in global fora and cricket matches, are increasingly aware of their role as voters in national elections, as consumers in national advertising campaigns, and so on. The ecumene of the nation is growing both wider and stronger, even as selective attention to some aspects of an ill-defined globalization may convince one that the nation-state is passe. Most of these visions of the nation are firmly trapped within the fiction of homogeneity; they are predicated on the belief that each unit of territory is ideally occupied by a singular conception of the national citizen. The nation as represented in the teleserials is often sectarian rather than inclusive; election campaigns invariably pander to the lowest common denominator of identity in their quest for a comparative advantage; competition in global fora (be it the United Nations or the World Cup for cricket) have become occasions for jingoism and tension with neighbor countries, not to speak of attacks on kindred minorities within one's own country; and diasporic populations, as if to compensate for their status as a marginal ethnic minority in the metropole, monetize their nostalgia through support for a univocal and hypermasculine vision of their homelands.

To begin thinking beyond the nation-state as currently constituted is to take seriously the argument that the enterprises of history writing and nation building are inextricably intertwined in the postenlightenment order: that the writing of history, at least since Hegel, has become nothing other than the story of how an enduring essence is finally realized as a sovereign subject in a clearly enclosed territory. As Prasenjit Duara notes, "We still do not know what histories will look like beyond the era of the nation-state. But we should seize the moment of the decoupling of History and the nation to think of how to write histories that open as they close" (1995, 49). In this concluding chapter, I begin from the view that one of the fundamental postulates of the post-Westphalian order of nation-states—the belief that territory must somehow, somewhere, align with identity—has to be taken apart, deconstructed, and demonstrated to be not an intrinsic or eternal truth so much as a hegemonic social convention susceptible to human agency and change. The recent history of South Asia suggests that every attempt at forcibly aligning territory and identity has unleashed ethnonationalist movements and violence, and has often resulted in precisely what was most feared — namely, secession. On the other hand, when state elites have responded to assertions of cultural or regional or linguistic or religious autonomy by according them a space within a pluralist conception of the nation, such movements have veered away from violent secession. Through a countermemorial reading of two significant events in twentieth-century South Asia, the partition of 1947 and the emergence of Bangladesh in 1971, and by pondering on the contrasting lessons offered by Dravidian and Sri Lankan Tamil nationalisms, I argue that a democratic and pluralist vision of national (indeed, subcontinental) space, reflected in greater degrees of decentralization and regional autonomy, might well be something worth struggling for. The entailments of such a countermemorial history are multiple: they force us to begin reconceiving the very fundamentals of the nationalist imaginary that undergirds international relations: territory, sovereignty, identity, and democracy. These are large tasks, and I see this conclusion as entering an ongoing dialogue on such a reconceptualization of South Asian space.

A COUNTERMEMORIAL READING OF SOUTH ASIAN HISTORY

With characteristic terseness, Michel Foucault captures the violence inherent in our efforts to comprehend reality: "if interpretation is the violent or surreptitious appropriation of a system of rules, which in itself has no meaning, in order to impose a direction, to bend it to a new will, to force its participation in a different game, and to subject it to secondary rules, then the development of humanity is a series of interpretations" (1977, 151–52). Ironically, for one routinely charged with nihilism, relativism, political passivity, and quietude, Foucault here reminds us that our inherited realities are residues of past, interpretive violences and consequently that our imagined worlds can become real to the extent that we make them through our own acts of interpretation and activism. The eternal verities of history are rendered instances of past dominations; all that remains is the relentless politicization of every fleeting crystallization of past, present, and future. Foucault refers to this never ending act of politicization as a practice of countermemory (1977, 139–64).

From such a perspective, the nation does not appear as an objective and immanent entity, but as one of a multiplicity of ways in which communities could have organized themselves. Within India, there is a stable and disambiguated history of Partition and Independence in 1947. According to this story, Indian nationalism was cleft along two contending principles: the Congress Party's secular, inclusive, and progressive version of history versus various retrogressive, communal interpretations of nationalism represented by Jinnah and the Muslim League, the Hindu Mahasabha, and other parochial parties based on religion, region, language, caste, class, or other inferior rubrics. Despite their best efforts, the story goes, secular and pluralist Congress leaders could not carry with them the insecure minority leader, Muhammad Ali Jinnah, who squandered the inheritance by leaving the family with his moth-eaten share. To many Indians, the post-1947 survival of a plural, secular India and the breakup of a Pakistan founded on the basis of religious nationalism demonstrate the historical veracity of the secular Congress position and the bankruptcy of religious nationalism. As the eminent Indian historian (and writer of Jawaharlal Nehru's biography) Sarvepalli Gopal notes in emblematic fashion, "the futility of seeking to hold the new state [Pakistan] together by the bond of a common religion was seen in the break-away, years later in 1971, of Bangladesh. No stronger proof is required that religious nationalism in South Asia is built on a foundation of sand" (1993, 11).

This particular narration of the origins of India and Pakistan is crucial in the Indian claim to a hegemonic status in the region. The belief that Indian nationalism constituted the only progressive (because it was secular, pluralist, and unified in diversity) variant of nation-building efforts in the subcontinent is the bedrock of India's assumed superiority in the region. Moreover, it is this same narration of India that has underlain the overweening domination of the center in the Indian postcolonial order. Following an initial period in which there was a greater recognition of the political rights of those in the states, since 1971 the tendency has been to lean in favor of the inexorable concentration of political power in India. Particularly since the so-called success in Bangladesh, every assertion of ethnic (that is, linguistic, religious, or regional) particularity or every demand for greater state or regional autonomy has invited the charge of being antinational and potentially secessionist, hence deserving of a hard-line response couched in the discourse of national security. The professed antinomy between nation and ethnicity has worked together in powerful ways to undergird state power and repression.

Despite its apparent solidity, problems abound in this narrative of Indian nationalism as built on the twin rubrics of secularism and pluralism (at least within the public sphere of Indian state elites and among most in the intelligentsia and middle class) and as singularly progressive, whereas other nationalisms are retrograde. First, the secular and pluralist character of the Congress Party's brand of nationalism is not easy to sustain through a close examination of the micropolitics of the preindependence period. As G. Balachandran notes in a recent essay that integrates an emerging literature,[2] Congress's mobilization strategies and symbolic repertoire in the first half of the twentieth century were often indistinguishable from a growing majoritarian northern Hindu identity:

> during the mid-1920s, the Congress, though professing a non-sectarian ideology, could seem to speak in the voice of the Hindu Mahasabha in northern India.... Although more overtly political than the Hindu revivalist or separatist movements of the late nineteenth and early twentieth centuries, the support bases of these movements and the Congress movements overlapped to a great extent. The Congress party at the local level was "sometimes indistinguishable from the movement for the protection of cattle or the propogation of Hindi," and there was a "sharp contradiction between the secular and non-communal catch-cries used in the Congress publicity or official pronouncements, and the idioms adopted by its orators." (1996, 97)[3]

The sometimes unself-reflexive and at other times uncaring majoritarian assumptions that accompanied the ascendancy of Congress through the 1930s and 1940s in the heartland of the Indian subcontinent were countered by various separatist and secessionist narratives all through the peripheries: in the Northeast, Punjab; in various princely states, Bengal, Madras; among the Muslims of the United Provinces and other regions; and so on. As ever, these narratives that sought to loosen the tight embrace of Congress nationalism were later either seamlessly integrated into the story of how the nation came to be rendered one (as seen in the revisionist history of the Dravidian movement, for instance) or consigned to the dustbin of history—paths not followed and rightly so (witness the breakup of Pakistan).

As a historian of the subaltern studies group, Shahid Amin (1995) demonstrates in a genealogy of Chauri Chaura (the infamous antipolice riot in a North Indian village in 1922 whose violence led Gandhi to call off his Non-Cooperation Movement against the British), the singular "Indian national movement" is better seen as a synchronous plenitude of specific events (each arising from a diversity of proximate provocations and often poorly understood subaltern specificities) that were progressively metaphorized by the narrative of the nation and finally memorialized as the story of how the nation was rendered one. It is against this modulation of a multiplex history into a univocal national movement that Chatterjee writes:

> It might be speculated that if there were many such alternative histories for the different regions of India, then the center of Indian history would not need to remain confined to Aryavarta or, more specifically, to "the throne of Delhi." Indeed, the very centrality of Indian history would then become largely uncertain. The question would no longer be one of "national" and "regional" histories: the very relation between parts and the whole would be open for negotiation. If there is any unity in these alternative histories, it is not national but confederal. But we do not yet have the wherewithal to write these other histories. Until such time that we accept that it is the very singularity of the idea of a national history of India which divides Indians from one another, we will not create the conditions for writing these alternative histories. (1993, 115)

Perhaps this self-anointed idea that Congress represented the sole progressive and historically viable notion of nationalism evoked the counternarrative that eventuated in Partition. Congress's disinclination to compromise with the Muslim leadership on a variety of issues through the decades leading up to the 1940s hinged on a distinction made between a national and progressive perspective on issues versus a communal and retrograde perspective. In this context, the dyad national/communal in the decades leading up to independence served a purpose identical to the dyad nation/ethnicity in contemporary times: *communal* and *ethnicity* were always decried as inferior and subversive terms, yet they also constituted the necessary and irreplaceable supplement for the very production of the terms *national* and *nation*. Despite the abstract level at which the national versus communal problematic was presented, the communal demands of the Muslims and of various other minorities often arose out of genuine fears and anxieties about their lot in a postcolonial order in which numerical majorities were going to be critical in deciding further distribution of resources and assets. In this context, Congress's attitude that it was the sole spokesman for all of British India (anyone speaking for any fraction thereof having been deemed parochial, antinational, or communal) sometimes translated into an overbearing attitude on a series of issues with regard to the minorities, specifically the Muslims, in the decades leading up to independence: constitutional reforms; reservation of seats for minorities in legislatures where they were numerically preponderant but economically so poor they weren't part of the franchise; residual powers of the provinces versus those of a central government; the broken promise to include members of the Muslim League in the cabinet after Congress secured overwhelming victories in the elections to the provincial councils in 1937;[4] the refusal to accept proposals that envisaged a loose confederal arrangement rather than an overcentralized government modeled as a direct legatee of the Raj. Such confidence was based on a belief in Congress that it represented the only progressive and secular version of nationalism at this time and that others were ab initio delegitimized by the narrative of history.[5] This supreme self-confidence and the concomitant refusal to take minority concerns and anxieties seriously can be seen in G. Balachandran's description of Congress as having been in many ways the "midwife in the birth of Pakistan" (1996, 106).

Conversely, the idea that Pakistan emerged as a result of a groundswell of religious nationalism is one that is at least as difficult to sustain in the face of historical evidence as the idea of Congress's professed secularism. There is the fact that the demand for a separate homeland for the Muslims on religious grounds did not emerge strongly in the provinces where they were a majority (Punjab and Bengal), but rather among Muslims in the United Provinces and other regions where they constituted a minority—a rather difficult fact to square with the idea that Pakistan represented the homeland of the subcontinent's Muslim peoples. There is the fact that the All-India Muslim League was routinely routed in elections in the preindependence period, barring the one held in 1945–46. Further, until the very eve of partition, an all-India Muslim sentiment or feeling or ideology or imagined community or commonality of interest is empirically very difficult, if not impossible, to establish for these decades. Like any other religious group, Indian Muslims were divided along grounds of class, region, language, and even the ways in which they practiced their religion. Just as with the Indian National Movement, the eventual creation of Pakistan was the telos that allowed for the retrospective disciplining and disambiguation of the specificities and particularities of regional struggles by the diverse Muslims of the subcontinent into the story of the founding of that nation. To see Pakistan as the outcome of a sustained and self-reflexive agitation for a homeland by the subcontinent's Muslims would be to traduce the complex and conjunctural histories that preceded that outcome.[6]

Among recent historians, Ayesha Jalal (1985) has suggested an alternative explanation to the one in which the creation of Pakistan is seen as the subcontinental Muslims' immanent destiny. Staying closer to the domain of an archival haute politique and refreshingly unenamored of metaphysics, she argues that the threat of an unspecified Pakistan was Jinnah's critical bargaining chip from a position of weakness in negotiations with Congress. His ambition was to secure parity for the Muslims with the Hindu majority, for the Muslim League with the Congress, and to find a way to ensure the safety of Muslims in the provinces in which they would constitute minorities. In attempting to achieve this ambition, Jinnah was severely constrained by at least two limitiations. First, the tremendous diversity of the subcontinent's Muslims rendered his self-anointed status as their sole spokesman a precarious one at best. Second, he could not specify the exact content of his Pakistan demand precisely because of the diverse interests that informed the subcontinent's Muslims: what was vital for the Muslims in Punjab or Bengal might prove disastrous for those in Kerala or the United Provinces. The culmination of his negotiations with Congress and with the departing colonial government in the creation of a new country was, in many ways, both a disappointment and an unexpected turn of events for him. Jalal suggests that Jinnah was playing a game of brinkmanship, hoping that the threat of an unspecified Pakistan with the possibility of partition would make Congress agree to a political dispensation with a weak center presiding over strongly autonomous parts united in a confederation. When, in 1946, under the Cabinet Mission Plan, a confederal dispensation for the postindependent order, one that would have retained the boundaries of British India, was mooted,

Jinnah accepted the offer, but Congress, after initially agreeing, vacillated and finally refused. Given the choice between a highly decentralized (but united) India and a strongly centralized (but partitioned) India, the Congress leadership, at the last moment, chose the latter option.

Jinnah's gamble failed largely for two reasons. First, the end game was rendered utterly chaotic by the newly elected Labour government in postwar Britain, which suddenly telescoped its withdrawal plans to a few months rather than the anticipated year.[7] More importantly, his gamble failed because the Congress leadership, specifically Nehru and Vallabhbhai Patel, belying their public commitment to an undivided India, increasingly came around to the view that a strong and centralized government was so important that Partition was a price worth paying for it. Asim Roy summarizes the main thread of this argument:

> Confronted with a choice between "unity" and a "strong centre," the Congress had been steadily coming to realize what might very well have to become the price of freedom namely, division. The unqualified commitment of the Congress to a strong centre stemmed from its vision of a strong, united and modernized India. Congressmen like Nehru, with socialist streaks in them, found the concept of a strong centre inseparable from the need and demand for India's economic reconstruction based on centralized planning. The bitter communal experiences of the provincial Congress ministeries after 1937 as well as that in the interim government in the nineteen-forties reinforced the Congress reluctance to seek political accomodation with the League. Finally, the Congress could hardly have been expected to overlook the supreme importance of a strong centre to ensure its own dominance in India after independence. (1993, 123)

Thus, in the anarchy of 1946–47, the emergence of Pakistan seemed not so much the coming to fruition of a mass-based ideology of religious nationalism as it was "an aberration, a historical accident, caused by a complex configuration of forces at a particular juncture" (Hasan 1993b, 108).

In the unpredictability and uncertainty surrounding their birth, India and Pakistan are hardly unique. Nations, whatever their illusions about their timeless existence, have invariably emerged out of accidents and conjunctures. What I would prefer to emphasize, however, is this: the creation of two nations in 1947 did not so much represent the realization of immanent destinies or a struggle between secular and religious versions of nationalism, as it did the unintended result of an unsuccessful effort by a minority to secure a more federal political dispensation and the unwillingness of the party of the majority, because of a fear of impending balkanization, to countenance political arrangements that gave the (minority) provinces a high degree of autonomy. In other words, the desire to have a strong, centrally dominated nation even at the cost of alienating those at its margins or peripheries produced precisely the outcome so assiduously sought to be avoided—namely, partition and the breakup of the nation itself.[8]

It is important to recognize that Partition represented the reductio ad absurdum of the nationalist imaginaire. The centuries-long coexistence of Hindu and Muslim communities in the subcontinent, the reality of an inseparably composite culture that had emerged from that encounter, the intertwined lives of thousands of families and individuals, all were now negated with one stroke of a cartographer's quill. Based on outdated census data detailing the eviscerated, numerical distributions of Hindus and Muslims, two nations were created out of an enduringly plural and cosmopolitan civilization. Unsurprisingly, nothing, but nothing, has been solved by Partition: all across the subcontinent, its bloody legacy lives on in dismembered families, forced migrations, material and cultural dispossession, ethnic ghettoization and enclaves, communal riots, so-called illegal immigration, wars, and the continued state of insecurity from low-intensity conflicts. Partition as a solution to the minority "problem" was premised on an ethnic imaginaire that underlies international relations, the belief that territory and identity must be brought into alignment. It is, consequently, hardly a suprise that the solution has proven to be the fount of a whole series of problems in postcolonial South Asia.

Twenty-five years after Partition, the secession of Bangladesh is routinely ascribed in India as proof of Pakistan's founding folly (religious nationalism) and the superiority of India's professedly secular and pluralist basis,[9] whereas in Pakistan, the emergence of Bangladesh is attributed primarily to Indian malfeasance, one deserving of a similar retribution through Kashmir. And, of course, contemporary Bangladesh, sees itself as an immanent destiny that achieved fruition in 1971.[10] Again, one could more plausibly argue that rather than any disproof of religious nationalism, the secession of Pakistan's eastern wing in 1971 was the result of overcentralization and the western wing's self-anointed "majoritarian" disregard for the sentiments and anxieties of peripheral "minorities."[11] Pre-1971 Pakistan, with its two wings separated by more than a thousand miles of Indian territory, was in reality no more (or no less) absurd than most other collectives that have willed themselves to be nations. The failure of that experiment owes less to some a priori weakness than it does to a postcolonial dispensation that concentrated political power, economic profits, and cultural superiority within West Pakistan and regarded the eastern wing as provincial and inferior. As Jalal observes, "The breakaway of the eastern wing and the creation of Bangladesh was simply the most dramatic manifestation of the tussle between a centralized and undemocratic state structure and the forces of regionalism. . . . [T]he source of provincial disaffections in Pakistan originate in the highly centralized nature of political and economic power" (1995, 252).

Just as partition has failed in resolving the question of nationhood, the emergence of Bangladesh has hardly settled the issue either. Thus, a movement that began as a secular and democratic assertion of linguistic and regional difference from West Pakistan (despite the common religion) has now jettisoned its secular baggage for an increasingly Islamic notion of self-identity, has rendered the status of Hindu and Christian minorities there ever more precarious, has proved to be highly intolerant of women's rights or of freedom of expression, has traduced its democracy through the repeated interventions of the military and authoritarian regimes, and so on.

Neither Partition nor Bangladesh can be considered proof of the folly of religious nationalism, but both are indicative of the perils of majoritarian overcentralization and a concomitant disregard for the aspirations of so-called peripheral minorities. Nationalisms everywhere are built on imagined bonds of community, be they religious, linguistic, racial, historical, or whatever. Their success or failure to endure as coherent entities hinges to a greater extent on how they treat those perceived to be outside some self-defined majority than on their particular charters of fictive community. The overcentralization and concentration of power by state elites on behalf of majorities they supposedly represent cannot be dissociated from what I have described as a postcolonial anxiety in previous chapters: the fear of national disunity and fragmentation produces actions and policies that hasten precisely that very outcome.

The purpose of this countermemorial reading of the events surrounding partition and the emergence of Bangladesh in 1971 is straightforward: I wish to mitigate the messianic zeal that has come to animate postcolonial nationalism in South Asia. By demonstrating that these represent false promises and failed solutions premised on the impossible belief that territory and identity can be brought into alignment, I seek to direct our energies toward reimagining existing notions of sovereignty and identity in this space.

A powerful counterexample to the tendency to seek secession as a result of overcentralization is the case of Dravidian Tamil nationalism. Dravidian nationalism peaked in the twentieth century in 1938–39 and 1964–65. On both occasions, the impetus was the same: the decision of the center to impose Hindi as a national language. The vehemence of Tamil response to this envisaged homogenization of the country scuttled the center's impulse. Unlike in Sri Lanka, the Indian government backed off from the idea of making Hindi the national language by deferring to the wishes of antagonized minorities. The veering away of Dravidian Tamil nationalism from the idea of secession can be plausibly seen as one of the few success stories of Indian federalism. Conceding linguistic statehood within an overall federal framework, indefinitely deferring the idea of imposing Hindi as a national language, and countenancing a regional party as the legitimate government in a state — all combined effectively to cement the state of Tamil Nadu more securely to the union. In this regard, it is the opportunities offered to a regional party within the Indian postcolonial order that explain the domestication of Dravidian ideology, not threats (the Sixteenth Amendment, which requires one to swear allegiance to the Constitution of India upon taking political office) or sanguinary patriotism (the Sino-Indian conflict of 1962) or assassination (of Rajiv Gandhi in 1991).

Ironically, it is precisely this success story of Indian federalism (limited as it was) that was thoroughly besmirched in the 1980s when the central government under Mrs. Gandhi inaugurated its twin-track policy with regard to Sri Lanka. The supposed secessionist history of Tamil Nadu served as the perfect alibi for a regime intent on destabilizing its neighbor to bring it in line with Indian hegemonic interests and on recovering a state lost to the ruling party for more than a decade. If, in the future, Tamil Nadu does become home to a violent insurgent movement based on the idea of Tamil ethnicity, the major contributor to that movement will have been not some innate proclivity for secession on the part of the people of that state or the seductions of Eelamist nationalism from across the Palk Straits, but the actions of the Congress regimes at the center in the 1980s.

Buttressing the example of Dravidianism in India through its obverse is the tragedy of Sri Lankan Tamil nationalism. Sri Lankan Tamils could have been folded within the national family with relative ease in the early 1950s. Yet, the majoritarian impulse of Sinhalese nationalism (and the political opportunities emergent in its wake) precluded a compromise. Sri Lanka is proof yet again that majoritarian overcentralization produces both irredentist violence and precisely what it fears most—namely, partition or secession. The desire for Eelam emerges as a direct consequence of the very imagination that animates most nationalists in South Asia. In that sense, the question of Eelam is not one confined to Sri Lanka but one faced by all the nation-states in the region.

Together, the countermemorial reading of Partition and Bangladesh and the contrasting examples offered by Sri Lankan Tamil and Dravidian nationalisms point to two conclusions: (1) the fiction of homogeneity or the homogenizing impulse that underlies postcolonial nationalism is a recipe for a partition that produces nothing but endless sectarian violence; (2) a possible way out of the postcolonial aporia is to reenvision the nation not as a space for the realization of a unified sense of identity but one with a pluralist ethos where alterity is respected rather than disciplined, suppressed, or assimilated.

REIMAGINING SOUTH ASIA

A few points are worth remembering as one reenvisions South Asian space along pluralist directions. First, it is critical to realize that in contemporary South Asia, the fiction of homogeneity reigns hegemonic over both the managers of the nation-state and the many insurgent movements fighting against them. The various Eelams of South Asia share the monological imagination that forever seeks to align territory with identity in a singular and final fashion.[12] They are essentially partition redux, and for that reason they constitute the farcical sequels to the initial tragedy. Hence, most insurgent movements in the region do not constitute an alternative to the existing spatial imaginaires of the nation, nor are they worthy of support by those committed to a pluralist and democratic ethos.

Second, it is pragmatic to remember Partition occurred fifty years ago, and three nation-states eventually emerged from that act. Reversing that act, however desirable it may seem to those committed to the syncretic civilization that characterized South Asia for centuries, is unlikely in the short run.[13] I would emphasize that the move toward regional autonomy and devolution of power within each of these countries as an important step in mitigating the contemporary violences. The initiation of such provincial autonomy and decentralization within each of these countries, combined with ongoing (if still preliminary) efforts at creating an economic trading bloc at the level of the South Asian region, may some day make talk of a South Asian confederation less utopian. But here and now, it would seem that the task of decentralizing political and economic decision making in the separate nations is itself sufficiently daunting.

Third, the debate over the unit of devolution captures the enormous complexity of the issues at hand. Although most in South Asia would probably agree that highly centralized and unitary nation-states are simply no longer viable (whether for political or economic reasons), there is a parallel recognition that devolution by itself is no panacea. Recollect the issue of traditional homelands outlined in an earlier chapter. The Sri Lankan Tamil claim for a homeland is interpreted, from a modernist standpoint, as a historically untenable and primordialist argument. As I suggested, faced with majoritarian chauvinism and discrimination, the Sri Lankan Tamils have latched on to the idea of traditional homelands as a crucial resource in their struggle for equality with the Sinhalese. In the political, economic, and cultural context of their marginalization, it is both politically and normatively unjustifiable to dismiss the Tamils claim regarding their traditional homeland. It is only in the context of a nondiscriminatory and egalitarian Sri Lankan (not Sinhalese) nation-state that one can demonstrate the historical vacuity of the Tamil claim to a homeland. In other words, I am suggesting that the initial unit of devolution of power can conceivably be a linguistic or religious or ethnic enclave, but such devolution must be accompanied by a simultaneous commitment to creating a society that does not anoint some communities as mainstream or more authentic and others as peripheral and alien.

Fourth, although the enumerated regimes of modernity have rendered it difficult to think outside of the categories of majority and minorities, we constantly have to foreground the reality that every geographical unit is an inventory of centuries of miscegenation, adulterated histories, cultural interminglings, nonorchestrated migrations, and multiplex affiliations. A majority at the national level is often a minority in select provinces; conversely, national minorities can constitute oppressive majorities in other provinces. Devolution of power envisaged along permanent ethnic fault lines will, at best, achieve a temporary deterrence based on a fear of the mutually assured destruction of minority hostage communities and, at worst, culminate in the impossible efforts at ethnic cleansing currently underway in Bosnia. Consequently, even if the initial dispensation is one that creates provincial boundaries based on linguistic or ethnic particularity, it has to be constantly accompanied by a resistance to the idea of ethnic enclaves and by the promotion of cultural, economic, political, and social linkages with the rest of the nation. In other words, a freezing of the enumerated demographics of regional dispersion has to be resisted. As Darini Rajasingham-Senanayake notes in regard to recent efforts at devolution of power in Sri Lanka,

> The danger with devolving on the basis of ethnic demographics alone is that reproduces the logic of ethnic chauvinists, Sinhala, Tamil, Muslim alike. It turns the idea of regional self-determination into an ethnic homeland or ethnic enclave. Devolution on the basis of ethnicity as conceived by Colombo based politicians who have been schooled to believe that the tryanny of the majority whether local or national is just only officialises the ethnic enclave mentality and fear and suspicion of cultural difference which has built up during the years of war. It will destroy the historically multicultural fabric of Sri Lankan society. (1997, 15)

Finally, although these steps are critical in terms of political and administrative engineering, perhaps the most crucial component lies in the cultivation of a democratic and pluralist ethos that radically revisions our existing notions of territoriality, identity, and security. As William Connolly notes in a summarization of this ethos that I find congenial to my countermemorial reading of South Asian space,

> The key to a culture of democratization is that it embodies a productive ambiguity at its very center, always resisting attempts to al-

low one side or the other to achieve final victory: *its role as a mode of governance is balanced and countered by its logic as a cultural medium of the periodic denaturalization of settled identities and conventions.* In a world where the paradox of politics is perpetually susceptible to forgetfulness, there is a perpetual case to be made for the renewal of democratic energies of denaturalization. For if the second dimension of democracy ever collapsed under the weight of the first, state mechanisms of electoral accountability would become conduits for fascist unity. (1995, 154–55, emphasis original)

It is in this task of repeated denaturalizations that one may find the vocation of the postcolonial intellectual: to decouple our histories from the narrative of the nation, to miscegenate the stories of our origins, and, perhaps most importantly, to decolonize our vision of the future by liberating that space from the modulations of ersatz pasts.

CONCLUSION

The enterprise of making the nation in South Asia, as elsewhere, has largely been premised on the idea of recovery. In this quest for a prelapsarian essence, the nation is metonymous with efforts to comprehend social reality itself: the practice of intellectual inquiry has invariably been inscribed within a narrative of recovering once pure and clear meanings. As Jacques Derrida observes, the effort to pacify forever the agonistic encounter between opposites underlies nearly all social analyses; it is

> the enterprise of returning 'strategically,' in idealization, or to a 'priority' seen as simple, intact, normal, pure, standard, self-identical, in order *then* to conceive of . . . derivation, complication, deterioration, accident etc. All metaphysicians have proceeded thus . . . : good before evil, the positive before the negative, the pure before the impure, the simple before the complex, the essential before the accidental, the imitated before the imitation, etc. This is not just *one* metaphysical gesture among others; it is the metaphysical exigency, the most constant, profound, and potent procedure. (1977, 66, 236, emphases original)

The effort at recovering pure origins is inscribed with an incredible degree of violence, both epistemic and physical. Resisting such an impulse, I have tried throughout this book to regard the narratives that constitute us as open-ended. Drawing on a different tradition, I have emphasized the miscegenation and adulteration that have always characterized our pasts, presents, and likely futures. All we have left are representations as the endless play of power that seeks to impose a decipherable code on a reality that ever eludes us. The quest for transcendence—the overcoming of difference—contained in the supposedly emancipatory narrative of the nation is nothing other than one more in an endless series of efforts to corral the future and subject various peoples to yet another arbitrary discipline.

Accompanying this resolute refusal to engage in any politics of transcendence is a desire to engage pragmatically and provisionally with the politics of our time and space. If history cannot be tamed, its ambiguities ever resistant to resolution and ever hostile to immutable notions of truth, it becomes critical to create and maintain space for a democracy conceived in terms of a pluralist ethos that respects alterity and refuses to banalize difference into synthesis. The purpose or telos of such a politics is precisely to render one's position and place unremarkable as it were, to go beyond them into a world where identity and differences are not the occasion for either chauvinistic celebration or annihilatory violence, but just simply are. And yet, we know that telos will never be reached, the "beyond" will never one day become the "here." It is precisely because it is ever over the horizon that it serves as the ennobling lie on which we premise our endless and agonistic politics.

Appendix 1
List of Interviewees

Thomas Abraham Sr., July 20, 1992, Madras
Mani Shankar Aiyar, June 15, 1994, New Delhi
A. X. Alexander, May 21, 1993, Madras
Gopi Arora, June 14, 1994, New Delhi
Lalith Athulathmudali, July 29, 1992, Colombo
Romesh Bhandari, July 13, 1993, New Delhi
P. R. Chari, July 5, 1993, New Delhi
P. Chidambaram, June 24, 1993, New Delhi
Stephen Cohen, June 9, 1993, New Delhi
Merwyn De Silva, August 4, 1992, Colombo
Gen. Yashwant Deva, June 21, 1993, New Okhla Industrial
    Development Area (NOIDA), Uttar Pradesh
P. P. Devaraj, Ceylon Workers Congress (CWC), July 30, 1992,
    Colombo
Gamini Dissanayake, August 4, 1992, Colombo
J. N. Dixit, June 21, 1994, Gurgaon, Haryana
Muchkund Dubey, July 20, 1993, New Delhi
Cheri George, August 5, 1992, Colombo
Era Janarthanan, July 22, 1992, Madras
Dayan Jayatilleka, August 7, 1992, Colombo
J. R. Jayewardene, August 5, 1992, Colombo
Narendra Nath Jha, June 29, 1993, New Delhi
V. Kanesalingam, July 31, 1992, Colombo

R. Kumaramangalam, MP, June 9, 1994, New Delhi
"Murasoli" Maran, May 20, 1993, Madras
Lakhan Lal Mehrotra, June 21, 1993, NOIDA, Uttar Pradesh
Gen. Ashok Mehta, July 23, 1993, New Delhi
K. P. S. Menon, July 22, 1992, Madras
K. Mohandas, June 12, 1992, Madras
M. R. Narayan Swamy, June 25, 1993, New Delhi
P. Nedumaran, June 7, 1992, Madras
A. S. Panneerselvam, May 24, 1993, Madras
Aditi Phadnis, June 26, 1993, New Delhi
Anita Pratap, July 21, 1993, New Delhi
Suresh Premachandran, EPRLF MP, August 4, 1992, Colombo
R. K. Raghavan, May 24, 1993, Madras
Sam Rajappa, *Statesman,* June 10, 1992, Madras
Mohan Ram, journalist, June 15, 1993, New Delhi
N. Ram, *Frontline,* June 2, 1992, Madras
Panruti Ramachandran, June 7, 1992, Madras
"Cho" Ramaswamy, June 1, 1992, Madras
M. K. Rasgotra, June 19, 1994, New Delhi
R. Ravindran, May 27, 1993, Madras
M. Senadhiraja, TULF MP, August 4, 1992, Colombo
Era Sezhiyan, May 29, 1992, Madras
D. Siddharthan, PLOTE, August 2, 1992, Colombo
Gen. Depinder Singh, July 2, 1993, Chandigarh, Haryana
Bhagwan Singh, *Sunday Mail,* May 22, 1993, Madras
Natwar Singh, July 22, 1993, New Delhi
S. K. Singh, July 6, 1993, New Delhi
T. S. Subramanium, June 6, 1992, Madras
P. S. Suryanarayana, July 25, 1992, Madras
Shyam Tekwani, May 23, 1993, Madras
Neelan Tiruchelvam, August 1 and 5, 1992, Colombo
K. Veeramani, May 21, 1993, Madras
S. H. Venkat Ramani, July 15, 1992, New Delhi
A. P. Venkateswaran, July 7, 1993, New Delhi
B. G. Verghese, July 6, 1993, New Delhi
Bradman Weerakoon, August 1, 1992, Colombo

Appendix 2
Text of the Indo–Sri Lanka Agreement to Establish Peace and Normalcy in Sri Lanka, Colombo, July 29, 1987

The Prime Minister of the Republic of India, His Excellency Mr. Rajiv Gandhi and the President of the Democratic Socialist Republic of Sri Lanka, His Excellency, Mr. J. R. Jayewardene having met at Colombo on 29 July 1987.

Attaching utmost importance to nurturing, intensifying and strengthening the traditional friendship of India and Sri Lanka and acknowledging the imperative need of resolving the ethnic problem of Sri Lanka, and the consequent violence, and for the safety, well-being and prosperity of people belonging to all communities in Sri Lanka.

1. Having this day entered into the following Agreement to fulfill this objective.

1.1 *desiring* to preserve the unity, sovereignty and territorial integrity of Sri Lanka

1.2 *acknowledging* that Sri Lanka is a multi-ethnic and multi-lingual plural society consisting inter alia, of Sinhalese, Tamils, Muslims (Moors) and Burghers;

1.3 *recognising* that each ethnic group has a distinct cultural and linguistic identity which has to be carefully nurtured;

1.4 *also recognising* that the Northern and the Eastern Provinces have been areas of historical habitation of Sri Lankan Tamil speaking peoples, who have at all times hitherto lived together in this territory with other ethnic groups;

1.5 *conscious* of the necessity of strengthening the forces contributing to the unity, sovereignty and territorial integrity of Sri Lanka, and preserving its character as a multi-ethnic, multi-lingual and multi-religious plural society, in which all citizens can live in equality, safety and harmony, and prosper and fulfil their aspirations;

2. *Resolve that:*

2.1 Since the Government of Sri Lanka proposes to permit adjoining Provinces to join to form one administrative unit and also by a Referendum to separate as may be permitted to the Northern and Eastern Provinces as outlined below:

2.2 During the period, which shall be considered an interim period (i.e.) from the date of the elections to the Provincial Council, as specified in para 2.8 to the date of the Referendum as specified in para 2.3, the Northern and Eastern Provinces as now constituted, will form one administrative unit, having one elected Provincial Council. Such a unit will have one Governor, one Chief Minister and one Board of Ministers.

2.3 There will be a Referendum on or before 31 December 1988 to enable the people of the Eastern province to decide whether:

(A) The Eastern Province should remain linked with the Northern Province as one administrative unit, and to continue to be governed together with the Northern Province as specified in para 2.2, or

(B) The Eastern Province should constitute a separate administrative unit having its own distinct Provincial Council with a separate Governor, Chief Minister and Board of Ministers.

The President may, at his discretion, decide to postpone such a Referendum.

2.4 All persons who have been displaced due to ethnic violence, or other reasons, will have right to vote in such a Referendum. Necessary conditions to enable them return to areas from where they were displaced will be created.

2.5 The Referendum, when held, will be monitored by a committee headed by the Chief Justice, a member appointed by the President, nominated by the Government of Sri Lanka, and a member appointed by the President, nominated by the representatives of the Tamil speaking people of the Eastern Province.

2.6 A simple majority will be sufficient to determine the result of the Referendum.

2.7 Meeting and other forms of propoganda, permissible within the laws of the country, will be allowed before the Referendum.

2.8 Elections to Provincial Councils will be held within the next three months, in any event before 31 December 1987. Indian observers will be invited for elections to the Provincial Council of the North and East.

2.9 The emergency will be lifted in the Eastern and Northern Provinces by 15 August 1987. A cessation of hostilities will come into effect all over the island within 48 hours of the signing of this Agreement. All arms presently held by militant groups will be surrendered in accordance with an agreed procedure to authorities to be designated by the Government of Sri Lanka. Consequent to the cessation of hostilities and the surrender of arms by the militant groups, the army and other security personnel will be confined to barracks in camps as of 25 May 1987. The process of surrendering of arms and the confining of security personnel moving back to barracks shall be completed within 72 hours of the cessation of hostilities coming into effect.

2.10 The Government of Sri Lanka will utilise for the purpose of law enforcement and maintenance of security in the Northern and Eastern Provinces the same organisations and mechanisms of Government as are used in the rest of the country.

2.11 The President of Sri Lanka will grant a general amnesty to political and other prisoners now held in custody under the Prevention of Terrorism Act and other emergency laws, and to combatants, as well as to those persons accused, charged and/or convicted under these laws. The Government of Sri Lanka will make special efforts to rehabilitate militant youth with a view to bringing them back to the mainstream of national life. India will co-operate in the process.

2.12 The Government of Sri Lanka will accept and abide by the above provisions and expect all others to do likewise.

2.13 If the framework for the resolutions is accepted, the Government of Sri Lanka will implement the relevant proposals forthwith.

2.14 The Government of India will underwork and guarantee the resolutions, and cooperate in the implementation of these proposals.

2.15 These proposals are conditional to the acceptance of proposals negotiated from 4.5.1986 to 19.12.1986. Residual matters not finalised during the above negotiations shall be resolved between

India and Sri Lanka within a period of six weeks of signing this Agreement. These proposals are also conditional to the Government of India cooperating directly with the Government of Sri Lanka in their implementation.

2.16 These proposals are also conditional to the Government of India taking the following actions if any militant group operating in Sri Lanka does not accept this framework of proposals for a settlement, namely:

(A) India will take all necessary steps to ensure that Indian territory is not used for activities prejudicial to the unity, integrity and security of Sri Lanka.

(B) The Indian Navy/Coast Guard will cooperate with the Sri Lanka Navy in preventing Tamil militant activities from affecting Sri Lanka.

(C) In the event that the Government of Sri Lanka requests the Government of India to afford military assistance to implement these proposals the Government of India will cooperate by giving to the Government of Sri Lanka such military assistance as and when requested.

(D) The Government of India will expedite repatriation from Sri Lanka of Indian citizens to India who are resident there concurrently with the repatriation of Sri Lankan refugees from Tamil Nadu.

(E) The Governments of India and Sri Lanka, will cooperate in ensuring the physical security and safety of all communities inhabiting the Northern and Eastern provinces.

2.17 The Government of Sri Lanka shall ensure free, full and fair participation of all voters from all communities in the Northern and Eastern Provinces in electoral processes envisaged in this Agreement. The Government of India will extend full cooperation to the Government of Sri Lanka in this regard.

2.18 The official language of Sri Lanka shall be Sinhala. Tamil and English will also be official languages.

3. This agreement and the annexure there-to shall come into force upon signature.

In witness whereof we have set our hands and seals hereunto. Done in Colombo, Sri Lanka, on this the twenty ninth day of July of the year one thousand nine hundred and eighty seven, in duplicate, both texts being equally authentic.

Rajiv Gandhi
Prime Minister of the Republic of India
Junius Richard Jayewardene
President of the Democratic Socialist Republic of Sri Lanka

ANNEXURE TO THE AGREEMENT

1. His Excellency the Prime Minister of India and His Excellency the President of Sri Lanka agree that the Referendum mentioned in paragraph 2 and its subparagraphs of the Agreement will be observed by a representative of the Election Commission of India to be invited by His Excellency the President of Sri Lanka.

2. Similarly, both Heads of Government agree that the elections to the Provincial Council mentioned in paragraph 2.8 of the Agreement will be observed by a representative of the Government of India to be invited by the President of Sri Lanka.

3. His Excellency the President of Sri Lanka agrees that the Home Guards would be disbanded and all paramilitary personnel will be withdrawn from the Eastern and Northern Provinces with a view to creating conditions conducive to fair elections to the Council.

The President, in his discretion, shall absorb such paramilitary forces, which came into being due to ethnic violence, into the regular security forces of Sri Lanka.

4. The Prime Minister of India and the President of Sri Lanka agree that the Tamil militants shall surrender their arms to authorities agreed upon to be designated by the President of Sri Lanka. The surrender shall take place in the presence of one senior representative each of the Sri Lankan Red Cross and the Indian Red Cross.

5. The Prime Minister of India and the President of Sri Lanka agree that a joint Indo–Sri Lankan observer group consisting of qualified representatives of the Government of India and the Government of Sri Lanka would monitor the cessation of hostilities from 31 July 1987.

6. The Prime Minister of India and the President of Sri Lanka also agree that in terms of paragraph 2.14 and paragraph 2.16(C) of the

Agreement, an Indian Peace Keeping contingent may be invited by the President of Sri Lanka to guarantee and enforce the cessation of hostilities, if so required.

Prime Minister of India
New Delhi
29 July 1987

Excellency,

Conscious of the friendship between our two countries stretching over two millenia and more, and recognising the importance of nurturing this traditional friendship, it is imperative that both Sri Lanka and India reaffirm the decision not to allow our respective territories to be used for activities prejudicial to each other's unity, territorial integrity and security.

In this spirit, you had, during the course of our discussions, agreed to meet some of India's concerns as follows:

(i) Your Excellency and myself will reach an early understanding about the relevance and employment of foreign military and intelligence personnel with a view to ensuring that such presences will not prejudice Indo–Sri Lankan relations.

(ii) Trincomalee or any other ports in Sri Lanka will not be made available for military use by any country in a manner prejudicial to India's interests.

(iii) The work of restoring and operating Trincomalee oil tank farm will be undertaken as a joint venture between India and Sri Lanka.

(iv) Sri Lanka's agreement with foreign broadcasting organisations will be reviewed to ensure that any facilities set up by them in Sri Lanka are used solely as broadcasting facilities and not for any military or intelligence purposes.

In the same spirit, India will:

(i) deport all Sri Lankan citizens who are found to be engaging in terrorist activities or advocating separatism or secessionism.

(ii) Provide training facilities and military supplies for Sri Lankan security forces.

India and Sri Lanka have agreed to set up a joint consultative mechanism to continuously review matters of common concern in the light of the objectives stated in para 1 and specifically to monitor the implementation of other matters contained in this letter.

Kindly confirm, Excellency, that the above correctly sets out the agreement reached between us.

Please accept, Excellency, the assurances of my highest consideration.

Yours Sincerely,
(Rajiv Gandhi)
His Excellency
Mr. J. R. Jayewardene

President of Sri Lanka
29 July 1987

Excellency,

Please refer to your letter dated the 29th of July 1987, which reads as follows:

Excellency,

Conscious of the friendship between our two countries stretching over two millenia and more, and recognising the importance of nurturing this traditional friendship, it is imperative that both Sri Lanka and India reaffirm the decision not to allow our respective territories to be used for activities prejudicial to each other's unity, territorial integrity and security.

2. In this spirit, you had, during the course of our discussions, agreed to meet some of India's concerns as follows:

(i) Your Excellency and myself will reach an early understanding about the relevance and employment of foreign military and intelligence personnel with a view to ensuring that such presences will not prejudice Indo–Sri Lankan relations.

(ii) Trincomalee or any other ports in Sri Lanka will not be made available for military use by any country in a manner prejudicial to India's interests.

(iii) The work of restoring and operating Trincomalee oil tank farm will be undertaken as a joint venture between India and Sri Lanka.

(iv) Sri Lanka's agreement with foreign broadcasting organisations will be reviewed to ensure that any facilities set up by them in

Sri Lanka are used solely as broadcasting facilities and not for any military or intelligence purposes.

3. In the same spirit, India will:

(i) deport all Sri Lankan citizens who are found to be engaging in terrorist activities or advocating separatism or secessionism.

(ii) Provide training facilities and military supplies for Sri Lankan security forces.

4. India and Sri Lanka have agreed to set up a joint consultative mechanism to continuously review matters of common concern in the light of the objectives stated in para 1 and specifically to monitor the implementation of other matters contained in this letter.

5. Kindly confirm, Excellency, that the above correctly sets out the agreement reached between us.

Please accept, Excellency, the assurances of my highest consideration.

Yours Sincerely,

(Rajiv Gandhi)

His Excellency
Mr. J. R. Jayewardene
President of the Democratic Socialist Republic of Sri Lanka,
Colombo

This is to confirm that the above correctly sets out the understanding reached between us. Please accept, Excellency, the assurances of my highest consideration.

(J.R. Jayewardene)
President

Notes

INTRODUCTION

1. In contrast, I find most of Rushdie's political essays unmarked by the prim-and-proper liberal correctness, the passé social democracy, and banality that Nandy sees in them. Even under the Damoclean sword of the *fatwa* (edict), Rushdie has resisted the temptation to find refuge in a transcendent ethic that declares speech sacred and free or to declaim mawkishly the authorial right to freedom of expression so sacrosanct that it must be protected at any cost. Given his predicament after the publication of *Satanic Verses,* many would have gladly indulged Rushdie any self-pity or a strident plea by him for the eternal verity of universalist values of liberal tolerance and respect for dissent. He has rarely pleaded such indulgence. Despite his moments of doubt, on the whole he has remained stubbornly committed to something he wrote before he wound up in his present, itinerant, lifestyle: "But human beings do not perceive things whole; we are not gods but wounded creatures, cracked lenses, capable only of fractured perceptions. Partial beings, in all senses of that phrase. Meaning is a shaky edifice we build out of scraps, dogmas, childhood injuries, newspaper articles, chance remarks, old films, small victories, people hated, people loved; perhaps it is because our sense of what is the case is constructed from such inadequate materials that we defend it so fiercely, even to the death.... [T]hose of us forced by cultural displacement to accept the provisional nature of all truths, all certainties, have perhaps had modernism forced upon us. We can't lay claim to Olympus" (1991, 12–13).

2. See William Shakespeare, *The Life and Death of King Richard II*:

This royal throne of kings, this scepter'd isle
This earth of majesty, this seat of mars,
This other Eden, demi-paradise;
This fortress built by Nature for herself
Against infection and the hand of war;
This happy breed of men, this little world;
This precious stone set in the silver sea...
Against the envy of less happier lands;
This blessed plot, this earth, this realm, this England. (act 2, scene 1)

3. For a delightful excoriation of the various hypocrisies of English cricket (by an American settled in Britain, no less!), see Marqusee (1994).

4. Ashley and Walker's (1990a and 1990b) responses to critiques of critical international relations theory are remarkable essays. Despite their insightful depiction of the dichotomous choices offered by mainstream scholars in their efforts to discipline every potential renegade, they replicate a series of similarly effective dichotomies themselves. These choices work effectively in delegitimating all critiques of critical international relations, even those that do not stem from a self-assured notion of sovereign subjectivity or out of a desire to discipline the ineffable ambiguities of representational practices. Ironically, for a critique premised on the essentially contestable character of social reality, it winds up reading like a jeremiad in its own way.

5. The enormous debt this work owes to the insights of Rick Ashley and Ashis Nandy should be obvious. By deconstructing the settled antinomies that were a never-ending seam for mainstream narratives on world politics and studies on colonialism, they created the intellectual space and provided the epistemic ammunition for a slew of works that have substantially remade these disciplines. The engaged interventions into particular arenas of conflict and contestations in world politics, the debates over the relevance of a situational ethic in different contexts, the question of whether strategic essentialism or the momentary anchoring of one's politics in identity can be a progressive step in certain contexts, and a host of similar and unrelated issues in both international relations and postcolonial studies reflected in a number of recent works are testament to the critical import of the writings of Ashley and Nandy. Although it would be impossible to list all the works in critical theory in recent years that have examined the question of political agency under postmodern conditions, the following are representative in their engagement with these issues: Campbell (1993, 1994), Critchley (1992), Ó' Tuathail (1996), and Warner (1991). Similarly, the innumerable citations in this book on recent works in postcolonial studies nearly all bear the mark of Nandy's insights concerning colonialism and modernity.

6. Janatha Vimukthi Peramuna (People's Liberation Front) — originally a Maoist guerrilla movement that acquired a tremendous following among

Sinhalese youth (especially in the more impoverished rural areas) in Sri Lanka. In mid-1971, the JVP insurgency constituted a serious challenge to the Sri Lankan state and was quelled with the help of military troops from India and other countries. In the late 1980s, the JVP would resurge, this time shorn of its Maoist ideology and as an ultranationalist, Sinhala-Buddhist movement committed to the violent overthrow of the Sri Lankan state. See Moore (1993) and Gunaratna (1990) for more on the JVP.

1. MIMETIC HISTORIES

1. One of the clearest expositions of such a view on foreign policy is in Campbell (1992). For more on such a process of worlding in the context of critical international relations, see Walker (1993).

2. In contrast to this discourse of danger regarding the peninsular coastline, see the understated evocation of the same zone as the crucible of a genuinely cosmopolitan and cultured transoceanic civilization in medieval times in Ghosh (1992).

3. Lest anyone think that Panikkar's work is now long forgotten, a recent book on Indian security reminds us that "Even today, Pannikar [sic] is extensively used in teaching in Indian (military) staff colleges" (Gordon 1995, 319–20).

4. The literature on the material and ideological underpinnings of the developmental state is vast. For works that historicize the emergence of such states, are aware of the differential empowerment of various groups and classes as such developmental ideology takes a hold, and recognize the spatialization of the world that it rests upon, see Alavi (1982), Basu (1985), Escobar (1995), and most importantly, Fanon (1963).

5. The prescience and comprehensiveness of Gandhi's critique of modernity and industrial civilization are perhaps best appreciated by reading his own works. Specifically, see his essay "Hind Swaraj," written as early as 1909 and reproduced in full in Rudranghsu Mukherjee's *Gandhi Reader* (1993). For insightful essays on the degree to which Gandhi represented a genuine moment in decolonization (in the sense that he was one of the few nationalists who did not see the postcolonial future as a mirror image of imperial pasts and presents), see Nandy (1980) and Chatterjee (1986). The introduction in Mukherjee (1993) is useful in this regard as well.

6. For the definitive work mapping how science and the project of postcolonial modernity were imbricated, see Abraham (1998).

7. For three analyses that succinctly demonstrate why the commitment to socialism remained populist or merely rhetorical, see Frankel (1978), Kohli (1987, chapter 2), and Kaviraj (1996).

8. There have been a small handful of works sensitive to the imbrication between Nehruvian notions of science and the scientific temper, on the one hand, and the role these notions played in enabling the state to estab-

lish a hegemonic presence relative to civil society. Important among these works are Abraham (1998), Chakrabarti (1982), and Vanaik (1990).

9. For details on the degree of economic pervasiveness of the Indian state circa early 1980s, see Bardhan (1984), Chakravarty (1987), and Rudolph and Rudolph (1987).

10. It is not my intention to imply that Ayoob is personally complicit with the human rights records of his government (which happens to be mine as well). I am suggesting, rather, that his text is an excellent illustration of the intertwined character of power and knowledge, of how the narrative of mainstream international relations allows us to square away our consciences on the question of violence in nation building.

11. As Pasha (1996) notes, Ayoob's views on the security predicament are echoed by a large number of other international relations theorists who construct an ideal model of nation building (out of the western experience) and can consequently regard postcolonial countries only as "quasi-states" and other sorry, lack-ey aberrations. See Doty (1996) for an excellent critique on similar lines.

12. As Ayoob notes, "The quest for predominance derives not only from all the objective factors that are used to measure power (size, population, resources, and industrial and technological capacity), but also from the Indian elite's perception that it inherited the Raj's strategic and political legacy, including the strategic unity that Britain had imposed on the subcontinent" (1989–90, 109).

13. On Punjab, see Tully and Jacob (1985), Jeffrey (1986), Kaur et al. (1984), Brass (1991), and Gupta (1985). On Assam, see Baruah (1994a and 1994b). On Kashmir, see the essays collected in Thomas, ed. (1992). On the Northeast, generally, see Hazarika (1994).

14. On Indian intelligence-based destabilization efforts in neighboring countries see Ahmad (1993), Ali (1993), Rose (1987), Bradnock (1990), and Gunaratna (1993).

15. For a sprinkling of such eulogies, see especially Sethi (1972), Mukherjee (1972), and Mankekar (1972).

16. For some important works that argue that Mrs. Gandhi concentrated power in her hands and did considerable damage to the institutional legacy she inherited, see Kohli (1990), Kochanek (1976), Dua (1981), Hart (1988), Kothari (1989, vols. 1, 2), Rudolph and Rudolph (1987), and Weiner (1989). Even sympathetic biographers do not mince words when it comes to Mrs. Gandhi's personal insecurity and often paranoid style of decision making. See, for example, Malhotra (1989).

17. For two pieces that make the point that Indian expansionism or attempted hegemony is not territorial but has to be understood at a different, more symbolic level, see Rose (1987) and Bradnock (1990).

18. For a recent work that anchors Indian foreign policy since independence in terms of such a self-serving and aggrandizing framework, in the context of the recent intervention in Sri Lanka, see Muni (1993).

2. PRODUCING SRI LANKA FROM CEYLON

1. Keeping in mind that the category *ethnic* and other categories are socially constructed, are embedded in an enumerated discourse of modernity that has an intimate connection to contemporary violence, and can deceive us into believing they are both immutable and timeless, I summarize data from the 1981 census of Sri Lanka below to give us a sense of the political universe in which the ethnic conflict is occurring. As of this census, Sri Lanka was made up of about 17.7 million people, 74 percent of whom were classified as Sinhala speaking, 25 percent were Tamil speaking, and the remaining 1 percent consisted of Burghers (people with Dutch and/or Portuguese ancestry), Malays, and Veddas (aboriginal/tribal peoples). The Sinhalese are mainly (90 percent of them) Theravada Buddhist, their language is related to the northern Indian family of languages (often described as Indo-Aryan or Indo-Germanic), and they live predominantly in the central and southwest parts of the island. About 12.6 percent of the population are Sri Lankan Tamils, and they reside primarily in the northern and the eastern provinces, though there is a sizable community in and around Colombo as well. Sri Lankan Tamils claim an antiquity in Sri Lanka at least as ancient as the Sinhalese, speak a language related to the Dravidian system of languages common across South India (where about fifty-five million Tamil-speaking people live in the Indian state of Tamil Nadu) and are primarily Saivite Hindus. Sri Lankan Tamils can further be divided into Jaffna Tamils, who dominate the northern province, and Batticaloa Tamils, who form about a third of the eastern province's population. Historically, relations between northern and eastern Tamils have not been uniformly congenial, and there has been little intermarriage between the communities. About 7 percent of the population consist of Tamil-speaking Muslims who are spread throughout the country but with a dense concentration in the eastern province. Although they share a language with Sri Lankan Tamils, the affinity of Muslims for the political causes espoused by the former is a complex and varying matter. About 6 percent of the Sri Lankan population are Estate Tamils who were "exported" to Ceylon from India in the nineteenth and early twentieth centuries to work on British-owned coffee and tea plantations in the Central Highlands. These Estate Tamils and their descendants have had an uneasy relationship with Sri Lankan Tamils, the latter being largely oblivious to their plight when the Sinhala-dominated state attempted to strip them of their citizenship rights (1948–49) and resident status (1964), besides viewing them as inferior in every way to themselves. Although at independence

they constituted nearly 12 percent of the population (exceeding even the Sri Lankan Tamils), the Estate Tamils' share in the overall population declined sharply to half of that by the early 1980s (largely on account of repatriation to India) as a result of a series of extraordinarily inhumane and discriminatory measures visited on them by the Sri Lankan government and condoned by both Sri Lankan Tamils and various Indian governments. For a work that sensitively portrays the differences within the Sri Lankan Tamils, see Wilson (1994b). For a superb mapping of Sri Lankan Muslim identity, see Ismail (1995), and for the definitive work on the Estate Tamils, see Daniel (1996).

2. The connection to modernity is succinctly made by Adorno and Horkheimer: "Bourgeois society is ruled by this kind of equivalence. It makes the dissimilar comparable by reducing it to abstract quantities. To the Enlightenment, that which does not reduce to numbers, and ultimately to the one, becomes illusion; modern positivism writes it off as literature" (1973, 11).

3. For a clear discussion regarding myth and history in the context of Sri Lanka, drawing heavily on Barthes (1972), see Daniel's (1990) piece "Sacred Places and Violent Spaces."

4. For a concise colloquial summary of the same argument that I elaborate from Tambiah, see Obeyesekere's (1993) presentation at a conference organized by the American Friends Service Committee. See Gunawardana (1990) for a historical detailing of the originary miscegenation of contemporary identities as well as of the recent origins of the "invented traditions" of racial purity. The opposite argument is made by Dharmadasa (1992). For an insightful essay that deconstructs the "miscegenation versus purity" opposition that undergirds this debate between Gunawardana and Dharmadasa (a debate itself premised on a very modernist overvalorization of history), see the essay "Dehistoricising History" by David Scott in Jeganathan and Ismail, S. (1995), 10–24.

5. The phrases within quotation marks in this excerpt are from the *Mahavamsa* or *The Great Chronicle of Ceylon* (Colombo: Ceylon Government Information Department, 1950) vol. 7, 48–58. The italicized word *Sihala* is Pali for *Sinhala*.

6. I borrow the notion of adulteration from an insightful piece by Lloyd (1994). In this context, as Coomaraswamy points out, many Tamil nationalists have in recent years jumped on this bandwagon and have similarly used the *Mahavamsa* as a mythic charter to date their own antiquity in Sri Lanka as well as to point out the mixed character of all the races of Sri Lanka. She, correctly, cautions that any such use of "legend as empirical fact must be challenged and discredited, regardless of the biases of the author or text" (1987, 81).

7. It must be mentioned that including Sri Lankan and English royalty in a single chronicle does have some precedent. As Kemper (1991, 22) details, when the Buddhist monk Yagirala Pannananda extended the *Mahavamsa* in the 1930s, he incorporated the British governors and royalty into the lineage of rulers.

8. For a systematic demonstration of the discrimination visited upon the Sri Lankan Tamils since independence (gradual underrepresentation in public-sector and general employment in terms of income levels, educational access, and agricultural support systems, especially irrigation facilities; in private-sector employment, as recipients of government expenditures for development and as victims of political violence), see the figures, tables, and data summarized in Committee for Rational Development (1984, 1–69). The CRD's painstaking and lucid empirical demonstration of many of the fallacies and myths that govern Sinhala perceptions of Tamils as a pampered minority and of themselves as a discriminated majority is especially commendable because most of its data is culled from governmental sources. That the myth of Tamil overrepresentation and Sinhala underrepresentation has not only persisted through the decades since the mid-1950s but has actually strengthened in recent years ought to sensitize one to the fact that the material basis of such myths are of limited relevance. Their salience has to be seen at the level of the political and communal needs they fulfill.

9. For details on the pogrom of July 1983, see, among others, Spencer (1990a), Hyndman (1988), *India Today,* August 31, 1983, Obeyesekere (1984), and Tambiah (1986 and 1996).

10. The author's punch line to this paragraph, which I have left out of the quote, is the following: "Indeed, as I write these lines the question which rings in my ears is what the intellectual elite of Egypt repeatedly asked me during my tour of duty in Cairo: 'Ambassador, in your opinion which is the more difficult minority, the Tamils or the Jews?'" (Dissanayaka 1993, 124). Once again, what is stunning is not the presence of such bigotry at the highest levels of the diplomatic corps, but rather the author's complete unawareness that what he says might be viewed as bigoted at all.

11. Interview, J. R. Jayewardene, August 5, 1992, Colombo.

12. Jayewardene had, just prior to the riots, already conditioned himself to such an indifferent response to the fate of the Tamils. On July 11, 1983, two weeks before the killings, in an interview he had observed, "I am not worried about the opinion of the Jaffna people.... Now we can't think of them. Not about their lives or of their opinions about us" (Wilson 1988, 137).

13. To put it baldly, post-1956 Sri Lanka is the future that the majoritarian Hindu fundamentalist parties in India under the leadership of the Bharatiya Janata Party wish to replicate. For those who still believe that

majoritarian Hindu nationalism provides a benign alternative to Nehruvian "pseudosecularism," contemporary Sri Lanka ought to serve as a grim reminder that it does not.

14. It is very important that, at this juncture, I distinguish the argument I am making here from an influential and controversial argument made by Kapferer in his 1988 book on Sinhalese and Australian nationalisms. To drastically summarize, Kapferer attributes an ahistorical and timeless essence to something called a Sinhala-Buddhist "ontology" that works at one level to hierarchize the national space with Sinhalese at the apex and others below, and at another level, to interpret every threat to this hierarchy as an assault on both the state and the individual citizen. My problem with Kapferer's argument is the timeless continuity he attributes to the essentialized nature of Sinhalese Buddhists and the impertubable doggedness with which this ontology remains pristine in its encounters with colonialism, modernization, and postcolonial politics. In contrast, I see the contemporary violence in Sri Lanka not so much as an instance of such an enduring ontology going back 2,500 years, but as arising out of the effort to produce a modern nation-state premised on singular notions of territoriality, identity, and sovereignty. For a charged debate that foregrounds precisely these differences of interpretation, see the debate between Spencer (1990b) and Kapferer (1990) in the pages of the journal *Current Anthropology*.

3. ESSENTIALLY TAMIL

1. I undertake a close textual analysis of Dixit's speech at a later point in this book (chapter 7) because it frames the issue of postcolonial nationalism in a way that inevitably produces an aporia. At the moment, I wish only to show that Dixit's reasoning follows many others in asserting what needs to be demonstrated—namely, that Tamil ethnicity in India and Sri Lanka were closely interrelated and informed each other in the twentieth century.

2. As I argue later in this chapter, De Silva is correct when he discerns a "vicarious nationalism" in the Dravida Munnetra Kazhagam (DMK), the political party that emerged in 1948 from the non-Brahmin, anticasteist, and anti–Hindi language movements in the Madras presidency in the 1930s and 1940s. However, there are two crucial differences in our interpretations. Whereas he argues that DMK's secessionist threat was "effectively checked," I argue that DMK was formed as a political party in 1948 by a new guard in its leadership to distance itself from the secessionist ideology of some of its antecedent social and political movements, and that it wanted accommodation within a federal Indian fold after 1947. In other words, DMK's secessionism was not so much checked as it was given up willingly. Second, De Silva exaggerates the degree and substance of such vicarious nationalism.

In my view, DMK support for Tamil nationalism in Sri Lanka was largely rhetorical and symbolic, hardly ever material or substantive. It was, moreover, intended primarily for domestic consumption in Tamil Nadu.

3. My narrative of Sri Lankan Tamil history is largely culled from the following works: Arasaratnam (1979 and 1986), Manogaran and Pfaffenberger, eds. (1994), Wilson (1988 and 1994a), Tambiah (1986 and 1996), TULF (1988), and Balasingham (1983).

4. The Estate Tamils would have a long and checkered history in the decades thereafter as their citizenship rights became a political football between the Indian and the Sri Lankan governments. Although the Estate Tamils exceeded even the Sri Lankan Tamils in terms of their share of the total population in 1948 (they were 12 percent to the latter's 11 percent), a series of policies — all of them unjustifiable on any human rights grounds or on definitions of citizenship from the United Nations — resulted in their disfranchisement, many thousands of them being declared stateless, being forced into bonded labor in the northern province and in Tamil Nadu, and being forced into repatriation back to India. By the early 1980s, under the leadership of S. Thondaman, a minister in the UNP cabinet under Jayewardene, the issue of stateless Estate Tamils had been solved, and those that remained in Sri Lanka had substantially recovered their right to vote as citizens. Jayewardene's motives in suddenly settling an issue that had supposedly defied resolution for more than four decades was simple: as long as the issue of stateless Estate Tamils existed, it gave Mrs. Gandhi's government a legitimate reason to intervene in Sri Lankan affairs. The last point was made to me by D. D. Devaraj, an Estate Tamil leader who served as minister in the UNP regime of Premadasa, in an interview, July 30, 1992, in Colombo.

5. In his biography of Bandaranaike, James Manor describes his caving into the demands of the Buddhist clergy and unilaterally abrogating his pact with Chelvanayagam as "the most grievous blunder of his career" (1989, 286).

6. The assessments of the Federal Party's collaboration with the UNP during Dudley Senanayake's term (1965–70) vary sharply. Whereas Wilson sees it as a period that, despite the nonimplementation of the Senanayake-Chelvanayagam Pact, "marked the golden years of Sinhala-Tamil reconciliation" (1994a, 111), a prominent Tamil politician of the Federal Party saw it as a period of unprincipled collaboration and naive faith in the Sinhalese on the part of the Tamils. See Navaratnam (1991), chapters 18–21.

7. The *veshti* is a flat white cloth wrapped around the lower half of the body by Tamil men, and the *jibba* is a shirtlike covering for the upper body.

8. For an analysis of the bifurcated lives led by Brahmins, combining a public liberal face with a personal lifestyle steeped in notions of ritual purity and pollution that demoted the vast majority of Tamil society (ap-

proximately 97 percent in fact!) as being incurably inferior to themselves, see Pandian (1994).

9. In Periyar's (and the Dravidian movement's) cosmology, the Brahmins of South India were originally from North India and had in past centuries emigrated southward, bringing with them the perfidious institutions of caste, Sanskritic culture, idolatry, inferior status for women, and a host of other social ills that destroyed the ingrained equality and self-respect of Dravidian society.

10. An astute observer (a participant in much of this history and one-time member of Parliament and the Tamil Nadu legislative assembly) put it to me rather succinctly: "Justice was a political party without an ideology, while the Self-Respect movement was an ideology without a political party." Era Sezhiyan, Interview, May 29, 1992, Madras.

11. For a recent article that persuasively argues that the vision of the Tamil nation that animated Periyar and the Self-Respecters was one of the few instances of a nationalist imaginaire not rooted in some classical past but rather located in an anticipatory and ever-fluid notion of the future, see Pandian (1993).

12. For an essay that insightfully integrates much of the subaltern studies material on this question, see Chatterjee's essay "The Nation and Its Peasants" in his 1993 work.

13. Once again, although DMK was often vociferous in its critique of such Sri Lankan state policies, their record is a sorry one in terms of actually helping the Estate Tamils repatriated to Tamil Nadu. See Daniel (1996) for a moving description of the plight of the Estate Tamils caught between a Sri Lankan state bent on expelling them, the Jaffna Tamils who deemed them inferior, and their supposed kinfolk and politicians in Tamil Nadu, who treated them in a contemptible manner upon their repatriation.

14. Indeed, throughout the 1960s and 1970s, relations between the two countries were excellent. In large part, Sri Lankan regimes adroitly followed a "keep India happy" policy, which translated into Indian neutrality or even into a pro–Sri Lankan government tilt on the Tamil question in Sri Lanka. This cordiality peaked during the 1970s, when Mrs. Gandhi and Mrs. Bandaranaike were in power (1970–77) and during the time when Jayewardene and Morarji Desai were heads of state (1977–79). Relations would deteriorate sharply thereafter, upon Mrs. Gandhi's return to power in January 1980, as detailed in chapter 4.

4. MODULATING BANGLADESH

1. To quote Foucault yet again on this distinction between a quest for a transcendent truth and seeing truth as embedded in discursive formations that are themselves nexuses of power and knowledge: "by truth I do not

mean 'the ensemble of truths which are to be discovered and accepted,' but rather 'the ensemble of rules according to which the true and the false are separated and specific affects of power are attached to the true,' it being understood also that it's not a matter of a battle 'on behalf' of the truth, but of a battle on the political status of truth and the economic and political role it plays" (1980a, 122).

2. Interview, Thomas Abraham Sr., Madras, July 20, 1992.

3. In a footnote to the quoted passage, Ali states, "Non-Congress state administrations, example, in Punjab, West Bengal and Tripura were also subjected to similar machinations." In pointing to this common pattern of covert destabilization of both regional and domestic regimes, Ali buttresses the point made by Thomas (1986) and by Phadnis and Jetly (1990). Bradnock (1990, 37) and Raina (1981) also support the argument that covert intelligence operations were more prominent under Mrs. Gandhi but played a relatively lower profile under Janata.

4. On the face of it, U.S. interest in a naval base at Trincomalee at this time seems improbable. As one analyst notes, "India's concerns here were somewhat excessive as the United States seemed unlikely to seek port facilities in another Asian country considering the...availability, in any case, of a major naval–air base in Diego Garcia" (Chari 1994, 6). Diego Garcia is an island about a thousand miles south of Sri Lanka, and South Asia hardly figured high enough in U.S. calculations (Indian delusions in this regard notwithstanding) to warrant serious interest in Trincomalee. Stephen Cohen, who works on security issues concerning South Asia, was at this time (late 1970s, early 1980s) affiliated with the Arms Control and Disarmament Agency of the State Department. At the time of my interview with him, he remembered no serious discussion about U.S. interest in Trincomalee in the State Department, especially at the higher levels. Although an occasional report may have been authored by some bureaucrat regarding such possibilities, nothing serious was ever afoot according to him. To the extent that there existed such a thing as a "South Asia policy at all," he described the mood in the State Department as being more on the lines of "keep India happy" at this time. Interview with Stephen Cohen, New Delhi, June 9, 1993.

5. For specifics on the District Development Councils, and Jayewardene's characteristic waffling, see Wilson (1988, 134–74). He regards the DDCs as inadequate in the context of Tamil demands for a more federal structure and devolution of autonomy to the Tamil regions. For a viewpoint more sympathetic to Jayewardene and critical of TULF's "intransigence," see De Silva and Wriggins (1994, 423–49). They emphasize the degree to which Jayewardene was constrained by the attitudes of his own ministers and MPs, not to speak of a belligerently conservative Sinhalese

civil society, especially the Buddhist clergy. They also note that TULF had begun to ride with the extremist Tamil militant movement at this time, and their compromising with the president on the DDCs would have been unacceptable to these groups.

6. Also see Obeyesekere (1984, 163). For a report on the events leading up to the incident, and specifically the impact of draconian legislation such as the Prevention of Terrorism Act passed by Jayewardene's regime (an act modeled on the South African Terrorist Act of 1967) in 1979, see Leary (1983).

7. Book-length studies on the origins, social base, and early activities of the Tamil militant groups of Sri Lanka are only beginning to emerge. Perhaps the pick of the lot published so far is Swamy (1994). Other sources include Hellmann-Rajanayagam (1994), Gunaratna (1993), Ram (1989), and Hoole et al. (1990). Much useful material can be found in newsmagazines and journals, especially *Frontline* (Madras), the *Lanka Guardian,* and *Pravada* (Colombo).

8. The reference in Mohandas's comment regarding MGR and Indira Gandhi coming closer together politically in 1982–83 requires some background information. Although he had allied with Mrs. Gandhi's Congress Party in the elections of 1977 (to both Parliament and state assembly), MGR had cozied up to the Janata regime when she was out of power. He further alienated Mrs. Gandhi when he reneged on a promise to support her contesting a by-election to Parliament from Thanjavur in Tamil Nadu in 1978 (she eventually returned to Parliament from Chikmagalur in neighboring Karnataka state). He backed out on his promise to ensure Mrs. Gandhi's reelection from Thanjavur ostensibly under pressure from the Desai regime. As a consequence of their rift, in the parliamentary elections of 1979, Congress allied with the DMK. Once Mrs. Gandhi was back in the saddle, MGR feared his government's unseating by the center and initiated a slow rapprochement with Mrs. Gandhi beginning in the early 1980s. This information is critical for another reason: allegations that he and the AIADMK harbored secessionist proclivities and sympathies for the cause of Eelam and acted in ways that went against or led central government policy on the Sri Lankan Tamil issue do not mesh with the picture drawn above: that of a chief minister always keen on being on the right side of the ruling party at the center.

9. This point was made by a variety of different individuals in the course of interviews. In the Tamil Nadu police, it was made by K. Mohandas, director general of police (retired), interview: Madras, June 12, 1992; R. Ravindran, inspector general of police (retired), interview: Madras, May 27, 1993; and former inspector general of police (intelligence), A. X. Alexander, interview: Madras, May 21, 1993. Among Sri Lankan Tamil militants,

the point that the pre-1983 training was largely done by the groups them-selves, without any involvement of either central or state support, was echoed by D. Siddharthan of PLOTE in an interview in Colombo, on August 2, 1992, and by K. Premachandran (Suresh) of the EPRLF, interview: Colombo, August 4, 1992. As Daniel notes, "As late as May 1983, the sum total of Tamil militants in the Jaffna peninsula numbered no more than three hundred, armed with largely primitive weapons" (1996, 140).

10. Interviews, Colombo, July 29 and August 4, 1992, respectively.

11. For details on the pogrom of July 1983, especially on its planned character and some evidence regarding the role of UNP officials and gov-ernment employees in the event, see Piyadasa (1984), Hoole et al. (1990, 64–65), Obeyesekere (1984), Hyndman (1988), Tambiah (1986 and 1996), and *India Today*, August 31, 1983.

12. Details in these paragraphs are taken from Tambiah (1986) and Nissan (1984, 177–84).

13. Interview, Merwyn De Silva, August 4, 1992, Colombo. It was also in 1983–84 that the Jayewardene administration was being cautioned by General Vernon Walters of the United States on the imminent possibility of an Indian invasion if they didn't work toward a resolution of the ethnic question (De Silva and Wriggins 1994, 590–91). The idea of an Indian in-vasion of Sri Lanka in mid-1984, which initially sounded utterly ludicrous to me, was something that a number of Sri Lankan politicians thought highly probable. According to the recollections of many in Sri Lanka, at this time it was strongly rumoured that airfields were being readied, army units were being mobilized, and various kinds of preparations were underway in India. Whether this was one more instance of Mrs. Gandhi attempting to pres-sure Jayewardene into making concessions on the diplomatic track or some kind of military gaming exercise or the handiwork of an intelligence disin-formation campaign, it does indicate the frame of mind of many in Sri Lanka, including Jayewardene, vis-à-vis India at this time. The Sri Lankans took the threat seriously enough for their foreign secretary, S. Jayasinghe, to request an emergency meeting with his Indian counterpart, M. K. Ras-gotra, and to rush into New Delhi within hours to clarify his doubts. As Rasgotra recalled it: "Jayasinghe telephoned me from Colombo and he said he wanted to come to Delhi urgently. I have very high respect for the man, very sober, sensible thoughtful official...so I said come. He said he had something very urgent and serious to talk about....They arrived....I said you are most welcome, but what brings you here? He said: 'I want to speak to you very, very openly, I consider you a friend and we look to you as a friend of Sri Lanka. We have an apprehension that India is going to attack Sri Lanka.' And I burst out laughing. I said: 'Jayasinghe, what are you... what is the matter with you?' 'No, no,' he said, 'Krishna [Rasgotra's middle

name], I am being very serious. . . . We have some information in Sri Lanka, rumours, that India is going to attack and do the job for the Sri Lankan Tamils. Separate Jaffna, make Jaffna a country.' So I, with all the sincerity and earnestness I could command, told him that if you want to meet anybody, I'll make the arrangements, but if my word is worth anything to you, please understand very clearly that there is no question of India intervening in any way in this situation." Interview, June 19, 1994, New Delhi.

14. The authors suggest that some of the delays in the APC were at Mrs. Gandhi's behest because she didn't want this controversy to impinge on the election prospects of Congress in Tamil Nadu (elections to both Parliament and the state assembly were to be held in late 1984 or early 1985). This suggestion does not sound very plausible to me. First, it is highly unlikely that the APC's acceptance of Annexure C, or otherwise, could have any significant impact on elections in Tamil Nadu. Second, if anything, the acceptance of Annexure C by the Sri Lankans at this point may have given a small boost to Congress, which could use it to portray itself as an able defender of Tamils everywhere. Third, if De Silva and Wriggins are right, they need to face the question why, then, on Mrs. Gandhi's death, did Jayewardene set about winding up the APC and ditching Annexure C altogether?

15. Interviews with TULF MPs Neelan Tiruchelvan, Colombo, August 1, 1992, and M. Senadhiraja, Colombo, August 4, 1992. They recalled that particularly Prime Minsiter Premadasa and the Buddhist clergy conducted themselves in the APC in a manner that indicated no desire to compromise or work with the political process.

16. Interview, Thomas Abraham Sr. Madras, July 20, 1992.

17. Although what actually transpired at the meetings between Amirthalingam and Mrs. Gandhi might never be known, one is struck by Amirthalingam and TULF's naivete. It was apparent that many in TULF continued to retain the impression that Mrs. Gandhi was truly a champion of their cause and would have gone to any length to help out Sri Lankan Tamils. Mrs. Gandhi was never in the business of fighting other people's struggles for them: she supported the Sri Lankan Tamils at this point in time because they offered a perfect way to get under Jayewardene's skin and to destabilize Sri Lanka — just as she had been quite indifferent to their plight in the 1970s when relations with Sri Lanka were excellent.

18. Interview, A. X. Alexander, inspector general, Tamil Nadu Police, May 21, 1992. Also see Mohandas (1992).

19. Shekhar Gupta was the first to report on RAW's arming and training of Tamil militants, "Sri Lanka Rebels: An Ominous Presence in Tamil Nadu," *India Today*, March 31, 1984, 84–94. This article was followed by reports in the *Sunday Times*, London, April 1, 1984, and then in Sri Lankan newspapers, *Island*, May 25, 1984, and *Sun*, May 23, 1984. Another detailed report was published in *South*, March 1985.

20. MGR's motivations in picking the LTTE for sponsorship are difficult to divine. When I suggested that he chose LTTE because of their obvious discipline and commitment to the cause of Eelam, two of his closest advisers, his inspector general of police, K. Mohandas, and a minister in his cabinet, "Panruti" Ramachandran, thought it unlikely — such causes were never particularly dear to his heart. They preferred a more mundane explanation, such as "Karunanidhi was close to TELO so MGR started supporting LTTE." Nor did these two advisers find it particularly plausible that MGR picked LTTE because the latter was already showing signs of autonomy from RAW and the central government. They were both very clear that as far as the center went, for all his on-screen heroics, the cinema star turned politician preferred discretion to valor. Interviews: K. Mohandas, June 12, 1992, Madras, and "Panruti" Ramachandran, June 7, 1992, Madras.

21. For a gruesome description of the torture and violence in these camps and of the incredible barbarity with which some Sri Lankan Tamil militant leaders ran them, see Daniel (1996, 140–42).

22. In 1998, Mohandas would finger G. Parthasarathi (the very same person conducting negotiations with Jayewardene on Annexure C!) as the "senior policy maker" of the quoted excerpt. See "Former D. G. P. Blames Government Policy for Spread of Bomb Culture," in Rediff on the Net [cited February 16, 1998]; @www.rediff.com./news/1998/feb/16dgps.htm. Interview with Mohandas. It must be mentioned that Mohandas blamed the actions of Sri Lankan militants in Tamil Nadu on policy makers in New Delhi who served as their protectors, while officials in New Delhi just as routinely ascribed these law-and-order problems to the Eelamist sympathies of Tamil Nadu's populace and the inability or unwillingness of the political parties there to rein in their enthusiasm. Plausible deniabilities all around.

23. This precocity of LTTE was reiterated in interviews with, among others, D. Siddharthan, PLOTE, August 2, 1992, Colombo, Era Janarthanan, July 22, 1992, Madras, a former member of the Legislative Council in Tamil Nadu and long-standing supporter of the Sri Lankan Tamils who knew Prabhakaran and others in the LTTE during the 1970s, long before they became prominent (or prosperous); P. Nedumaran, June 7, 1992, Madras, Tamil Nadu politician who explicitly espoused the cause of Eelam and had visited Jaffna at the invitation of the LTTE in 1984; and "Panruti" Ramachandran, June 7, 1992, Madras.

5. HEGEMONY AS SPECTACLE

1. For details on the pogrom against the Sikhs and the involvement of the Congress Party and state machinery, see Citizens Commission (1985), Peoples Union for Democratic Rights (PUDR) and Peoples Union for Civil Liberties (PUCL) (1984), Das, ed. (1990), Kothari and Sethi, eds. (1985), and Chakravarty and Haksar (1987). For an especially comprehensive dis-

cussion of the anti-Sikh riots, see Tambiah (1996, 101–62), and for an examination of the political culture inaugurated by Mrs. Gandhi that allowed for something like this pogrom to occur, see Krishna (1994).

2. During Rajiv's entire five-year term as prime minister, not a single person involved in the Delhi riots would be brought to justice. By 1992, ten persons had been convicted, none of them the prominent politicians who had been sighted by innumerable eyewitnesses as leading and directing the rioters. Government figures put the number murdered at 2,733 people, and the real figures are probably much higher. More than 5,000 were reported killed during these riots, according to an unofficial report (see *New York Times,* September 16, 1996). In September 1996, an Additional Sessions judge, S. N. Dhingra, sentenced 89 persons involved in the riots to five years of rigorous imprisonment and a fine of Rs. 5,000 each. He derided the Delhi police for their "suppression of truth," charged the administration with being "interested in nonprosecution" of the rioters, and described previous government investigations into the riots as a "farce." Justice Dhingra also passed the only death sentence so far in the Delhi riots case, against a butcher named Kishor Lal, who is alleged to have been involved in more than 150 killings. See *India Network News Digest* II, vol. 2, issue 1032, report by Prafulla Das, September 9, 1996.

3. In mid-1985, Rajiv Gandhi met with Rajni Kothari and a prominent Sikh architect, Patwant Singh. After the various reports cited in note 1 were published, two Congress leaders allegedly responsible for the riots were assassinated by Sikh militants in Delhi. Referring to this, "Rajiv Gandhi turned on Kothari and said angrily: 'I will hold you responsible if any more killings of this kind take place.'" Kothari, an eminent political scientist and human rights activist, was president of PUCL at this time. Astoundingly enough, Rajiv Gandhi was threatening the person who had exposed the murderers, rather than seeking justice for the Sikhs of Delhi. See Singh (1994, 141–42).

4. Interview, July 13, 1993, New Delhi.

5. Neelan Tiruchelvam, TULF MP, felt that very little serious preparation went into Thimpu, with all the energy and effort going into bringing the parties together rather than into the substance of the discussions. Moreover, he felt that too many agencies and organizations, working at cross-purposes, were involved in getting the conference together, resulting in chaos. Interview, August 1 and 5, 1992, Colombo.

6. This summarization of talks on the July proposals is from Wilson (1988, 192–98). For a somewhat different reading, see De Silva and Wriggins (1994, 620–23). The latter point to TULF's refusal to give up on a united northeastern province as the main stumbling block. But this refusal was hardly unexpected as it had been a staple of Tamil demands going back

at least to the APC of 1983–84. Chidambaram himself saw the changes introduced by Jayewardene as indicating that the latter was never serious about negotiating with the Tamils. His own insistence on meticulously documenting all drafts and proposed amendments and getting Jayewardene to commit himself in writing was motivated by his negative assessment of Jayewardene's bona fides as a negotiator. Interview, June 24, 1993, New Delhi. Similar assessments of Jayewardene and the reasons for the breakdown of talks on the Chidambaram proposals were given by Neelan Tiruchelvam and M. Senadhiraja, both representatives of TULF. Interviews, August 4 and 5, 1992, respectively, Colombo.

7. As Shyam Tekwani, photojournalist with *India Today,* recalled, goodwill for the militants lasted a very brief while. Soon, locals began to question why citizens of a foreign country were being housed in camps and provided with rations, while they themselves often went hungry and were destitute. He remembered many instances of fishermen in coastal villages having serious differences with militants about poaching. Moreover, the militants regarded themselves as different and superior to the locals, adding to the anger of the latter. Interview, May 23, 1993, Madras. Such instances of differences, which occasionally broke out into fights, were also confirmed by A. X. Alexander (then inspector general of Tamil Nadu Police); K. Mohandas (former inspector general of police, June 12, 1992, Madras); N. Ram (editor, *Frontline,* June 2, 1992); "Cho" Ramaswamy (a well-known journalist and playwright, editor of *Tuglak,* June 1, 1992); and Bhagwan Singh (journalist with the *Sunday Mail,* May 22, 1993, Madras). All agreed that although sympathy for the Sri Lankan Tamils was at a peak in July–August 1983, by mid-1986 it had ebbed considerably, and they were regarded as nuisances at minimum and often as dangerous.

8. Anita Pratap, interview, July 21, 1993, New Delhi. However, Prabhakaran had made clear his intention to shift his base back to Jaffna in October, even before SAARC.

9. Many foreign service officers in India held RAW mainly responsible for the fiasco at the SAARC summit. In their view, RAW officials exaggerated their influence on the LTTE and convinced Rajiv Gandhi the latter would acquiesce with Indian desires for a grand peace announcement. Moreover, they alleged RAW officials were probably telling LTTE that India was behind their quest for Eelam (but could not come out openly on that front) in order to secure LTTE's cooperation in announcing such a breakthrough. Although these contending versions are interesting as instances of bureaucratic politics, the more important point here is that various institutions of the Indian state were working at cross-purposes.

10. The description of Brasstacks based on a superb report published under the auspices of the Program in Arms Control, Disarmament and In-

ternational Security at the University of Illinois at Urbana-Champaign. See Bajpai et al. (1995).

11. On the question of the three men's attitude against the Tamils, one could array them in ascending order of chauvinism: Premadasa, Athulath-mudali, Dissanayake. Although there was no doubt about Premadasa's deep hatred of the Indian regime, he was perhaps the least tainted by anti-Tamil bigotry. Athulathmudali, it must be said to his credit, took the trouble of learning Tamil and could speak the language fluently. As an earlier chapter indicated, Dissanayake was, of the three, given to the most sanguinary comments about Tamils. However, his growing proximity to India would lead him to mute overt chauvinism in his rhetoric. Finally, I feel compelled to add, these shades of difference are minor in comparison to a glaring fact: none of the three politicians or Jayewardene was free from a virulent anti-Tamil and pro-Sinhala sentiment. At a fundamental level, all four believed and acted as if Sri Lanka was exclusively the land of Sinhala Buddhists and the rest were, at best, tolerated minorities.

12. For a brief mention about the line that Dissanayake inaugurated in a note submitted to Jayewardene on June 10, 1985, see De Silva and Wriggins (1994, 614–15).

13. A comment by one of Sri Lanka's more insightful analysts perfectly captured Dissanayake's stratagem: "If Sri Lanka was going to be India's Afghanistan, Gamini was going to be Babrak Karmal." Interview, Dayan Jayatilleka, August 7, 1992, Colombo.

14. Much has been made of this grant, both by Sri Lankan academics and by many in India. The conventional interpretation is that it is one more indicator of the degree to which New Delhi's policy on Sri Lanka was tied down because of the Tamil Nadu factor, and of how the state and its chief minister had a propensity to lead, instead of follow, the center in foreign policy. By now, it ought to be evident that I disagree completely. At the risk of sounding repetitive: to me, it is inconceivable that MGR would have publicly paid out such a large sum of money to Tamil militants without first getting the center's permission. More likely, the center wanted to aid the militants against the Sri Lankan army, and the ever-obliging MGR did their dirty work for them. It must be remembered, in this context, that RAW's training of the militants, which had ground to a halt in late 1986, was resumed in April–May of 1987 and went on until the Indo–Sri Lanka Agreement was signed on July 29, 1987. So the central government had already initiated a policy of helping the militants defend themselves before MGR announced his monetary award to them.

15. S. H. Venkat Ramani, correspondent, *India Today*, interview, July 15, 1992, New Delhi. Like any good journalist, that was enough for Venkat Ramani to head toward Galle Face Green, opposite the Sri Lankan president's office and the center stage of the Sri Lankan political theater. Sure

enough, that evening around five P.M, two of the Mirage 2000s, which were only supposed to escort the AN 32s and be on their way back to Bangalore, made a lazy turn over Colombo city and could be seen plainly over the Indian Ocean, off Galle Face.

16. Dixit, interview, June 21, 1994, Gurgaon, Haryana.

17. Sunanda K. Datta-Ray, "Pranks for Diplomacy: Picking Up the Pieces Afterwards," *Statesman,* June 7, 1987; "India's Gunboat Diplomacy," *Statesman,* June 4, 1987; B. G. Verghese, "Another View on Sri Lanka," *Indian Express,* June 3, 1987; and Pran Chopra, "Fiasco in Sri Lanka—I and II," *Indian Express,* June 17 and 18, 1987. Datta-Ray was especially trenchant. He noted in concluding his essay, "Meanwhile, if relations between the two countries are not irreparably damaged, it will be entirely because of the neglected diplomatists in South Block. They may not be consulted, the files they put up may be disregarded, but like conscientious nursery attendants, they are always there to pick up the pieces after each reckless children's romp. No previous government has needed the constant services of such a salvage squad as much as this one."

18. Interview, J. R. Jayewardene, August 5, 1992, Colombo.

19. Although it would take us too far afield to go into details, Rajiv Gandhi was under tremendous pressure at this time as well, albeit for different reasons. The preceding months had seen his regime lurch from one crisis to another. In June 1987, he was locked in a battle for the very survival of his regime with President Zail Singh, who was spearheading a move by some dissidents within the Congress Party to unseat him using a corruption scandal (Bofors) as their reason. His party had lost state-level elections in Andhra Pradesh, Karnataka, Assam, and Punjab in the preceding year, and dissatisfaction within the party was at a peak. With assembly elections in the state of Haryana around the corner, his regime desperately needed something to reverse their declining fortunes. He had broken with two close advisers and friends, Arun Nehru and Arun Singh, and his relations with his very popular finance minister turned defense minister, V. P. Singh, had taken a sharp turn for the worse. The shifting of V. P. Singh from finance to defense was widely seen as a move to take him out of the loop in the ongoing investigations into corruption, and his resignation came at the height of the current crisis. Ironically, although Jayewardene was the one who seemed paranoid about his survival as president, it would appear that in reality Rajiv Gandhi was closer to the edge of the precipice. Given all this, Sri Lanka seemed to be an opportune theater in which to stage a spectacular foreign policy success and redeem Gandhi's leadership in some measure.

20. All quotations are from the text of the Indo–Sri Lanka Agreement to Establish Peace and Normalcy in Sri Lanka (Colombo, July 29, 1987) as reprinted in Kumar, ed. (1988, 233–37). The agreement (rather confusingly) also has an "Annexure to the Agreement" and an exchange of letters be-

tween Rajiv Gandhi and Jayewardene. Although quibblers may separate various parts and attach different emphases to each, I regard the entire package as the "agreement": I believe that is why the two governments published all these documents together as the agreement in the first place.

21. The distance between the India's presumed centrality in world affairs (in the minds of many Indian bureaucrats, politicians, academics, and journalists) and the relatively peripheral attention given to subcontinental matters generally in the world media is often vast. The sociohistorical reasons for such narcissism in a postcolonial elite has long intrigued me, but for the moment I shall confine myself to noting that many in the Indian establishment were convinced that the agreement of 1987 made banner headlines in western capitals and was the stuff of intense debate there.

22. The underlined sentence is a fascinating one. It is (most probably) an error by Gunaratna. It should read, "The referendum will never take place." In a truly Freudian slip, Gunaratna ventriloquates either Rajiv Gandhi's innermost intentions or Jayewardene's or his own by mistakenly quoting Rajiv to the effect that "The merger will never take place," instead of suggesting that the referendum would be endlessly postponed. In a recent conversation, Gunaratna averred it was simply a typo and ought to read that the referendum would never take place, but the slip remains fascinating for all the above reasons. Conversation with Gunaratna, June 7, 1997, Honolulu.

23. This was an important moment of truth for Premadasa. There was a huge opposition to the agreement, and many attempts were being made to woo him, including by SLFP. By biting back his disgust and playing along, Premadasa ensured that he would remain the front-runner for the UNP's presidential nomination the next year. If he had succumbed to his own feelings and jumped on the anti-agreement bandwagon, he would have faced a very uncertain political future, especially considering that SLFP's presidential nomination was locked up by Sirima Bandaranaike. At the same time, his explicitly supporting the agreement would ensure his defeat against Sirima in the next year's presidential election.

24. Interview, K. P. S. Menon, July 22, 1992, Madras.

25. An interesting aspect of my interviews with Athulathmudali and Jayewardene was their virtually identical replies to a question regarding what they would have liked to have happened differently if they had their druthers. Both men replied that when New Delhi had Prabhakaran there during the deliberations just prior to the signing of the agreement, they ought not to have let him go. Rather, as Athulathmudali pointed out, if Sheikh Abdullah could have spent more than fifteen years in exile in a hill station in Tamil Nadu, and the Dalai Lama could be similarly housed in Dharamsala in Himachal Pradesh, Prabhakaran could jolly well have been sent to some place such as Kashmir for that duration. Both men believed

this step could have dramatically increased the probability of the success of the agreement. Athulathmudali, interview, July 29, 1992, Colombo, and Jayewardene, interview, August 5, 1992, Colombo.

26. For a detailed explanation of his version of what transpired in his meetings with Puri and then with others in Delhi, including Rajiv Gandhi, see Prabhakaran's interview with Anita Pratap in *India Today*, August 15, 1987, 78–79. Incidentally, Anita Pratap herself is of the view that the Indians strong-armed Prabhakaran in Delhi and got him to agree under duress. Interview, July 21, 1993, New Delhi.

27. Interview, June 21, 1994, Gurgaon, Haryana.

28. Interviews, Dixit, June 21, 1994, Gurgaon, Haryana, and Chidambaram, June 24, 1993, New Delhi. In my interview with Jayewardene, he did not back off from such an interpretation of his actions. As he put it, Churchill had smartly got the Americans to die for Britain in huge numbers during World War II, so what was the big deal? Moreover, the president had always been convinced that India's aid and abetting of the militants was entirely responsible for Sri Lanka's so-called terrorist problem, so there was an element of justice in the Indian army coming into Sri Lanka to disarm the militant groups. Interview, August 5, 1992, Colombo.

29. The speed at which the troops were inducted merits some explanation. As I note in chapter 6, as early as April 1987, the Indian army had been asked to game out various scenarios for Sri Lanka, including the large-scale induction of Indian troops into the northern province there. The precise nature of these operations weren't spelled out (there was no need to), but it ranged from peacekeeping operations to a conflict with the Sri Lankan army. This prior preparation explains how the Indian army's divisions were moved to Palaly within hours of the signing of the agreement.

30. In this regard, a noteworthy aspect of Geertz's (1980) descriptions of Negara is his insistence that its theatricality was neither hostile to nor merely derivative of the more mundane and material aspects of statehood. The Negara fulfilled multiple important functions as a state: the huge and complex system of water management, the regulation of trade, the ceremonial cremations, and the like, and did so in an envelope of ceremony, pomp, and splendor that rendered the state a uniquely participatory phenomenon, not merely a distant leviathan dominating from above and without.

6. NARRATIVES IN CONTENTION

1. From the visitor's log book, the entry by Sqdn. Ldr. K. J. Bhatt, Indian Air Force, September 15, 1987. Trincomalee Oil Tank farm guest house, Trincomalee.

2. Interview, Lt. Gen. Depinder Singh, retired, Panch Kula, Chandigarh, Haryana, July 2, 1993.

3. Interview, General Singh. In his book, the general is more explicit: "What he did say was that he would never again trust the External Affairs Ministry of India and the Research and Analysis Wing (RAW). Considering the time and place, I did not ask him to elaborate" (n.d., 48).

4. The second Prabhakaran uttered this phrase, the crowd erupted with cheers and acclamation. It was the first public indication of LTTE's stance on disarming. The cheers took Prabhakaran by surprise and "a momentary spasm of annoyance pass[ed] over [his] face" (Hoole et al. 1990, 145). It indicated that the people were tired of the war and euphoric about the presence of the IPKF and that LTTE was, at the moment at any rate, out of sync with popular sentiment in Jaffna.

5. Many in India regard Prabhakaran's speech at Sudumalai, often described as his "we love India" speech (!), as indicating his acceptance of the agreement. In the face of such passages, I fail to see how.

6. Interview, Maj. Gen. Yashwant Deva, retired, Signals, NOIDA, June 21, 1993, Uttar Pradesh.

7. Foreign service officers regarded RAW officials as heavy-footed "spooks" who had no business conducting foreign policy, whereas intelligence agency personnel felt that the diplomats ought to confine themselves to throwing parties and leave the hard-nosed business of relations with neighboring regimes to them. Underlying these petty bureaucratic rivalries between the Indian Foreign Service (IFS) and RAW is a more substantive issue that I examine in chapter 7. From the time of its inception in the late 1960s, RAW has grown tremendously in importance. The emergence of a well-endowed, completely secretive intelligence agency and its increasing prominence in the conduct of foreign policy would seem to indicate the rise of what Der Derian (1992) insightfully calls "antidiplomacy."

8. Interview, A. S. Panneerselvam, May 24, 1993, Madras. In fact, in their propaganda against the agreement, LTTE used many references to alledge Indian army atrocities in Bangladesh during the war of 1971. Photojournalist Shyam Tekwani distinctly remembers this about the days in Jaffna immediately after its signing (interview, May 23, 1993, Madras). LTTE wasn't the only group on to Indian designs in this regard. PLOTE was equally sophisticated in their analysis of Indian intelligence agencies and the role they had played in Bangladesh. A warning on this account, as far back as 1984, was published by them in a book in Tamil that was titled, interestingly enough, *Vangam Thanda Padam* (The Lessons of Bangladesh). See Swamy (1994, 179).

9. Dixit, interview, June 21, 1994.

10. On August 18, when the Sri Lankan Parliament convened for the first time since the signing of the agreement, two hand grenades exploded on the podium that seated the president and his entire cabinet. Besides injuring Athulathmudali badly, the explosions killed a district minister from

Matara (Keerthi Abeywickrema). A right-wing Sinhala chauvinistic group, Deshapremi Janatha Peramuna or Patriotic Peoples Front, claimed credit for the explosions.

11. Dixit, interview, June 21, 1994, Gurgaon, Haryana. Relations between Dixit and Harkirat Singh had already soured considerably. During Thileepan's fast, fearing what might happen if he died, Singh had sent an angry memo to Dixit telling him to stop dragging his feet in talks with LTTE and to settle the matter speedily (Singh, n.d., 78). Outraged at this, Dixit in turn had dashed off a memo to New Delhi alleging that Singh had gone soft in his heart (if not head) on LTTE and had best be sacked forthwith (Gunaratna 1993, 229). More generally, this exchange revealed a problem that continually bedeviled India's operation in Sri Lanka: a lack of clarity as to who called the shots and what the chain of command was.

12. Interview, July 29, 1992, Colombo.

13. Jayatilleka mentions one more angle to all of this: it was the Indians who had leaked the whereabouts of the boat carrying the seventeen men to the Sri Lankan navy in the first place as a prelude to softening up the LTTE (1995, 16).

14. Details on the heli-landing operation are culled primarily from an interview with Lt. Gen. (retired) Depinder Singh, July 2, 1993, Panch Kula, Chandigarh, Haryana. Also see Kadian (1990, 41–44) for more information on this episode.

15. Singh interview, July 2, 1993.

16. Interview, Maj. Gen. Yashwant Deva (retired), June 21, 1993, NOIDA, Uttar Pradesh.

17. Among many who repeated this inaccurate version of events were Dixit (interview, June 21, 1994) and Narendra Nath Jha, Indian high commissioner in Sri Lanka between 1990 and 1993 (interview, June 29, 1993, New Delhi).

18. Deepavali (literally, "row of lamps") is the most popular of Hindu festivals, commemerating the triumph of good over evil and the return of King Rama to his throne after his fourteen-year exile in the jungle, recounted in the epic *Ramayana*.

19. Interview, Maj. Gen. (retired) Ashok Mehta, July 23, 1993, New Delhi.

20. See Dixit quoted in *India Today,* December 15, 1995, 53. Implicit in Dixit's comment is an oft-encountered stereotype among India's civilian elite that the army top-brass are a bunch of Colonel Blimpish characters without much capacity for subtle thought. At least one foreign secretary mentioned that jokes and merciless caricatures about them were popular at the highest levels of the Rajiv Gandhi government. Interview, Muchkund Dubey, July 20, 1993, New Delhi.

21. Interview, N. Ram, June 2, 1992, Madras. Also see Hellman-Rajanayagam (1994, 130) for details on such public opinion polls.

22. Despite such insights, Hellmann-Rajanayagam, like many others who have analyzed the relationship between Tamil Nadu and Sri Lanka, is prone to exaggerate connections between the two Tamil communities and to overestimate support for the cause of Eelam amongst Tamils in Tamil Nadu. See, for example, her confused and convoluted analysis in the sections surrounding this quote, which tries, against her own evidence, to argue that the DMK and Karunanidhi represented a genuine threat of secession (in the 1980s) and support for the Sri Lankan Tamil quest for Eelam at this time. The DMK, like the AIADMK when it was in power and the Indian government ever since 1983, tried to make political (especially electoral) capital out of its purported sympathy for the Sri Lankan Tamil cause. To confuse this opportunistic display of sympathy with a serious effort at secession is to misunderstand the entire trajectory of Dravidian politics in the preceding decades, as chapter 3 argued at some length.

23. Premadasa obtained 50.43 percent of the votes, Bandaranaike obtained 44.95 percent, and Abeygunasekara got 4.63 percent of the vote. Given the low turnout, Premadasa had secured only 27.4 percent of the registered voters in the country. In terms of actual numbers, Premadasa obtained 2,569,199 votes to Bandaranaike's 2,289,860 votes, with Abyegunasekara getting 235,719 votes. The margin between Premadasa and Bandaranaike was 279,339 votes. This discussion of numbers and turnouts is a necessary prelude to off-the-record comments made by two high-ranking Indian diplomats who were in Sri Lanka during these times. Both stated that the Indians supported Premadasa in the elections and basically delivered his victory. They did this, according to diplomats, in at least two ways: first, in many places in the North and East, the elections were conducted by IPKF, who stuffed the ballot boxes with UNP votes. Second, the Indians contributed huge amounts of money to Premadasa's election coffers. As one of these two individuals noted, "We got the damn fellow elected. Look at the results, it was very, very close. Bottom line was this, we delivered all three: the Tamil votes in the northeastern region; the Muslim votes in the eastern province; and Tamil plantation votes in the hill country.... Rajiv Gandhi supported this line totally. It was not an off-the-cuff decision. It was 'Mrs. Bandaranaike will screw you now; Premadasa may screw you later. Go with Premadasa for now.'" The other individual was equally blunt: "it was the IPKF which stuffed the ballot boxes in favor of Premadasa. He won by only 200,000 votes. It was a wafer-thin majority. Another 200,000 votes and the second preference votes would have been counted, and they were all for Mrs. Bandaranaike, not for Ossie [Abeygunasekara]. And she

would have won.... [O]ur army did it." (Under Sri Lankan electoral rules, if none of the candidates secured more than 50 percent of the popular vote, the second preferences of the voters would determine the winner.) As noted earlier, Premadasa obtained 50.43 percent of the vote. The claims by the two Indian officials that the Indians got Premadasa elected don't sound as far-fetched in this light.

24. Interview, Suresh Premachandran, EPRLF MP, August 4, 1992, Colombo.

25. There is more to this tangled web of intrigue and counterintrigue. After Rajiv Gandhi was assassinated and the history of India's role in Sri Lankan affairs came under close scrutiny, Karunanidhi would reveal a startling fact. According to him, in mid-1989, when he was chief minister and Rajiv still prime minister, in retaliation for Premadasa's provocations (in calling for the immediate exit of the IPKF and arming of the LTTE), Rajiv used Karunanidhi to convey to the LTTE that India would even back LTTE in its quest for Eelam if it ditched Premadasa at this time. Evidently, LTTE did not rise to this newly proferred bait.

26. Interview, J. R. Jayewardene, August 5, 1992, Colombo. The president explicitly mentioned that Ranjan Wijeratne, the defense minister under Premadasa, often dropped in on him and expressed his incredulity at Premadasa's action in handing over the Northeast to the LTTE without a fight.

7. POSTCOLONIAL APORIAS

1. Precise numbers of casualties in these enduring low-intensity conflicts are difficult to come by. Certain figures are routinely cited as representing the numbers dead: for example, fifty thousand dead in the ethnic conflict in Sri Lanka; forty thousand killed in the Sri Lankan state's quelling of the JVP insurgency in the late 1980s and early 1990s; about forty thousand killed in the ongoing civil war in Kashmir since 1987; more than fifty thousand killed in Assam in India since 1982; over forty thousand killed in Punjab during the 1980s; and similar numbers in the Northeast in the last decade. Although these estimates may not be strictly accurate, their magnitude ought to serve as a reminder of the pervasiveness and costs of so-called low-intensity conflicts in South Asia.

2. I find Wagner's (1995) translation of this passage more lucid than the stilted prose in the edition by Zone, translated by Carolyn Fawcett wherein the same passage is rendered as: "The normal is not a static or peaceful, but a dynamic and polemical concept.... To set a norm, to normalize, is to impose a requirement on an existence, a given whose variety, disparity, with regard to the requirement, present themselves as a hostile, even

more than an unknown, indeterminant. It is, in effect, a polemical concept which negatively qualifies the sector of the given which does not enter into its extension while it depends on its comprehension" (Canguilhem 1989, 239).

3. In the years 1987–89, the JVP was suspected of killing Vijaya Kumaratunga, the leader of the Sri Lanka Mahajana Party (SLMP), which was a member of the United Socialist Alliance, and one of the few politicians who supported the agreement of 1987 because it envisioned Sri Lanka as a multiethnic polity. The JVP was also suspected in the assassination of Harsha Abheyewardene, UNP party chairman, in late 1987, his successor Nandalal Fernando in April 1988, and another MP, G. V. S. De Silva, shortly thereafter.

4. The complicity of some in the media in this effort to selectively cover up the details of past interactions between the Indian government and the Sri Lankan Tamil militants, on the predictable ground that it was a matter of national security, is reflected in a recent editorial from *India Today*: "Justice M. C. Jain has confirmed what was once India's worst kept secret: that through the '80s, the government of this country effectively sponsored the terrorism of the Liberation Tigers of Tamil Eelam (LTTE) in Sri Lanka. Deposing before the Jain Commission, a variety of senior functionaries, including former prime ministers, attempted to excel each other in unveiling the manner in which the LTTE used India as a safe haven cum training camp. While much of the government's Sri Lanka policy in the past decade cannot be condoned, it is regrettable that Jain has, clumsily and crudely, brought into public gaze documents that can be profoundly damaging to India's strategic interests.... Covert operations, undesirable as they may be in theory, are part of statecraft. The imperatives which go into shaping a nation's exchange with its external environment are that nation's privilege.... Some of the damage can still be undone if Parliament agrees to have put before it only those portions of Jain's report which are relevant to Rajiv's assassination. Let issues not be confused further—nor India compromised" ("Confusing Issues," November 24, 1997). Setting aside the incredible obtuseness of an editorial that argues that covert operations in Sri Lanka were not relevant to Rajiv Gandhi's assassination, the passage is a fascinating instance of how the discourse of realpolitik structures social reality for us. Of course, the greater irony is that a leading editor of a much-vaunted democratic and free press is here literally begging for more secrecy and less transparency in the affairs of state.

5. A presidential commission set up to inquire into Athulathmudali's assassination completed its report in October 1997. Although its findings are yet to be made public, certain portions were leaked to newspapers. According to the *Midweek Mirror* (Colombo), the report avers that Athulathmudali was not assassinated by the LTTE as originally alleged, but was a

"contract killing by the underworld," done "because he was posing a major political challenge to Premadasa." It further noted, "evidence of premeditated murder was seen in the non-provision of proper security for the fatal meeting, the planting of evidence and wrong information given to the inquiring magistrate in an apparently planned and deliberate manner." Meanwhile, the government-owned *Daily News* reported that the commission concluded that an assassination of such magnitude could not have occurred without the command of Premadasa. Similarly, a separate inquiry into the death of Gen. Kobbekaduwa suggested that, contrary to initial reports, the general's Jeep did not explode because it went over a mine, but because a bomb had been planted in the vehicle. Once again, the report implicated former president Premadasa in the assassination of the general. Both commissions of inquiry, incidentally, were headed by a Supreme Court judge. See "Sri Lankan President Ranasinghe Premadasa implicated in the death of a senior politician," *SLNet News Digest,* October 8, 1997 (Reuter).

6. "Decriminalisation of Politics," editorial in *Pravada* 3 (1994): 1–2.

7. See, among others, Chakravarty and Haksar (1987), Citizens Commission (1985), Kothari and Sethi, eds. (1985), Padgaonkar (1993), and Peoples Union for Democratic Rights and Peoples Union for Civil Liberties (1984). For a compelling depiction as to how politicians, bureaucrats, and the media intersect to determine how and when communal riots in India are staged, see Brass (1997). More generally, on the criminalization of politics and the tremendous growth of the politician-criminal nexus, see *India Today International,* specifically issues dated August 25, 1997, and October 6, 1997.

8. In an interesting piece written after a trip through the ethnonationalist cauldron of northern Myanmar, Amitav Ghosh makes a related observation: "There are thousands of putative nationalities in the world today; at least sixteen of them are situated on Burma's borders. It is hard to imagine that the inhabitants of these areas would be well served by becoming separate states. A hypothetical Karenni state, for example, would be landlocked, with the population of a medium-sized town: it would not be less dependent on its larger neighbors simply because it had a flag, and a seat at the UN" (1996, 49).

9. It is worth noting that most insurgent groups in Punjab, Kashmir, and Afghanistan have what are best described as fundamentalist ideas on the "appropriate" role of women in public life, on religion, on popular participation in decision making, and on a number of other issues. Through their actions and their espoused positions, most of these groups have made it clear that neither minorities nor anyone who disagrees with the leader of the insurgent movement will be tolerated should their imagined communities ever become real.

10. Sir John Strachey, former lt. governor in India, quoted in Sarkar (1983, 2).

11. Quoted in Gopal (1993, 10).

8. DECOLONIZING THE FUTURE IN SOUTH ASIA

1. Some recent titles should suffice to indicate this disenchantment: *Unravelling the Nation* (Basu and Subrahmanyam, eds., 1996); *Unmaking the Nation* (Jeganathan and Ismail, eds., 1995); *The Illegitimacy of Nationalism* (Nandy 1994); *The Nation and Its Fragments* (Chatterjee 1993); *Contesting the Nation* (Ludden, ed., 1996); *Rescuing History from the Nation* (Duara 1995).

2. Although it would take us too far afield to give a comprehensive description of how Congress's avowedly secular nationalism seamlessly ingested the ideology and icons of a northern Indian Hindu religious ethos as it expanded its ecumene and just as effectively decried all alternative imaginaries based on class, language, religion, and gender as ab initio sectarian and inferior, a rapidly growing list of works have charted this development. See, in particular, Amin (1988), Bayly (1975), Fox (1990), Freitag (1989), Gilmartin (1989), Hasan (1991), Kesavan (1988 and 1989), McLane (1987 and 1988), Page (1982), Pandey (1990), and Robinson (1974) for details on this process. At minimum, these works disabuse one of the facile contrasts drawn between the secular, progressive and pluralist vision of the nation represented by Congress and the sectarian, reactionary and monological visions represented by Jinnah, Ambedkar, Periyar, Saraladevi Chaudhurani, and all the others who serve as little more than provincial straw men in the grand narrative of India.

3. The quotes within Balachandran's quote are from Bayly (1975, 132, 142) and McLane (1987, 322–51). The argument made here by Balachandran is evocative of a point I made earlier (in chapter 3) regarding the process of vernacularizing an ideology such as nationalism: as it works its way through the colonial and postcolonial landscape, the liberal democratic version of nationalism and its emphasis on the putative equality of all citizens as individuals inevitably seems to partake more and more strongly of local, sectarian, and provincial flavorings. Nationalism acquires content and meaning not through a universalist and abstract discourse of uniform citizenship but through a strongly particularist and sectarian appeal to various proximate affiliations, relying upon a symbology that inevitably reflects the cultural ethos of the majority community in that specific terrain.

4. It has to be remembered that this overwhelming Congress victory in the provincial elections of 1937 did not include either (united) Bengal, where the Krishak Praja Party won, or (united) Punjab, where the Union-

ists won the day. In other words, Congress could not carry the two largest Muslim-majority provinces.

5. For example, a recent collection of essays examines the micropolitics of Congress ascendancy in the preindependence period and meticulously details how the idea of the "primary contradiction" being defined as British colonialism enabled the Congress leadership to exercise a tight control over the national movement. Dalits, subaltern peasant classes, urban working classes, and of course Muslims were all sought to be integrated into the nation but exclusively on the terms of Congress's notion of the primary contradiction and not on the basis of recognizing the autonomy and agency of these inevitably subnational groups. For example, peasant insurgencies directed against the Raj would be supported by Congress, but not those directed against Indian landlords; Dalit demands could be accommodated within a framework of religious or social reformism but not by granting their demand for separate electorates; workers' rights deserved support but not at the expense of domestic capitalists; and so on down the line. See the essays in Sisson and Wolpert, eds. (1988).

6. This troubling historical fact, however, has not stood in the way of a whole slew of works that have traced the predication of eventual destiny of Pakistan farther and farther back in history. Recently, Akbar Ahmed (1997) has posited a genealogy for Pakistan going back to the twelfth-century Muslim ruler Saladin. He is effortlessly topped by Aitzaz Ahsan (1996), who discerns a subcontinental divide as far back as 6,000 (!) years as he makes a distinction between what he terms "Indic culture" (India) and the culture of the "Indus" (Pakistan). To Ahsan, India and Pakistan have been distinctive and separate entities from, literally, time immemorial.

7. It must be emphasized that Jalal's thesis, for all its perspicacity, is not without problems. The notion that Jinnah was such a federalist and one so interested in the autonomy of provincial governments against an overbearing center is somewhat hard to credit (especially when one considers the fact that the Muslim-majority provinces of the Northwest tended to prize their autonomy and rather reluctantly recognized Jinnah and the league's authority to dictate matters to them). Further, there is sufficient ground to believe that his support for the Cabinet Mission Plan arose more from a desire to retain an enlarged geographical ecumene for a Pakistan that was seen as the eventual goal in any event. Although Jinnah's refusal to spell out the precise content of his "Pakistan" was tactically a brilliant ploy for someone arguing from a position of weakness, strategically it ran the risk of "being too clever by half" (Stern 1993, 179). In the event Congress called his bluff, not only would he be left with a "moth-eaten Pakistan," it would leave the Muslims of postpartition India even more precarious than

before, which is in some ways precisely what happened. See Stern (1993, 175–79) and Roy (1993, 127–32) for an elaboration of these issues with regard to Jalal's arguments.

8. Thomas (1996) makes the same point: "In 1946, the British put forward the Cabinet Mission Plan to preserve the unity of India as it moved towards independence. According to the plan, a confederation of three parts that approximately followed the lines of the existing states of India, Pakistan (including all of Punjab) and Bangladesh (including all of Bengal and Assam) was proposed. The plan was accepted by Mohammed Ali Jinnah, the leader of the All-India Muslim League who led the struggle for Pakistan, but rejected by Jawaharlal Nehru, leader of the Indian National Congress. Failure to agree to what would have been a confederal India led to the partition of India in 1947. Although Nehru's rejection had much to do with his rivalry with Jinnah and his unwillingness to accept what was perceived to be a British plan, it had also to do with his unwillingness to accept a state that was so decentralized that it amounted to de facto partition" (34).

9. To cite just two examples of writing Bangladesh in this manner: the journalist Sanjoy Hazarika, in an otherwise excellent ethnography of the Northeast in India, noted that the emergence of Bangladesh "destroyed for good the political idiocy that assumed that two nations — for that was what Pakistan was even at the best of times between East and West — could live as a political unit under the banner of Islamic nationhood, separated as they were by distance, language, culture and politics" (1994, 28). In similar vein, Maj. Gen. (retired) Jogindar Singh noted the Indian "victory" in 1971 "logically... laid to rest the two-nation theory which led to the break-up of our great country in 1947" (1993, 245). In attributing the emergence of Pakistan in 1947 to a historically untenable religious nationalism, proved so by the secession of Bangladesh in 1971, Hazarika and Singh are emblematic of literally innumerable Indian analysts.

10. Consider these recent titles: Sirajul Islam, *History of Bangladesh: 1704–1941*, 3 volumes (1992), and Dilip Chakrabarti, *Ancient Bangladesh: A Study of Archaeological Sources* (1992). As ever, it is the task of the historian to trace retrospectively the origins of the nation in the distant past, proving yet again that the distinctive sign of the modern is history (Dirks 1990).

11. I place the words "majoritarian" and "minorities" in quotation marks because the Punjabi domination of Pakistan in the period 1947–71 was not based on its numerical superiority (in fact, the eastern wing's population was way more than all of the western wing, not to speak of the Punjabis) as it was on the fact that bureaucratic, military, and political power were concentrated in that group. Similarly, the numerical preponderance of the Bengalis did not seem to alter their "minority" status in

terms of political, economic, or cultural impact on decision making in the nation.

12. As Connolly notes, "Even when the fragment within the state seeks to break this monopoly it usually does so by imagining itself as a state" (1995, 135).

13. As Ghosh observes in the context of India's neighbor, "Burma's borders are undeniably arbitrary, the product of a capricious colonial history. But colonial officials cannot reasonably be blamed for the arbitrariness of the lines they drew. All boundaries are arbitrary: there is no such thing as a 'natural' nation, which has journeyed through history with its boundaries and ethnic composition intact. In a region as heterogeneous as Southeast Asia, any boundary is sure to be arbitrary. On balance, Burma's best hopes for peace lie in maintaining intact the larger and more inclusive entity that history, albeit absent-mindedly, bequeathed to its population almost half a century ago" (1996, 49).

Bibliography

Abeyesekera, Charles, and Newton Gunasinghe, eds. 1987. *Facets of Ethnicity in Sri Lanka*. Colombo: Social Scientists Association.

Abraham, Itty. 1998. *The Making of the Indian Atomic Bomb: Science, Secrecy and the Postcolonial State*. London: Zed.

Adorno, Theodor, and Max Horkheimer. 1973. *The Dialectic of Enlightenment*, translated by J. Cumming. London: Verso.

Ahmad, Imtiaz. 1993. *State and Foreign Policy: India's Role in South Asia*. New Delhi: Vikas.

Ahmed, Akbar S. 1997. *Jinnah, Pakistan and Islamic Identity: The Search for Saladin*. London: Routledge.

Ahsan, Aitzaz. 1996. *The Indus Saga and the Making of Pakistan*. Karachi: Oxford University Press.

Akbar, M. J. 1986. *India: The Siege Within*. New Delhi: Penguin.

Alavi, Hamza. 1982. "State and Class under Peripheral Capitalism." In *Introduction to the Sociology of "Developing" Societies*, edited by Hamza Alavi and Teodor Shanin, 289–307. New York: Monthly Review.

Ali, Mahmud. 1993. *The Fearful State: Power, People and Internal War in South Asia*. London: Zed.

Amin, Shahid. 1988. "Gandhi as Mahatma: Gorakhpur District, Eastern UP, 1921–22." In *Selected Subaltern Studies*, edited by Ranajit Guha and Gayatri Chakravorty Spivak, 288–342. New York: Oxford University Press.

———. 1995. *Event, Metaphor, Memory: Chauri Chaura 1922–1992*. Delhi: Oxford University Press.

289

Amirthalingam, Appapillai. 1988. Introduction to *Towards Devolution of Power in Sri Lanka: Main Documents August 1983 to October 1987*. Tamil United Liberation Front, iii–vi. Madras: Jeevan Press.

Anderson, Benedict. 1991. *Imagined Communities: Reflections on the Origin and Spread of Nationalism*. London: Verso.

Appadurai, Arjun. 1993. "Numbers in the Colonial Imagination." In *Orientalism and the Postcolonial Predicament*, edited by Carol Breckenridge and Peter Van der Veer, 314–339. Philadelphia: University of Pennsylvania Press.

———. 1996. *Modernity at Large: Cultural Dimensions of Globalization*. Minneapolis: University of Minnesota Press.

Appiah, Kwame Anthony. 1992. *In My Father's House: Africa in the Philosophy of Culture*. New York: Oxford University Press.

Arasaratnam, Sinnappah. 1979. "Nationalism in Sri Lanka and the Tamils." In *Collective Identities, Nationalism and Protest in Sri Lanka*, edited by Michael Roberts, 500–522. Colombo: Marga Institute.

———. 1986. *Sri Lanka after Independence: Nationalism, Communalism, and Nation-Building*. Madras: University of Madras.

Arooran, K. Nambi. 1980. *Tamil Renaissance and Dravidian Nationalism 1905–1944*. Madurai: Koodal Publications.

Ashley, Richard K. 1983. "Three Modes of Economism." *International Studies Quarterly* 27: 463–96.

———. 1984. "The Poverty of Neorealism." *International Organisation* 38: 225–86.

———. 1987. "The Geopolitics of Geopolitical Space: Toward a Critical Social Theory of International Politics." *Alternatives* 12: 403–34.

Ashley, Richard K., and R. B. J. Walker. 1990a. "Speaking the Language of Exile: Dissident Thought in International Studies." *International Studies Quarterly* 34: 259–68.

———. 1990b. "Reading Dissidence and Writing the Discipline: Crisis and the Question of Sovereignty in International Studies." *International Studies Quarterly* 34: 367–416.

Ayoob, Mohammed. 1989–90. "India in South Asia: The Quest for Regional Predominance." *World Policy Journal* 7: 107–33.

———. 1995. *The Third World Security Predicament: State Making, Regional Conflict and the International System*. Boulder, Colo.: Lynne Rienner.

Bajpai, Kanti, and Stephen Cohen, eds., 1993. *South Asia after the Cold War: International Perspectives*. Boulder, Colo.: Westview.

Bajpai, Kanti, Stephen Cohen, Sumit Ganguly, P. R. Chari, and Pervaiz Cheema. 1995. "Brasstacks and Beyond: Perception and Management of Crisis in South Asia." *ACDIS Occasional Paper: Research Program in Arms Control, Disarmament and International Studies.* Urbana: University of Illinois Press.

Baker, Christopher. 1976. *The Politics of South India 1920–1937.* Cambridge: Cambridge University Press.

Baker, Christopher, and David Washbrook. 1975. *South India: Political Institutions and Political Change 1880–1940.* Delhi: Macmillan.

Balachandran, G. 1996. "Religion and Nationalism in Modern India." In *Unraveling the Nation: Sectarian Conflict and India's Secular Identity,* edited by Kaushik Basu and Sanjay Subrahmanyam, 81–128. New Delhi: Penguin.

Balasingham, Anton. 1983. *Liberation Tigers and the Tamil Eelam Freedom Struggle.* Madras: Makkal Acchakam.

Balibar, Etienne. 1991. "The Nation Form: History and Ideology." In *Race, Nation, Class: Ambiguous Identities,* edited by Etienne Balibar and Immanuel Wallerstein, 86–106. London: Verso.

Bardhan, Pranab. 1984. *The Political Economy of Development in India.* Delhi: Oxford University Press.

Barnett, Marguerite Ross. 1976. *The Politics of Cultural Nationalism in South India.* Princeton, N.J.: Princeton University Press.

Barthes, Roland. 1972. "Myth Today." In *Mythologies,* translated by Annette Leavers, 109–59. New York: Noonday.

Baruah, Sanjib. 1994a. "'Ethnic' Conflict as State-Society Struggle: The Poetics and Politics of Assmese Micro-Nationalism." *Modern Asian Studies* 28: 649–72.

———. 1994b. "The State and Separatist Militancy in Assam: Winning a Battle and Losing the War?" *Asian Survey* 34: 863–82.

Bastian, Sunil. 1990. "Political Economy of Ethnic Violence in Sri Lanka: The July 1983 Riots." In *Mirrors of Violence: Communities, Riots and Survivors in South Asia,* edited by Veena Das, 286–304. Delhi: Oxford University Press.

Basu, Kaushik, and Sanjay Subrahmanyam, eds. 1996. *Unravelling the Nation: Sectarian Conflict and India's Secular Identity.* New Delhi: Penguin.

Basu, Sanjib. 1985. "Nonalignment and Economic Development: Indian State Strategies 1947–1962." In *States Versus Markets in the World-System,* edited by Peter Evans, Dietrich Rueschmeyer, and Evelyn Huber Stephens, 193–213. New York: Sage.

Bayly, Chris A. 1975. *Local Roots of Indian Politics: Allahabad, 1880–1920.* Oxford: Clarendon.

Benjamin, Walter. 1969. "The Work of Art in the Age of Mechanical Reproduction." In *Illuminations,* edited by Hannah Arendt and translated by Harry Zohn, 217–51. New York: Schocken Books.

Berman, Marshall. 1982. *All That Is Solid Melts into the Air: The Experience of Modernity.* New York: Penguin.

Bhabha, Homi, ed. 1990. *Nation and Narration.* London: Routledge.

———. 1991. " 'Race,' Time and the Revision of Modernity." *Oxford Literary Review* 13: 193–219.

Billig, Michael. 1995. *Banal Nationalism.* London: Sage.

Bourdieu, Pierre. 1977. *Outline of a Theory of Practice.* Cambridge: Cambridge University Press.

Bradnock, Robert W. 1990. *India's Foreign Policy Since 1971.* London: Pinter.

Brass, Paul. 1991. *Ethnicity and Nationalism: Theory and Comparison.* New Delhi: Sage.

———. 1997. *Theft of an Idol: Text and Context in Representations of Collective Violence.* Princeton, N.J.: Princeton University Press.

Byres, Terry J. 1982. "India: Capitalist Industrialisation or Structural Stasis?" In *The Struggle of Development: National Strategies in an International Context,* edited by Martin Godfrey and M. Bienefeld, 135–64. Chichester: Wiley.

Campbell, David. 1992. *Writing Security: United States Foreign Policy and the Politics of Identity.* Minneapolis: University of Minnesota Press.

———. 1993. *Politics without Principle: Sovereignty, Ethics, and the Narratives of the Gulf War.* Boulder, Colo.: Lynne Rienner.

———. 1994. "The Deterritorialization of Responsibility: Levinas, Derrida and Ethics after the End of Philosophy." *Alternatives* 19: 455–84.

Canguilhem, Georges. 1989. *The Normal and the Pathological.* Trans. Carolyn R. Fawcett. New York: Zone.

Carter, Paul. 1987. *The Road to Botany Bay: An Essay in Spatial History.* London: Faber and Faber.

Chakrabarti, Dilip. 1992. *Ancient Bangladesh: A Study of Archaeological Sources.* Delhi: Oxford University Press.

Chakrabarti, Radharaman. 1982. *The Political Economy of Indian Foreign Policy.* Calcutta: K.P. Bagchi.

Chakrabarty, Dipesh. 1992. "Postcoloniality and the Artifice of History: Who Speaks for 'Indian' Pasts?" *Representations* 37: 1–26.

Chakravarty, Sukhamoy. 1987. *Development Planning: The Indian Experience.* Oxford: Clarendon Press.

Chakravarty, Uma, and Nandita Haksar. 1987. *The Delhi Riots: Three Days in the Life of a Nation.* New Delhi: Lancer International.

Chandra, Bipan. 1979. *Nationalism and Colonialism in Modern India.* New Delhi: Orient Longman.

Chari, P. R. 1994. "The IPKF Experience in Sri Lanka." *ACDIS Occasional Paper: Research Program in Arms Control, Disarmament and International Security.* Urbana-Champaign: University of Illinois Press.

Chatterjee, Partha. 1986. *Nationalist Thought and the Colonial World: A Derivative Discourse.* Delhi: Oxford University Press.

———. 1993. *The Nation and Its Fragments: Colonial and Postcolonial Histories.* Princeton, N.J.: Princeton University Press.

Cheran, R. 1992. "Cultural Politics of Tamil Nationalism." *South Asia Bulletin* 12: 42–56.

Chopra, Pran. 1987. "Fiasco in Palk Straits: Options and Illusions." *Indian Express,* New Delhi, 18 June.

Citizen's Commission. 1985. *Report on the New Delhi Riots against the Sikhs, October 31–November 4, 1984.* New Delhi: Tata.

Cohen, Stephen, and Richard Park. 1978. *India: An Emergent Power?* New York: Crane, Russak and Co.

Cohn, Bernard. 1987a. "The Census, Social Structure and Objectification in South Asia." In *An Anthropologist among Historians and Other Essays,* 224–54. Delhi: Oxford University Press.

———. 1987b. "Representing Authority in Victorian India." In *An Anthropologist among Historians and Other Essays,* 632–82. Delhi: Oxford University Press.

Comaroff, John. 1991. "Humanity, Ethnicity, Nationality." *Theory and Society* 20: 661–83.

Committee for Rational Development. 1984. *Sri Lanka, the Ethnic Conflict: Myths, Realities and Perspectives.* New Delhi: Navrang.

Connolly, William. 1991. *Identity/Difference: Democratic Negotiations of Political Paradox.* Ithaca, N.Y.: Cornell University Press.

———. 1995. *The Ethos of Pluralization.* Minneapolis: University of Minnesota Press.

Coomaraswamy, Radhika. 1987. "Myths without Conscience: Tamil and Sinhalese Nationalist Writings of the 1980s." In *Facets of Ethnicity in Sri Lanka,* edited by Charles Abeyesekera and Newton Gunasinghe, 72–99. Colombo: Social Scientists Association.

Critchley, Simon. 1992. *The Ethics of Deconstruction: Derrida and Levinas.* Cambridge: Blackwell.

Daniel, Valentine E. 1990. "Afterword: Sacred Places, Violent Spaces." In *Sri Lanka: The Roots of Conflict,* edited by Jonathan Spencer, 227–46. London: Routledge.

———. 1996. *Charred Lullabies: Chapters in an Anthropology of Violence.* Princeton, N.J.: Princeton University Press.

Das, Veena, ed. 1990. *Mirrors of Violence: Communities, Riots and Survivors in South Asia.* New Delhi: Oxford University Press.

DeLillo, Don. 1988. *Libra.* New York: Viking.

Der Derian, James. 1992. *Antidiplomacy: Spies, Terror, Speed, and War.* Cambridge: Blackwell.

———. 1994. "The Pen, the Sword and the Smart Bomb: Criticism in the Age of Video." *Alternatives* 19: 133–40.

Derrida, Jacques. 1976. *Of Grammatology.* Translated by Gayatri Spivak. Baltimore: Johns Hopkins University Press.

———. 1977. *Writing and Difference.* Translated by Alan Bass. London: Routledge.

———. 1982 (1968). In *Margins of Philosophy.* Translated by Alan Bass. Chicago: University of Chicago Press.

De Silva, Chandra R. 1977. "Education." In *Sri Lanka: A Survey,* edited by Kingsley M. De Silva, 403–31. Honolulu: University of Hawaii Press.

———. 1984. "Sinhala-Tamil Ethnic Rivalry." In *From Independence to Statehood: Managing Ethnic Conflict in Five African and Asian States,* edited by Robert Goldman and A. Jeyaratnam Wilson, 100–121. London: Pinter.

De Silva, Kingsley M. 1981. *A History of Sri Lanka.* London: C. Hurst and Co.

———, ed. 1986. *Managing Ethnic Tensions in Multi-Ethnic Societies: Sri Lanka 1880–1985.* Lanham, Md.: University Press of America.

———. 1987. *The "Traditional Homelands" of the Tamils of Sri Lanka: A Historical Appraisal.* Colombo: International Center for Ethnic Studies.

———. 1988. "Nationalism and the State in Sri Lanka." In *Ethnic Conflict in Buddhist Societies: Sri Lanka, Thailand and Burma,* edited by Kingsley M. De Silva, Pensri Duke, and Nathan Katz, 62–76. London: Pinter.

De Silva, Kingsley M., and Howard Wriggins. 1994. *J. R. Jayewardene of Sri Lanka: A Political Biography.* Vol. 2. Honolulu: University of Hawaii Press.

Dharmadasa, K. N. O. 1992. *Language, Religion, and Assertiveness: The Growth of Sinhalese Nationalism in Sri Lanka.* Ann Arbor: University of Michigan Press.

Dillon, Michael. 1995. "Security, Philosophy and Politics." In *Global Modernities,* edited by Mike Featherstone, Scott Lash, and Roland Robertson, 155–77. London: Sage.

Dirks, Nicholas. 1990. "History as a Sign of the Modern." *Public Culture* 2: 25–32.

Dissanayaka, T. D. S. A. 1993. *The Dilemma of Sri Lanka.* Colombo: Swastika.

Dixit, J. N. 1989. "IPKF in Sri Lanka." *United Services Institution of India Journal* 69: 248–62.

Doty, Roxanne. 1996. *Imperial Encounters: The Politics of Representation in North-South Relations.* Minneapolis: University of Minnesota Press.

Dua, Bhagwan. 1981. "India: A Study in the Pathology of a Federal System." *Journal of Commonwealth and Comparative Politics* 19: 257–75.

Duara, Prasenjit. 1995. *Rescuing History from the Nation: Questioning Narratives of Modern China.* Chicago: University of Chicago Press.

Dutt, Srikant. 1984. *India and the Third World: Altruism or Hegemony?* London: Zed.

Escobar, Arturo. 1995. *Encountering Development: The Making and Unmaking of the Third World.* Princeton, N.J.: Princeton University Press.

Fanon, Frantz. 1963. *The Wretched of the Earth.* Trans. Constance Farrington. New York: Grove.

———. 1967. *Black Skin, White Masks.* Trans. Charles Lam Markham. New York: Grove.

Feldman, Allen. 1991. *Formations of Violence: The Narrative of the Body and Political Terror in Northern Ireland.* Chicago: University of Chicago Press.

Fernando, Tyronne. 1988. *100 Days in Sri Lanka '87.* Colombo: Chromographic Ltd.

"Former D. G. P. Blames Government Policy for Spread of Bomb Culture." In Rediff on the Net. [dated February 16, 1998]. Available @ www.rediff.com/news/1998/feb/16dgps.htm.

Foucault, Michel. 1977. "Nietzsche, Genealogy, History." In *Language, Counter-Memory, Practice: Selected Essays and Interviews,* edited by Donald F. Bouchard, 139–64. Ithaca, N.Y.: Cornell University Press.

———. 1980a. "Truth and Power." In *Power/Knowledge: Selected Interviews and Other Writings 1972–1977,* edited by Colin Gordon, 109–33. New York: Pantheon.

———. 1980b. "Two Lectures." In *Power/Knowledge: Selected Interviews and Other Writings 1972–1977,* edited by Colin Gordon, 78–108. New York: Pantheon.

———. 1982. "Afterword: the Subject of Power." In *Michel Foucault: Beyond Structuralism and Hermeneutics,* edited by Hubert L. Dreyfus and Paul Rabinow, 208–26. Chicago: University of Chicago Press.

Fox, Richard G. 1990. "Gandhian Socialism and Indian Nationalism: Cultural Domination in the World-System." In *South Asia and World Capitalism,* edited by Sugata Bose, 244–61. Delhi: Oxford University Press.

Frankel, Francine. 1978. *India's Political Economy 1947–1977.* Princeton, N.J.: Princeton University Press.

Freitag, Sandria. 1989. *Collective Action and Community: Public Arenas and the Emergence of Communalism in North India.* Berkeley and Los Angeles: University of California Press.

Geertz, Clifford. 1980. *Negara: The Theater State in Nineteenth-Century Bali.* Princeton, N.J.: Princeton University Press.

Ghosh, Amitav. 1992. *In an Antique Land: History in the Guise of a Traveler's Tale.* New York: Vintage.

———. 1996. "A Reporter at Large: Burma." *New Yorker,* 12 August, 38–54.

Gilmartin, David. 1989. *Empire and Islam: Punjab and the Making of Pakistan.* Berkeley and Los Angeles: University of California Press.

Gopal, Sarvepalli, ed. 1991. *Anatomy of a Confrontation: The Babri Masjid-Ramajanmabhumi Issue.* New Delhi: Viking.

———. 1993. "Crisis of Secularism in South Asia." *Pravada* 2: 10–16.

Gordon, Sandy. 1995. *India's Rise to Power: In the Twentieth Century and Beyond.* New York: St. Martin's.

Gramsci, Antonio. 1971. *Selections from the Prison Notebooks.* Edited and translated by Quintin Hoare and Geoffrey Nowell Smith. New York: International.

Guha, Ranajit. 1983. "The Prose of Counter-Insurgency." In *Subaltern Studies II: Writings on South Asian History and Society,* edited by Ranajit Guha, 1–42. New Delhi: Oxford University Press.

Gunaratna, Rohan. 1990. *Sri Lanka: A Lost Revolution? The Inside Story of the JVP.* Colombo: Institute of Fundamental Studies.

———. 1993. *Indian Intervention in Sri Lanka: The Role of India's Intelligence Agencies.* Colombo: South Asian Network on Conflict Research.

Gunawardana, R. A. L. H. 1990. "The People of the Lion: The Sinhala Identity and Ideology in History and Historiography." In *Sri Lanka: History and the Roots of Conflict,* edited by Jonathan Spencer, 45–86. London: Routledge.

Gupta, Anirudha. 1990. "A Brahmanic Framework of Power in South Asia?" *Economic and Political Weekly* 25: 711–14.

Gupta, Dipankar. 1985. "The Communalizing of Punjab 1980–1985." *Economic and Political Weekly* 20: 1185–90.

Hagerty, Devin. 1991. "India's Regional Security Doctrine." *Asian Survey* 31: 352–72.

Hardgrave, Robert L., Jr. 1965. *The Dravidian Movement.* Bombay: Popular Prakashan.

Hart, Henry. 1988. "Political Leadership in India: Dimensions and Limits." In *India's Democracy: An Analysis of Changing State-Society Relations,* edited by Atul Kohli, 18–61. New Delhi: Orient Longman.

Hasan, Mushirul. 1991. *Nationalism and Communal Politics in India, 1885–1930.* New Delhi: Oxford University Press.

———, ed. 1993a. *India's Partition: Process, Strategy and Mobilization.* New Delhi: Oxford University Press.

———. 1993b. "Competing Symbols and Shared Codes: Inter-Community Relations in Modern India." In *Anatomy of a Confrontation: Ayodhya and the Rise of Communal Politics in India,* edited by Sarvepalli Gopal, 99–121. London: Zed.

Hazarika, Sanjoy. 1994. *Strangers in the Mist: Tales of War and Peace from India's Northeast.* Delhi: Viking.

Hellmann-Rajanayagam, Dagmar. 1994. *The Tamil Tigers: Armed Struggle for Identity*. Stuttgart: Franz Steiner.

Holt, John Clifford. 1991. *Buddha in the Crown: Avalokitesvara in the Buddhist Traditions of Sri Lanka*. New York: Oxford University Press.

Hoole, Rajan, Daya Somasundaram, K. Sritharan, and Rajani Thiranagama. 1990. *The Broken Palmyrah: The Tamil Crisis in Sri Lanka, an Inside Account*. Claremont, Calif.: Sri Lanka Studies Institute.

Hyndman, Patricia. 1988. *Sri Lanka: Serendipity under Siege*. Nottingham: Spokesman.

Irschick, Eugene F. 1969. *Politics and Social Conflict in South India: The Non-Brahman Movement and Tamil Separatism, 1916–1929*. Berkeley and Los Angeles: University of California Press.

———. 1986. *Tamil Revivalism in the 1930s*. Madras: Cre-A.

Islam, Sirajul. 1992. *History of Bangladesh: 1704–1941*. 3 volumes. Dhaka: Asiatic Society of Bangladesh.

Ismail, Qadri. 1995. "Unmooring Identity: The Antinomies of Elite Muslim Self-Representation in Modern Sri Lanka." In *Unmaking the Nation: The Politics of Identity and History in Modern Sri Lanka*, edited by Pradeep Jeganathan and Qadri Ismail, 55–105. Colombo: Social Scientists Association.

Jalal, Ayesha. 1985. *The Sole Spokesman: Jinnah, the Muslim League and the Demand for Pakistan*. Cambridge: Cambridge University Press.

———. 1995. *Democracy and Authoritarianism in South Asia: A Comparative and Historical Perspective*. Cambridge: Cambridge University Press.

Jayatilleka, Dayan. 1995. *Sri Lanka: The Travails of Democracy, Unfinished War, Protracted Crisis*. New Delhi: Vikas.

Jayewardene, J. R. 1984. *Golden Threads*. Sri Lanka: Dept. of Government Printing.

Jeffrey, Robin. 1986. *What's Happening to India? Punjab, Ethnic Conflict, Mrs. Gandhi's Death and the Test for Federalism*. London: Macmillan.

Jeganathan, Pradeep, and Qadri Ismail, eds. 1995. *Unmaking the Nation: The Politics of Identity and History in Modern Sri Lanka*. Colombo: Social Scientists Association.

Kadian, Rajesh. 1990. *India's Sri Lanka Fiasco: Peacekeepers at War*. New Delhi: Vision.

Kapferer, Bruce. 1988. *Legends of People, Myths of State: Violence, Intolerance, and Political Culture in Sri Lanka and Australia*. Washington, D.C., and London: Smithsonian Institution Press.

———. 1990. "Comment." *Current Anthropology* 31: 291–94.

Kapur, Ashok. 1988. "Indian Security and Defense Policies under Indira Gandhi." In *India: The Years of Indira Gandhi*, edited by Yogendra K. Malik and D. K. Vajpeyi, 42–59. Leiden: E. J. Brill.

Kaur, Amarjit, Shekhar Gupta, J. S. Aurora, and Raghu Rai. 1984. *The Punjab Story.* New Delhi: Roli.

Kaviraj, Sudipta. 1992. "The Imaginary Institution of India." In *Subaltern Studies VII,* edited by Partha Chatterjee and Gyanendra Pandey, 1–39. Delhi: Oxford University Press.

———. 1996. "Democracy and Development in India." Mimeo. Center for South Asia Studies, International and Area Studies. University of California, Berkeley.

———. n.d. "Democracy and Development in India." Unpublished manuscript.

Kearney, Robert N., and Barbara Diane Miller. 1987. *Internal Migration in Sri Lanka and Its Social Consequences.* Boulder, Colo.: Westview.

Kemper, Steven. 1991. *The Presence of the Past: Chronicles, Politics, and Culture in Sinhala Life.* Ithaca, N.Y.: Cornell University Press.

Kesavan, Mukul. 1988. "1937 As a Landmark in the Course of Communal Politics in the U.P." *Occasional Papers in History and Society,* 2d series, no. 11. Nehru Memorial Museum and Library. New Delhi, November.

———. 1989. "Invoking a Majority: The Congress and the Muslims of the United Provinces 1945–47." In *Self Images, Identity and Nationality,* edited by P. C. Chatterji, 91–111. New Delhi: Allied.

King, Anthony D. 1995. "The Times and Spaces of Modernity." In *Global Modernities,* edited by Mike Featherstone, Scott Lash, and Roland Robertson, 108–23. London: Sage.

Klein, Bradley S. 1994. *Strategic Studies and World Order: The Global Politics of Deterrence.* Cambridge: Cambridge University Press.

Kochanek, Stanley. 1976. "Mrs. Gandhi's Pyramid: The New Congress." In *Indira Gandhi's India: A Political System Reappraised,* edited by Henry C. Hart, 93–124. Boulder, Colo.: Westview.

Kodikara, Shelton. 1992a. *Foreign Policy of Sri Lanka.* New Delhi: Chanakya.

———. 1992b. "Defence and Security Perceptions of Sri Lankan Foreign Policy Decision-Makers: A Post-Independence Overview." In *Security Dilemma of a Small State,* edited by P. V. J. Jayesekera, 206–33. New Delhi: South Asian.

Kohli, Atul. 1987. *The State and Poverty in India: The Politics of Reform.* Cambridge: Cambridge University Press.

———. 1990. *Democracy and Discontent: India's Growing Crisis of Governability.* Cambridge: Cambridge University Press.

Kothari, Rajni. 1989. *Politics and the People: In Search of a Humane India,* vols. 1, 2. New Delhi: Ajanta.

Kothari, Smitu, and Harsh Sethi, eds. 1985. *Voices from a Scarred City: The Delhi Carnage in Perspective.* New Delhi: Lokayan.

Krishna, Sankaran. 1992. "Transition in the Era of U.S. Hegemony: Indian Economic Development and World-Systems Analysis." In *Pacific-Asia and the Future of the World-System,* edited by Ravi Arvind Palat, 119–31. Westport, Conn.: Greenwood.

———. 1993. "The Importance of Being Ironic: A Postcolonial View on Critical International Relations Theory." *Alternatives* 18: 385–417.

———. 1994. "Constitutionalism, Democracy, and Political Culture in India." In *Political Culture and Constitutionalism: A Comparative Approach,* edited by Daniel Franklin and Michael Baun, 161–83. Armonk, N.Y.: M.E. Sharpe.

———. 1996. "Cartographic Anxiety: Mapping the Body Politic in India." In *Challenging Boundaries: Global Flows, Territorial Identities,* edited by Michael J. Shapiro and Hayward R. Alker Jr., 193–214. Minneapolis: University of Minnesota Press.

Kumar, Satish, ed. 1988. *Yearbook on India's Foreign Policy, 1987/1988.* New Delhi: Sage.

Leary, Virginia. 1983. *Ethnic Conflict and Violence in Sri Lanka: Report of a Mission to Sri Lanka in July–August 1981.* Geneva: International Committee of Jurists.

Lefebvre, Henri. 1991. *The Production of Space.* Translated by Donald Nicholson. Cambridge: Blackwell.

Little, David. 1994. *Sri Lanka: The Invention of Enmity.* Washington, D.C.: United States Institute of Peace.

Lloyd, David. 1994. "Adulteration and the Nation: Monologic Nationalism and the Colonial Hybrid." In *An Other Tongue: Nation and Ethnicity in the Linguistic Borderlands,* edited by Alfred Arteaga, 53–92. Durham, N.C.: Duke University Press.

Ludden, David. 1993. "Orientalist Empiricism: Transformations of Colonial Knowledge." In *Orientalism and the Postcolonial Predicament,* edited by Carol Breckenridge and Peter van der Veer, 250–78. Philadelphia: University of Pennsylvania Press.

———, ed. 1996. *Contesting the Nation.* Philadelphia: University of Pennsylvania Press.

Majumdar, R. C., H. C. Raychaudhuri, and K. Datta. 1960. *An Advanced History of India.* London: Macmillan.

Malhotra, Inder. 1989. *Indira Gandhi: A Personal and Political Biography.* London: Hodder and Stoughton.

Manikkalingam, Ram. 1992. "Tigerist Claims: A Critique." *Pravada* 1: 11–15.

Manivannan, R. 1992. "Tamil Nadu Elections: Issues, Strategies and Performance." *Economic and Political Weekly* 26: 164–65.

Mankekar, D. R. 1972. *Pakistan Cut to Size: The Authentic Story of the 14-Day Indo-Pakistan War.* New Delhi: India Book Company.

Manogaran, Chelvadurai. 1994. "Colonization as Politics: Political Use of Space in Sri Lanka's Ethnic Conflict." In *The Sri Lankan Tamils: Eth-*

nicity and Identity, edited by Chelvadurai Manogaran and Bryan Pfaffenberger, 84–125. Boulder, Colo.: Westview.

Manogaran, Chelvadurai, and Bryan Pfaffenberger, eds. 1994. *The Sri Lankan Tamils: Ethnicity and Identity*. Boulder, Colo.: Westview.

Manor, James. 1989. *The Expedient Utopian: Bandaranaike and Ceylon*. Cambridge: Cambridge University Press.

Marqusee, Mike. 1994. *Anyone But England: Cricket and the National Malaise*. London: Verso.

McLane, John R. 1987. *Indian Nationalism and the Early Congress*. Princeton, N.J.: Princeton University Press.

———. 1988. "The Early Congress, Hindu Populism, and the Wider Society." In *Congress and Indian Nationalism: The Pre-Independence Phase*, edited by Richard Sisson and Stanley Wolpert, 47–61. Berkeley and Los Angeles: University of California Press.

Mellor, John, ed. 1979. *India: A Rising Middle Power*. Boulder, Colo.: Westview.

Meyer, Eric. 1984. "Seeking the Roots of Tragedy." In *Sri Lanka: In Change and Crisis*, edited by James Manor, 137–52. New York: St. Martin's.

Mohandas, K. 1992. *MGR: The Man and the Myth*. Bangalore: Panther.

Moore, Mick. 1992. "Retreat from Democracy in Sri Lanka." *Journal of Commonwealth and Comparative Politics* 30: 70–84.

———. 1993. "Thoroughly Modern Revolutionaries: The JVP in Sri Lanka." *Modern Asian Studies* 27: 593–642.

Mosse, George L. 1985. *Nationalism and Sexuality: Respectability and Abnormal Sexuality in Modern Europe*. New York: H. Fertig.

Mukherjee, Dilip. 1972. *Yahya Khan's "Final War": India Meets Pakistan's Threat*. New Delhi: Bennett and Coleman.

Mukherjee, Rudrangshu, ed. 1993. *The Penguin Gandhi Reader*. New Delhi: Penguin.

Muni, S. D. 1993. *Pangs of Proximity: India and Sri Lanka's Ethnic Crisis*. New Delhi: Sage.

Nandy, Ashis. 1980. *At the Edge of Psychology: Essays in Politics and Culture*. Delhi: Oxford University Press.

———. 1983. *The Intimate Enemy: Loss and Recovery of the Self under Colonialism*. Delhi: Oxford University Press.

———. 1990a. "The Politics of Secularism and the Recovery of Religious Tolerance." In *Contending Sovereignties: Redefining Political Community*, edited by R. B. J. Walker and Saul Mendlovitz, 125–44. Boulder, Colo.: Lynne Rienner.

———. 1990b. "The Discreet Charms of Indian Terrorism." *The Journal of Commonwealth and Comparative Politics* 12: 25–43.

———. 1994. *The Illegitimacy of Nationalism: Rabindranath Tagore and the Politics of Self*. Delhi: Oxford University Press.

——. 1995. *The Savage Freud and Other Essays on Possible and Retrievable Selves.* Princeton, N.J.: Princeton University Press.

Navaratnam, V. 1991. *The Rise and Fall of the Tamil Nation.* Madras: Kaanthalakam.

Nayar, Baldev Raj. 1972. *The Modernization Imperative and Indian Planning.* Bombay: Vikas.

——. 1975. "Treat India Seriously." *Foreign Policy* 18: 133–54.

Nehru, Jawaharlal. 1936. *An Autobiography.* London: John Lane.

——. 1946. *The Discovery of India.* Delhi: Oxford University Press.

——. 1950. *Independence and After: A Collection of Speeches 1946–1949.* New York: John Day.

——. 1956. *Speeches on Science and Planning.* New Delhi: Government of India.

Nietzsche, Friedrich. 1954. "On Truth and Lie in an Extra-Moral Sense." In *The Portable Nietzsche,* edited and translated by Walter Kaufmann, 42–47. New York: Vintage.

Nissan, Elizabeth. 1984. "Some Thoughts on Sinhalese Justifications for the Violence." In *Sri Lanka: In Change and Crisis,* edited by James Manor, 177–84. New York: St. Martin's.

Obeyesekere, Gananath. 1984. "The Origins and Institutionalisation of Political Violence." In *Sri Lanka: In Change and Crisis,* edited by James Manor, 153–74. London: St. Martin's.

——. 1993. "Peace in Sri Lanka: Obstacles and Opportunities." Paper presented at a conference organized by the American Friends Service Committee, 12 June.

Padgaonkar, Dileep. 1993. *When Bombay Burned.* New Delhi: UBS.

Page, David. 1982. *Prelude to Partition: The Indian Muslims and the Imperial State System of Control 1920–1932.* New Delhi: Oxford University Press.

Palanithurai, G. 1993a. "Ethnic Political Parties and Electoral Behavior in Tamil Nadu." In *Ethnic Movement in India: Theory and Practice,* edited by G. Palanithurai and R. Thandavan, 157–78. Delhi: Kanishka.

——. 1993b. "Tamil Nationalism as a Factor in Indian Politics." In *Ethic Movement in India: Theory and Practice,* edited by G. Palanithurai and R. Thandavan, 69–82. Delhi: Kanishka.

Palanithurai, G., and K. Mohanasundaram. 1993. *Dynamics of Tamil Nadu Politics in Sri Lankan Ethnicity.* New Delhi: Northern Book Centre.

Pandey, Gyanendra. 1990. *The Construction of Communalism in Colonial North India.* Delhi: Oxford University Press.

——. 1994. "The Prose of Otherness." In *Subaltern Studies VIII: Essays in Honour of Ranajit Guha,* edited by David Arnold and David Hardiman, 188–221. Delhi: Oxford University Press.

Pandian, Jacob. 1987. *Caste, Nationalism and Ethnicity: An Interpretation of Tamil Cultural History and Social Order.* Bombay: Popular Prakashan.

Pandian, M. S. S. 1993. "'Denationalising' the Past: 'Nation' in E. V. Ramasamy's Political Discourse." *Economic and Political Weekly* 28: 2282–87.

———. 1994. "Notes on the Transformation of 'Dravidian' Ideology: Tamilnadu, c. 1900–1940." *Social Scientist* 22: 84–104.

———. 1995. "Beyond Colonial Crumbs: Cambridge School, Identity Politics and Dravidian Movement(s)." *Economic and Political Weekly* 30: 385–91.

Panikkar, K. M. 1969. *Geographical Factors in Indian History.* Bombay: Bharatiya Vidya Bhavan.

Parthasarathy, Malini. 1985. "Saga of a Doctor... Political Prisoner... Liberation Activist." *Frontline,* 23 March–5 April.

Pasha, Mustapha Kamal. 1992. "Beyond the Two-Nation Divide: Kashmir and 'Resurgent' Islam." In *Perspectives on Kashmir: Roots of Conflict in South Asia,* edited by Raju G. C. Thomas, 369–87. Boulder, Colo.: Westview.

———. 1996. "Security as Hegemony." *Alternatives* 21: 283–302.

Peoples Union for Democratic Rights (PUDR) and Peoples Union for Civil Liberties (PUCL). 1984. *Who Are the Guilty? Report of a Joint Inquiry into the Causes and Impact of the Riots in Delhi from 31 October to 10 November.* New Delhi: Excellent Printing Services.

Pfaffenberger, Bryan. 1982. *Caste in Tamil Culture: Religious Foundations of Sudra Domination in Tamil Sri Lanka.* Syracuse, N.Y.: Maxwell School for Foreign and Comparative Studies.

Phadnis, Urmila, and Nancy Jetly. 1990. "Indo-Sri Lankan Relations: the Indira Gandhi Years." In *Indian Foreign Policy: The Indira Gandhi Years,* edited by A. K. Damodaran and U. S. Bajpai, 146–61. New Delhi: Radiant.

Piyadasa, L. 1984. *Sri Lanka: The Holocaust and After.* London: Marram.

Ponnambalam, Satchi. 1983. *Sri Lanka: The National Question and the Tamil Struggle.* London: Zed.

Radhakrishnan, R. 1993. "Communal Representation in Tamil Nadu, 1850–1916: The Pre-Non-Brahmin Movement Phase." *Economic and Political Weekly* 28: 1585–97.

Raina, Asoka. 1981. *Inside RAW: The Story of India's Secret Service.* New Delhi: Vikas.

Rajasingham-Senanayake, Darini. 1997. "After Devolution: Protecting Local Minorities and Mixed Settlements." *Pravada* 4–5: 12–15.

Ram, Mohan. 1989. *Sri Lanka: The Fractured Island.* New Delhi: Penguin.

Ram, N. 1985. Troubled Island. *Frontline,* 1–14 December.

Ramaswamy, Sumathi. 1994. "The Nation, the Region, and the Adventures of a Tamil 'Hero.'" *Contributions to Indian Sociology,* n.s., 28: 295–322.

Ricoeur, Paul. 1984–1988. *Time and Narrative,* vols. 1–3. Translated by Kathleen McLaughlin and David Pellauer. Chicago: University of Chicago Press.

———. 1991. "Life in Quest of Narrative." In *On Paul Ricoeur: Narrative and Interpretation,* edited by David Wood, 20–33. London and New York: Routledge.

Roberts, Michael. 1979. "Elite Formation and the Elites, 1832–1931." In *Collective Identities, Nationalisms and Protest in Modern Sri Lanka,* edited by Michael Roberts, 153–213. Colombo: Marga Institute.

———. 1996. "Filial devotion in Tamil Culture and the Tiger Cult of Martyrdom." *Contributions to Indian Sociology* 30: 245–72.

Robinson, Francis. 1974. *Separatism among Indian Muslims: The Politics of the United Provinces Muslims, 1880–1923.* Cambridge: Cambridge University Press.

Rose, Leo. 1987. "Non-Military Dimensions of India's Regional Policy." In *The Security of South Asia: American and Asian Perspectives,* edited by Stephen Philip Cohen, 3–33. Urbana: University of Illinois Press.

Roy, Asim. [1990] 1993. "The High Politics of India's Partition: The Revisionist Perspective." Reprinted in *India's Partition: Process, Strategy, Mobilization,* edited by Mushirul Hasan, 102–32. Delhi: Oxford University Press.

Rudolph, Lloyd I., and Susanne Hoeber Rudolph. 1987. *In Pursuit of Lakshmi: The Political Economy of the Indian State.* Chicago: University of Chicago Press.

Rushdie, Salman. 1980. *Midnight's Children.* New York: Avon.

———. 1991. *Imaginary Homelands: Essays and Criticism 1981–1991.* London: Granta.

Russell, Jane. 1982. *Communal Politics under the Donoughmore Constitution 1931–1947.* Dehiwela: Tisara.

Said, Edward. 1978. *Orientalism.* New York: Vintage.

———. 1988. "Identity, Negation, Violence." *New Left Review* 171: 46–59.

———. 1993. *Culture and Imperialism.* New York: Alfred Knopf.

Sarkar, Sumit. 1983. *Modern India: 1885–1947.* New Delhi: Macmillan.

Schalk, Peter. 1994. "Women Fighters of the Liberation Tigers in Tamil Ilam: The Martial Feminism of Atel Palacinkam." *South Asia Research* 14: 163–83.

Scott, David. 1995. "Dehistoricising History." In *Unmaking the Nation: The Politics of Identity and History in Modern Sri Lanka,* edited by Pradeep Jeganathan and Qadri Ismail, 10–24. Colombo: Social Scientists Association.

Sen Gupta, Bhabhani. 1983. "Regional Security: the Indian Doctrine." *India Today,* 31 August.

Sethi, Surinder Singh. 1972. *Decisive War: Emergence of a New Nation.* New Delhi: Sagar.

Shapiro, Michael. 1993. *Reading Adam Smith: Desire, History and Value.* Newbury Park, Calif.: Sage.

Singh, Depinder. n.d. *The IPKF in Sri Lanka.* New Delhi: Trishul.

Singh, Jogindar. 1993. *Behind the Scene: An Analysis of India's Military Operations.* New Delhi: Lancer International.

Singh, Patwant. 1994. *Of Dreams and Demons: An Indian Memoir.* New Delhi: Rupa and Co.

Sinha, Mrinalini. 1995. *Colonial Masculinity: The 'Manly' Englishman and the 'Effeminate Bengali' in the Late Nineteenth Century.* Manchester: Manchester University Press.

Sisson, Richard, and Leo E. Rose. 1990. *War and Secession: Pakistan, India, and the Creation of Bangladesh.* Berkeley: University of California Press.

Sisson, Richard, and Stanley Wolpert, eds. 1988. *Congress and Indian Nationalism: The Pre-Independence Phase.* Berkeley and Los Angeles: University of California Press.

Sivarajah, Ambalavanar. 1992a. "Dravidian Sub-Nationalism and Its Regional Implications." In *Security Dilemma of a Small State,* edited by P. V. J. Jayasekera, 122–45. New Delhi: South Asian.

———. 1992b. "Indo-Sri Lanka Relations in the Context of Sri Lanka's Ethnic Crisis (1976–1983)." In *Security Dilemma of a Small State,* edited by P. V. J. Jayasekera, 506–23. New Delhi: South Asian.

Sivaram, D. P. 1992. "The Twin Narratives of Tamil Nationalism"; "Barathy and the Legitimation of Militarism"; "Tamil Miltary Castes"; "Bishop Caldwell and the Tamil Dravidians"; "Militarism and Caste in Jaffna"; "The Suppression of Tamil Military Castes"; and "Tamil Militarism: The Code of Suicide," *Lanka Guardian,* Colombo, May–August.

Sivaramani. 1992. "Poems of Sivaramani." Introduced by Sitralega Maunaguru and translated from Tamil by "a group of Tamil poets and scholars." *Pravada* 1: 21–22.

Sivasithamparam, M., and A. Amirthalingam. 1988. "Our Reservations on the Agreement." In *Towards Devolution of Power in Sri Lanka: Main Documents August 1983–October 1987,* Tamil United Liberation Front. Madras: Jeevan.

Sivathamby, K. 1985. *Tamil Nationalism and Social Conflicts: An Effort to Understand the Current Ethnic Crisis.* Handy Perinbanayagam Memorial Lecture, Jaffna, Sri Lanka.

———. 1993. "Understanding the Dravidian Movement: Problems and Perspectives." In *Ethnic Movement in India: Theory and Practice,* edited by G. Palanithurai and R. Thandavan, 13–47. Delhi: Kanishka.

Spencer, Jonathan. 1990a. "Collective Violence and Everyday Practice in Sri Lanka." *Modern Asian Studies* 24: 603–23.

———. 1990b. "Writing Within: Anthropology, Nationalism and Culture in Sri Lanka." *Current Anthropology* 31: 283–91.

———, ed. 1990c. *Sri Lanka: History and the Roots of Conflict.* London: Routledge.

Spivak, Gayatri C. 1988a. "Subaltern Studies: Deconstructing Historiography." In *Selected Subaltern Studies,* edited by Ranajit Guha and Gayatri C. Spivak, 3–34. New York: Oxford University Press.

———. 1988b. "Three Women's Texts and a Critique of Imperialism." *Critical Inquiry* 12: 243–61.

Stern, Robert W. 1993. *Changing India: Bourgeois Revolution on the Subcontinent.* Cambridge: Cambridge University Press.

Subrahmanyam, K. 1982. *Indian Security Perspectives.* New Delhi: ABC.

Subramanium, T. S. 1992. "A Role Unveiled: On India and Sri Lankan Militants." *Frontline,* 17–31 January.

Suntheralingam, R. 1967. *Eylom: Beginnings of Freedom Struggle.* Colombo: Arasan.

Swamy, Narayan M. R. 1994. *Tigers of Lanka: From Boys to Guerrillas.* Delhi: Konark.

Tambiah, Stanley J. 1955. "Ethnic Representation in Ceylon's Higher Administrative Services, 1870–1946." *University of Ceylon Review* 13: 91–115.

———. 1986. *Sri Lanka: Ethnic Fratricide and the Dismantling of Democracy.* Chicago: University of Chicago Press.

———. 1990. "Presidential Address: Reflections on Communal Violence in South Asia." *Journal of Asian Studies* 49: 741–60.

———. 1992. *Buddhism Betrayed? Religion, Politics, and Violence in Sri Lanka.* Chicago: University of Chicago Press.

———. 1996. *Leveling Crowds: Ethnonationalist Conflicts and Collective Violence in South Asia.* Berkeley: University of California Press.

Tamil United Liberation Front. 1988. *Towards Devolution of Power in Sri Lanka: Main Documents August 1983 to October 1987.* Madras: Jeevan.

Thandavan, R. 1993. "AIADMK: Counter Ethnic Political Party." In *Ethnic Movement in India: Theory and Practice,* edited by G. Palanithurai and R. Thandavan, 205–50. Delhi: Kanishka.

Thapar, Romila. 1993. *Interpreting Early India.* Delhi: Oxford University Press.

Thomas, Raju G. C. 1986. *India's Security Policy.* Princeton, N.J.: Princeton University Press.

———. ed. 1992. *Perspectives on Kashmir: Roots of Conflict in South Asia.* Boulder, Colo.: Westview.

———. 1996. *Democracy, Security and Development in India.* New York: St. Martin's.

Tuathail, Gearóid, Ó'. 1996. *Critical Geopolitics: The Politics of Writing Global Space.* Minneapolis: University of Minnesota Press.

Tully, Mark, and Satish Jacob. 1985. *Amritsar: Mrs. Gandhi's Last Battle.* London: Cape.

University Teachers for Human Rights (Jaffna). 1991. *The Debasement of the Law, Humanity and the Drift towards Total Violence.* Report no. 8, August 28. Thirunelvely, Jaffna: University of Jaffna.

———. 1993. *A Sovereign Will to Self-Destruction*—the Continuing Saga of Dislocation and Disintegration. Report no. 12, November 15. Thirunelvely, Jaffna: University of Jaffna.

Uyangoda, Jayadeva. 1994. "Ethnicity, Nation and State Formation in Sri Lanka: Antinomies of Nation-Building." *Pravada* 3: 11–17.

Vanaik, Achin. 1990. *The Painful Transition: Bourgeois Democracy in India.* London: Verso.

Varshney, Ashutosh. 1991. "India, Pakistan and Kashmir: Antinomies of Nationalism." *Asian Survey* 31: 997–1019.

Venkatachalapathy, A. R. 1995. "Dravidian Movement and Saivites 1927–1944." *Economic and Political Weekly* 30: 761–68.

Visswanathan, E. S. 1983. *The Political Career of E. V. Ramasami Naicker: A Study in the Politics of Tamilnadu 1920–1949.* Madras: Ravi and Vasanth.

Vittachi, Tarzie. 1958. *Emergency '58: The Story of the Ceylon Race Riots.* London: Andre Deutsch.

Wagner, Benno. 1995. "Normality — Exception — Counter-Knowledge: On the History of a Modern Fascination." In *Global Modernities,* edited by Mike Featherstone, Scott Lash, and Roland Robertson, 178–91. London: Sage.

Walker, R. B. J. 1993. *Inside/Outside: International Relations as Political Theory.* Cambridge: Cambridge University Press.

Waltz, Kenneth. 1979. *Theory of International Relations.* Reading, Mass.: Addison-Wesley.

Warner, David. 1991. *An Ethic of Responsibility in International Relations.* Boulder, Colo.: Lynne Rienner.

Washbrook, David. 1976. *The Emergence of Provincial Politics.* Cambridge: Cambridge University Press.

———. 1989. "Caste, Class and Dominance in Modern Tamil Nadu: Non-Brahmanism, Dravidianism and Tamil Nationalism." In *Dominance and State Power in Modern India: Decline of a Social Order.* 2 vols. Edited by Francine R. Frankel and M. S. A. Rao, 1: 204–65. Delhi: Oxford University Press.

Weber, Eugen. 1976. *Peasants into Frenchmen: The Modernization of Rural France 1870–1914*. Stanford: Stanford University Press.

Weiner, Myron. 1989. *The Indian Paradox: Essays in Indian Politics*. New Delhi: Sage.

White, Hayden. 1978. *Tropics of Discourse: Essays in Cultural Criticism*. Baltimore, Md.: Johns Hopkins University Press.

Wilson, Alfred Jeyaratnam. 1988. *Break-Up of Sri Lanka: The Sinhalese-Tamil Conflict*. London: C. Hurst and Co.

———. 1994a. *Chelvanyakam and the Crisis of Sri Lankan Tamil Nationalism, 1947–1977*. London: C. Hurst and Co.

———. 1994b. "The Colombo Man, the Jaffna Man, and the Batticaloa Man: Regional Identities and the Rise of the Federal Party." In *The Sri Lankan Tamils: Ethnicity and Identity*, edited by Chelvadurai Manogaran and Bryan Pfaffenberger, 126–42. Boulder, Colo.: Westview.

Winichakul, Thongchai. 1994. *Siam Mapped: The History of the Geo-Body of a Nation*. Honolulu: University of Hawaii Press.

Index

Sankaran Krishna is associate professor of political science and director of the Center for South Asian Studies at the University of Hawai'i at Manoa. The author of numerous journal articles and chapters in edited books, Krishna focuses primarily on postcolonial studies and critical international relations theory, especially as they pertain to South Asia.